Habsburg Sons
Jews in the Austro-Hungarian
Army 1788-1918

Publication of this book is supported in part by grants from the Austrian Cultural Forum New York and the University of Graz.

Habsburg Sons
Jews in the Austro-Hungarian Army 1788-1918

Peter C. Appelbaum

BOSTON
2022

Library of Congress Cataloging-in-Publication Data

Names: Appelbaum, Peter C., author.

Title: Habsburg sons : Jews in the Austro-Hungarian Army, 1788-1918 / Peter C. Appelbaum.

Other titles: Austro-Hungarian Army, 1788-1918

Description: Boston : Cherry Orchard Books, 2021. | Includes bibliographical references and index.

Identifiers: LCCN 2021022360 (print) | LCCN 2021022361 (ebook) | ISBN 9781644696897 (hardback) | ISBN 9781644696903 (paperback) | ISBN 9781644696910 (adobe pdf) | ISBN 9781644696927 (epub)

Subjects: LCSH: Austro-Hungarian Monarchy. Heer--History--20th century. | World War, 1914-1918--Austria. | Jewish soldiers--Austria--History--20th century. | Jews--Austria--History--20th century. | Austro-Hungarian Monarchy. Heer--Chaplains--History--20th century. | World War, 1914-1918--Chaplains. | Military chaplains--Austria--History--20th century. | Jews--Austria--History--19th century. | Austro-Hungarian Monarchy. Heer--History--19th century. | Jewish soldiers--Austria--History--19th century.

Classification: LCC D539 .A67 2021 (print) | LCC D539 (ebook) | DDC 940.4/13436089924--dc23

LC record available at https://lccn.loc.gov/2021022360
LC ebook record available at https://lccn.loc.gov/2021022361

Copyright © 2021 Academic Studies Press All rights reserved
ISBN 9781644696897 (hardback)
ISBN 9781644696903 (paperback)
ISBN 9781644696910 (adobe pdf)
ISBN 9781644696927 (epub)

Book design by Kryon Publishing Services, Ltd.
Cover design by Ivan Grave

Published by Cherry Orchard Books, an imprint of Academic Studies Press
1577 Beacon Street
Brookline, MA 02446, USA
press@academicstudiespress.com
www.academicstudiespress.com

For all those who wouldn't or couldn't leave and were murdered in cold blood.

Contents

Foreword: A History of a Bygone Era, by Manfried Rauchensteiner   vii

Foreword: Jewish Soldiers in Habsburg Austria, by Gerald Lamprecht   xi

Author's Introduction   xxiv

Plates   xxx

Chapter 1. Setting the Stage   1

Chapter 2. Jews in the Armies of Austro-Hungary before the Great War: A Comparative Framework   24

Chapter 3. The Kaiser Needs You! Initial Reaction to the Declaration of War   49

Chapter 4. Snapshots from the Eastern Front: Diaries, Memoirs, Reports   67

Chapter 5. Snapshots from Other Fronts: The Balkans, Italy, and Palestine   127

Chapter 6. Austro-Hungarian *Feldrabbiner*: Tallit, Torah, and Tobacco   172

Chapter 7. Captives of the Tsar in European Russia, Siberia, and Central Asia   238

Chapter 8. Epilogue. The Fate of Habsburg Jewish Veterans and Their Influence on Postwar Europe   290

Bibliography   307

Index   317

Praise   324

Foreword

A History of a Bygone Era

Manfried Rauchensteiner

Consulting the 1914 volume of one of the most helpful reference books of the Austro-Hungarian Monarchy—the *Schematismus für die k.u.k. Armee und Flotte* (Schematics for the Imperial and Royal Army and Navy)—one finds not only a list of the regiments, garrisons, and the names of the officers on active duty and in the reserves, but also names of clergymen and their religions: Roman Catholic, Greek Catholic, Greek Orthodox, Protestant (Augsburg Confession), Evangelical Reformed (Calvinists), "Israelitic" (Jewish), and "Mohammedanic" (Muslim).

The total of seven officially approved confessions mirrors the diversity of the army, which, for its part, was a replica of the construction of the polyglot Habsburg Empire, and therefore difficult to understand. In 1867, Austria-Hungary was divided into two halves, each of which had its own government and parliament, with only three common ministers. Over all of this stood the emperor and king, until 1916 Franz Joseph I (Ferenc József in Hungary), and after him Emperor Karl I (Charles I)—in Hungary, King Károly IV. The Monarchy consisted of eleven nationalities, which had identical rights and obligations, but beyond that, they had very few similarities.

The mention of eleven nationalities is misleading insofar as there existed an additional group of people, which had the qualities of a nationality but did not see itself as such: the Jews.

The total number of Jews in the Habsburg Monarchy was approximately four percent of its total population of fifty-two million; therefore, the number of Jews was more than the percentage of Italians, Romanians, and Austrian Serbs put together. Compared to other nationalities, who settled in wide but definable regions, the Jews were scattered over the entire Monarchy; thus, one could not count them exclusively as part of one or the other kingdom, principality, or county. And there was yet another problem: Most Austrian Jews counted themselves as being of German nationality, notwithstanding the fact that approximately half of them lived in Galicia—today part of Poland and the Ukraine—and in Bukowina—which today is divided between Ukraine and Romania. Their spiritual capital was not L'viv (Lemberg) or Černivci (Czernowitz), but Vienna, where the percentage of Jews was about eight percent of the population. In Budapest, the percentage was slightly higher.

Jews played an important role in the politics, administration, economy, science, and especially in the culture of the Habsburg Empire—but they also played a significant role in the army, Most people, even in Austria and Poland, may be surprised to know that Austrian emperors proudly held the title of Duke of Auschwitz and Sator. This fact should be emphasized, since it was ignored and suppressed during the Nazi period in Austria.

Long before the implementation of compulsory military service in the Habsburg Monarchy in 1868, the Jews of Galicia, like German-Austrians, were liable for the draft and military service. This was one of the consequences of the annexation of the southern parts of Poland by Austria in 1772. Jews regarded compulsory military service with mixed feelings: some looked on it as an unpleasant obligation, but others as a great opportunity. Austria was a much more modern and liberal state than Poland or Russia; it opened up all sorts of possibilities for a career and, in the case of the Jews, for emancipation. Religious tolerance, beginning with the *Toleranzpatent* of Emperor Joseph II (1780–1790), also enlarged the scope of religious freedom. The military also opened up opportunities for social advancement. Jewish officers could attain the ranks of staff officers and generals. Of course, the journey was painstaking, for the mass of professional officers were Roman Catholics, as was the emperor and king. Still, opportunities for promotion were available. By contrast, in Prussia Jews were not allowed to become reserve officers and not permitted into the Prussian officers' corps; thus, Germany entered World War I without a single Jewish officer.

Since Austria-Hungary was not involved in great military conflicts in the years between 1866 and 1914, service in the army as well as in the navy was comparatively comfortable. Every male Austrian able to serve in the military was obliged to serve for twelve years, three years on active duty and nine in the reserves. In 1912, the period for active duty was reduced to two years. Then, World War I broke out, changing everything.

Like most other European countries, a euphoric atmosphere reigned in most parts of the Austro-Hungarian Empire, and reserve soldiers were keen to join up for active service. Tumultuous scenes occurred in many parts of the country; nobody wanted the be absent when the most important event of the twentieth century thus far took place. At the end of July and in early August 1914, two million Austro-Hungarian soldiers were sent to war against Serbia and Russia, a war whose reality proved to be completely different from the one expected. Nevertheless, the soldiers did not hesitate and went off to fight for God, emperor, and fatherland.

Jewish soldiers were no exception. They fought in the lines of the Habsburg armies in Serbia, Poland, Russia, Montenegro, Albania, and Italy. They were part of the Austro-Hungarian Expeditionary Corps, which was sent to the Ottoman Empire in the Near and Middle East, and some of the most haunting and touching photos of the war show Austro-Hungarian Jewish soldiers praying at the Western Wall in Jerusalem in the midst of the Great War.

During the war, 5,091 Jewish Austro-Hungarian officers were killed in action or died from wounds or illness. This made up 6.78 percent of all officer losses and lay far beyond expectation, given that Jews comprised 4 percent of the population. Officer losses of the Honvéd (Royal Hungarian), one of the three parts of the Austro-Hungarian Army, were even higher: One third of the Honvéd officers killed in the numerous battles were Jews. The fact that the overall number of Jewish soldiers killed remained below the estimated number gave rise to derogatory comments, but did not reflect the true situation.

Altogether, more than 300,000 Jewish soldiers served in the infantry and other branches. They fought, were decorated, suffered, and died like their comrades from other nationalities.

One additional fact should also to be mentioned: Tens of thousands of Jewish soldiers were taken as prisoners of war and became part of the 1.5 million prisoners that the Austro-Hungarian Army lost to the Russians. Because they viewed themselves as German-Austrians or Hungarians, most were brought to the prisoner of war camps beyond the Ural Mountains and to the Asiatic provinces of the Russian Empire. There, they had to remain until the Russian Revolutions and the peace treaty with Bolshevik Russia in 1918.

One of the chapters in this book stands out as especially significant.to the history of the Austro-Hungarian War. It is the history of the Jewish chaplains (*Feldrabbiner*) who accompanied Jewish soldiers during both the good and the bad days of the war. The importance of the role and history of the *Feldrabbiner* cannot be overestimated. It was the *Feldrabbiner* who supported the faith of the soldiers in their prosecution of a "just" war. It was the *Feldrabbiner* who supported the religious conviction of the Jewish soldiers, explained the Holy Scriptures, and gave the soldiers the feeling of some normality, which was put to its sternest test during the war. It was also the *Feldrabbiner* who gave them comfort and consolation in their darkest hours. Their story is part of the larger history of the end of Austria-Hungary in World War I, and is an essential part of the subject of this book.

Peter Appelbaum deserves our thanks for having so thoroughly researched the role of Jewish soldiers as part of the Austro-Hungarian Army. He has made a large amount of previously unpublished texts, articles and correspondence available for the first time in the English language, most especially the history of the *Feldrabbiner*, which he describes in an excellent manner. This is a practically unknown part of the history of World War I, detailing aspects far beyond the usual operational, tactical or logistical levels of the original catastrophe of the twentieth century: This vast war can only be understood by accompanying these suffering men individually through their history of pain and suffering. A history of Austro-Hungarian Jewish soldiers during the war is much more than simply closing a gap in our knowledge. It also offers insights that can enable us to better understand the many good points of the Austro-Hungarian Empire.

One of the most beautiful and poignant epitaphs for the old monarchy was written by the author Joseph Roth, who was born in Brody. When Roth explained his motives for writing his great novel *Radetzky March*, he noted:

> A cruel will of history has shattered my old fatherland, the Austro-Hungarian Monarchy. I loved this fatherland that enabled me to be both a patriot and a citizen of the world at the same time, an Austrian and a German among all Austrian peoples. I loved the virtues and advantages of this fatherland, and now that it is lost and gone, I still love its faults and weaknesses. It had many. It atoned for them with its death.

There is really nothing to add to Roth's epitaph.

Jewish Soldiers in Habsburg Austria

Gerald Lamprecht

In autumn 1933 the famous Austrian author Joseph Roth, who had already fled from Berlin into exile to Paris in January of that year, wrote the powerful text *Das Autodafé des Geistes*. In this text, he accusingly wrote:

> They all [the burned authors] have fallen on the field of honor of the spirit. They all have a common flaw in the eyes of German murderers and arsonists: *Jewish blood and European spirit.*
>
> The threatened and terrorized world must account for the fact that penetration of Private Hitler into European civilization does not only mean the beginning of a new chapter in the field of antisemitism: far from it! What the arsonists say is true, but in a different sense; this Third Reich is the beginning of its downfall! By destroying the Jews, one persecutes Christ. For the first time Jews are beaten to death not because they crucified Jesus, but because they produced him. When one burns the books of Jewish or suspicious authors, one actually sets fire to the Book of Books: to the Bible. If one expels or imprisons Jewish judges and lawyers, one turns in spirit at the same time against right and justice....
>
> We German writers of Jewish descent were the first to fall for Europe. We were spared folly and remorse. All we have left is honor...!
>
> Many of us served in the field during the war, and many fell. We wrote for Germany, we died for Germany. We shed our blood for Germany in two ways: the blood that nourishes our physical life and the blood with which we write. We have sung of Germany, the true Germany! That is why we are being burned by Germany today![1]

Joseph Roth, who had repeatedly mourned the downfall of the multi-ethnic Habsburg monarchy with his texts, wrote the *Autodafé des Geistes* as a response to book burnings by the National Socialists from May 1933 onwards and the beginning persecution and expulsion of Jews. For him, Jewish authors and expatriates were soldiers who fought for the spirit of Europe.

Only a few years later, in the summer of 1940, Jakob Kellmann opened his memoirs—addressed to his daughter—with the words:

> . . . and many generations will tell of their great-great-grandfathers, who fought and bled as Austrians in the Great War of 1914–1918, but had to leave their Fatherland when a former war comrade came to power in this country, and decided that for people who belong to the Jewish *Volksstamm* [tribe] there is no longer any place in their own Fatherland, regardless of their merits for the same.[2]

Kellmann was born in Galicia, moved to Vienna shortly before the beginning of the Great War, fought in the Habsburg army from 1915 to 1918, and became an Austrian citizen after 1918, having overcome numerous bureaucratic obstacles. He led a successful life in Vienna before persecution began in March 1938 for him and all those defined as Jews by the National Socialists through the 1935 Nuremberg Laws. The consequences were first loss of their middle-class existence and then loss of homeland and potentially of life. Kellmann and his family first managed to flee to Panama and then on to the United States, where he lived until his death.

A third example. The story is told that Major General Emil Sommer, the first Federal Leader of the Austrian Federation of Jewish Front Soldiers and later head of the Legitimist Jewish Front Fighters, was torn out of his apartment by young SA-men in the course of the *Anschlusspogrom* (annexation-pogrom) in Vienna in March 1938, to be publicly humiliated in a so-called *Reibpartie*, where Jews were forced to clean the city streets and pavements with hand brushes. But before he was taken out, the story goes, he asked the SA-men to be allowed to go back to his apartment to dress differently. After a short while, he returned dressed in his uniform with all his war decorations, whereupon the SA-men "shamefacedly" let him go. As Thomas Chaimowicz put it in his memoirs: "A k.u.k. general, kneeling on the ground washing the streets, could lead to a disturbance of people passing by, many of whom had noticed a few days after the invasion where the wind was blowing."[3]

All three abovementioned examples bear witness to the National Socialist policy of expulsion and extermination of the Jewish population, after loyal and patriotic military service to their respective homelands during World War I. They loudly denounce the betrayal by Private Adolf Hitler of his former war comrades, and cast the logic of modern military service into the balance against Nazi barbarism. The modern state assures the individual "citizen soldier," ready to fight in times of war, civil rights and security as well as equal position in society and state. In this way, the "hero's death" or willingness to suffer in war has been the ultimate proof of each individual citizen's unbreakable loyalty to the state and society in which he lived.[4] Joseph Roth, Jakob Kellmann, Emil Sommer, and many thousands of other former soldiers of World War I referred to this fundamental relationship between military service and civil rights in the face of the Nazi threat. They drew attention to achievements of Jewish emancipation, and deplored the National Socialists' betrayal of the promise of emancipation.

Military service and Emancipation

In 1783, before emancipation and Jewish military service were first considered in Prussia, Government Councilor Christian Wilhelm Dohm published an enlightened paper *Über die Bürgerliche Verbesserung der Juden*.[5] Dohm, who had been inspired by Moses Mendelssohn to write this paper, dedicated an entire chapter to the question of Jewish military service, first listing all the traditional arguments of opponents of Jewish military service, alleging that Jews were generally incapable of military service. The religious commandments of "Sabbath rest" and Jewish dietary laws would complicate Jewish military service. Alleged Jewish social segregation, as well as their "unfamiliarity with physical labor" or "lack of physical stature" would also be problems. But, above all, there was the religious principle that the only just war is a "defensive war," and that wars of aggression are forbidden. The prevailing opinion was that Jews would not, when compelled to do so, fight against Jewish soldiers of opposing armies, thus behaving disloyally towards their homeland. For all these reasons, emancipation opponents concluded that "citizens who do not defend the society to which they belong are not citizens like others, cannot demand equal rights, and must tolerate a measure of oppression."[6]

Dohm responded:

> One has the right to demand unqualified military service from Jews as well. Now, of course, they cannot do this because oppression, in

which they have lived for so long, has stifled their warlike spirit and personal courage, and their religious speculations have led them to antisocial paradoxes. They had no Fatherland for a millennium and a half, so how could they fight and die for something that didn't exist? I am convinced that once they have been given a Fatherland, they will fight with the same ability and loyalty as everyone else.[7]

Dohm's writings represent the central discourses of debates on Jewish war service throughout the nineteenth century up to World War I. In essence, they touch on the question of the extent to which Jews could become full citizens of emerging liberal national-civic societies. Accordingly, development of European Jewish emancipation can also be seen through the prism of admission of Jews to military service and the question of their opportunities for military promotion.

In France, emancipation took place in 1791, when Jews were able to serve without restrictions in the military. Consequently, Jewish soldiers fought in all Napoleonic wars. Despite some setbacks and restrictions at the beginning of the 19th century by the *Décret Infâme* (1808), Jews were able to rise to the highest military ranks within the army, especially in the Third French Republic.[8] French Jewish military chaplains (*aumôniers*) had existed since the beginning of the nineteenth century. But complete integration into the French army did not mean that there was no antisemitic discrimination. Rather, the Dreyfus affair is to be seen as the birth of political antisemitism in France.[9] It must be borne in mind that, despite the catastrophic social and political consequences of *l'Affaire*, Dreyfus was permitted to join the French general staff—something that was impossible in Prussia and unthinkable in Imperial Russia.

The United States, Great Britain, and Italy emancipated their Jewish population very early and, despite some individual antisemitism, there were no structural restrictions in the military careers of Jewish soldiers. In all these armies, Jews were able to rise to general rank, and in the case of Great Britain, during World War I, there was also a separate Jewish volunteer unit, the Jewish Legion.[10]

In the Russian Empire, emancipation was only a consequence of World War I and the Revolution of 1917. Until 1827, no Jews were drafted into the army, instead they had to pay a substitute tax. As in other European countries, enlistment of Jews into the army, which began in 1827, was primarily aimed at greater integration into society, which in Russia meant that Jewish soldiers were to be forced to convert through numerous discriminations. As a result of these politics, opportunities for career advancement in the army were limited, and many Jews tried to escape military service for religious reasons, fear of discrimination, and baptism.[11] With enactment of general compulsory military service in 1874, numerous decrees were issued to force Jews into military service. In the last third of the nineteenth and at the beginning of the twentieth century, the army also introduced numerous restrictions for Jews. In 1908, for example, right-wing parties in the Duma demanded that Jews be completely exempted from military service and that substitute taxes should be paid instead. The aim of this initiative was to undermine demands for emancipation. Liberal, enlightened Jewish authorities repeatedly argued for military service as an argument for emancipation, to no avail.[12]

In an expert opinion of the *Oberkriegskollegium*, Prussian Jews were considered unsuitable for military service in 1790,[13] and not admitted into the army until the emancipation edict of 1812. Subsequently, Jews fought as Prussian soldiers in the wars of liberation and again, with numerous restrictions, in the reactionary wars against Denmark (1864) and Austria (1866). These restrictions were gradually lifted (at least on paper) with foundation of the German Empire and the emancipation of 1871. In the Franco-Prussian war of 1870/71, many Jews again fought for the German Empire, in an attempt to gain national integration within the framework of the German army.[14] But despite legal emancipation and active patriotic participation in the war, it was impossible for Jews in the Prussian army to become officers until World War I. Jews were also not allowed to become reserve officers.[15] Although there was no legal foundation for this rejection, the aristocratic status of the Protestant Prussian nobility and the idea of a Christian Germany in which Jews were under no circumstances allowed to give orders to Christians, made it impossible in the Prussian army even for Jews who were largely bourgeois. By contrast, Catholic Bavaria was more liberal, allowing a small number of Jews to become officers. This military rejection, also found in other societal areas, was perceived as a deep insult. The industrialist and future foreign minister of the Weimar Republic, Walter Rathenau, wrote, after repeated attempts at an officer's career had failed:

> In the adolescence of every German Jew there is a painful moment which he remembers throughout his life: when he becomes fully aware for the first time that he has entered the world as a second-class citizen and that no capability or merit can free him from this situation.[16]

The impossibility of an officer's career for Jews in the German Empire was finally abolished after massive losses in the officer's corps during the early months of the war. During the war's course, despite the antisemitism already described, about 3,000 Jews were promoted to officer rank (but none higher than captain).[17]

In the Habsburg Monarchy, the beginnings of Jewish military service were linked to Joseph IIs *Toleranzpatent* (edict of tolerance). Starting in 1782, he gradually implemented the ideas set forth by Christian Wilhelm Dohm, against considerable resistance from the Court War Council. Austria was the first European country to introduce military duty for Jews in 1788, even before France.[18] At first, Jews were only used in transportation, but from 1789 onwards they could also serve in other units. As in other countries, there were initially supporters and resolute opponents of military service within the Jewish population. Supporters associated military service with the chance of emancipation and societal integration, while the mostly Orthodox opponents, who were critical of the Age of Enlightenment (*haskalah*), expressed fears with regard to observance of religious laws.[19]

After a brief period of regression following the death of Joseph II, Jews were readmitted to military service in 1806, and allowed to rise to officer's and finally to general's rank within the Habsburg Army by the time of the *Ausgleich* (compromise) and emancipation in 1867.[20] It is noteworthy that, after enactment of general conscription in 1869, a very high proportion of reserve officers in the Habsburg Army towards the end of the nineteenth and beginning of the twentieth century were Jews. István Deák shows that, in 1911, seventeen percent of the reserve officers were Jews and that during World War I around 25,000 Jewish officers served.[21] Besides the fundamental denominational tolerance of the Habsburg Monarchy and importance of the army as one of the three columns of the supranational state (bureaucracy, dynasty, army), this was certainly also due to the high proportion of Jewish high school graduates.[22]

If one understands the history of Jewish military service as part of the history of emancipation, then at the beginning of World War I both parallels and differences emerge in the different countries. Jews served as soldiers for their homeland in all belligerent states, to gain or confirm their legal and social acceptance. The total number of Jewish soldiers who served during the war is difficult to quantify, as only limited reliable statistics are available. According to a contemporary list from the 1930s, a total of c. 1.25 to 1.5 million Jews served in all warring countries. For the Habsburg Army, about 300,000–350,000 soldiers are assumed to have served, of whom between 30,000 and 35,000 were killed. In the Tsarist army, the figure is estimated at 600,000, of whom between 60,000 and 70,000 were probably killed. In the German Empire about 100,000 served and 12,000 were killed, while, in the British Army corresponding numbers were 60,000 and 2,324, respectively.[23] In the French army, 35,000 soldiers served and 7,000 fallen are reported to have been killed.[24] Most Jewish soldiers during the World War came from Central and Eastern Europe, and Jewish soldiers fought on the Eastern Front in all armies.

It should also be emphasized that Eastern European Jewish civilians were particularly affected by the war, because their settlement areas in the Russian Pale of Settlement, Galicia, and Bukovina were central theaters of operations. Furthermore, the World War did not end sensu stricto in November 1918, but immediately passed into the Baltic wars of independence as well as Polish-Ukrainian, Polish-Soviet and Russian Civil Wars. Many Jews died between 1914 and 1920 in pogroms, and as a result of diseases and famines. With the continuation of the war, antisemitism also became radicalized; about 60,000 Jews were murdered in pogroms in affected areas during these years, and by mid-1921 about 200,000 Jews were homeless in those "bloodlands."[25]

Expectations, Experiences, Memories

Against the backdrop of promises of emancipation, thousands of Jews with very specific expectations of their military service followed their beloved Emperor Franz Joseph I's call to arms, and volunteered at the beginning of the war in 1914. For them, equality of rights achieved in 1867 was to be followed by social equality through military service, and, finally, all forms of antisemitism would be overcome. Another war goal was liberation of Jews from the Tsarist yoke, and the slogan "revenge for Kishinev" was on everyone's lips. These expectations comprised specific Jewish experiences and subsequent war memories from 1914 onwards.[26] Jewish war experience did not result from events that only Jewish soldiers would have experienced, but also from the specific Jewish interpretation and endowment with meaning of military violence. This means that, with the exception of decidedly antisemitic violence, the experience of warlike violence, suffering and deprivation shared by millions of other people, was not specifically Jewish. The specific Jewish endowment of meaning, in addition to general war discourses of the time, was founded above all in the history of emancipation and struggle for citizenship as well as in Jewish religion and tradition. The focus of these experiences was always on the questions of social equality and recognition of the Jewish population and, closely linked to this, defense against antisemitism. They centered on the area of tension between Jewish particularism and national egalitarianism, equal and recognized possibilities of existence of a Jewish "minority," and Jewish identity in a liberal, national-civic society. This tension is reflected in all debates about Jewish war expectation, war experience and war memories, suffered by all soldiers as well as the mourning and overcoming of trauma and the assurance of collective identity.[27] These Jewish endowments of meaning become visible as narratives in the reports of soldiers' experiences, memoirs, sermons of rabbis and chaplains, narratives in Jewish newspapers and magazines, and Jewish war memorials and other memory signs.[28]

Based on expectations and experiences, foundations for future Jewish war memory were already laid during the war period. Particularly in newspapers and magazines, names of the fallen heroes were memorialized and special sections for the Jewish heroes were built in the Jewish cemeteries. From 1918, cemeteries and synagogues were to become the central locations of Jewish war memory. After the Great War, almost every Jewish community in Austria erected war memorials, normally in the center of the war grave sections, or memorial plaques in synagogues or in Jewish cemeteries. The list of the fallen was placed at the center of all these memorials and plaques, just as in non-Jewish memorials, usually without making any reference to their military or social status. Inscribed names were framed by religious or patriotic symbols and followed by some religious references.[29] All of these memorials carried the typical abbreviations that appear on Jewish tombstones such as פ״נ and תנצב״ה.

Responsibility for the erection of Jewish war memorials and memorial plaques all over Austria from 1919 onwards lay with Jewish communities, burial associations (*chevra kadishas*) and the *Bund jüdischer Frontsoldaten* (BJF, Federation of Jewish War Veterans) of Austria, founded in Vienna in 1932. The BJF was founded by former Austrian Jewish Soldiers after a drastic increase in the number of antisemitic agitations and assaults by National Socialists.[30] Its main aims were to protest the "permanent defamation and daily defilement of the Jewish name and Jewish honor,"[31] actively resist antisemitism, and preserve and maintain Jewish civil rights in Austria. Members of the BJF legitimized their activities by citing their loyal military service to the Habsburg Army and referring to the narrative of emancipation and military service. The head of the BJF, off-duty Captain Sigmund Edler von Friedmann (the future Eitan Avisar of the Israeli Defense Forces) argued in his speech at the general muster on May 5, 1935:

Was Jewish blood that was shed worth less than the blood of non-Jews? No! It was the same lifeblood that was shed, the same lifeblood wept over by Jewish and non-Jewish mothers alike. We do not beg for equality, we do not beg for equal rights, we demand them![32]

Conclusion

In the end, all efforts by men like Joseph Roth, Jakob Kellmann, and Emil Sommer, former Jewish soldiers, and members of the BJF to fight for their rights as citizens and remember their military service, ultimately afforded no protection whatsover. The Holocaust marked the end of traditions of Jewish war memory in Austria. All those who returned to Austria after 1945 could not continue the war memorial discourses of the prewar period because history of their heroic struggle for the Fatherland was robbed of legitimacy due to betrayal by the very Fatherland they had so much loved and for which they had sacrificed so much.[33] The National Socialists not only expelled and destroyed the milieu of remembrance necessary for every form of memory, they also destroyed many material memorial signs like monuments and plaques in synagogues and cemeteries. Furthermore, memory of the Jewish soldiers of World War I was overshadowed by the catastrophe of the Holocaust, and in Austria, like the history of the Jews in general, was largely erased from public consciousness for many years.

If one looks at the academic literature on Austrian Jewish soldiers, it can be seen that Jews in general and Jewish soldiers in the Habsburg Army in particular, were hardly noticed for a long time and thus were not researched.[34] The first scientific work on the situation in Austria was done by Wolfgang von Weisl in 1971,[35] followed by Erwin A. Schmidl (1989),[36] István Déak (1990),[37] Martin Senekowitsch (1994 and 1995),[38] Beatrix Hoffmann-Holter (1995),[39] Marsha Rozenblit[40] and David Rechter,[41] both in 2001. What they all have in common is that in the end they did not lead to any greater public or historical knowledge with regard to Jewish participation in the war, either as soldiers or as supporters, victims or opponents. A noticeable change resulted from the centennial of 2014-2018,[42] which witnessed publication of a new edition of Erwin Schmidl's standard work (1989)[43] and realization of a number of exhibitions[44] and book projects.[45] These include publication of the war diaries of the physician Bernhard Bardach[46] as well as this important book by Peter Appelbaum.

Finally, looking at the specific practice of memory in Austria after 1945, it can be observed that in contrast to Germany, where the first signs and activities of memory of the Jewish soldiers of World War I are noticeable from the 1960s onwards,[47] Austrian public debate about Jewish war memories and Jewish soldiers, Jewish culture and history, began late. One of the first memorial activities dates from 1982 and is closely linked to the move of the Austrian Jewish Museum into the Wertheimer house in Eisenstadt. On the museum's initiative, a memorial plaque for fallen Jewish soldiers, first erected in June 1934 and probably destroyed by the National Socialists, was redesigned and installed in the museum's inner courtyard.[48] Although representatives of the Austrian armed forces attended the inauguration by Chief Rabbi Eisenberg in 1982, it was not until the 1990s that the army became aware of individual Jewish war memorials from the interwar period that had not been destroyed. Since 1995 a wreath has been laid in front of the Jewish war memorials at the Jewish cemetery in Graz and for some years now also at the Jewish memorial and cemetery at the Vienna *Zentralfriedhof* on All Saints' Day during Austrian Armed Forces' commemoration of the fallen.[49] Thus, more than a hundred years after the end of the World War I, Austrian Jewish soldiers are now part of official Austrian hero's memory and, at least in the field of the military preservation of tradition, they finally receive the recognition that they so deeply desired in the years from 1914 to 1938.

Endnotes

1. Joseph Roth, "Das Autodafé des Geistes," in *Joseph Roth Werk*, vol. 3: *Das journalistische Werk 1929–1939*, ed. Klaus Westermann (Frankfurt am Main and Vienna: Büchergilde Gutenberg, 1989), 494–503.
2. Memoirs of Jacob Kellmann, Leo Baeck Institute (LBI), ME 1639; Martin Moll and Herbert-Ernst Neusiedler (eds.), *Woher du kommst. Die wahre Geschichte ihres Lebens, die Jacob und Paula Kellmann für ihre Tochter aufgeschrieben haben* (Vienna: edition a, 2014).
3. See Thomas Chaimowicz, "'Lacht nicht, ich wasche Gottes Erde'. Als Jude und Legitimist im Wien von 1938," in *1938—Anatomie eines Jahres*, ed. Thomas Chorherr (Vienna: Ueberreuter, 1987), 292–299, here 293; see also: "Austrian General Disclaims Role in Jewish Street-Sweeping 'Epic'," *New York Times*, October 15, 1946.
4. See Ute Frevert, *Die kasernierte Nation. Militärdienst und Zivilgesellschaft in Deutschland* (Munich: C.H. Beck, 2001), 15f.; Nikolaus Buschmann, "Vom 'Untertanensoldaten' zum 'Bürgersoldaten'? Zur Transformation militärischer Loyalitätsvorstellungen um 1800," *Jahrbuch des Simon-Dubnow-Instituts* 12 (2013): 105–126, here 105.
5. Christian Wilhelm Dohm, *Ueber die buergerliche Verbesserung der Juden* (Berlin and Stettin: Friedrich Nikolai, 1783).
6. Ibid., 223.
7. Ibid., 236f.

8   See Anne Külow, "Jüdische Soldaten in der Französischen Armee—Ein Erfolgsmodell für Integration?," in *Jüdische Soldaten: Jüdischer Widerstand in Deutschland und Frankreich*, ed. Michael Berger and Gideon Römer-Hillebrecht (Paderborn, Munich, Vienna, and Zürich: Verlag Ferdinand Schöningh, 2012), 145–148.
9   Detlev Zimmermann, "Eine Bewährungsprobe für die Republik. Frankreich und die Dreyfus-Affäre," in *J'Accuse . . . ! . . . ich klage an! Zur Affäre Dreyfus. Eine Dokumentation*, ed. Elke-Vera Kotowski and Julius H. Schoeps (Berlin: Verlag für Berlin-Brandenburg, 2005), 33–46.
10 See Martin Watts, *The Jewish Legion and the First World War* (Basingstoke: Palgrave Macmillan, 2005).
11 Military service in the Russian Empire also triggered migration. See, for example, the biography of the Hebrew author Gershon Shoffmann: Gerald Lamprecht, "Gerschon Schoffmann—eine biographische Annäherung," in Gerschon Schoffmann, *Nicht für immer. Erzählungen* (Graz and Vienna: Literaturverlag Droschl, 2016), 337–350, here 339.
12 "Militärdienst der Juden," in *Jüdisches Lexikon. Ein enzyklopädisches Handbuch des jüdischen Wissens in vier Bänden*, vol. 4, part 1: *Me–R* (Berlin: Jüdischer Verlag, 1930), 182–191, here 188–191; Yohanan Petrovsky-Shtern, "Military Service in Russia," in *The YIVO Encyclopedia of Jews in Eastern Europe*, vol. 2, ed. Gershon David Hundert (New Haven and London: Yale University Press, 2008), 1170–1174.
13 See "Militärdienst der Juden," 183.
14 See Christine G. Krüger, *"Sind wir denn nicht Brüder?" Deutsche Juden im nationalen Krieg 1870/1871*, vol. 31 of *Krieg in der Geschichte* (Paderborn, Munich, Vienna, and Zürich: Verlag Ferdinand Schöningh, 2006), 191–297.
15 See Michael Berger, *Eisernes Kreuz—Doppeladler—Davidstern. Juden in deutschen und österreichisch-ungarischen Armeen. Der Militärdienst jüdischer Soldaten durch zwei Jahrhunderte* (Berlin: Trafo Wissenschaftsverlag, 2010), 27–47; idem., *Für Kaiser, Reich und Vaterland. Jüdische Soldaten. Eine Geschichte vom 19. Jahrhundert bis heute* (Zürich: Orell Füssli, 2015).
16 Walter Rathenau, quoted in Shulamit Volkov, *Walther Rathenau. Ein jüdisches Leben in Deutschland 1867–1922* (Munich: C.H. Beck, 2012), 33.
17 See Berger, *Eisernes Kreuz*, 50.
18 See Erwin A. Schmidl, *Habsburgs jüdische Soldaten 1788–1918* (Vienna, Cologne, and Weimar: Böhlau Verlag, 2014), 29–32.
19 See Michael K. Silber, "From Tolerated Aliens to Citizen-Soldiers. Jewish Military Service in the Era of Joseph II," *Austrian Studies* 6 (2005): *Constructing Nationalities in East Central Europe*, ed. Pieter M. Judson and Marsha L. Rozenblit (New York and Oxford: Berghahn Books, 2004) 19–36, here 27–29.
20 "Militärdienst der Juden," 186.
21 See István Deák, *Der k.(u.)k. Offizier 1848–1918* (Vienna: Böhlau Verlag, 1995), 206, 208.
22 Ibid., 211.
23 Felix Aron Teilhaber, "Der Weltkrieg und die Juden," in *Jüdisches Lexikon. Ein enzyklopädisches Handbuch des jüdischen Wissens in vier Bänden*, vol. 4, part 2: *S–Z* (Berlin: Jüdischer Verlag, 1930), 1379–1381, here 1380. Current data put the number of Russian Jewish soldiers at c. 180,000. No accurate fatality statistics are available (Yohanan Petrovsky Shtern, personal communication). Thus, the total of Jews serving in all armies was nearer to one million.
24 See Jay Winter, "Jüdische Erinnerung und Erster Weltkrieg: Zwischen Geschichte und Gedächtnis," in *Jahrbuch des Simon-Dubnow-Instituts* 13 (2014): 111–129, here 117f.

25 David Rechter, "Die große Katastrophe: die österreichischen Juden und der Krieg," in *Weltuntergang. Leben und Sterben im Ersten Weltkrieg*, ed. Marcus G. Patka (Vienna, Graz, and Klagenfurt: Styria Premium, 2014), 14; Timothy Snyder, *Bloodlands. Europe between Hitler and Stalin* (New York: Basic Books, 2010).

26 See Jörg Rogge, "Kriegserfahrungen erzählen—Einleitung," in *Kriegserfahrungen erzählen. Geschichts- und literaturwissenschaftliche Perspektiven*, ed. Jörg Rogge (Bielefeld: Transcript Verlag, 2016), 9–30, here 13f.

27 See Jay Winter, *Sites of Memory, Sites of Mourning. The Great War in European Cultural History* (Cambridge: Cambridge University Press, 1995); Reinhart Koselleck, "Einleitung," in *Der politische Totenkult. Kriegerdenkmäler in der Moderne*, ed. Reinhart Koselleck and Michael Jeismann (Munich: Wilhelm Fink Verlag, 1994), 9–20.

28 See Gerald Lamprecht, "Erinnern an den Ersten Weltkrieg aus jüdischer Perspektive 1914–1938," *Zeitgeschichte* 41 (2014): 242–266; idem, "Jewish Soldiers in the Austrian Collective Memory 1914 to 1938," in *Jewish Soldiers in the Collective Memory of Central Europe. The Remembrance of World War I from a Jewish Perspective*, ed. Gerald Lamprecht, Eleonore Lappin-Eppel, and Ulrich Wyrwa, vol. 28 of Schriften des Centrums für Jüdische Studien (Vienna, Cologne, and Weimar: Böhlau Verlag, 2019), 311–330.

29 See "Protocol of the meeting of the committee for the erection of the war memorial on the central cemetery," April 4, 1926 and the "Program of the call for bids," August 1926, Central Archives for the History of the Jewish People; Archiv der IKG Wien, A/W 1176 a–d.

30 See Gerald Lamprecht, "The Remembrance of World War One and the Austrian Federation of Jewish War Veterans," *Quest. Issues in Contemporary Jewish History. Journal of Fondazione CDEC* 9 (October 2016): *The Great War. Reflections, Experiences and Memories of German and Habsburg Jews (1914–1918)*, ed. Petra Ernst, Jeffrey Grossman, and Ulrich Wyrwa, accessed October 13, 2018, www.quest-cdecjournal.it/focus.php?id=381, accessed April 4, 2021.

31 "Aufruf zur Gründungsversammlung des Bundes Jüdischer Frontsoldaten im Juli 1932," in *Drei Jahre Bund jüdischer Frontsoldaten Österreichs* (Vienna, n.d.), 18.

32 *Drei Jahre Bund jüdischer Frontsoldaten Österreichs*, 54.

33 This can also be seen, for example, in the failure of the reactivation attempts of the Austrian Federation of Jewish Front Soldiers after 1945. See, for example, Wiener Stadt- und Landesarchiv (WStLA), 1.3.2.119.A32.1932.6959/1932.

34 See Derek J. Penslar, *Jews and the Military. A History* (Princeton and Oxford: Princeton University Press, 2013); Sarah Panter, *Jüdische Erfahrungen und Loyalitätskonflikte im Ersten Weltkrieg*, vol. 235 of Veröffentlichungen des Instituts für Europäische Geschichte Mainz (Göttingen: Vandenhoeck & Ruprecht, 2014); Ulrich Sieg, *Jüdische Intellektuelle im Ersten Weltkrieg. Kriegserfahrungen, weltanschauliche Debatten und kulturelle Neuentwürfe* (Berlin: Akademie Verlag, 2001).

35 Wolfgang von Weisl, *Die Juden in der Armee Österreich-Ungarns* (Tel Aviv: Olamenu, 1971).

36 Erwin A. Schmidl, *Juden in der k.(u.)k. Armee 1788–1918* (Eisenstadt: Österreichisches Jüdisches Museum, 1989).

37 István Déak, *Beyond Nationalism. A Social and Political History of the Habsburg Officer Corps* (Oxford: Oxford University Press, 1990).

38 Martin Senekowitsch, *Ein ungewöhnliches Kriegerdenkmal. Das jüdische Heldendenkmal am Wiener Zentralfriedhof* (Vienna: Militärkommando Wien, 1994); idem, *Verbunden mit diesem Lande. Das jüdische Kriegerdenkmal in Graz* (Graz: Militärkommando Steiermark, 1995).

39 Beatrix Hoffmann-Holter, *"Abreisendmachung" Jüdische Kriegsflüchtlinge in Wien 1914 bis 1923* (Vienna, Cologne, and Weimar: Böhlau Verlag, 1995).

40 Marsha Rozenblit, *Reconstructing a National Identity. The Jews of Habsburg Austria during World War I* (Oxford: Oxford University Press, 2001).
41 David Rechter, *The Jews of Vienna and the First World War* (London: Littman Library of Jewish Civilization, 2001).
42 Among other things, the Center for Jewish Studies at the University of Graz has established a research focus on this topic. This has resulted in the following publications, among others: *Zeitgeschichte* 41, no. 4 (2014): *Der Erste Weltkrieg aus jüdischer Perspektive. Erwartungen—Erfahrungen—Erinnerungen*, ed. Gerald Lamprecht, Eleonore Lappin-Eppel, and Heidrun Zettelbauer; *Yearbook for European Jewish Literature Studies/Jahrbuch für europäisch-jüdische Literaturstudien* 1 (2014): *Europäisch-jüdische Literaturen und Erster Weltkrieg/European-Jewish Literatures and World War One*, ed. Petra Ernst and Eleonore Lappin-Eppel (eds.), *Jüdische Publizistik und Literatur im Zeichen des Ersten Weltkriegs*, vol. 25 of Schriften des Centrums für Jüdische Studien (Innsbruck, Vienna, and Munich: Studienverlag, 2016); Gerald Lamprecht, Eleonore Lappin-Eppel, and Ulrich Wyrwa (eds.), *Jewish Soldiers in the Collective Memory of Central Europe. The Remembrance of World War I from a Jewish Perspective*, vol. 28 of Schriften des Centrums für Jüdische Studien (Vienna, Cologne, and Weimar: Böhlau Verlag, 2019).
43 Schmidl, *Habsburgs jüdische Soldaten*.
44 Marcus G. Patka (ed.), *Weltuntergang. Leben und Sterben im Ersten Weltkrieg* (Vienna, Graz, and Klagenfurt: Styria Premium, 2014).
45 See Ulrich Wyrwa, "Zum Hundertsten nichts Neues. Deutschsprachige Neuerscheinungen zum Ersten Weltkrieg," *Zeitschrift für Geschichtswissenschaft* 62, no. 11 (2014): 921–940 (part 1), and 64, nos. 7/8 (2016): 683–702 (part 2).
46 *Carnage and Care on the Eastern Front. The War Diaries of Bernhard Bardach 1914–1918*, trans. and ed. Peter C. Appelbaum (New York and Oxford: Berghahn Books, 2018).
47 See Tim Grady, *The German-Jewish Soldiers of the First World War in History and Memory* (Liverpool: Liverpool University Press, 2011); and the new edition of the book from 1935, *Kriegsbriefe gefallener deutscher Juden*, intr. Franz Josef Strauß (Stuttgart: Seewald Verlag, 1961); or Egmont Zechlin, *Die deutsche Politik und die Juden im Ersten Weltkrieg* (Göttingen: Vandenhoeck & Ruprecht, 1969).
48 See *Neue Eisenstädter Zeitung*, July 1, 1934, 5; *Burgenländische Freiheit*, June 1982, 43.
49 See Manfred Oswald, "Traditionspflege von Widerstand und Verfolgung im österreichischen Bundesheer," *DÖW Jahrbuch* (1997): 180–185; here 182.

Author's Introduction

A book about Jewish soldiers and chaplains in the Habsburg armies is a daunting prospect that, many times during its gestation, I doubted I could complete. Unlike the relatively homogenous German army, the Austro-Hungarian military was a polyglot of many nationalities and languages. Whereas a knowledge of English, German, and Hebrew had previously sufficed for my purposes, the current project necessitated an additional knowledge (which I do not possess) of Yiddish, Hungarian, Czech, Polish, Serbo-Croatian, Italian, and Russian, and access to books and archives around the world, which was nearly impossible for an amateur working alone, with no funding.

I began with German-speaking Austrians and, even there, pickings were slim compared to those of Germans. Austro-Hungarian Jewish solders seemed less likely to put their thoughts on paper, compared to German counterparts. There are, of course, significant exceptions, such as diaries of Bernhard Bardach and Teofil Reiss, and books by Egon Erwin Kisch, Hans Kohn, Kaspar Blond, Adolf Epstein, Georg Breithaupt, and Lavoslav Kraus, but most of these are either handwritten in Sütterlin, or difficult to obtain. The Epstein and Breithaupt books, for example, are available in only two or three libraries in the world.

Habsburg Jews were admitted into the military before the French Revolution, but unlike French Jews to whom Napoleon gave full equality, Jews under Joseph II did not have equal rights. Although far from being an enlightened monarch, Joseph II understood that allowing Jews to serve in the military might be of financial benefit to his Empire. This started through his series of *Toleranzpatente* in the last two decades of the eighteenth century. This liberalization continued, with ups and some downs, until the beginning of World War I, with Jews promoted to high rank and even ennobled. By contrast, in Prussia, only one Jew, Meno Burg, was promoted to officer's rank: Jews were not allowed to become reserve officers; Germany entered the war without a single Jewish commissioned officer. The relatively benign rule of Emperor Franz Joseph—who saw no reason to discriminate against "his" Jews—succeeded in retaining rights for Habsburg Jews, in and out of the military, despite prevalent bourgeois antisemitism.

Understanding of the role played by Jews in the Habsburg Empire requires knowledge of the history of Hungary, in particular the Kossuth Rebellion of 1848 and the *Ausgleich* (compromise) of 1867. Jews played a significant role in the Kossuth Rebellion, and were, for a short time, punished for their activities. The rebellion raised their Magyar sentiment and, when the *Ausgleich* occurred, they entered the military in large numbers. They assimilated (or tried to), Magyarized their names, and mixed marriages were common. By contrast, Orthodox Galician Jews initially attempted to escape military service by buying themselves out or leaving the area. This gradually ceased, but Orthodoxy remained.

When contrasted with the two countries against which the Central Powers would fight on the Eastern Front and in the Alps during the war, Italy was the most liberal in its treatment of Jews. After the *risorgimento*, Jews were granted full rights, and progressed through the general staff to ministerial status without problem. Every effort was made during the war to comply with religious laws, and Italy had the highest per capita number of serving Jews of all warring parties. By contrast, Tsarist Russia oppressed its Jews with pogroms and the Pale of Settlement; there were no Jewish chaplains, and Jews were not promoted to officer's rank. Despite this, Russian Jews volunteered enthusiastically in large numbers when war began.

Identifying the primary culprit who caused World War I has occupied historians for decades. Austro-Hungary entered the war with the mistaken idea that they could deal with the Serbs in a short, sharp, limited war. The Austro-Hungarian army was not properly modernized, and its leaders, personified by Conrad von Hötzendorf, lacked insight and modern thinking of their German counterparts. It could be said that Habsburg generals were fighting the previous war, and it became rapidly clear to the German Army that they were "shackled to a corpse." Nevertheless, there was no lack of bravery in the Austro-Hungarian army, only bad and disorganized leadership, which the men recognized quickly and complained about vociferously. The ease with which troops on the Eastern Front gave up and went into imprisonment had multiple causes other than cowardice. On the Italian Front, Austrians fought with determination and bravery, on perhaps the worst front in the war.

Definitive statistics are not available, but between sixteen and thirty-one percent of Austro-Hungarian soldiers were taken captive, and spent prolonged periods of time in prisoner of war camps all over Russia and Central Asia. In Central Asia, Austro-Hungarian Jews came into contact for the first time with Bukharan communities, in distant towns and cities of which they had previously never heard. A large number of Jewish civilians from Przemyśl and other occupied cities were caught up in the prisoner-of-war net, and shared the same fate as captured soldiers. Jewish prisoners of war often found civilians in nearby towns who tried to be of assistance. Descriptions of Bukharan synagogue services and a Pesach seder in Turkestan are unique. The master of the house, who has two wives, is astonished when told that polygamy is not permitted amongst Ashkenazi Jews. Kaspar Blond describes an escape odyssey through Persia and Mesopotamia, and reports effects of the Armenian genocide in Aleppo.

As with my previous two books, my desire in the current volume was to give voices to long-dead men: expressing their feelings, desires, and impressions of the war. In recent years, historians have reanalyzed and rethought the contents of World War I diaries and memoirs, modifying and sometimes changing the original narrative. This has not been my aim. My belief is that thoughts and concepts of a conflict such as World War I must be analyzed with insights of the times during which they were written. Exaggerated patriotism may seem ridiculous today with a century's hindsight but at the time feelings were real and cogent.

The more than twenty nationalities of the polyglot Habsburg Empire, each with their own culture and traditions, complicated military communication, making language an important issue in troop coordination. Jewish soldiers' knowledge of languages, including German and Yiddish, gave them important places as translators and liaison with local civilian *Ostjuden*. Austro-Hungarian soldiers came into contact with *Ostjuden* on a long-term basis; Christians and the majority of Jews in the army regarded them as a curiosity, something outside their normal purview. Influx of expelled *Ostjuden* refugees into large cities such as Vienna did not improve their acceptance in the community.

Whereas the less than fifty German Jewish chaplains left sufficient written material (monographs, festival and other sermons) to fill more than one book, their Austro-Hungarian counterparts yielded scant archival material, and I was left with newspaper articles and letters to describe the feelings and activities of more than 130 chaplains from all over the Empire. A picture emerges of chaplains who were perhaps less secularly learned than their German counterparts, but whose chief interest lay in action, not writing. In contrast to their more liberal German counterparts, Austro-Hungarian chaplains dealt with Orthodox Jewish soldiers from Galicia and Bukowina, who were much more interested in mutual expounding of a page of Torah or Talmud than food, cigarettes, or newspapers. In this regard, the newspaper articles of Rabbi Leo Bertisch are instructive. The fifty-six-year-old Rabbi Adolf Kelémen is also unique, because he died from wounds received on the front. I could find no other Jewish chaplain of the Central Powers who died in the field.

The diary of Bernhard Bardach, published recently in my English translation for the first time, reports almost each day of the war in minute detail. It includes people, places, offensives (with a detailed description of the Brusilov Offensive), personal family details, description of *Ostjuden*, and of mounting food shortages as the war progressed. It also includes photographs from his unique collection of over 900 photographs. Teofil Reiss, from a large Lemberg family with relatively little education, participates wherever needed as cook, food-gatherer, and medical orderly. He has at least one young lady (sometimes more than one) in almost every town he visits. His description of one of these ladies, who arrived at the camp and announced herself as his wife, is comical. Dolu Rawitz's diary from the Italian front is full of scathing criticisms of bad leadership.

The two Hebrew novels by Avigdor Hameiri—a Hungarian from Carpatho-Ruthenia—about his participation in World War I are unique. Hameiri volunteered as soon as the war began, and served on the Carpathian and Eastern Fronts from the beginning of the war until he was taken prisoner during the Brusilov Offensive in June 1916. Both books are excerpted in this volume. The first book, *The Great Madness*, includes a wide cast of characters from all over the Habsburg Empire: Galician and Hungarian Jews (converted, assimilated, and Orthodox), Austrians, Croats, Poles, Ruthenians, Czechs, even a Gypsy or two. His reports, spiced with his acerbic humor, are mostly historically correct but he sometimes lapses into "autofiction."

Hameiri's second book, *Hell on Earth*, which was recently published for the first time in my English translation, deals with Hameiri's imprisonment in camps all over European Russia, Siberia, and Turkestan during 1916–1917. He is accompanied by three faithful friends: a faithful Calvinist Magyar, a *yeshiva* student with an agile sense of humor, and a humble Gypsy. All three die en route, the first two in gruesome ways. Some of the material is historically accurate, but some is presented as "auto-fiction" amidst a great deal of seeming hallucination due to extreme suffering. The book also includes a description of Russian Jewry suffering under Tsarist oppression, the geography of the entire area, historical personalities of all types, and camp life and its attendant corrupting influences. Hameiri was liberated in spring 1918 and spent the time until his immigration to Palestine in 1921 in Ukraine. There, he witnessed the Ukrainian anti-Jewish pogrom of 1918–1920. Like the journalist John Reed, he was there to observe everything.

The palette of Jews in the Austro-Hungarian Army is so wide that no one single book can hope to do it justice. It is my hope that this book will stimulate other researchers—with a broader command of languages than myself—to complement and broaden my findings.

This book could not have been written without the cooperation of a great many people from many countries who provided advice, information on books and memoirs, and archival assistance. Frank Mecklenburg, Michael Simonson, and Tracey Felder (Leo Baeck Institute, New York), Inka Arroyo Altezana and her staff (Central Archives for the History of the Jewish People, Jerusalem), Irene Aue Ben David (Leo Baeck Institute, Jerusalem), Lia Toaff and Sylvia Haia Antonucci (Archivio Storico della Comunità Ebraica di Roma), Christoph Tepperberg and his staff (Österreichisches Staatsarchiv/Kriegsarchiv, Vienna), Tomáš Krákora (Czech Jewish Museum, Prague). Translation and other valuable advice and assistance was given by Ljiljana Dobrovšak and Mihaela Peric (Croatian), PierLuigi Briganti (Italian), Rudolf Kučera, Kateřina Kuklíková, Pavla Urbaśkova, Katariná Pomorska (Czech), Jan Rybak, Konrad Zielinski, Marek Gałęzowski, Maciej Gorny, Michał Czajka, Stanislava Caravoulias (Polish), Yochanan Petrovsky Shtern (Russian). I thank Manfried Rauchsteiner for continued support, manuscript critique, and gracing the book with a foreword. Similarly, I thank Gerald Lamprecht for his scholarly introduction and the photograph of the Jewish Soldiers' Memorial in Vienna. Jay Winter, Marc Saperstein, and Georg Wurzer critiqued various parts of the manuscript and offered valuable suggestions. A special thanks to Georg Wurzer for sharing unique references on the Austro-Hungarian prisoner-of-war experience, obtaining (with permission) and translating documents from the State Archives of the Russian Federation, Moscow into German, and assistance with Sütterlin transcriptions. I thank Paul Bihari for sharing his doctoral dissertation with me. Ernst Schmidl, Marcus Patka, and Martin Senekowitsch are thanked for valuable advice, and Annette Hübner for transcribing cursive German. I thank Glenda Abramson for help with works by Uri Zvi Greenberg.

The following are thanked for copyright approval of archives and photographs: Leo Baeck Institutes in New York and Jerusalem; Austrian National Library; Vienna War Archives; Archiv der Republik; Jewish Museum, Vienna; Central Archives of the History of the Jewish People, Jerusalem; Museum of Czech Literature and Prague Jewish Museum, Prague; Altona Museum, Goldberg Collection; Jewish Historical Museum, Amsterdam; the Jewish Historical Archives in Rome; Katya Krausova; Buchhandlung Stöhr Verlag; Foto Fayer & Co. I thank Eva Buchberger (Böhlau Verlag) for permission to cite material from E. A. Schmidl, *Habsburgs jüdische Soldaten*; Ktav Publishing for permission to cite J. Schoenfeld, *Shtetl Memoirs*; Tuvia Erez for permission to translate and excerpt portions of his grandfather Teofil Reiss's diary; Yoni Shapira and his brothers for giving me permission to publish my own and other translations of works by their grandfather; Jonathan Orr Stav and Ilana Hairston for permission to paraphrase portions of their mother Yael Lotan's translation of Hameiri's *The Great Madness*; Tim Demy and Joseph Phillips (Stone Tower Books and Black Widow Press) for permission to cite excerpts of my recent edited version of *The Great Madness*; Wayne State University Press for permission to cite sections of my translation of Hameiri's *Hell on Earth*; the Random House Group for permission to quote From *Chronicle of a Life* by S. Trebitsch, published by William Heinemann; Cahill, Gordon, and Reindl LLP for permission to cite excerpted material by Hans Kohn. I thank Alessandra Anzani, Matthew Charlton, Ekaterina Yanduganova, Kira Nemirovsky, Ilya Nikolaev, and the staff at Academic Studies Press for their kind cooperation. Esther Dell and Robin Long provided invaluable library assistance, and Eleanor Leo took care of all things software.

The first shall come last: I thank my dearest wife Addie (*eishet chayil mi yimtza*) for her Job-like patience and forbearance during many years of travail and doubts, carefully reading through the entire manuscript, and providing valuable insights. This book would not have been possible without her. I thank my daughter Madeleine for a daughter's love.

Any errors in facts or presentation are all mine.

Peter C. Appelbaum
Land O Lakes, FL
August 2020

Plates

Plate 1. Teofil Reiss (courtesy of Tuvia Erez)

Plate 2. Avigdor Hameiri (courtesy of Yoni Shapira)

Plates | xxxi

Plate 3. Egon Kisch in uniform, 1913 (Courtesy Museum of Czech Literature, Prague)

Plate 4. Adolf (Dolu) Rawitz (courtesy of Leo Baeck Institute, Jerusalem).

Plate 5. Taste testing of kosher field kitchen for Russian prisoners of war by *Feldrabbiner* Salomon Bock (third from right) (courtesy of Katya Krausova)

Plate 6. Russian soldiers praying in an Austrian prisoner of war camp (courtesy of Austrian War Archives, Vienna)

Plates | **xxxiii**

Plate 7. Rabbi Arnold Frankfurter, flanked by Rabbis Ernst Deutsch (left), and Rudolf Ferda (right) (courtesy of Jewish Museum, Vienna).

Plate 8. Rabbi Adolf Altmann (courtesy Jewish Historical Museum, Amsterdam).

Plate 9. *Feldrabbiner* on the Isonzo front (courtesy of the Central Archives for the History of the Jewish People, Jerusalem).

Plate 10. *Feldrabbiner* conference of the the 5th Army in Trieste, 1917. Back row (left to right): S. Hirsch, A.D. Deutsch, M. Margel, E. Deutsch; Middle row (left to right): A. Schweiger, B. Hausner, S. Nagelberg, B. Diamant, M. Schwarz; Front row (left to right): A. Kelémen, Oberrabbiner P.H. Chayes, J. Frank, M. Tauber (courtesy of Jewish Museum, Vienna).

Plate 11. Simchat Torah celebration Isonzo, 1917 (courtesy Central Archives of the History of the Jewish People, Jerusalem)

Plate 12. Georg Popper, taken 1915 in Przemyśl (courtesy Austrian National Library)

Plate 13. Bukharan Jews (courtesy Austrian National Library)

Plate 14. Officers of the Austrian detachment in Persia. Kaspar Blond is second from the right (courtesy of Verlagsbuchhandlung Stöhr, Vienna)

Plate 15. Mudjahids (courtesy of Verlagsbuchhandlung Stöhr, Vienna)

Plate 16. Monument to Jewish war dead, *Zentralfriedhof*, Vienna (courtesy Gerald Lamprecht)

Plate 17. Emil Sommer, 1935 (courtesy of Martin Senekowitsch and Foto Fayr, Vienna).

Plate 18. Emil Sommer in Theresienstadt (courtesy Stiftung Historische Museen Hamburg, Altonaer Museum, Sammlung Goldberg)

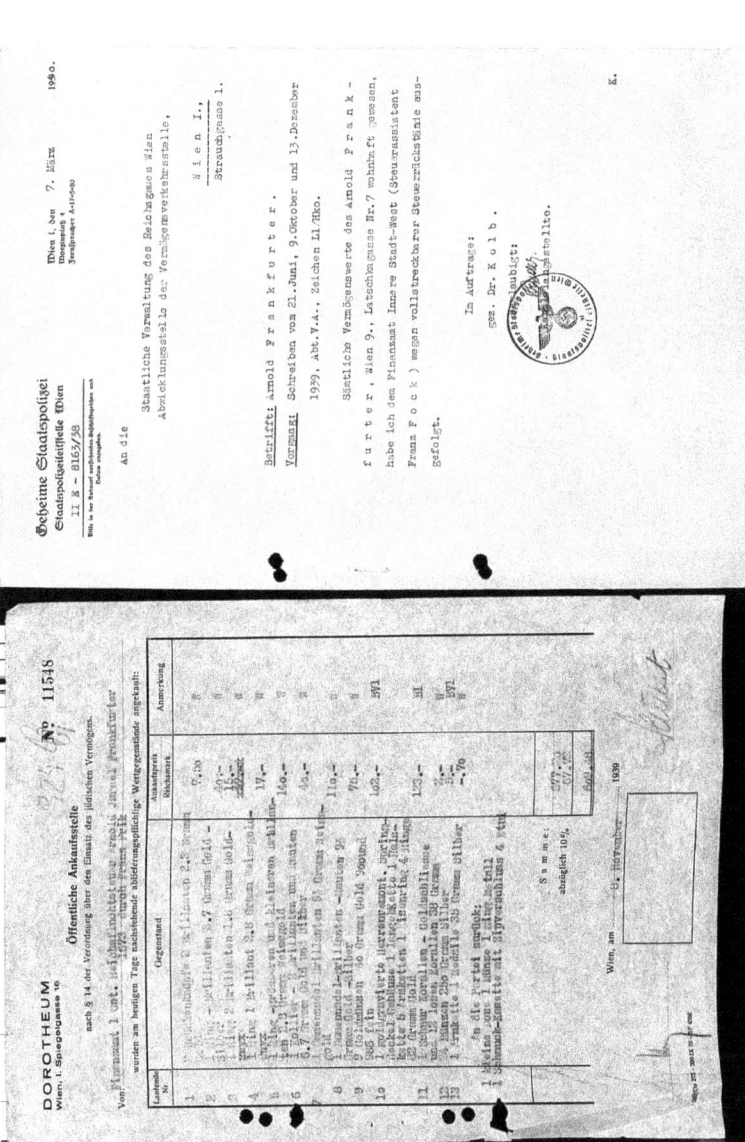

Plate 19. Gestapo correspondence regarding jewellery impounded from Rabbi Arnold Frankfurter after having deported to Buchenwald. (Archiv der Republik, VA 924).

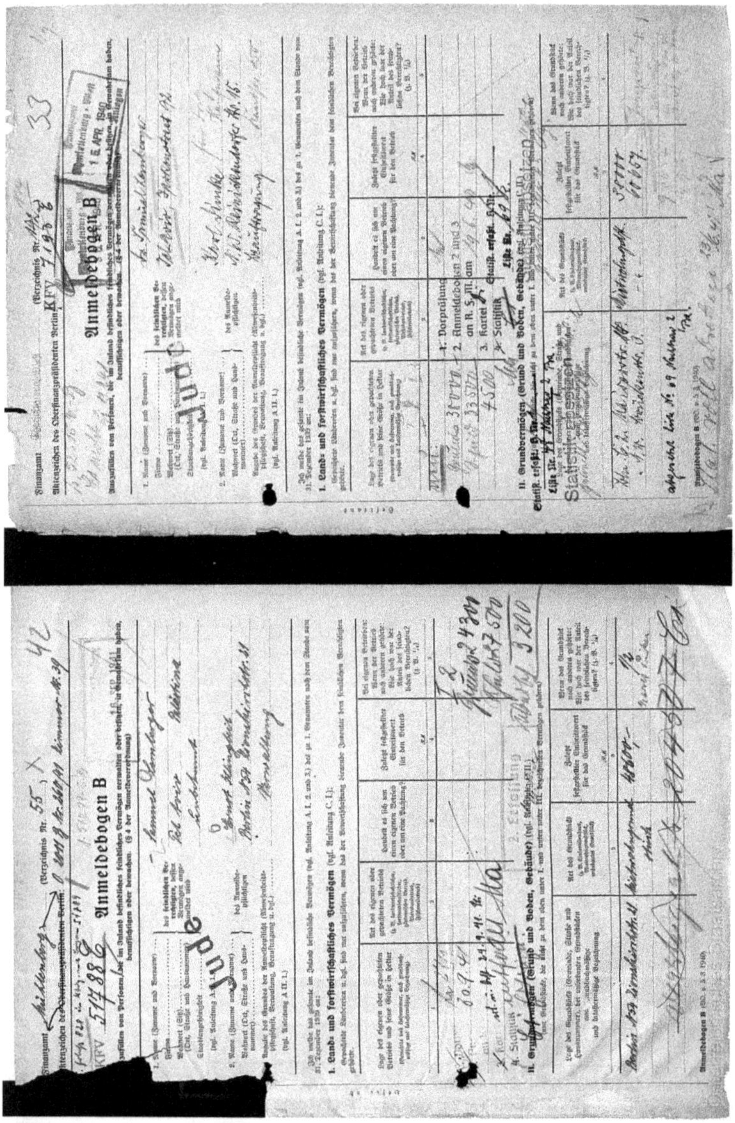

Plate 20. Gestapo correspondence on property confiscated from Rabbi Samuel Lemberger after emigration to Israel (Archiv der Republik, VA 35.248).

CHAPTER 1

Setting the Stage

World War I was the first global war, and had unprecedented Jewish participation. Never before (nor since) have Jews fought in the armies of so many countries, on both sides of a conflict simultaneously. The total number of Jewish soldiers on all sides was approximately one million.[1] Building on the findings of my two previous studies of Jews in the German Army,[2] the aim of this book is to add to existing scholarship that compares Jews in the Austro-Hungarian Army to those in Prussia and the German Reich, and to delineate the different national experiences of soldiers in the Habsburg Army, with emphasis on the Great War.

My findings may be summarized as follows: Austro-Hungary was the first country in Europe to allow Jews into the army, and, throughout the sixty-year reign of Kaiser Franz Joseph, overt antisemitism in the army was rare. Austro-Hungarian soldiers fought bravely, but often surrendered to the enemy out of exhaustion, bad leadership, atrocious weather, poor nutrition, and incompetence. Unlike their German counterparts, who were well led, Habsburg soldiers recognized and complained loudly about incompetent leadership. Czech regiments had a reputation for disloyalty, but closer analysis reveals that their performance was often due to bad leadership and other factors. Language problems with Hungarian and Slavic speakers in the multiethnic army complicated smooth functioning, but were largely overcome by Jewish soldiers, who usually spoke German and/or Yiddish.

Although Jewish soldiers were more likely than German soldiers to live in contact with *Ostjuden*, the latter were still regarded as foreign and "exotic" beings, approached with suspicion and thinly veiled dislike. This book enlarges on experience of Jewish and non-Jewish Austro-Hungarian soldiers living and fighting in close proximity with *Ostjuden* throughout the war on the Eastern Front.

A unique feature of my scholarship details prisoner-of-war experiences (mainly in Russia and Turkestan) of Austro-Hungarian soldiers; at least one fourth of all Habsburg soldiers were imprisoned throughout Russia and

Central Asia. I have included the diaries and memoirs of Jewish soldiers imprisoned as far afield as Siberia, Turkestan, Transbaikalia, and Bukhara, travel odysseys of prisoners escaping from Turkestan through Persia and Mesopotamia, and Pesach seders amongst Bukharan Jews.[3] New information on Austro-Hungarian *Feldrabbiner* has been gleaned from contemporary Jewish publications. A précis of a diary by Bernhard Bardach, an Austro-Hungarian Jewish physician who kept an extensive diary throughout the war, is provided. Finally, Jewish experiences in the Russian and Italian armies—against whom the Austro-Hungarian Army fought—are briefly analyzed.

After the *Ausgleich* [settlement] of 1867, three distinct Habsburg Armies were formed: 1) the Common Royal and Imperial (k.u.k.) Army and Marines; 2) the Royal Imperial (k.k.) Austrian (Cisleithanian) *Landwehr* (standing army); 3) the Royal Hungarian (k.u.) Honvėdsėg, or Honvėds, together with a separate Croatian *Landwehr*. General conscription was introduced in 1869 and was in effect when the war began.[4] This system, which was significantly more complex than that used in the German Army, will be used throughout this book.

I have used a wide array of documents to provide insight into the Habsburg Jewish frontline war experience: 1) newspaper articles written about, and in many cases, by serving soldiers, physicians, and chaplains; 2) diaries and memoirs, some from archives. It is important to realize that memoirs published years after the fact—such as those of Egon Kisch and especially Lavoslav Kraus (chapters 4 and 5)—must be interpreted with caution as they may not accurately reflect the status quo. However, properly analyzed, they yield valuable information. Many newspaper articles have been translated into German from original Hungarian in *Egyenlőség* (Equality—the weekly Budapest Jewish newspaper). Hungarian, Czech, Croatian, and Polish sources have been consulted, to reflect as wide a variety of soldiers in the multinational Habsburg Army as possible, outlining differences and similarities. This is of particular importance for Czech soldiers, often reported as disloyal, shirkers, and prone to change sides, culminating in formation of the Czech Legion, which played an important part in the aftermath of the October Revolution and resultant civil war.[5] Avigdor Hameiri, a Hungarian Jew from Carpatho-Ruthenia who experienced the entire war, first as a soldier and later as a Russian prisoner of war, describes Czechs as cruel prisoner-of-war guards in Russian internment camps.[6] By contrast, Egon Kisch exemplifies a Czech soldier who fought bravely during the 1914 Austro-Hungarian invasion of Serbia.[7] Corporal Siegfried Spitzer, another Czech, served for thirteen months on the Russian Front and was awarded the Silver Medal for Bravery Second Class, and Fritz Mändel served in Italy (chapters 4 and 5). I could not find disloyal sentiments in writings of these three soldiers, only complaints about inept leadership. Rozenblit asserts that bad leadership, not disloyal sentiments, were often responsible for problems with Czech units.[8] Her assertions are borne out when this issue is examined closely. I have thought that this issue requires clarification from the outset, to put individual reports of Czech disloyalty into proper perspective.

On December 5, 1917, six members of the German nationalist faction in the *Reichsrat* handed Minister of Defense von Georgi an inquiry entitled "Conduct of the Czechs in the World War."[9] Czechs were accused of having resisted mobilization, neglecting duties at the front, and committing treason by defecting to the enemy in large numbers. No authoritative documents were produced, and accusations were never disproved or commented on by authorities.

Incidents of Czech noncompliance or failure to follow orders had occurred repeatedly before the war. During the Bosnia-Herzegovina annexation crisis of 1908, mutinies in the Thirty-Sixth Infantry Regiment occurred. Severe national tensions resulted in the Twenty-Eighth Infantry Regiment (Prague House Regiment) being relocated to the Tyrol. During partial mobilization that occurred in the First Balkan War, reservists in the k.u.k. Eighth Dragoon and Eighteenth Infantry Regiments refused to board trains to Galicia. High command remained distrustful of non-German and non-Hungarian minorities, so it was easy for the myth of "Czech perfidy" to gain currency at home and abroad.[10] The reality was more complicated.

When war began, Czechs joined in patriotic demonstrations, with no signs of disloyalty, and mobilization occurred without incident. Accusations of Czech perfidy began after the k.u.k. army suffered a series of defeats in Russia and Serbia in summer and fall 1914, forcing them to withdraw across a broad front. However, failures during the 1914 Serbian campaign were mostly due to inadequate war plans and incompetent leadership. Chief of Staff Conrad von Hötzendorf was seen as chiefly responsible for the debacles, but managed to deflect responsibility by putting blame on army commanders.[11] This went down the chain of command, with many commanders digging up old prejudices against Czech, Slovak, Slovene, or Serbian soldiers, blaming them for defeats. Opening months of the war witnessed high losses (Lein asserts more than half)[12] amongst peacetime officers and men in all troop bodies, including those from Bohemia and Moravia.[13] By December 1914, the army's depleted strength was filled by middle-aged men who had never served before and were given only eight weeks of training before being sent to the front, compared to fallen or captured comrades, who had served two years in the peacetime army. Problems in army leadership continued.[14]

Initial reports of fighting by Bohemian troops appeared to lay concerns to rest: the 102nd Infantry Regiment (ninety-one percent Bohemian), was one of the first units to receive praise, followed by the Twenty-Eighth Infantry Regiment and Seventeenth Infantry Corps.[15] During the second Russian advance across the San in October 1914, the k.u.k. Nineteenth Infantry Division, mainly Czech, performed admirably. However, there were other incidents. The Seventh, Eighth, Ninth, and Twenty-First *Landwehr* Divisions, mostly composed of Czechs, gained a reputation of flight, surrender, and self-mutilation during the first days of the 1914 Serbian campaign, resulting in imposition of severe disciplinary measures due to cowardice.[16]

Subsequent reports of repeated Czech disloyalty came to a head when the Twenty-Eighth Prague House Infantry Regiment (ninety-five percent Czech) collapsed on April 3, 1915, in a battle near Zborow against numerically superior Russians.[17] Czechs were blamed for disloyalty. The case stood out because neighboring Slovene, Italian, and German units held their positions well. What passed unnoticed was that the unit had almost been destroyed in December 1914, and never fully regained its fighting spirit. When the thin line of soldiers—who had been fighting for days in heavy snow and frost—was hit by a Russian attack on April 3, surrounded, and forced to surrender, about 300 soldiers retreated in time, while approximately 1,000 officers and men were taken captive. During the battle, more than 100 officers and men of the Twenty-Eighth were killed. Austro-Hungarian high command saw this collapse as proof of Czech unreliability, and the commander of the third army, General Boroević, disbanded the regiment.[18] However, subsequent investigation, which failed to provide any proof that the Twenty-Eighth had willingly defected, proved this decision to be premature. Rather, collapse was caused by multiple factors, chiefly dismal leadership. While military courts were investigating this, one of the Twenty-Eighth's replacement platoons, which had not been disbanded owing to Italy's May 1915 war declaration, was transferred to the Isonzo, where they performed admirably.[19] Emperor Franz Joseph reestablished the regiment on December 21, 1915. However, k.u.k. high command had already announced that the regiment had been disbanded for treachery, so damage was done in the public eye.[20]

Another incident adduced for Czech treachery was mutiny on May 1, 1915 in the replacement battalion of the Twenty-First Infantry Regiment, followed by destruction of the Twenty-First and Thirty-Sixth Infantry Regiments (eighty-five percent Czech) in a Russian attack near Sieniawa (Poland). Investigation laid primary blame on the Thirty-Sixth Regiment, which was permanently disbanded on August 13, 1915.[21]

Lein argues that defeat of the Thirty-Sixth was due to other factors, suggesting that the unit's fighting ability had suffered from supply problems, frequent command changes, poorly trained reservists, and errors by superior officers.[22] Plaschka adds a history of abusive training methods to collapse of morale in the Twenty-Eighth Regiment.[23] Similarly, Rauchensteiner asserts that there was no indication that, despite all the above incidents, Czechs were especially susceptible to desertion or collaboration.[24]

K.u.k. leadership remained suspicious of Czech troops, using alleged inferior performance to shift blame for their known failures. This is especially evident during the Brusilov Offensive.[25] Since it became clear that the crippling attack was due to careless combat tactics, which failed to consider Russian shock troop tactics, k.u.k. leadership again decided to shift the blame onto the Czechs.[26] As will be discussed later (chapter 7), lack of supplies and equipment, extreme weather, and bad leadership can discourage even the hardiest soldier (Jew and Christian alike), and lead to lack of fighting spirit, collapse of morale, and desertions.

As 1918 progressed and chances for a Central Powers victory disappeared, non-German nationalities within the empire agitated increasingly for independence. Czechs and Slovaks were encouraged by efforts of the Czechoslovak nationalist Tomáš Masaryk (1850–1937), but similar nationalist sentiments were voiced by Hungarians, Poles, and Southern Slavs (Serbs, Croats, Slovenes, and Bosnians). Ultimately, Emperor Karl I (Charles I) was unable to keep the empire together, and it disintegrated into its component parts.

Apart from Czechs, Ruthenians are described negatively in many reports.[27] Bernhard Bardach describes Bosnian cowardice in his unit, but Paul Amman stresses their bravery (chapter 4). I argue that generalities cannot be made regarding the loyalties of Habsburg minorities in the army: many other factors, including a desire for their own homeland and lack of desire to fight when the war appeared to be lost, need to be considered.[28]

Experiences between nationalities differed significantly. Language played an important role: many soldiers, especially from Slavic countries, knew no more German than the eighty standard army commands, and each nationality had unique cultural heritages. Hungarians in the empire had been given full rights only in 1867, less than fifty years before the war began, and Jews were at the forefront of the Kossuth rebellion (chapter 2). The lingua franca of educated Czech Jews was German, not Czech; problems of Czech loyalty have been discussed. Poland ceased to exist as a nation with its third partition in 1795, and nationalist feelings simmered during the approximately 120 years before the war began.[29] Portions of Austro-Hungarian Poland like Galicia and Bukowina contained large Jewish populations, many Orthodox, whose loyalty to the supranational Habsburg monarchy was bolstered by antipathy to the oppressive Tsarist regime with its Pale of Jewish Settlement, pogroms, and persecutions. In the case of Christian Southern Slavs, loyalties were complicated. Croats were more loyal to the empire than Habsburg Serbs, and portions of Slovenia and the Tyrol had strong Italian influences. Lavoslav Kraus, a Croatian Jew from Osijek, doubted the moral underpinning of the war, but nevertheless fought bravely, with medals to prove it (chapter 4).[30]

The composition of the Austro-Hungarian Army reflected the empire's ethnic and linguistic composition. For every 1,000 soldiers, 267 spoke German, 223 Hungarian, 135 Czech, eighty-five Polish, eighty-one Ukrainian, sixty-seven Serbo-Croatian, sixty-four Romanian, thirty-eight Slovakian, twenty-six Slovenian, and fourteen Italian.[31] Deák has reported that, at the start of the war, 142 units in the Habsburg Army were monolingual, 162 bilingual, and twenty-four trilingual, with a handful of units in which four or more languages were spoken.[32] Engle has asserted that language barrier was a significant cause of miscommunications and misunderstandings amongst polyglot Habsburg nationalities, especially Hungarians and Slavs.[33] I argue that Jews in the Habsburg Army were more capable of communicating with military authorities than Slavic or Hungarian soldiers. Jewish educated classes throughout the empire used German as lingua franca, or were well conversant with the language. Additionally, Orthodox Jewish soldiers from regions like Galicia, Bukowina, and Poland spoke Yiddish, a descendant of *Mittelhochdeutsch*, comprehensible (although looked down upon) by German-speakers, allowing soldiers to follow orders more easily. Yiddish also allowed easier communication with civilian *Ostjuden*. The above did not apply to Sephardic Jews from the Balkans and Italy, whose mother tongue was Ladino (Judeo-Spanish).

I also argue that postwar experiences of different nationalities differed, with Jewish veterans often playing an important part in political developments. The Hungarian Communist party was founded by Béla Kun (who became a Russian prisoner of war in 1916 and was sent to a camp in the Urals, where he first became interested in communism). After overthrow of the immediate postwar Social Democratic Károlyi government, the short-lived 1919

Hungarian Soviet Republic—led by the Garbai government—comprised a majority of Jewish veterans and non-veterans such as Béla Kun, Vilmos Böhm, Tibor Szamuely, Jenő Varga, Zsigmond Kunfi, József Pogány, Jenő Landler, György Lukács, and others.[34] Lavoslav Kraus became a Communist during the war and fought with Béla Kun to defend the 1919 Hungarian Communist Revolution.[35] Josip Broz Tito, future postwar leader of Yugoslavia, spent his formative years as a Habsburg soldier.

The role of Jewish veterans in antidemocratic political activities in postwar Poland and Czechoslovakia was less marked. In Czechoslovakia, the enlightened, democratic leadership of Tomáš Masaryk prevented postwar bloodshed and revolution. Jewish veterans in regions such as Transylvania that were annexed by Romania found themselves living under increased antisemitic conditions which affected loyalty to the newly enlarged Romanian state. Carpatho-Ruthenian Jews were absorbed into the eastern portion of Czechoslovakia under Masaryk's benign rule. In the newly created Polish state, immediate postwar years saw horrific pogroms (especially in Lemberg, Pinsk [Belarus], Vilna)[36] against Jewish veterans and non-veterans alike, with wars between Poland and Ukraine/Russia, until Marshal Józef Piłsudski (1867–1935) stabilized the government in the early 1920s; however, a degree of antisemitism remained. In postwar Italy, Mussolini's black shirts held the appeal of order, but its authoritarianism left most Italian Jews (including veterans) feeling uneasy.

The situation of the Austro-Hungarian Army was unique in that, according to Rachamimow, as many as 2.77 million Austro-Hungarian soldiers became Russian prisoners of war. This occurred in large "catches," for example the surrender of Przemyśl on March 22, 1915, the "Black and Yellow Offensive" of September 1915, and the Brusilov Offensive starting in June 1916, which saw approximately 750,000 Austro-Hungarian soldiers killed, wounded, missing, or captive. Entire regiments refused to fight, and were captured. Germany, the other major member of the Central Powers fighting on the Eastern Front, sent troops only when the Austro-Hungarian Army failed, or to bolster a large offensive, and had approximately 167,000 soldiers captured by the Russians.[37] Russian imprisonment was unique, in that large numbers of civilians—many Jewish—from occupied cities such as Przemyśl were sent into captivity, many in Central Asia. Before the Russian Revolution, treatment of officer prisoners was remarkably benign; monthly allowances of fifty rubles bought a comfortable standard of living (with exemption from work), better than in prisoner-of-war camps of other Entente members (chapter 7). At large assembly camps near Moscow and Kiev, prisoners were separated by ethnicity. In general, soldiers of Slavic origin and those from Alsace-Lorraine were incarcerated in European Russia. Other nationalities, including Hungarians and German-Austrians, were sent to Siberia and Turkestan. That does not mean that conditions were better in European Russia: some of the best run camps were in Siberia.[38]

Many Jewish soldiers' prisoners of war diaries written by in what was at the time called Turkestan (modern day Uzbekistan, Kazakhstan, Kyrgyzstan), have not been seen before in English translation. Prisoners found themselves as far afield as Tashkent, Osh, Kokand, Transbaikalia, and Astrakhan. Hans Kohn describes his journey to a remote outpost in the Pamir Mountains near Chinese Turkestan,[39] while Adolf Epstein describes Bukharan synagogue services and Pesach family seders.[40] The complex escape stories of some Austro-Hungarian prisoners such as Kaspar Blond from Turkestan through Persia, Mesopotamia via Ottoman Turkey, are unique. Blond witnessed the effects of the Armenian genocide, the first of its kind, and a pivotal event in the twentieth century, at first hand in Aleppo.[41] By contrast, written experiences of German soldiers in Russian captivity are scarce.

Prisoner experiences of officers and enlisted men in Russia—at least until the February Revolution of 1917—were very different because of the officers' generous monthly allowance. There is no evidence that Jewish prisoners were at least overtly discriminated against. By contrast, Jewish prisoners (both officers and men) had the advantage of support from local civilian Jewish communities.[42] The best description of enlisted compared to officer prisoners of war that I could find comes from a fictitious (but probably fact-based) description by Breithaupt of officers, enlisted men, and civilians from Przemyśl side by side (but separated) in a Transbaikalian camp (chapter 7).[43] I have divided Austro-Hungarian prisoner experiences by region, for comparison and differentiation of experiences and opinions of each group.

An additional aspect addressed in this book is the unique nature of contact between Austro-Hungarian soldiers, and Jewish civilians living on the Eastern Front. This is touched upon in my two previous volumes and expanded in this book. I assert that the Austro-Hungarian soldier's exposure to Eastern European and Russian Jewish civilians was broader, and occurred over longer periods of time, than that of his German counterpart. Whereas German-and Austro-German Jewish soldiers—especially those from large cities—had little previous contact with *Ostjuden*, Austro-Hungarian Jews from regions such as Galicia and Bukowina were well acquainted with them. Indeed, many soldiers from the latter two regions were themselves Orthodox *Peyes-* (side locks) and *Kaftanjuden*, who must have appeared otherworldly to their assimilated brethren. That does not mean that they regarded them as equals: indeed, their feeling of strangeness was almost as strong as their Christian counterparts.[44] Orthodox Jews fought as fiercely, if not more so, as did assimilated coreligionists, stoked by hatred of Russian oppressors (see chapter 4).

Tamara Scheer asserts that, in and out of the army, Jews in the prewar Habsburg Army were, with other nationalities, considered in the "other" category. This despite their strong feeling for the supranational nature of the empire.[45] That Jews themselves recognized antisemitism, covert or obvious, always present in Kaiser Franz Joseph's empire, and their problem with Austrian identity, is obvious from the play "Professor Bernhardi" by Arthur Schnitzler (1862–1931).[46] Karl Lueger (1844–1910), Mayor of Vienna, was openly antisemitic.

Germans—apart from Battles of Tannenberg and the Masurian Lakes and their campaign in Courland (Western Latvia)—served on the Eastern Front only to bolster their Central Powers partners such as during the 1915 Gorlice-Tarnów Offensive, or to stem the Russian advance during the Brusilov Offensive of 1916. Apart from the Battle of Caporetto (October 24 to November 19, 1917), Austro-Hungarians fought the Italians alone.

Vejas Gabriel Liulevicius asserts that German troops in *Ober Ost* developed a "mindscape" of revulsion towards the "East," and came to think of it as a timeless region beset by chaos, frozen winters, spring flooding, disease and barbarism, instead of what it really was, a region suffering from ravages of warfare. He claims that the encounter with the East formed an idea of "spaces (*Raum*) and races" that needed to be cleared and cleansed by German *Kultur*.[47] This does not seem to have been the case with Austro-Hungarian soldiers, who served uninterruptedly on the Eastern Front until hostilities ceased after the Russian Revolution in 1917.

In my recent book, I have made available for the first time an annotated English translation of the diaries of Bernhard Bardach (see above), who spent the entire war on the Eastern (and later on the Italian) Front. These meticulous diaries shed light on a hitherto neglected theater of World War I.[48] Bardach describes day-to-day activities of the Austro-Hungarian Army, including bad leadership, unpreparedness for battle, bad planning. His criticism of inept leadership is echoed in other diaries on both Eastern and Italian Fronts (chapters 4 and 5).

Unlike German Jewish physicians such as Nathan Wolf and Hugo Natt, whose diaries are replete with descriptions of their medical duties,[49] Bardach's medical activities are not emphasized. Still, it is clear that they were onerous, dangerous, and performed in all weather and road conditions: hot dusty summers, icy, snowy winters, thawing periods, and fall rains that turned roads into seas of mud making transportation almost impossible. Dr. Isidore Segall, like the Germans Nathan Wolf and Hugo Natt, describes bandaging wounds in the middle of the firing line, surrounded by blood and wounded men. Mention must also be made of Dr. Alfred Adler, the first to describe "war neurosis" in his treatment of soldiers from the front line (chapter 4).

Bardach describes the battles for the Carpathians in 1914–1915, the Gorlice-Tarnów Offensive of 1915 and in particular the 1916 Brusilov Offensive. He is right in the middle of the Brusilov Offensive from the outset, and his hour-by-hour description of its first desperate days and weeks, followed by repeated attacks by both sides that achieved nothing but casualties and exhaustion, is unique. Adolf Mechner, serving in Brody (Ukraine), confirms chaos and bloodshed at the start of the Brusilov Offensive (chapter 4). Bardach acidly names the Austro-Hungarian commanders (especially General Kralowetz) responsible for the debacle, and describes how arrival of Hindenburg, and bolstering of the front with German troops, helped stem the tide. He reports endless attacks and counter-attacks that made both Austro-Hungarian and Russian Armies spent forces after the offensive petered out.[50] Like the journalist John Reed, he was there. Things calm down in 1917, which he spends in Volhynia.[51] Towards the end of the war he is transferred to the Italian Front, and he ends the war on the Piave.

Bardach's diary is replete with personal anecdotes, weather reports, long periods of boredom, and detailed descriptions of other fronts. As befits an officer in Kaiser Franz Joseph's army, he is a bit of a snob and sets great store by seating arrangements at meals and efflorescence of rank and medals. At various points, we obtain insight on his family in Vienna, who are the fulcrum of his life during long periods away from home.[52] Starting in 1916 and with increasing desperation, food and other shortages are reported. He sends regular food packages home, with amounts and costs reported in detail.[53] By 1918, shortages have become catastrophic and he believes that a weakening of the home front played a major role in Austrian defeat. Some of his views approximate the "stab in the back myth" (*Dolchstosslegende*).

A unique aspect of the Bardach legacy is the collection of over 900 photographs he took, on all aspects of the war. His diary must be taken in conjunction with these, often masterful, photographs, which depict cruelty of war, often in chilling detail. Text and photographs show an almost physical distancing of Bardach—an assimilated Austrian Jew—from the exotic-looking *Ostjuden*, whom he observes as if he were on the outside looking in. He regards Russian Jews whom he meets in synagogue on High Holidays in the same light.[54]

Additional soldiers' diaries offer other insights. Teofil Reiss (chapter 4), one of sixteen children of a poor Galician family, served as factotum, cook, and medical orderly, predominantly on the Russian Front. His language is that of a man of limited education, and his unique diary is studded with affairs with a girl (sometimes more than one) in every village. He comes from Lemberg, capital of Galicia, and, like the much more educated, assimilated Bernhard Bardach (see below) describes Tarnów as a "dirty, typically Jewish town." It is evident that greater or lesser feelings of disdain for poor rural *Ostjuden* was not limited to Jewish educated classes.[55]

Reading these sources has led me to conclude that suffering Jewish civilians of Eastern Europe frequently looked on the armies of the Central Powers as liberators. Most spoke Yiddish, allowing them to communicate with German speaking troops more easily than their non-Jewish counterparts whose mother tongue was Slavic or Hungarian. Cruelty and depredations of Russian troops against Jewish civilians are well documented, sometimes reaching grotesque proportions. However, the situation was complicated, as exemplified by the file of Jewish State Representative to the Fourth Duma in Łódź Meer Khaimovich Bomash (1861–1947) in the GARF (*Gosudarstvenny Arkhiv Rossiiskoi Federatsii*, Moscow) archives.

Bomash, a physician, was elected to the Łódź Duma in 1912. In fall 1914 he founded, with the Duma representative from Kovno N. M. Fridman, an association to assist Jewish soldiers and civilians suffering as a result of the war.[56] In February and March 1915, the two men met with members of the government, including Foreign Minister Sergei Dmitrievich Sazonov (1860–1927) and Finance Minister Piotr Lvovich Bark (1869–1937), to discuss the situation of the Jewish civilians in the front lines; nothing was done. In August 1915 and 1916 Bomash testified in the Duma about antisemitic publications and closure of Jewish presses—again, no response.

From August 1914, several Jewish (Yiddish) printing presses (even for children's books) were closed, and the sale of books in Yiddish and performance of Yiddish plays were banned, in Vilna, Vitebsk, Kiev, Odessa, and other locations.[57] The ban on writing letters from the front in Yiddish prevented soldiers in trenches and field hospitals from communicating with their families, sometimes for the last time. Most Russian Jews were locked up in the Pale of Settlement, powerless to do anything to help the motherland. The folly of these measures—which could only serve to further alienate the Russian Jewish masses—was pointed out to Bomash by S. A. (probably a member of the Jewish soldiers' assistance association), to no avail.

Bomash's file includes an anguished description of:

> . . . a significant portion of the population plunged into misery and despair. Conditions are similar to what they were in the Middle Ages, when Jews were accused of well poisoning and host desecration. Jews are blamed for the war and its accompanying suffering and misery. Instead of burning copies of the Talmud in the village square [as was done during the thirteenth and fourteenth centuries], Jewish cultural and political thought is choked off by censorship. There is, however, a significant part of the population who understand that the "Jewish" question is in reality a Russian question. Jewish freedom of expression and thought really means Russian freedom of expression and thought. Expression and publication in Yiddish must be allowed, and restrictions lifted.

The scene changes to the town of Wilkomir, with a population of 15,000, two-thirds of these Jewish.[58] At best, relations between Jews and non-Jews (Poles, Lithuanians) were strained. But in April 1915, as S. A. reported, rumor spread that Jews had gathered to celebrate the Central Powers occupation of Kovno, and had defaced a portrait of the Tsar. In early May, an order came down expelling Jews from the entire province. Because there was no railway, and other forms of transport were difficult to obtain, most left on foot, taking the little that they could carry with them. Most merchants were Jews, and the economy quickly collapsed, with rampant inflation, impoverishment, and desolation.

S. A. also described depredations from Western Galicia in early 1915. The entire area was either partially or totally destroyed. Cossacks plundered everything, starting with Jewish stores and properties that the fleeing Jews had let behind. Stores were broken into and goods plundered, or sold without regard for financial order. Successive towns were completely looted. Russians retreated and then advanced again; each time destruction worsened. The ground was so covered with filth that the only dry ground was in what was left of the houses. In Tuchów (Poland), which had 400 families (150 Jewish), only two houses were left standing, crowded with fifteen to twenty people (two invalids). The beautiful synagogue ark was chopped up and used for wood, and horses stabled inside the building, which soon filled with stinking dung. Cossacks found and desecrated the Torah scrolls that the congregation had carefully hidden.

S. A. continued that all wealthy Jews had departed first, leaving only the poor behind. All forms of civilian life had been destroyed: schools closed, and children begged, allowing themselves to be sold in the streets. When Cossacks arrived in Brody (eighty percent Jewish), Jewish girls were used for bayonet practice, and more than a hundred houses burned to the ground with kerosene and sulfur. Rumors of Jewish espionage abounded, and served to increase Cossack barbarity against Jews, many of whom were forced into compulsory labor. Rape of Jewish women was the norm. One young boy was told that his life would be spared if he hanged his father. He hanged his father and then the Cossacks hanged him. In one case, a dying Russian begged for a rabbi to cleanse his guilty conscience: he had killed an old Jew with a bayonet because he refused to hand over his money. The rabbi, not knowing what to do, promised to return but by the time he did, the Russian had died. Tearful prayers were offered up in the local synagogue. As was routine, hostages were taken and some executed.

Instead of dealing with their Jewish question honestly and directly, the government resorted to diversions. In January 1916, Director of Police K. D. Kefafov sent a circular to district and police leaders accusing Jews of economic sabotage. Fridman and Bomash complained about this in the Duma, but the cadet party felt that this would lead to a split in the progressive block. Bomash requested a toned-down version of the circular, but this too was denied, whereupon he bemoaned inability of a Jewish Duma delegate to have any influence on politics.[59]

Russian Jews (even those in positions of some authority) were in an invidious position. Even when their few elected representatives tried to improve their condition, nothing happened. During the course of the war, several hundred thousand Jewish civilians were expelled from their homes, becoming wandering refugees.[60] Suspicion of espionage (for example after Russian occupation of Przemyśl) led to many Jewish civilians being sent to prison camps in Russia and Central Asia (chapter 7). Jewish civilians often suffered at the hands of soldiers of the Central Powers as well; provisions, livestock, and other war material were requisitioned, leaving civilians with little. However, wholesale burning, plundering, mass expulsions, rape, synagogue desecration, and murder carried out by the Tsar's soldiers did not occur during German or Austrian occupation. Thirty years later, the situation would be reversed: those same soldiers exterminated Eastern European Jewish culture, and the Red Army liberated the remnant that was left. Soldiers on the Eastern Front encountered an entire civilization shortly before it was destroyed in the Holocaust.

Another finding of my research is that, unlike the German Army, Austro-Hungarian soldiers—Jewish and non-Jewish alike—criticized and complained vociferously about the disorganized, inefficient military command structure of their own army. Although Habsburg's Jews understood, perhaps better than anyone else, the supranational nature of the empire, and their love for Kaiser Franz Joseph (Ephraim Yossele, as some called him) was deep, this did not blind them to their army's inefficiencies.[61] Germans were confident of the army's ability and did not question it until the last months of the war. German military leadership was superior to that of Austro-Hungary and their soldiers more disciplined, but that did not mean that Austro-Hungarian soldiers were less brave—as witnessed on the Italian Front. Austro-Hungarian military bureaucracy—described by the serving painter Joseph Floch—was largely ossified, fighting the previous war. Arnold Höllriegel describes the good-natured stupidity of Austrian officials (chapter 4); Adolf (Dolu) Rawitz spends much of his diary making sarcastic remarks about inept leadership on the Italian Front (chapter 5), and Bernhard Bardach (see above) rails against bad leadership that brought about the initial collapse at the start of the Brusilov Offensive.

Due to Joseph II's early Jewish *Toleranzpatente*, Austro-Hungary was the first European state that allowed Jews to serve in the army, even before the French Revolution. The more than sixty-year relatively benign reign of Kaiser Franz Joseph gave Austro-Hungary's Jews considerable upward mobility in the army and possibility of ennoblement, without, like Germany, the need to convert. In the Hungarian Honvéd army, Jews served (including as officers) and died in disproportionate numbers (chapter 2). Although no formal *Burgfrieden* was decreed in Austria-Hungary, as it was in Germany (chapter 3), overt antisemitism was much less marked in the Austro-Hungarian compared to the German Army, with its noxious *Judenzählung* of 1916.[62] Antisemitism increased during the last two years of the war, when it became clear that the Central Powers could not win. A *Judenzählung* was suggested for Austria-Hungary, but refused outright.[63] Jewish Austro-Hungarian soldiers' books and diaries do make mention of antisemitism, but often brush it off when it does occur. Bardach's diary of 557 handwritten pages mentions only two incidents of antisemitism in passing, both without special emphasis. In one incident, he is sitting at table next to an officer with antisemitic opinions, which he brushes off with a humorous remark and no further comment.[64] David Neumann describes disproving that he is a shirker by doing extra exercise during basic training, and Eugen Hoflich is falsely accused of cowardice. Teofil

Reiss mentions antisemitism several times in his diaries, and Avigdor Hameiri comments acidly on a Hungarian colonel, the unit's arch antisemite (chapter 4). Lilian Bader, reporting on her husband Edwin Bader's service on the Italian front as a physician with the *Meraner Scharfschützen* (Meran/Tyrolean sharp-shooters)—the cream of the Habsburg Army—briefly mentions antisemitic comments at dinner on the Italian Front. At first no one could believe that the blond-haired Bader was Jewish, but antagonism soon disappeared when they experienced his abilities first-hand (chapter 5).

Russia and Italy reflected two polar opposites: blatant antisemitism and no rights on the one hand, freedom and equal rights on the other. In the Russian army Jews were tolerated, but not promoted to officer's rank, and received no special treatment whatsoever, including no spiritual care. Despite pogroms and discrimination, Russian Jews volunteered enthusiastically when war began.[65] By contrast, Italian Jewish soldiers received every possible special consideration. The ratio of Italian Jews who served relative to the entire Jewish population was perhaps highest of all warring parties, and Italian Jewish officers, many with very high rank, were the norm, not the exception (chapter 5).

As in my previous two books, I have endeavored to add to information by historiographers and demographers, by providing qualitative accounts, restoring a voice to Jewish soldiers from many nationalities and languages, whose experiences in the Great War have hitherto been ignored or undervalued. Reports have been accessed from as many nationalities from the polyglot Empire as possible, compared and contrasted with one another. One of the best sources of information about the multinational Habsburg army is Avigdor Hameiri's first war book, *The Great Madness*. According to Hameiri, the army was composed of simple Magyar peasants, sophisticated Budapest artistic types, including assimilated and converted Hungarian Jews who tried their best to hide their Jewishness, shady underworld characters, Italian workmen, Orthodox Talmudic scholars who attacked the enemy wrapped in tefillin crying *Sh'ma Yisrael*, haughty Austrian nobility, Croats, and secretly nationalistic Czechs, spiced with a Gypsy or two. They are all there, in this great work.[66]

What were the similarities and differences between Jewish experiences in the Habsburg Armies and those in the German Reich? When dealing with statistics and demography, numbers must be leavened with the fact that there were five times more Jews living in Austro-Hungary than in all German states combined, complicating accurate statistical analysis. Unlike Germany, Austro-Hungary did not keep precise statistics, and there are no exact data on the number of Jewish soldiers who served in the Habsburg Army during the war.

Figures between 275,000 and 400,000 have been adduced: it is likely that 300,000–350,000 served. Of these, 30,000–40,000 died of wounds or illness. Approximately 25,000 Jews (c. 10% of the total number who served) were professional or reserve officers, a much larger number than that in the German army, and the Austro-Hungarian army entered the war with many Jewish officers. More than 1,000 Jewish officers were killed in action, and at least 7% of all officers killed in action were Jews; however, it is likely that this number is much higher.[67] According to Hungarian government statistics, 155,799 of a total of 378,000 soldiers (41.1%) active in the war in Hungary were fatally wounded, including those who died as a consequence of their wounds. Out of these 155,799 soldiers, 5,116 were Jews. Among 352,292 wounded soldiers, 15,339 were Jews, as were 3,770 of 74,860 war disabled. Some Hungarian historians believe these figures to refer to only some cities (Szeged, Pècs, Miskolc, Budapest), meaning that the actual number of killed, wounded, and missing is probably significantly higher. The number of Jewish soldiers from contiguous Croatia and Slavonia is unknown, but some believe that nine of every 100 inhabitants (including Jews) served in the army. According to the 1910 census, Croatia's 21,103 Jews represented around 0.8% of its 2,621,954 inhabitants. After outbreak of the war, young Croatian and Slavonian Jewish men were mobilized into field units. At least seven divisions were recruited when war began, mainly the k.u.k. Thirty-Sixth and Seventh Infantry Divisions, and the Hungarian-Croatian Forty-Second Croatian *Landwehr* Division. Croatian divisions fought in the 1914 and 1915 Serbian campaigns, and were transferred to the Eastern Front in late 1915, then to the Tyrol in 1918. Dobrovšak has enumerated 107 Croatian Jews killed during the war, but statistics are incomplete.[68] By contrast, the numbers of Jews in the Serbian Army are more exact (150 of 600 mobilized Jews killed, wounded, or dead of other causes).[69]

Czechs living in Bohemia and Moravia comprised approximately 13% of the Austro-Hungarian Army, and comprised two thirds in more than twenty-five regiments of the k.u.k. army, and thirteen regiments of the k.k. *Landwehr*. Certain regiments could be regarded as exclusively Czech, while dozens of others had significant numbers of Czech soldiers.[70] The approximately one million Czech-speaking soldiers included 12,000 active and 22,500 reserve officers (excluding officer-candidates).[71] The role played by Austrian Poles is complicated by the fact that, during World War I, Poland did not exist as a country but was divided into Congress Poland (administered by Russia until the Gorlice-Tarnów Offensive, with occupation of Warsaw and points east, including Vilna) and Western Poland, including Galicia, Bukowina (Austro-

Hungary), and Pomerania and Silesia (Germany). Poles comprised the majority of soldiers in several k.k. *Landwehr* and k.u. Honvéd regiments, and were distributed throughout other regiments and branches. Out of approximately 630,000 Polish speaking Habsburg soldiers, 3,800 were active and 6,600 reserve officers (excluding officer candidates). A separate voluntary formation, the Polish Legions under Piłsudski, with more than 600 Jewish soldiers, took the *Landsturm* oath and gave valuable service through 1916 (chapter 4).[72] The exact number of Czech and Polish Jews in the Habsburg Army is unknown, but must have corresponded with the general population in each region.

In Germany, more precise overall figures are available: Approximately 100,000 Jews served in the Kaiser's army; of these, about 80,000 served on the front, and 12,000 were killed, died from other causes, or went missing. Approximately 35,000 were decorated, and 23,000 promoted. Despite there not being a single Jewish officer in the pre-World War I German Army, more than 2,000 became officers during the war, not including more than 1,100 medical orderlies and assistants.[73] These promotions took place in the presence of increasing antisemitism, especially after the October 1916 *Judenzählung* (see above).

In my first book, I set out details about *Feldrabbiner* in the German Army.[74] The forty-five chaplains and assistant chaplains who served were mostly Liberal, from a relatively homogenous Jewish background. They served on Western and Eastern Fronts, and saw to religious needs of Jewish (and if necessary non-Jewish) soldiers. The tone of their writing is formal, reflecting a learned secular and non-secular background, with little emphasis on Orthodoxy.[75] By comparison, the approximately 133 Austro-Hungarian Jewish chaplains (chapter 6) reflect larger numbers of Jewish soldiers in the Habsburg than in the German Army. I argue that Austro-Hungarian Jewish soldiers were unique because of their varied nationalities, languages, backgrounds, and religious affiliations. One chaplain, Rabbi Adolf Kelémen, was fifty-three when he volunteered; he died after being wounded by a shell fragment on the Romanian Front in 1917 (chapter 6). The Habsburg Army was the only fighting force on either side in which needs of large numbers of Orthodox Jewish soldiers (mainly from Galicia and Bukowina) were addressed. This included kosher dining facilities, where possible, provided at government expense. This convenience even extended in some cases to Russian prisoners of war. Dietary and other regulations for Pesach were published in the official military gazette, and chaplains from both Orthodox and Progressive backgrounds, speaking different languages of the empire, were made available. Each unit had its own liturgical objects such as Torah scrolls, prayer books, and prayer shawls. Russian and Serbian Jewish prisoners of war participated in services and festive meals, and in some cases even had their own prayer rooms.[76] By contrast, the German Army did not provide kosher kitchens or liturgical objects, but assisted in other ways such as leave and assembly points, provision of cooking material and potatoes. German chaplains had to provide provisions and liturgical objects from private sources, mainly their own communities and lodges.[77] Orthodox soldiers also served in the Russian Army, but no official allowances for them were made, and no chaplains provided.[78]

Compared to German chaplains, Austro-Hungarian chaplains wrote significantly less about military experiences, perhaps because they were less formal, less prolix in words, and more deeply involved in the day-to-day lives of their charges. Their writings demonstrate men of few words but great humility, kindness, and dedication. Jewish chaplains served nearby civilian communities and refugees without let or hindrance, whereas German chaplains had to go through an often onerous command procedure before this was permitted.[79] The result was the same, but bureaucratic hurdles differed.

In contrast to German chaplains, some of whom wrote lengthy monographs and published their sermons, newspaper articles (mainly in *Dr. Bloch's Österreichische Wochenschrift*) were my principal source for the writings of Austro-Hungarian *Feldrabbiner*. The writings of Rabbi Leo Bertisch (chapter 6) are unique: they are the only ones I could find that deal in detail with Biblical and Talmudic texts, expounding on the role of the priests as chaplains. Rabbi Bertisch stresses that mutual learning of a page or two of Talmud or Torah was more important to Orthodox soldiers than tangible gifts from home. This is not reported in writings of German *Feldrabbiner*, who emphasize material gifts from home, smoking, and reading material.

As was the case with respect to the Jews in Germany, a special role was played by Austro-Hungarian Jews in financing the war effort. Their share in war loans, through a corporation or individually, reached ten percent of the total amount. They also played an important role in production of war materials. Some were rewarded by the rulers with aristocratic titles and honors.[80]

This book makes no pretense at historiographic hypotheses. Instead, as was the case with my other books, it attempts to put flesh, sinews, and blood vessels on bones of the long dead, allowing their voices to be heard after a century has passed. Other more formal analyses should be used to examine these issues from different points of view.

In addition to the current introduction, this book contains seven more chapters. The second chapter traces the fate of Habsburg Jewish soldiers from the *Toleranzpatent* of Joseph II through 1914. Chapter 3 uses books, memoirs, journals, and newspaper articles from all parts of the empire, to describe and compare initial feelings and writings of Austro-Hungary's Jews during early August days of the war. The following two chapters deal with diaries and memoirs of Jewish soldiers on the Eastern (chapter 4), and Italian, Balkan, and Ottoman Fronts (chapter 5). I have attempted to break down diaries by nationality, comparing and contrasting war experiences of Jewish soldiers from as many parts of the empire as possible. The sixth chapter reflects service of Austro-Hungarian *Feldrabbiner*. Chapter 7 deals with prisoner-of-war experiences of Austro-Hungarian Jewish soldiers, broken down by area of imprisonment. The book concludes with the postwar fate of Austro-Hungarian Jewish veterans, with special reference to the Shoah. The divergent fate of Jewish veterans from different nationalities is described, especially with regard to their role in the short-lived postwar Hungarian Communist Revolution.

Endnotes

1. J. Karp, M. L. Rozenblit, "Introduction. On the Significance of World War I and the Jews," in *World War I and the Jews. Conflict and Transformation in Europe, the Middle East, and America*, ed. M. L. Rozenblit and J. Karp (New York and Oxford: Berghahn Books, 2017), 5.
2. P. C. Appelbaum, *Loyalty Betrayed. Jewish Chaplains in the German Army During the First World War* (London and Portland, OR: Vallentine-Mitchell, 2014); idem, *Loyal Sons. Jews in the German Army in the Great War* (London and Portland, OR: Vallentine-Mitchell, 2014).
3. The Emirate of Bukhara was a Central Asian state that existed from 1785 to 1920 on the territory of the modern-day Uzbekistan. It occupied the land between the Amu Darya and Syr Darya rivers, and was home to a large Jewish population.
4. E.A. Schmidl, *Habsburgs jüdische Soldaten, 1788-1918* (Vienna, Cologne and Weimar: Böhlau Verlag, 2014), 70–71; M. Rauchensteiner, *The First World War and the End of the Habsburg Monarchy* (Vienna, Cologne, and Weimar: Böhlau Verlag, 2014), 51.
5. D. Bullock, *The Czech Legion 1914–20* (Oxford: Osprey Publishers, 2008).
6. A. Hameiri, *Hell on Earth*, trans. from the original Hebrew (*Bagehinom shel Mata*) P. C. Appelbaum (Detroit: Wayne State University Press, 2017), 253–260, 394–409.
7. E. E. Kisch, *"Schreib das auf Kisch!" Das Kriegstagebuch von Egon Erwin Kisch* (Berlin: Erich Reiss Verlag, 1930).
8. M. Rozenblit, *Reconstruction of a National Identity. The Jews of Habsburg Austria during World War I* (Oxford and New York: Oxford University Press, 2001), 85, 88
9. "Anfrage betreffend das Verhalten der Tschechen im Weltkrieg," in *Stenographische Protokolle des Hauses der Abgeordneten des Reichsrates*, session 22, May 30, 1917–November 12, 1918 (Vienna: Staatsdruckerei, 1920), inquiry 1749/I, December 5, 1917.
10. M. Rauchensteiner, *The First World War*, 335–338.

11 R. Lein, "The Military Conduct of the Austro-Hungarian Czechs in the First World War," *The Historian* 76, no. 3 (2014), 524–525.
12 Ibid., 525.
13 Rauchensteiner, *The First World War*, 336.
14 Ibid., 319–354; Lein, "Military Conduct," 518–549.
15 Rauchensteiner, *The First World War*, 336.
16 Ibid., 335–336.
17 Zboriv (Ukraine).
18 Field Marshal Svetozar Boroević von Bojna (1856–1920), described as one of the finest defensive strategists of World War I.
19 "Bericht über das Verhalten des XI./MB/28 an der Front," K-M Präs 49/2/11 ex 1916, August 10, 1915, *Österreichisches Staatsarchiv/Kriegsarchiv/KM- Präs*, box 1729.
20 Rauchensteiner, *The First World War*, 347–349; Lein, "Military Conduct," 526–529.
21 Rauchensteiner, *The First World War*, 349–350.
22 Lein, "Military Conduct," 529–532.
23 R. Plaschka, "Zur Vorgeschichte des Überganges von Einheiten des Infantrieregiments Nr. 28 an der russchischen Front 1915," in *Österreich und Europa: Festschrift für Hugo Hantsch zum 70 Geburtstag*. (Graz: Verlag für Geschichte und Politik, 1965), 455–464.
24 Rauchensteiner, *The First World War*, 350.
25 The Brusilov Offensive was Russia's greatest feat of arms during World War I, and among the most lethal offensives in history. The offensive involved a major Russian attack against the armies of the Central Powers on the Eastern Front. Launched on June 4, 1916, it lasted until late September when it petered out due to exhaustion and lack of supplies.
26 Lein, "Military Conduct," 531–532.
27 In the Austro-Hungarian context, "Ruthenian" signifies "Ukrainian."
28 B. Bardach, *Carnage and Care on the Eastern Front. The War Diaries of Bernhard Bardach, 1914–1918*, ed. and trans. from the original hand-written German P. C. Appelbaum (New York and Oxford: Berghahn Books, 2018). The Brusilov Offensive is reported in detail on 127–194, Ruthenian cowardice on 92, and the real culprits of the Austro-Hungarian debacle on 131.
29 N. Davies, *God's Playground: A History of Poland*, revised edition. (Oxford: Clarendon Press, 2005).
30 F. Hameršak, L. Dobrovšac, "Croatian-Slavonian Jews in the First World War," in *Quest. Issues in Contemporary Jewish History. Journal of Fondazione CDEC* 9 (October 2016): *The Great War, Reflections, Experiences and Memories of German and Habsburg Jews 1914-1918*, ed. P. E. J. Grossman, and U. Wyrwa, 94-121, Accessed 6 April 2021, www.quest-cdecjournal.it/focus.php?id=378.
31 G. Rothenberg, "The Habsburg Army in the First World War," in *The Habsburg Empire in World War One*, ed. R. A. Kann, B. K. Király, and P. S. Fichtner (Boulder, CO: East European Quarterly, 1977), 74–75.
32 I. Deák, *Der k(u.)k Offizier 1848–1818* (Vienna: Böhlau Verlag, 1995), 122, cited in R. Lein, *Pflichterfüllung oder Hochverrat? Die tschechischen Soldaten Österreich-Ungarns im ersten Weltkrieg* (Vienna: Lit Verlag, 2011), 44.
33 J. C. Engle, "'This Monstrous Front will Devour Us All.' The Austro-Hungarian Soldier Experience, 1914–15," in *1914: Austro-Hungary. The Origins and the First Year of World War I*, ed. G. Bischof, F. Karlhofer, and S. R. Williamson (New Orleans: New Orleans University Press, 2014), 145–152.

34 B. Menczer, "Bela Kun and the Hungarian Revolution of 1919," *History Today* 19, no. 5 (May 1969): 299–309; P. Pastor, *Hungary between Wilson and Lenin: The Hungarian Revolution of 1918–1919 and the Big Three* (Boulder, CO: East European Quarterly, 1976); F. P. Zsuppán, "The Early Activities of the Hungarian Communist Party, 1918–19," *Slavonic and East European Review* 43, no. 101 (June 1965): 314–334.
35 Hameršak and Dobrovšac, "Croatian-Slavonian Jews in the First World War," 110–111.
36 F. M. Schuster, *Zwischen allen Fronten. Osteuropäische Juden während des ersten Weltkrieges (1914–1919)* (Cologne, Weimar, and Vienna: Böhlau Verlag, 2004), 427–437. Lviv (Ukraine), Vilnius (Lithuania).
37 A. Rachamimow, *POWs and the Great War. Captivity on the Eastern Front.* (Oxford and New York: Berg, 2002), 31–33.
38 Ibid., 54–58.
39 H. Kohn, *Living in a World Revolution. My Encounters with History* (New York: Pocket Books, 1964), 95–96. Originally published New York: Simon and Schuster, 1964.
40 A. Epstein, *Kriegsgefangenen in Turkestan. Erinnerungen von Georg Popper und Adolf Epstein* (Vienna: Selbstverlag, 1935), 17–37.
41 K. Blond, "Ein unbekannter Krieg. Persönliche Aufzeichnungen als k.u.k. Sanitätsfähnrich in Persien während der Jahre 1915/16," in Österreichische Militärgeschichte 5 (1997): *Ein unbekannter Krieg 1914-1916. Das k.u.k. Gesandtschaftsdetachement Teheran von Persien bis nach Wien* (Vienna: Verlagsbuchhandlung Stöhr), 33–93.
42 Rachamimow, *POWs and the Great War*, 50.
43 G. Breithaupt, *Der Kampf ums Dasein. Ein Ausschnitt aus der sibirischen Gefangenschaft'* (Berlin: Verlag Carl Curtius, 1919).
44 T. Scheer, "Habsburg Jews and the Imperial Army before and during the First World War," in *Beyond Inclusion and Exclusion. Jewish Experience of the First World War in Central Europe*, ed. J. Crouthamel, M. Geheran, T. Grady, and J. B. Köhne (New York and Oxford: Berghahn Books, 2018), 55–62.
45 Ibid., 59–60; D. Rechter, *The Jews of Vienna and the First World War* (Oxford and Portland, OR: The Littman Library of Jewish Civilization, 2008), 187.
46 The setting is Vienna, 1900. Professor Bernhardi is a Jewish physician, director of the Elizabethinum. A young woman in his care is dying of sepsis following an abortion. Unaware that she is on the brink of death, she is happy and believes herself to be recovering. Father Reder, a priest summoned by a nurse, arrives to give the patient the last rites but Bernhardi refuses him admission. He wants to spare her the anguish she would suffer were she to realize that she is about to die. The priest argues that she must be absolved of sin before she dies, especially since she has undergone an abortion. While Bernhardi and Father Reder are arguing, the girl dies, having been told by the nurse that the priest arrived. Her death was hastened by the realization that her condition was terminal, and she died in a state of fear. A press campaign causes public outcry. False testimony and fabrications about Bernhardi striking the priest inflame endemic Viennese antisemitism. Bernhardi faces trial. He loses his post in the clinic he helped found, is sentenced to two months in prison, and loses his medical license. He refuses to appeal the decision. The play ends with a philosophical discussion on Jewish identity.
47 V. G. Liulevicius, *War Land on the Eastern Front: Culture, National Identity, and German Occupation in World War I. Studies in the Social and Cultural History of Modern Warfare* (New York: Cambridge University Press, 2005), 151–175.
48 Bardach, *Carnage and Care*.
49 Appelbaum, *Loyal Sons*, 159–206.

50 Bardach, *Carnage and Care*, 127–166.
51 A historic region in Central and Eastern Europe, situated between south-eastern Poland, south-western Belarus, and western Ukraine.
52 Bardach, *Carnage and Care*, 236, 250.
53 Ibid., 249, 257, 260–261.
54 Ibid., xii–xiii.
55 T. Reiss, *Tagebuch eines jüdischen Soldaten*, Leo Baeck Institute, DS 135 A93 R45 [1919]; idem, *In the Line of Fire: A Soldier's Story 1914–1918*, trans. T. Erez (n.p.: CreateSpace Independent Publishing Platform, 2016). The comment on Tarnów appears in his entry of June 25, 1915.
56 Kaunas (Lithuania).
57 Vitebsk (Belarus), Kyiv (Ukraine).
58 Ukmergė (Lithuania)
59 GARF, fond 9458, opis 1, delo 168, *Arkhiv chlena Gosudarstvennoi Dumy Bomasha Meera Khaimovicha* (Archive of the member of the State Duma, Meer Khaimovich Bomash); "Bomash, Meer Khaimovich," accessed March 8, 2021, https://ru.wikipedia.org/wiki/Бомаш,_Меер_Хаимович.
60 Schuster, *Zwischen allen Fronten*, 125; R. Klein-Pejšová, "The Budapest Jewish Community's Galician October," in *World War I and the Jews. Conflict and Transformation in Europe, the Middle East, and America*, ed. M. L. Rozenblit and J. Karp (New York and Oxford: Berghahn Books, 2017), 113; P. Ernst, "Der erste Weltkrieg in deutschsprachig-jüdischer Literatur und Publizistik in Österreich," in *Krieg. Erinnerung. Geschichtswissenschaft*, ed. S. Mattl, G. Botz, S. Karnern, and H. Konrad (Vienna, Cologne, and Weimar: Böhlau Verlag, 2009), 68–72.
61 Michael Freund, "Fundamentally Freund: What American Jewry can learn from Emperor Franz Joseph," Jerusalem Post, November 23, 2016, accessed March 8, 2021, https://www.jpost.com/Opinion/Fundamentally-Freund-What-American-Jewry-can-learn-from-Emperor-Franz-Joseph-473487.
62 Appelbaum, *Loyal Sons*, 239–283.
63 Österreichisches Staatsarchiv/Kriegsarchiv, KM Präs. 1616, 34–17/3.
64 Bardach, *Carnage and Care*, 3, 6, 93.
65 M. Saperstein, *Preaching in Times of War 1800–2001* (Oxford and Liverpool: The Littman Library of Jewish Civilization, 2012), 303–304.
66 A. Hameiri, *The Great Madness*, trans. Yael Lotan (Haifa: Or Ron Publishing House, Ltd., 1984). Original published in 1930 as *Hashiga'on Hagadol*. See also idem, *The Great Madness*, ed. P. C. Appelbaum (Middletown, RI: Stone Tower Press, and Boston, MA: Black Widow Press, 2021).
67 M. Paul-Schiff, "Teilnahme der österreichisch-ungarischen Juden am Weltkrieg. Eine statistische Studie," in *Mitteilungen zur jüdischen Volkskunde. Jahrbuch für jüdische Volkskunde*, new series, 26/27 (1924/1925): 153–154; E. A. Schmidl, *Juden in der k.(u.)k. Armee 1788–1918. Jews in the Habsburg Armed Forces* (Eisenstadt: Eisenstadt Jewish Museum, 1989), 144; M. Berger, *Eisernes Kreuz, Doppeladler, Davidstern. Juden in deutschen und österreichisch-ungarischen Armeen. Der Militärdienst jüdischer Soldaten durch zwei Jahrhunderte* (Berlin: Trafo Verlag, 2010), 113; Schmidl, *Habsburgs Jüdische Soldaten*, 115; idem., "Jüdische Soldaten in der k.u.k. Armee," in *Weltuntergang. Jüdisches Leben und Sterben im ersten Weltkrieg*, ed. M. G. Patka (Vienna, Graz, and Klagenfurt: Styria Premium, 2014), 46.
68 L. Dobrovšak, "Fallen Jewish Soldiers in Croatia during the First World War," in *Jewish Soldiers in the Collective Memory of Central Europe. The Remembrance of World War I from a*

Jewish Perspective, ed. G. Lamprecht and E. Leppin-Eppel (Vienna, Cologne, and Weimar: Böhlau Verlag, 2019), 345–348.
69 *Spomenica Poginulih i Umrlih Srpskih Jevreja u Balkanskom i Svetskom Ratu 1912–1918* (Beograd: Odbor za podizanje spomenika palim jevrejskim ratnicima, 1927), 1–162; A. Budaj, *Vallis Judaea—Povijest požeške židovske zajednice* (Zagreb: D. Graff, d.o.o., 2007), 39; *Magyar Zsidó Lexikon Kiadása*, ed. P. Ujvári (Budapest: Pallas-nyomda, 1929), 950; R. Patai, *The Jews of Hungary, History, Culture, Psychology* (Detroit: Wayne State University Press, 1996), 460; L. Dobrovšak, "Fragments from the History of the Croatian Jews during the First World War (1914–1918)," *Review of Croatian History* 10, no. 1 (2014): 134–135; Hameršak and Dobrovšak, "Croatian-Slavonian Jews in the First World War," 110–111.
70 Rauchensteiner, *The First World War*, 335.
71 Rauchensteiner, personal communication.
72 Rauchensteiner, *The First World War*, 330; Rauchensteiner, personal communication. The Austro-Hungarian k.u.k. and k.u. *Landsturm* was a reserve force consisting of men aged thirty-four to fifty-five, intended to provide replacements for the front line units and provide a militia for local defense; see M. Gałęzowski, *Na Wzór Berka Joselewícza : Żołnierze i Oficerowie Pochodzenia Żydowskiego w Legionach Polskich* (Warsaw: Instytut Pamięci Narodowej, Komisja Ścigania Zbrodni przeciwko Narodowi Polskiemu, 2010).
73 Appelbaum, *Loyal Sons*, 272–273.
74 Appelbaum, *Loyalty Betrayed*.
75 S. Hank, H. Simon, U. Hank, *Feldrabbiner in den deutschen Streitkräften des ersten Weltkrieges* (Berlin: Hentrich & Hentrich, 2013).
76 P. Steiner, "Namensliste der Feldrabbiner in der österreich-ungarischen Armee des ersten Weltkrieges," in *Weltuntergang. Jüdisches Leben und Sterben im ersten Weltkrieg*, ed. M. G. Patka (Vienna, Graz, and Klagenfurt: Styria Premium, 2014), 77–79; D. J. Hecht, "Feldrabbiner in der k.u.k. Armee während des ersten Weltkriegs," in *Weltuntergang*, 69.
77 Appelbaum, *Loyalty Betrayed*.
78 Y. Petrovsky-Shtern, personal communication.
79 Appelbaum, *Loyalty Betrayed*, 206.
80 Patai, *The Jews of Hungary*, 460.

CHAPTER 2

Jews in the Armies of Austro-Hungary before the Great War: A Comparative Framework

Before emancipation of French Jews by the French Revolution and Napoleonic era, Emperor Joseph II began, in 1781, to issue (at a time when Jews in the German States were not even counted as citizens), a series of *Toleranzpatente* (edicts of tolerance), one for each of his many provinces. While not granting Jews equal rights, these edicts permitted them to officially serve in the army.[1] Prior to this, although Jews had fought in many European wars, they were only tolerated as volunteers.[2] On October 13, 1781, Joseph's first edict allowed Protestants and Jews in the empire to practice their religion freely. This was followed on January 2, 1782 with a second edict that gave Jews greater freedom.[3]

Joseph II was a man of limited vision, and these initial *Toleranzpatente*, and those that followed, reflected a mixture of renaissance idealism and traditional antisemitic prejudice:

> It is well known that Jews make a living in trade by illegal trafficking, theft, and deception of every kind against honest Christian customers. So it is most useful and necessary to turn them into functional members of society, diminishing their dishonest trade practices.[4]

Interesting details, copied from original hand-written documents on evolution of Jewish service in the Habsburg Army from 1782 through 1910, are provided by Rudolf von Hödl.[5] Emperor Joseph II was the first European head of state to grant Jews at least partial equality. In 1785, the United Bohemian Austrian Court Chancellery first posed the question whether and how Jews can be employed in the military. The idea was summarily rejected by the

Hofkriegsrat (Court War Council). On August 20, 1787, Graf Joseph von Brigido, Governor of Galicia, sent suggestions about Jews in the military to Joseph II. Brigido opined that Jews living in his area should be conscripted, and assigned to transportation or as artillery servants, but not allowed to carry arms for the present (although this could gradually change). In December 1787, another attempt was made by the Chancellery (six months after a Jew who volunteered for military service was rejected by the *Hofkriegsrat*).

On February 18, 1788, Joseph II decided that "Jews are suitable for military service, at least as artillery servants." Although this decision at first only applied to Galician Jews, on June 4, 1788 it was extended to all Habsburg Jews. The *Hofkriegsrat* pointed out problems of Jewish dietary and Sabbath laws, but were overruled.

In 1789, the new decree ordered the general Jewish conscription in Galicia potentially extended to all Habsburg Jews. This time, the *Hofkriegsrat* were powerless to obstruct. Initially, Orthodox Galician Jewry were against military service, and petitioned the Emperor for exemptions. When this wasn't granted, many fled to the forests, or across the border to Russian Poland.[6]

Joseph II, although a child of his time with all of its prejudices, was nevertheless a relatively tolerant monarch. Even if reasons for allowing his Jews into the military were less than pure, in Gershon Wolf's words he freed them from the "yellow stain of the poll tax, allowing them to develop a healthy feeling of self-consciousness and honor."[7]

In his fictional novelette *Moschko von Parma*, Karl Emil Franzos depicts reaction of a simple Galician Jewish shtetl boy to military service in an infantry regiment during the Italian campaigns of 1848 and 1849. He describes parents, rabbi, and community trying to convince Moshko by every means possible not to become a soldier, and commit treason against his faith. These descriptions must be leavened by the fact that Franzos—himself a Galician Jew—described his co-religionists as *fromm, faul und feige* (pious, lazy, and cowardly). However, he understood the fact that "each country has Jews that it deserves," and that Christian prejudices were largely responsible for lower socio-economic level of Galician shtetl Jews, compared to those in Germany or France.[8]

Orthodox attitudes soon softened somewhat. In 1789, swearing in of Jewish recruits on the Torah was introduced, and Jews were admitted into the infantry.[9] Reaction to this new ordinance was more positive, and was welcomed, amongst Jews in the more "enlightened" western territories of the empire such as Bohemia, Lower Austria and Trieste, as an encouraging sign for future equal rights.[10] In 1789 Chief Rabbi of Prague, Ezekiel Landau, perhaps the first to see the necessity of adjusting Jewish dietary laws and rituals to exigencies of military service, preached the following sermon at the swearing-in of the first Prague Jewish recruits:

> Enter into your destiny, follow unhesitatingly, follow your superiors, be loyal and obedient out of duty. Do not forget your religion, and do not be ashamed to be Jews amongst so many Christians. Pray to God every day, starting when you rise in the morning. God's service comes first. Even the Kaiser owes Him service, and all his attendants, present and past, pray to God. Do not be ashamed of this sign of your religion (handing over some tefillin, a package of tallitot, and prayer books to the soldiers). If you have time, pray daily as it beseems a Jew, and as you well know. If you don't have time, at least pray the *Sh'ma*. Observe the Sabbath where possible and conditions permit, because I hear that, in most cases, you are allowed to rest on that day. Always grease the wagons Friday, before evening. Do everything that can be done on Friday. Live in unity with your Christian comrades, and make sure that you and they become friends: then they will work on Sabbath in your place. And you will work for them on their Christian Sundays. The Kaiser was gracious enough to say that you will not be forced to eat meat. You can live from butter, cheese, and permitted foods, until you reach a place where Jews live, and your kind comrades permit you to eat there. If any of you becomes sick, nourish him, with tea for as long as possible, until necessity demands that he takes meat broth. Always remain true to God in your hearts. Never deviate from the faith of your forefathers, and serve our All-Highest Ruler with good will and indefatigable activity. Attain thanks and honor for us and for our entire nation, so all may see that our hitherto oppressed people love their leader and those who serve in positions of authority, and are prepared to sacrifice their lives when need be. I hope that, through you—if you, as befits all subjects, act loyally and faithfully—we will perhaps be able to be rid of the remaining fetters still oppressing us. And what kind of fame and honor that you bring back can be better for all righteous people, than for your fellow-citizens? I give you my innermost and most heartfelt blessing.[11]

After Joseph's death in 1790, many Jewish communities requested to pay for their son's military exemption: this was approved by Joseph's successor

Leopold II. The sum was eventually raised from 30 to 150 gulden. Jewish conscription in Hungary was abolished on April 12, 1790, but reinstated in 1799–1800. During wars against revolutionary France and Napoleon, the need for conscripts grew: after 1793, if Jews wanted to avoid service against payment, they had to raise the sum themselves, instead of relying on the community. Financial exemption of Jews lasted into the 1830s. Regardless of religion, a large sum of 500–700 gulden was now required, to purchase a substitute.

As in other European countries, Jewish dietary laws and Sabbath and festival observance were adduced as drawbacks of Jewish military service in the Habsburg Empire. Initial problems were gradually ironed out and non-Jewish officers learned at least a degree of tolerance for Jewish traditions. Jewish soldiers were compensated, after buying their own food, especially during festivals. Orthodox Jews obtained food from private sources within local communities, freeing them from having to eat in the mess. Duty on Sabbath and festivals was rabbinically permitted, if required by exigencies of war. Jews were sworn in on the Torah, Jewish laws such as prohibition against mixing clothing material with flax,[12] and the wearing of beards and side locks, were also dealt with. It must also be added that (then, as now), not all Jewish soldiers followed the letter of Jewish law and ritual.[13]

A side-by-side comparison between Germany and Austro-Hungary only becomes possible from the last three years of the Napoleonic wars, 1813–1815. Between 1793 and 1815, over 36,000 Jews—35,000 from Austrian lands, predominantly Bohemia, but only 1,200 from Hungary—served in the Habsburg army. In 1803—the short period of peace between the second and third coalition wars against France—increased Jewish conscription was reflected in 981.5 (*sic*) Jewish soldiers out of a total of 170,000. Jews served in transportation, and later infantry: throughout the entire nineteenth century the number of Jews in elite units such as cavalry and light cavalry remained small. Hospitalized Jewish soldiers were permitted rabbinical visits, if there was a nearby Jewish community.[14] Generalized mistrust of Jewish recruits remained commonplace, and difficult to overcome. A *Hofkriegsrat* decree of 1805 forbade them from home leave, to prevent desertion.[15]

Around 1808, Jews were allowed to become officers, and by 1809 Jews in the Austrian Army were an everyday occurrence. At the Battle of Aspern-Essling (May 21–22, 1809), Corporals David Friedländer and Josef Pollak distinguished themselves. In 1811, several Jewish soldiers—including one corporal—served in the Fourth (*Hoch und Deutschmeister*) Infantry Regiment, while forty-four Jewish soldiers served in the Forty-Fourth Infantry (one corporal, four privates first class). Twenty soldiers and one private first class served in the Tenth Infantry. Lieutenant Karl Wiener was killed 1809 in Baumersdorf during the battle of Wagram (July 5–6). Maximilian Arnstein(er), one of the first Habsburg Jewish officers, was already serving in the army before the war of 1805; he was taken prisoner by the French in 1805. After returning from captivity, he was promoted ensign in the Sixty-Third Infantry. On October 26, 1809 he was transferred to the Ninth Hussars, and promoted first lieutenant a year later. Arnsteiner was killed in Colmar on December 24, 1813, and buried by Jewish rite. Another Jewish officer, Franz Bernard Frankl, died in 1817 in the Prague garrison hospital from wounds received.[16] In contrast to Prussia, no diaries of serving Austro-Hungarian Jews could be found through the wars of the nineteenth century, and we are left with anecdotal reports.

Jewish officers were appointed for the first time in the Habsburg Army during the Napoleonic Wars. When, in 1815, the Prague Jewish pedagogue and scholar Peter Beer (1758–1838) asked whether his students could become officers, the *Hofkriegsrat* declared that "there are no reasons why hopeful students of the Israelite faith, who serve as volunteers, and pay for their own equipment, cannot be promoted to officer's rank."[17]

By comparison, after Frederick William III granted Jews citizenship in 1811, allowing them into the military in 1812, approximately two percent of all Jews living in Prussia volunteered for the Napoleonic Wars between 1813 and 1815. The diaries of Löser Cohen chronicle this experience.[18]

The number of Jews serving in the peacetime Prussian army slowly increased, but entry into the Prussian officers' corps was consistently denied.[19] Little information on Jews in the Habsburg Armies between 1815 and 1848 is available. The years immediately after the Napoleonic wars in Austro-Hungary were a time of reactionary politics, Jews were still barred from entering artillery and cavalry, and the *Hofkriegsrat* rejected the attempt of two Jewish corporals to join the Trabant Horse Guards, although no doubt was cast on their prior military service. Tricks were played on Jews with regard to their military service. Rafael König from Znaim,[20] who wanted to become a locksmith (a trade closed to Jews), first had to bring an affidavit that he had been found "unfit for military duty" before, after a delay of two years, he was allowed to enter the guild.[21] In other areas of the military, progress was made. Jews were permitted to enter the Military Medical Academy, the *Josephinum*, and in 1844 Dr. Simon Hirsch was appointed regimental physician of the Fourth Ulans. Promotion to captain of the Jewish First Lieutenant Moyses Almoslino (a Sephardic Jew living in Slavonia) was blocked, because he lived in part of the empire that, until the *Ausgleich* of 1867 (see below), did not grant its Jews equal rights.[22] When the matter was referred to the *Hofkriegsrat*, they opined that he shouldn't even have been promoted to lieutenant.[23]

Jews strove to assimilate, if necessary by baptism. Several baptized families were ennobled, and all sent their sons—as the crowning achievement of their assimilation—into the professional officers' corps. Three sons of the court factor Joel, ennobled to Ritter von Joelson, served. Two sons rose through the ranks to regimental commandant, while the third son was promoted, at fifty-nine, to field marshal, commandant of an infantry battalion, and baron.[24] Rabbi Max Grünwald mentions an officer named Hönig, who became a captain in the *Hoch und Deutschmeister* Regiment, and a Viennese named Emmanuel Eppinger who became an officer in 1811.[25] Throughout this book, I have endeavored to include only Jews who, as far as I could ascertain, retained their religion, and did not convert.

Heinrich Singer, one of the first Austrian Jews promoted to high rank, didn't convert and served throughout his career as a Jew. Born 1797 in Lemberg, at ten years of age he entered an "engineers' academy," which he left seven years later with a rank of junior lieutenant.[26] He was assigned to the Third Ulans under Archduke Karl, fought in Italy and France during 1814–1815, and was transferred as first lieutenant to one of the Kaiser's own elite cavalry regiments. Field Marshal Radetzky took him into his general staff, and Singer was promoted captain in 1831. By 1847 he had been promoted colonel, eighteen months later to major general and commandant of three brigades, which were sent to the then papal state of Romagna to "restore order" in the war against members of Garibaldi's *risorgimento*. During the First Italian War of Independence, it thus fell to the first Jewish general in the Austrian Army to reconquer Ancona, their main Adriatic port, for the Papal States, on June 19, 1849. Austria didn't take active part in the Crimean War, but mobilized and declared "armed neutrality." Singer was promoted field marshal and chief of staff of the Fourth Army, but didn't have a chance to show his ability, owing to Austria's neutrality. After demobilization, Singer retired at the age of sixty, but was reactivated and travelled widely until he died in 1871.[27]

From 1845 through the start of World War I, only one Jew (Meno Burg) served as a staff officer in the Prussian standing army, and that only with intercession by a close relative of King Frederick William IV, and under discriminatory, demeaning, circumstances. This, despite having written the first Prussian artillery textbook in geometry and trigonometry, and giving instruction to Werner, founding member of the Siemens family.[28] In the

Austro-Hungarian Army, after initial pitfalls, the experience was different. The long reign (1848–1916) of Kaiser Franz Joseph I, a relatively tolerant monarch who (with initial exception of Hungarians) saw no reason to discriminate based upon race or religion, gave Habsburg Jews consistent, stable, upward mobility, including advancement in army and civil service. In Germany, a succession of conservative monarchs, from Frederick William III through Wilhelm II, and the leadership of the reactionary Bismarck, gave the Jews no such leeway.

Deák and Mader delineate four periods of development for Jewish officers in Habsburg Armies: 1) the first half of the nineteenth century, when generally only converts could make a career in the military; 2) the liberal period between the 1860s and the end of the century, which witnessed rapid increase of Jews in the officers corps; 3) a period of decline in the years prior to 1914; 4) World War I, when the number of Jewish officers again increased rapidly and comprised a significant number of the corps.[29]

The role of Jewish soldiers in Hungary during the pivotal 1848 Kossuth Rebellion against the Habsburg monarchy in the person of Franz Joseph I is illuminating.[30] No comparative rebellion against Frederick William IV occurred in the German Reich. Lack of a similar armed uprising may be argued to have played a significant role—together with the "white revolutionary" Bismarck, and Kaiser William I's unexpectedly long reign after the death of his brother Frederick William IV—in the appearance of reactionary Prussian nationalism during the second half of the nineteenth century.

Before the rebellion, Hungary's Jews lived under greater oppression than their Austrian counterparts, by this time freed from many of the previous discriminatory laws dating from the time of Maria Theresia, who had expelled all Jews from the *Erblanden* (including Vienna and Bohemia). A recent pogrom in Pressburg—at that time seat of the Hungarian parliament—which plundered and destroyed all Jewish houses and stores outside the ghetto, moved even the Orthodox rabbi of Pressburg, the *Chatam Sofer*, to make common cause with the Hungarians.[31] Hungary's Jews (approximately 130,000 in 1805, rising to 400,000 three decades later), despite originally being German-speaking, quickly became Magyar patriots, especially during the so-called Reform Diet Period in 1830 and the 1840, and leading Hungarian liberals pushed for the transformation of Jews' legal status and for giving the Jews full rights, equal with the Magyars. Grateful for their new freedoms, Jews enthusiastically embraced Magyar culture, started to Magyarize their names, and learned Hungarian, replacing German and Yiddish as their lingua franca.[32]

When all connection with the Hungarian government and Kaiser Franz Joseph were broken, and Ludwig Kossuth, "President of the Republic of Hungary," opened the army to all faiths, Jews flocked to enlist, participating in numbers three to four times higher than the rest of the country. Many Jews in Austria served in the revolutionary National Guard. In 1848 the liberal political thinker and future chief rabbi of Vienna Noah Mannheimer repeatedly emphasized that Jews could not avoid conflicts related to the "rights of man and citizens," set out in the French Revolution declaration.

During the 1848–1849 rebellion, Jews fought in the imperial army and in the Hungarian national (Honvéd) army. Political interests led to a coalition of Hungarian liberals and reformist Jews, who supported Hungarian national interests, and hoped for equal rights under a new constitution.

The rump section of Hungary recognized by Kossuth had about ten million inhabitants, 3% of whom were Jews. In early 1849, when the uprising reached its peak, 20,000 (11%) of a total of 175,000–180,000 revolutionary fighters were Jewish. Despite rumors to the contrary, no non-professional Jewish soldier in the Kossuth Army reached a rank higher than captain. Little is known about war deeds of these Magyar revolutionaries: after the revolution had been crushed no one wanted to risk court-martial by drawing attention to themselves.[33] József Rosenfeld (Rozsay) served as physician-in-chief in a Honvéd military hospital, and Lipót Popper as a Honvéd first lieutenant. In Austria, many Jews fought in the democratic National Guard, which sometimes gave rise to antisemitic incidents and difference in loyalty of Jewish communities.[34]

Years immediately after the 1848–1849 rebellion were characterized by repression, for Jew and non-Jew alike, with an attempt by the young Emperor Franz Joseph to establish "neoabsolutist" rule. The Austrian High Command took a dim view of Jews serving in the revolutionary cause, with heavy fines on several Hungarian Jewish communities and imprisonment in some cases.[35] Four rabbis, including Rabbi Einhorn of the Pest Reform Synagogue who was appointed chaplain of Jews in the revolutionary army, were court-martialed, but later pardoned.[36]

Heinrich Oppenheimer, born in 1829, took part in the Kossuth rebellion, entering the Vienna "academic legion," becoming captain of the National Guard. After the rebellion was crushed, he joined the Second Infantry Regiment in May 1849 and was promoted lieutenant within a year. He scornfully turned down his superior's officer of baptism to speed up his career, and served in Italy (1859), South Tyrol (1866), and Bosnia (1878), retiring with the rank of major.³⁷ Karl Stras(s)/Strahs was born in Bohemia in 1828 and volunteered December 1848. Within four months, he was promoted second lieutenant and transferred from light infantry to cavalry. Five months later, he was promoted first lieutenant in the Emperor's Second Hungarian Hussars at the early age of twenty-one, but did not convert. He was pensioned as a semi-invalid at thirty-three, with the rank of captain first class. Deák asserts that Stras purchased his promotions.³⁸

Jewish soldiers served Austro-Hungary and the German states in ever-increasing numbers in all three Bismarckian wars: the number of German Jews who served in the 1870–1871 war against France could have been as high as 15,000. The Prussian Jewish experience is reflected in diaries by Siegismund Samuel and Oscar Rothman. The Hanoverian Georg Steinberg fought with Prussia against Denmark in 1864, but against Prussia in 1866.³⁹ No such diaries for Jewish Habsburg soldiers could be found. Otto von Bismarck ruled Prussia with Wilhelm I, bypassing parliament, for nearly three decades. Bismarck's innate Protestant antisemitism retained the status quo, and Jews continued to be excluded from the Prussian officers corps although they fought bravely in all three wars and loyally performed their military service in peacetime. This exclusion did not occur through the long, tolerant rule of Emperor Franz Joseph.

Between 1848 and 1866, Austria fought five wars: three against Italy, one each against Denmark and Prussia. According to Mader, between 10,000 and 30,000 Jews fought in the wars of 1859 and 1866.⁴⁰ These wars led to a thorough reform in the Habsburg Army, and increase in the number of serving Jews. Von Weisl cites Paul Diamant that sixteen officers serving in 1856 were probably Jews. A simple uneducated baggage train soldier named Bardach saved the regimental cash box during the 1866 battle of Chlum against Prussia.⁴¹ He was acting as a simple canteen proprietor, because no one expected any war-like activity by an *Ostjude*. However, this act of bravery won him the Gold Medal for Bravery, the highest award in the field: he was promoted non-commissioned officer, then hussar officer then major, and finally ennobled with the title Wolf, Edler von Chlumberg. He died greatly honored in 1914 in Czernowitz.⁴²

After the Battle of Königgrätz on July 3, 1866, the Prussian Army streamed into Northeast Bohemia and Moravia, in the direction of Olmütz and Brünn. The few fortresses under Austrian control that lay in the way were hard-pressed and full of wounded. Lieutenant Ignaz Goldstein volunteered to travel through enemy lines, and report this dangerous situation to *Feldzeugmeister* (General of the Infantry) Ritter von Benedek in Olmütz. In response, Benedek sent

Goldstein directly to Vienna, to report his findings to the Emperor's general adjutant, with a recommendation for recognition of his brave deeds.

Goldstein described his journey from the fortress as follows:[43]

> Punctually at midnight, a bomb fell on the casement where we had gathered, warning me that I must depart. A dreadful storm began: torrential rain fell, and it was pitch dark. This worked to my advantage, because it allowed me to break through the enemy's forward outpost unseen. I obviously couldn't use the main road, and swam through the enemy's moat around the fortress. Thunder and lightning allowed me to see the enemy outposts. I walked on, suddenly encountering a road. An enemy patrol appeared, but I confused them by speaking in an incomprehensible Slavic tongue, and they let me go. It was already 8.00 am and, exhausted, I travelled on. I met a man with a horse, and asked whether I could borrow it for a few hours against payment. He refused, probably because of my untrustworthy appearance, so I bought it outright for 200 crowns, and rode into the forest to rest, letting it loose to graze.
>
> Having rested for a few hours, I continued on the road. At 2.00 pm, I reached a railway station. Because a cavalry patrol was near, I fled to a nearby forest, where I climbed up a tree and awaited my fate. The patrol appeared to have heard about the horse affair and were searching the woods. Soon an Austrian patrol appeared, and, to my joy, chased the Prussians away. Much relieved I climbed down and walked into the nearby corn field. Relieved to have escaped the enemy area, I continued to a small town, where I met our Thurn and Taxis Cavalry Division. I reported to His Highness at once, showed him my report, and requested escort to Olmütz. I requested a horse, because in my exhausted and undernourished state I couldn't proceed on foot. While His Highness was giving orders, the alarm sounded: everyone lost their head, and I was left to my own devices. The division left and, in my pitiable state, I was unable to follow them. I dragged my weary bones into town, where I slaked my thirst in the village fountain. A village woman showed me the way to Olmütz via the nearby railway station. However the station master stopped me: I couldn't make myself understandable, and he was about to arrest me. A hefty push on the chest put paid to him, and I continued on. Soon,

I heard horses' hooves behind me: "Halt!" It was Colonel Schiller, and the vanguard of a rifle battalion. The colonel regarded me suspiciously, because he had been informed by the station master that a spy was lurking around the station. I showed the adjutant my orders, and again asked to requisition a horse and await arrival of the main troop body. The colonel requested names of my superiors, but this didn't appear to gain his trust, and he requested my report. I made the colonel aware of the officers' honor code, mandating that I could only deliver the report into the hands of *Feldzeugmeister* Benedek. I reminded him that, even if I were a spy, his duty was to hand me over to army high command. The colonel drew his sabre and threatened to run me through. I answered:

"Herr Oberst! We are in enemy country, and have no business sharpening our swords against unarmed men who are our brothers. Our situation is too serious, and every second counts. I will circumvent the officers honor code by handing over my report to you for the good of the army—but only if you give me your word of honor, and guarantee before your troops, that this important report be immediately sent on its way to *Feldzeugmeister* von Benedek."

The colonel gave his officers his word that the depeche would immediately be sent to its destination. I myself, however, was transported to Hohenstadt under armed guard.[44] In retrospect, I was lucky that the escort was so heavy, because otherwise the townspeople—having previously heard about the spy—would have lynched me. At around 6.00 pm, I was thrown into a cell in chains and left to await my fate. Despite the conditions, I was so exhausted that I went right to sleep. At around 11.00 pm, I was awakened by the door creaking: the provost appeared, to ask me what my last wishes were and told me to say my prayers, because I had been condemned to death by hanging.

While all this was occurring, I heard the call from afar: "Herr *Leutnant* Goldstein!" I couldn't believe my ears but, when the call was repeated, I replied: "Present!" Recognizing the situation, I ordered the provost, who had almost fainted: "Chains off! Lantern in front of you, quick march!" When we arrived at the prison entrance, Count

Thurn and Taxis's senior adjutant overtook me:

"Herr *Leutnant*, we are very sorry for this unpleasant incident! I hand the depeche back to you—please fulfil your original mission. You look exhausted, and have obviously received no nourishment recently. Please accompany me to the nearby inn, and join my officers in their meal."

Upon our arrival at the inn, he introduced me to the brigade officers present. Only Colonel Schiller, who was also present, cast his eyes down from embarrassment. I walked towards him excitedly, introduced myself, and said respectfully: "I will continue to do my duty, as I have done in the past, and will certainly make a point of reporting your actions to the highest authorities."

I bowed and left the colonel with his mouth hanging open, took my place at table next to Senior Adjutant Platz, and prepared finally to enjoy some food. But I had no appetite, and left without eating anything, instead requisitioning a wagon in order to immediately continue my trip to Olmütz. By the time I arrived at 8.00 am, high command was already there, I reported to *Feldzeugmeister* von Benedek, and was admitted immediately The Army Commander came up to me, not even waiting for the report, patted my head, and said: "Herr *Leutnant*, I've heard that you were wounded." "Not physically Excellency, but psychologically," I said, reporting the affair with Colonel Schiller. Benedek, incensed at what had happened, immediately promised me satisfaction.

Ignaz Goldstein was born 1839 in Alt-Becse, Hungary.[45] In March 1859 he joined no 6 infantry regiment. Following the reorganization of the infantry he was assigned to the Twenty-Third Infantry Regiment, and promoted lieutenant on May 1, 1866, just before the Battle of Königgrätz. He left the army in December 1866, and died 1909 in Budapest in reduced circumstances, but supported by a veteran's pension.[46] Several conclusions may be drawn from this report. Firstly, bravery was not lacking in the Habsburg Army, only sound leadership. Secondly, although suppressed, there was always a level of antisemitism in the army, particularly in higher officers' classes. But the most important lesson is that satisfaction, even by a lowly lieutenant against a colonel, was assured, irrespective of religion and social rank, ensuring equal treatment under the law (see below).

Dr. Moritz Frühling published a list of Vienna Jews who distinguished themselves in campaigns between 1859 and 1867. Major Karl Herzl served in the 1848–1849 and 1866 campaigns (against Denmark and Prussia, respectively), also in the 1878 occupation of Bosnia Herzegovina, and Captain Moritz Neustadl served in the 1848–1849 and 1859 Italian campaigns. In the latter he was so badly wounded that he had to be pensioned in 1860. Captain Wilhelm Löwy served in 1848–1849 and 1866, and Ignaz Ziffer served in the infantry against the Polish uprising of 1846, the 1848–1849 Italian campaign, the 1859 campaign against France and Sardinia-Piedmont, and the 1866 Prussian campaign. He was promoted captain, decorated with the Austrian Silver Medal of Bravery and the Russian St. George Order, and died in 1882. Senior artilleryman Ernst Semler from Vienna served in the Fourth Artillery Regiment, and was awarded the Silver Medal for Bravery in 1848. He was later captain in the military police in Milan and Hermannstadt,[47] and pensioned in 1855.[48]

Eduard Schweitzer from Hungary, who distinguished himself in the Prussian war of 1866, was a non-commissioned officer when war began. He was promoted lieutenant at the relatively young age of twenty-six, fought in the Bosnian campaign (1878) where he was awarded the Order of the Iron Crown, raised to nobility, and knighted. He ended his career as Field Marshal Eduard Ritter von Schweitzer, and died a Jew. A Jewish non-commissioned officer named Barber from Bukowina ended the war as *Rittmeister* (cavalry or other captain); his son later became an officer in the standing army. Alexander (later Ritter von) Eiss served, first as volunteer, cadet, then lieutenant, distinguished himself in the Italian war of 1859 before the eyes of Kaiser Franz Joseph, and was elevated to nobility. His career progressed more rapidly than that of his Christian comrades: he was promoted colonel, regimental commandant, and (honorary) major general after retirement, the case for most unbaptized Jews. Both his sons distinguished themselves during the World War I. The younger son Hermann was a captain in a sapper battalion and highly decorated, before falling in battle, while the younger son Karl was one of the few awarded the Golden Medal for Bravery both for ordinary soldiers and for officers. Heinrich Ulrich (Ritter von Trenckheim) served as an officer in the 1866 and 1878 (Italian) campaigns, and was promoted major general in 1906. The Hungarian Simon Vogel rose through the ranks to colonel and infantry commandant, and ended his career as honorary major general just before the beginning of World War I. Other post-1848 Jewish officers included Colonel

Adolph Beer, who rose through the ranks to become commandant of an artillery corps in Laibach.[49]

Several Jews already serving in the standing army were promoted major general during the course of World War I. Leopold Austerlitz from Prague volunteered as a one-year reserve officer in 1877. After qualifying in mathematics and physics he became a senior artillery instructor before, in 1900, he was appointed colonel in the artillery general staff. At the end of 1914, he commanded the heavy mortar division outside Belgrade. For this service he was decorated with the Franz Joseph Order, and retired a major general. Maximilian Maendel was a successful infantry officer, who began his professional career in 1878 with the elite Tyrolean sharp-shooters. He led an infantry in Galicia summer 1914 and in 1916, now a colonel, led a mountain brigade in the Italian campaign. In honor of his bravery at the defense of a bridgehead in Görz, he was ennobled (Maximilian Maendel von Bughart), and promoted major-general in 1917.[50] The Prague Jew Carl Schwarz was promoted lieutenant in 1878, became regiment commandant of a *Landwehr* infantry regiment, and was pensioned in 1913 as a major general. When war began he was reactivated and promoted to actual major general. The Honvéd officer Mór Grün(hut) served with distinction throughout World War I, and in 1918 was promoted to colonel and ennobled (Márton Zöld de Sióagárd).[51]

Jews also served in the *Kriegsmarine* (navy) during this time period. Tobias Oesterreicher, son of a Moravian merchant, joined the navy as a cadet in 1848 at age of fifteen. He was promoted *Fregattenleutnant* (captain) at twenty-five, before becoming baptized. During the Battle of Lissa, Oesterreicher captained the battleship "Elisabeth" so successfully, that he was awarded the Leopold Order. Ennobled to baron, he attained the rank of rear-admiral before being pensioned early due to illness. Another Jew, Dr. Karl Fleischmann, served in the navy for forty years and also attained admiral's rank, but as a physician. Two other Jews were promoted to captain of the line, one with the equivalent of colonel, the other to colonel.[52] The number of Jews serving in the navy rose from 0.9% in 1885 to 1.7% in 1911.[53]

The years immediately after the Kossuth Rebellion saw increased mistrust of Jews in the Austrian military because of participation in the revolt, and Jews were excluded from military academies. As late as 1865, Field Marshal Archduke Albrecht stated that "Jews should perhaps not serve in the mess and in hospitals, because of their well-known tendency towards corruption and lack of morals." Despite these transitory problems, between 10,000 and 30,000 men served in wars of 1859 and 1866. By 1855, contemporary reports indicate that there were already fifty-nine Jewish officers (eleven captains, fifteen first, and thirty-three second lieutenants), and 110 military physicians. By 1859 those numbers had grown to 157 officers and military physicians, and 1866 saw 200 Jewish officers. During the war of 1866, there were 168 Jews out of a total of 4,500 Viennese volunteers: four were killed in battle.[54]

The compromise (*Ausgleich*) of December 21, 1867 granted equal rights to all citizens regardless of religion, removing the last vestiges of Jewish discrimination. Franz Joseph became Emperor of Austria and King of Hungary (which was finally granted equal status). Thereafter, in Hungary, the Monarch was referred to as the King, or "His Royal and Imperial Majesty," and, in the Hungarian National Army, soldiers swore loyalty to the king (not the kaiser per se). Three distinct armies were formed (see chapter 1).This structure, and the polyglot nature of the Habsburg army, complicates any one single book on this subject. The army was run mainly from Vienna and Budapest, with lower rates of participation by Slavic and other minorities, which gave rise to dissatisfaction that had not been solved by the time war began.

The Jews of Habsburg Austria were amongst the empire's most loyal subjects and understood perhaps more than most what it meant to be loyal to a supranational state. Gershon Wolf, in his 1869 article entitled "Jews in the Austrian Army," quotes Schiller's Wallenstein that "The Austrian has a Fatherland which he loves with good reason," adducing this about the Jews in Austro-Hungary. This remained true even in times of oppression, and even more so after the 1867 compromise.[55] Hungarian Jews continued Magyarizing their names, and regarding themselves with true Magyar pride and loyalty.

According to the 1869 Cisleithanian Census, 822,220 Jews lived in "Austrian lands," and 522,113 in Hungary (including Siebenbürgen and Croatia.).[56] Jews constituted about 4% of the empire's population.[57] In 1872, the first year for which figures are available, 12,471 Jews served in the k.u.k. army, comprising 1.5% of the force. Corresponding numbers rose during the following decades, and by 1902 reached 59,784 (3.9%). By 1911, the figure had dropped to 3.1%, (46,064), possibly due to a decrease in the Jewish population from 4.8% (1890) to 4.6% (1910), or massive immigration to the United States. Numbers included unscripted soldiers, reservists, and one-year volunteers who, after finishing gymnasium, were officer-eligible after a year of service. In 1911, the last prewar year for which numbers exist, and ordinary soldiers and office aspirants were counted separately, 2,048 of the 46,064 Jewish soldiers were officer aspirants (including the reserves). In the same census, the number of Jewish career officers had dropped from 178 to 109.[58]

Numbers were lower in Galicia where, in 1871, around 30.3% of Jewish men (3,856 out of 12,693) liable for military duty did not appear before their draft board. Matters were particularly bad in the Eightieth Infantry, where 64.5% of Jewish draft age men did not appear for muster. However, even in Galicia from 1868 to 1870 the number of Jewish recruits rose from 198 to 805.[59] One Jewish author at the time spoke of "deep cultural and physical defects amongst Galician Jews," and mistrust of the military amongst Galician Jews, who were often very poor and badly equipped for military service.[60] In 1910, for example, in lower Austria, Bohemia, Moravia, and Silesia 0.5%–0.8% of the Jewish population served in the military, compared to only 0.3%–0.4% in Galicia and Bukowina, the two provinces where large numbers of the empire's Jews lived.[61]

Despite jokes about most Jews serving only in transportation and administration, Jews served in disproportionately higher numbers in the infantry and medical corps. Jewish non-commissioned officers were especially prized due to knowledge of languages in a polyglot Empire of many nationalities. The k.u.k infantry regiment no. 95 from Chortkow contained so many Jews, that it was called the "Rothschild Regiment."[62] In 1886, twenty-six of the thirty-eight students at non-commissioned officers' training school of the Fifth Corps Artillery Regiment in Komorn were Jews.[63] In a biographical compendium prepared in 1911, Frühling lists 987 Jewish career officers in the Joint Army between 1848 and 1910, more of them in the army medical corps than in combat branches. Amongst them, nineteen had been promoted to general before 1911.[64]

A comparison between the armies of Austro-Hungary with those of united Italy—where equality was quick and complete (chapter 5), Germany—where a great deal more prejudice occurred,[65] and Russia—where discrimination was almost absolute (chapter 4), is instructive. Frühling reported that "In favor of the Austrian military authorities, it must be said that the Double Monarchy is a unique country, with the most modern and liberal spirit toward its Jewish citizens, treating them with the purest, most faithful and knightly spirit."[66] The Hungarian Jew Theodor Herzl, as feuilletonist of the Vienna *Neue Freie Presse*, was delegated to cover the Dreyfus affair, an event that changed his life and made him a fervent Zionist.[67]

As noted, the first Jewish officers in the Habsburg Armies were commissioned during the Napoleonic wars, 1808–1809. Approximately 200 Jewish officers served in the wars of 1866. After 1867, the number of Jewish officers in the k.u.k. army was still not large: 178 by 1897, dropping to 109 in 1911 (see above).[68] Berger has listed one Jewish field marshal, one rear admiral, five major generals, and seventeen colonels in the 1911 Austrian Army.[69] However, these numbers may include baptized Jews. Numbers of Jewish officers in the k.k.(*Landwehr*) army were similar to those in the k.u.k. army, but significantly higher in the k.u. (Honvėd) army. An analysis of 800 Honvėd officers who died during World War I revealed that about 1/3 of professional and reserve officers were Jewish: in some regiments, numbers reached as high as 50% or greater.[70] Additionally in contrast to the k.u.k and k.k. armies, k.u. officers were not drawn predominantly from the upper classes and nobility, but also from middle and lower classes. Tamara Scheer asserts that, regardless of figures, the high numbers of Jewish reserve officers in autobiographical accounts may be exaggerated, but does not give any reason for this statement.[71]

By contrast, the Prussian Army entered World War I without a single Jewish officer. In the Bavarian Army, which was slightly more liberal than its Prussian counterpart, forty-six Jews served as reserve officers, and forty-two as territorial army officers, before the war began.[72] In Austro-Hungary, those who finished school were granted privileges: they only had to serve as one-year volunteers, after which, if their service was satisfactory, they went through a short training period and were promoted lieutenant or appointed reserve officer—usually in the artillery and medical corps and the baggage train, but also in the cavalry, Tyrolean sharp-shooters (the crème de la crème of the army), and other sections. Because of the high number of Jewish students, it is not surprising that between 1897 and 1911 about 18% (every fifth) of all reserve officers were Jewish (not including Jewish medical officers in the reserve and converts to Christianity). In the k.u.k. army of 1897, statistics differentiated for the first time between professional and reserve officers: 1,993 Jewish officers comprised 18.7% of the entire reserve officers' corps. In the same year, there were 680 Jewish reserve military officials, comprising 21% of that service group. The number of reserve officers in the k.u. army was higher than those in k.u.k. and k.k. armies, respectively. Reserve Jewish officers served in transportation, medical corps, and infantry, but were also well represented in elite corps such as the cavalry and Tyrolean sharpshooters.

Between 1885 and 1911, the number of Jewish officers serving in the navy (around 0.1%) remained small, mainly Jews from Dalmatia and other parts of the Adriatic coast. Friedrich Pick (Edler von Seewarth) served 1866 in Italy and 1869 in Dalmatia, retiring with a colonel's rank. Moritz (Ritter von) Funk served in campaigns of 1848–1849, 1859, 1864, and 1866, and in 1868–1871 as head of the war ministry naval chancellery section.[73]

The early nineteenth century saw a significant rise in antisemitism in Vienna, which became a hotbed of anti-Jewish agitation. Despite this, the religious tolerance of Emperor Franz Joseph as well as strictly enforced army rules not only mandated Jewish service, but permitted them into elite service branches (see above). In sharp contrast, the period after German unification between 1871 and 1914 was marked by ever-increasing racial antisemitism, not allayed by baptism. Although permitted on paper, Jews were still not allowed-in practice—into the Prussian officers' corps, "not so much on 'religious' as on *völkisch* grounds." The concept of racial antisemitism and exclusion of German Jews from the *Volk*, supported by influential men such as Treitschke and Stocker, gained traction.[74] Although antisemitism also increased in Austro-Hungary during the decades before the war, this was less evident than in Germany, and kept in check by Kaiser Franz Joseph and his advisors.

Why were there so many Jewish reserve officers? Simply because the army required a high school diploma or its equivalent for a young draftee to serve as a so-called one-year volunteer. This compulsory "volunteering" qualified him for reserve officers' school and a reserve officers' commission. The main beneficiaries of this highly biased class system were Jews, many of whom were well educated and well-off financially. While Jews represented only 5% of the population, they comprised about one third of high school students; it is therefore not surprising that they formed about one fifth of the reserve officers' corps. Meanwhile, youngsters of lesser education had to serve for three (or four) years and none rose above non-commissioned rank. Such a unique situation and opportunity should have led to the creation of Jewish political parties in both Austria and Hungary, but this was rarely attempted, and remained unpopular. The relatively large Jewish middle and upper classes wanted to assimilate, and saw in an officer's commission the final step in that direction. It is not surprising, therefore, that many Jewish officers served loyally during the war. Because the first bloody battles depleted the ranks of the younger career officers, reservists, among them many Jews, became platoon and company commanders, especially during the last years of the war. World War I was indeed a conflict fought by civilians in uniform. This, as well as the governmental prohibition of overt antisemitism within the armed forces, may explain why so many Jewish officers failed to note the rise of often ferocious personal antisemitism within the two halves of the Monarchy.

The main popular charge was that the Jews were shirkers, which was untrue. Because they were literate and at least bilingual—if not multilingual—in an army that contained eleven major ethnic groups, they were often employed in technical, administrative, or medical services. There were Jewish shirkers, but no more than amongst their Christian counterparts. Many Galician Jews did not serve, because they had become homeless refugees. However, as will be seen, a large number of even the most orthodox Jews served with bravery and honor.

The medical profession has always been prized by Jews, so it is no surprise to find Jews serving in the medical corps of all warring countries. Did Jews join the medical corps so as to shirk front-line service? Doctors like Isidore Segall (chapter 4) and Bernhard Bardach[75] from Austro-Hungary, and Nathan Wolf and Hugo Natt[76] from Germany lay that canard to rest. Jews were already well represented in the Austro-Hungarian medical corps during the nineteenth century. This was particularly the case in Galicia, a province in which large numbers of Jews lived. In 1876 General of the Cavalry Erwin Graf Neipperg (1813–1897), Commanding General of Galicia, noted that "there are more Israelites in the current medical officers' corps than is desirable, in light of their numbers in the general population."[77] Frühling listed over 300 Jewish members of the Austro-Hungarian medical corps (all armies) through the eighteenth century, from junior physician to surgeon general.[78] By 1911, 1.9% of career officers served in the medical corps, with 0.8% in the infantry.[79]

A few other examples of Jews in the Habsburg medical corps, who served through World War I, follow. Dr. Michael Waldstein (Edler von Heilwehr) served in the 1859 Italian campaign. He was promoted to general staff rank and retired with major general rank. Dr. Alois Pick entered the medical corps in 1884, and served as Professor at the University of Vienna medical school. By 1918, Pick was the fourth highest ranking member of the medical corps, with rank of field marshal. Dr. Leopold Herz, head of the Third Garrison Hospital in Przemyśl, penned an excellent study of medical aspects of the Second Anglo-Boer War (1899–1902). Dr. Siegfried Plaschkes, a junior physician when war began, served on the Serbian and Italian Fronts, and was awarded the Golden Service Cross with Crowns and the Knights' Cross of the Franz Joseph Order with War Decoration for bravery.[80]

Unbaptized Jews could reach the rank of colonel: according to an unwritten rule, however, further promotion became difficult (but did occur). At least a dozen Jews reached the rank of general; this does not include converted Jews such as Baron Samu(el) Hazai (1852–1942), who served as Hungary's Minister of Defense between 1910 and 1917.[81] It should be noted that in Hungary, unlike Prussia and other German states, the minister of defense played a crucial political and military role.

Importantly, each officer (including a one-year reserve officer), had not only the right, but the duty of "satisfaction" by sword or pistol if he felt his honor to be impugned. This rule was strictly adhered to, and woe betide the comrade, of any faith, who did not respond to being called out. Jewish students of the time were respected and feared as duelists with sword and pistol. If satisfaction was refused—for example, by a Christian to a Jew—the culprit was called in front of an *Ehrenrat* (honor court), with potentially extremely unpleasant consequences.[82] Antisemitism in the military reported by Scheer (chapter 1) must be leavened by this important fact. Indeed, she cites Deák that "although antisemitism was rampant amongst the middle classes, even the most rabid antisemite had to think twice before insulting a Jew."[83] Trebitsch describes an incident of a challenge being rejected on the grounds that the challenger, being a Jew, was not entitled to satisfaction:

> The gate of the Josefstadt cavalry barracks flew open and *Feldzeugmeister* Baron Gradl, Garrison Commander of Vienna appeared on his beautiful charger:
>
> "I have come today because an unpleasant incident has been reported to me. One of you—whose name I prefer not to mention—has gravely insulted a comrade and refused to give the offended comrade satisfaction because he is of another faith. Anyone who has been brought up from birth to think nobly and act chivalrously is entitled to demand satisfaction, no matter where his cradle may have stood—even if he were a fuzzy-wuzzy!"[84]

This strict officers' code affected reserve officers who later became writers or artists, and said or did something untoward in their professional capacity. The physician and writer Arthur Schnitzler (1862–1931) lost his officer's patent as first lieutenant, because he questioned the validity of dueling in his novelette *Lieutenant Gustl*. The fact that Schnitzler was a Jew apparently had no effect on this decision.[85] Joseph Roth (1894–1939), in his novel *Radetzky March*, describes how Jewish regimental physician Demant, grandson of an orthodox Jewish innkeeper, challenges an aristocratic officer comrade, who has made an antisemitic remark in a fit of drunkenness, to a duel. Demant fears that he will not survive the fight.

I will die like a so-called hero tomorrow, against the nature of my grandfather and race. In ancient books, one finds the sentence: "He who raises his hand against his fellow-man is a murderer." Tomorrow someone is going to raise a pistol against me, and I against him. I shall become a murderer. But I'm short-sighted, won't aim properly, and will have my small revenge. When I take off my glasses, I can see nothing. I will shoot, while seeing nothing! That will be more natural, honest, and suitable! . . . I have no strength to escape from this foolish duel. I will become a hero out of foolishness, according to rules of the honor code. A hero, I tell you!

In the novel, both duelists fire on each other, and are both killed.[86]

When examining and comparing statistics, care must be taken not to include baptized Jews or "Jews of Jewish origin" with one Jewish parent. This is not always easy, because exact records were not always kept. I have tried throughout this book to include only Jewish soldiers, but some errors may occur of which I am not aware. The following chapters will explore the role of Jewish soldiers (officers, physicians, chaplains, non-commissioned officers, and enlisted men) in the Austro-Hungarian army during World War I.

Endnotes

1. J. Karniel, *Die Toleranzpolitik Kaiser Josephs II*, vol. 9 of Schriftenreihe des Instituts für deutsche Geschichte, Universität Tel Aviv (Gerlingen: Bleicher, 1986), 378–474; H. M. Mader, "Judentum und altösterreichische Armee," in *Judentum und Militär. 18 Kulturwissenshatflicher Dialog vom 16 November 2010* (Vienna: Bundesministerium für Landesverteidigung und Sport, 2012), 18–24.
2. Examples include defense of Prague in the seventeenth century, and service in the Dutch navy in the war against England.
3. Mader, "Judentum," 18–19; E. A. Schmidl, *Habsburgs jüdische Soldaten 1788-1918* (Vienna, Cologne, and Weimar: Böhlau Verlag, 2014), 21–22.
4. Österreichisches Staatsarchiv/Kriegsarchiv, Vienna 1788 38-1182: Hofkanzelei an Hofkriegsrat, 1788, June 14.
5. Österreichisches Staatsarchiv/Kriegsarchiv, Vienna, Nachlass Rudolf von Hödl: *Die Juden im Österreich-Ungarischen Heere*, B/460, nr. 11.
6. Schmidl, *Habsburgs jüdische Soldaten*, 27–33; Mader, "Judentum," 18–20.
7. G. Wolf, "Juden im österreichischen Heere," *Österreichische Militärische Zeitschrift* 2 (1869): 126.
8. K. E. Franzos, *Moschko von Parma* (Stuttgart and Berlin: Cotta'sche Buchhandlung Nachfolger, 1921), 5, 12–31. Karl Emil Franzos (1848–1904) was a popular Austrian novelist of the nineteenth century. See also M. Klanska, "'Jedes Land hat die Juden, die es ver-

dient." Karl Emil Franzos und die Juden," in *Karl Emil Franzos: Schriftsteller zwischen den Kulturen*, ed. P. Ernst (Innsbruck, Bozen, and Vienna: Studienverlag, 2007), 37–50.

9 Karniel, *Die Toleranzpolitik Kaiser Josephs*, 444–449; I. Deák, *Jewish Soldiers in Austro-Hungarian Society*, vol. 34 of Leo Baeck Memorial Lectures (New York: Leo Baeck Institute, 1990), 1–29; Schmidl, *Habsburgs jüdische Soldaten*, 32–37.

10 G. Wolf, "Die Militärpflicht der Juden," *Ben Chananja. Wochenblatt der jüdischen Theologie*, February 21, 1862, 61–63.

11 R. Kestenberg-Gladstein, *Neuere Geschichte der Juden in den Böhmischen Ländern*, vol. 1, *Das Zeitalter der Aufklärung 1780-1830* (Tübingen: J. C. B. Mohr, Paul Siebeck, 1969), 71–72.

12 *Shatnez* is cloth containing both wool and linen (linsey-woolsey). Leviticus 19:19 and Deuteronomy 22:11 prohibit the wearing of wool and linen fabrics in one garment.

13 W. Žáček, "Zu den Anfängen der Militärpflichtigkeit der Juden in Böhmen im Neunzehten Jahrhundert," *Jahrbuch der Gesellschaft für Geschichte der Juden in der Czechoslovakischen Republik* 7 (1935): 265-303; Schmidl, *Habsburgs jüdische Soldaten*, 37–50.

14 Hödl, *Die Juden*, 46–51; Schmidl, *Habsburgs jüdische Soldaten*, 51–54.

15 Österreichisches Staatsarchiv/Kriegsarchiv, Vienna. Hofkriegsrat D 2—139/19.

16 M. Frühling, "Wiener Juden für die Österreich-Ungarische Armee," *Ost und West* (August–September 1910): 537–546; W. von Weisl, *Die Juden in der Armee Österreich-Ungarns. Illegale Transporte* (Tel Aviv: Olamenu, 1971), 6; Schmidl, *Habsburgs jüdische Soldaten*, 51–58.

17 Österreichische Staatsarchive/Kriegsarchive, Hofkriegsrat 1815 G I 7/657, Peter Beer to Hofkriegsrat, Prague, April 30, 1815; ibid., Hofkriegsrat to Peter Beer, Vienna, May 13, 1815.

18 P.C. Appelbaum, *Loyal Sons, Loyal Sons. Jews in the German Army in the Great War* (London and Portland, OR: Vallentine-Mitchell, 2014), 1–8.

19 Ibid., 10–11.

20 Znojmo (Czech Republic).

21 M. Grünwald (ed.), "Rafael König, der erste jüdische Schlosser-Meister Österreichs," in *Die Feldzüge Napoleons Nach Aufzeichnungen jüdischer Teilnehmer und Augenzeugen* (Vienna & Leipzig: Wilhelm Braumüller, 1913), 294–295.

22 Slavonia: eastern Croatian province.

23 Hofkriegsrat an Militärkommando Slawonien, August 31, 1838, cited in Schmidl, *Habsburgs jüdische Soldaten*, 59–61.

24 Schmidl, *Habsburgs jüdische Soldaten*, 57–61.

25 M. Grünwald (ed.), *Die Feldzüge Napoleons nach Aufzeichnungen jüdischer Teilnehmer und Augenzeugen* (Vienna and Leipzig: Wilhelm Braumuller, 1913), 25–28; von Weisl, *Die Juden*, 7–8.

26 Lviv (Ukraine).

27 von Weisl, *Die Juden*, 7–9.

28 Appelbaum, *Loyal Sons*, 12–18.

29 I. Deák, *Beyond Nationalism. A Social and Political history of the Habsburg Officers Corps, 1848-1918* (New York and Oxford: Oxford University Press, 1990), 172; Mader, "Judentum," 26.

30 I. Deák, *The Lawful Revolution. Louis Kossuth and the Hungarians, 1848-1849* (New York: Columbia University Press, 1979), 112–117. Lajos (Louis) Kossuth de Udvard et Kossuthfalva (1802–1894) was a Hungarian lawyer, politician and Governor-President of the Kingdom of Hungary during the revolution of 1848–1849 against the Habsburg Dynasty. A joint army of Russian and Austrian forces defeated Hungarian forces. After res-

toration of Habsburg power, Hungary was placed under brutal martial law, and it took until 1867 for it to regain equal status.

31 Bratislava (Slovak Republic). Rabbi Moses Schreiber/Sofer, also known as the *Chatam Sofer*, or Seal of the Book (1762–1839), was the head of the Pressburg yeshiva, the leading yeshiva in Central Europe.

32 W.O. McCagg, Jr., *A History of Habsburg Jews 1670–1918* (Bloomington, IN: Indiana University Press, 1989), 132; R. Klein-Pejšová, *Mapping Jewish Loyalties in Interwar Slovakia* (Bloomington, IN: Indiana University Press, 2015), 4–7.

33 von Weisl, *Die Juden*, 8–11; Mader, "Judentum," 27–28.

34 Schmidl, *Habsburgs jüdische Soldaten*, 62–63.

35 Deák, *Kossuth*, 116.

36 von Weisl, *Die Juden*, note 3, 22f; Mader, "Judentum," 27–28.

37 Frühling, "Wiener Juden," 541–542.

38 Deák, *Beyond Nationalism*, 173–174; Schmidl, *Habsburgs jüdische Soldaten*, 65–66.

39 Appelbaum, *Loyal Sons*, 18–31.

40 Mader, "Judentum," 29.

41 Chlum (Czech Republic).

42 Old capital of the old Habsburg province of Bukowina (currently split between Romania and Ukraine), latter-day Chernivtsi (Ukraine). Von Weisl, *Die Juden*, 11.

43 "Jüdische Kriegshelden. I. Leutnant Ignaz Goldstein," *Neue National-Zeitung* 16 (August 14, 1914): 124–125. The Battle of Königgrätz (near modern-day Hradec Králové and Sadová [Czech Republic]) was the defining battle in the 1866 Prussian-Austrian War. Olmütz: (Olomouc) and Brünn (Brno), both in the Czech Republic. *Feldzeugmeister* Ludwig August Ritter von Benedek (1804 –1881) commanded the Imperial Army at the Battle of Kőniggrätz.

44 Zábřeh (Czech Republic).

45 Bečej (Serbia).

46 "Jüdische Kriegshelden. II. Leutnant Ignaz Goldstein," *Neue National-Zeitung* 18 (September 4, 1914): 3–4.

47 Sibiu (Romania).

48 Frühling, "Wiener Juden," 538–545.

49 Ljubljana (Slovenia).

50 Gorizia (Italy).

51 von Weisl, *Die Juden*, 11–13; Schmidl, *Habsburg jüdische Soldaten*, 87–91.

52 von Weisl, *Die Juden*, 13. The Battle of Lissa (the Battle of Vis) took place on July 20, 1866 in the Adriatic Sea near the Dalmatian island of Lissa (Vis in Croatian) and was a decisive victory for an outnumbered Austrian Empire over a numerically superior Italian force. It was the first major sea battle between ironclads.

53 Schmidl, *Habsburgs jüdische Soldaten*, 76.

54 Frühling, "Wiener Juden," 543; Schmidl, *Habsburgs jüdische Soldaten*, 67–69.

55 G. Wolf, "Juden im österreichischen Heere," 129. The citation in *Wallenstein's Death*, act 1, lines 306–307, by Friederich von Schiller (1759–1805), is: *Der Österreicher hat ein Vaterland/und liebt's, und hat auch Ursach', es zu lieben*.

56 Transylvania (Romania).

57 W.-D. Bihl, "Die Juden," in *Die Habsburgermonarchie 1848–1918*, vol. 3: *Die Völker des Reiches*, ed. A. Wandruszka and P. Urbanitsch (Vienna: Verlag der Österreichischen Akademie der Wissenschaften, 1980), 881–890; Schmidl, *Habsburgs jüdische Soldaten*, 73.

58 Deák, *Beyond Nationalism*, 174; Mader, "Judentum," 29–30; Schmidl, *Habsburgs jüdische Soldaten*, 73–74.
59 Schmidl, *Habsburgs jüdische Soldaten*, 73–75.
60 M. Paul-Schiff, "Teilnahme der Österreich-ungarischen Juden am Weltkrieg," in *Mitteilungen der Gesellschaft für jüdische Volkskunde*, new series, 3 (1925),151–156; Deák, *Jewish Soldiers*, 1–29; Schmidl, *Habsburgs jüdische Soldaten*, 75–76.
61 Bihl, "Die Juden," 913.
62 Chortkiv (Ukraine).
63 Schmidl, *Habsburgs jüdische Soldaten*, 76–78. Komorn: Komárno (Slovak Republic), Komárom (Hungary).
64 M. Frühling, *Biographisches Handbuch der in der k.u.k. Österr-Ungar. Armee und Kriegsmarine aktiv gedienten Offiziere, Ärzte, Truppen, Rechnungs-Führer und Sonstige Militärbeamten jüdischen Stammes* (Vienna: Selbstverlag, 1911).
65 Appelbaum. *Loyal Sons*, 1–45.
66 Frühling, "Wiener Juden," 544–545.
67 Schmidl, *Habsburgs jüdische Soldaten*, 80–84. Theodor Herzl (1860–1904) was the founder of modern political Zionism. Alfred Dreyfus (1859–1935), a French Alsatian Jewish artillery officer, was unjustly convicted in 1894 and sentenced to life imprisonment for allegedly communicating French military secrets to the German Embassy in Paris, After nearly five years on Devil's Island, Dreyfus was returned to France and retried. He was acquitted in 1906.
68 I. Deák, *Jewish Soldiers*, 1–29. Schmidl, *Habsburgs jüdische Soldaten*, 85–86.
69 M. Berger, *Eisernes Kreuz, Doppeladler, Davidstern. Juden in deutschen und österreichisch-ungarische Armeen. Der Militärdienst jüdischer Soldaten durch zwei Jahrhunderte* (Berlin: Trafo Verlag, 2010), 108.
70 Paul-Schiff, "Teilnahme der österreich-ungarischen Juden," 151–156; Schmidl, *Habsburgs jüdische Soldaten*, 100.
71 T. Scheer, "Habsburg Jews and the Imperial Army before and during the First World War," in *Beyond Inclusion and Exclusion. Jewish Experiences of the First World War in Central Europe*, ed. J. Crouthamel, M. Geheran, T. Grady, and J. B. Köhne (New York and Oxford: Berghahn Books, 2018), 63.
72 Appelbaum, *Loyal Sons*, 35–45.
73 G. E. Rothenberg, *The Army of Francis Joseph* (West Lafayette, IN: Purdue University Press, 1976), 128; Deák, *Jewish Soldiers*, 16–21; Schmidl, *Habsburgs jüdische Soldaten*, 100–105; von Weisl, *Die Juden*, 3; Frühling, *Biographisches Handbuch*, 207–208; Mader, "Judentum," 31–33.
74 Appelbaum, *Loyal Sons*, 31–40. The remark by Kuno Graf von Westarp appears on 38. The word *völkisch* is untranslatable, but implies racial exclusion from the German nation.
75 B. Bardach, *Carnage and Care on the Eastern Front. The War Diaries of Bernhard Bardach 1914–1918*, ed. and trans. P. C. Appelbaum (New York and Oxford: Berghahn Books, 2018).
76 Appelbaum, *Loyal Sons*, 159–206.
77 Schmidl, *Habsburgs jüdische Soldaten*, 109.
78 Frühling, *Biographisches Handbuch*, 103–178.
79 Deák, *Beyond Nationalism*, 174–175.
80 "Dr. Siegfried Plaschkes. Arzt im Weltkrieg 1914–1918," *Zeitschrift für die Geschichte der Juden* 9–10 (1973): 173–174; Schmidl, *Habsburgs jüdische Soldaten*, 108–112.
81 Schmidl, *Habsburgs jüdische Soldaten*, 215.
82 von Weisl, *Die Juden*, 2–4.

83 Deák, *Beyond Nationalism*, 133. Cited by Scheer, "Habsburg Jews," 65.
84 S. Trebitsch, *Chronicle of a Life*, trans. E. Wilkins and E. Kaiser (London: William Heinemann Ltd., 1953), 27. "Fuzzy-wuzzy" is translated from the original German *Zulukaffir*.
85 Schmidl, *Habsburgs jüdische Soldaten*, 107–108.
86 J. Roth, *Radetzkymarsch* (Hamburg: Rowohlt, 1987), 77; Cited after I. Deák, *Der k.u.k. Offizier 1848–1918* (Vienna, Cologne, and Weimar: Böhlau Verlag, 1991), 163.

CHAPTER 3

The Kaiser Needs You! Initial Reaction to the Declaration of War

On July 29, 1914, one day after declaration of war against Serbia, Kaiser Franz Joseph appealed for loyalty to his Empire's multiethnic nationalities in face of war. The empire in 1910 contained more than 2.2 million Jews: Of these, more than 932,458 (4.5% of the total population) lived in the Kingdom of Hungary (Transleithania). The number of Jews in Budapest peaked by 1910: 203,687 or 23.1% of inhabitants of the capital. A total of 1,313,687 (4.6% of the total population) lived in the kingdoms and provinces represented in the imperial parliament of the *Reichsrat* (Cisleithania). The great majority of "Austrian" Jews lived not in "German-speaking" Austria, but in Galicia (871,906) and Bukowina (102,919), forming 11% and 13% of their total population, respectively. In cities like Lemberg and Czernowitz, Jews comprised, in 1900, 28% and 32% of the total population, respectively, and in the Bukowinan town of Brody, 72% of the population were Jewish. Virtually all remaining Jews of "Austria" lived in Vienna, Bohemia (especially Prague), Moravia, and Silesia. By 1910, 175,318 Jews lived in Vienna (9% of the city's population).[1] The long reign of Franz Joseph I witnessed great strides in Jewish equality, especially after the compromise of 1867 partially reestablished sovereignty of the Kingdom of Hungary, separate from and no longer subject to the Austrian Empire. Under the compromise, the Cisleithanian (Austrian) and Transleithanian (Hungarian) regions of the state were governed by separate parliaments and prime ministers. Unity was maintained through rule of a single head of state, the Emperor of Austria and King of Hungary, and common monarchy-wide ministries of foreign affairs, defense and finance under his direct authority. Armed forces were combined with the emperor-king as commander-in-chief. Jews, with their feeling of supranational loyalty, easily combined political loyalty to Austria, German culture, and Jewish ethnicity. The empire's Jewish population was heterogeneous, ranging from Orthodox Jews of Bukowina, Galicia, and Northern Hungary to assimilated Jews of Vienna, Western Austria, Budapest, and Prague.[2] Russia mobilized more rapidly than expected in August 1914 and invaded Austria, so it was easy for Austria's Jews to regard Tsarist Russia as their main enemy. Russia, with its Pale of Settlement and pogroms, was the country with most outward manifestations of antisemitism, and a war against Russia was seen by Habsburg Jews as a war to liberate Russia's Jews from Tsarist oppression.[3]

When war began, many assimilated, educated Austrian Jews were gripped by emotional patriotism, which choked off doubt about war's validity. In a previous book, I have pointed out that the "August enthusiasm" for the war in Germany was largely a myth.[4] Can the same may be said for Austro-Hungary? Rauchensteiner describes how some newspapers in Austro-Hungary only took a clear prowar position after the Serbian response to the Austrian demarche had been rejected. Austro-Hungarian academicians, philosophers, and intellectuals (including later pacifists) banded together in favor of the decision to go to war. An Austrian committee for the liberation of Russian Jews, formed mainly by Viennese Jews, numbered amongst its members a young Martin Buber. Rauchensteiner suggests an explanation for this initial enthusiasm based upon the third Vienna school of psychiatry. A search for the meaning of life had proved futile and, to compensate, masses of intellectuals volunteered as soldiers, or at least, like Stefan Zweig, wished to work for the war in the rear.[5] Intellectuals seized the opportunity to matter, move to the center of their society, and escape social and political marginalization.[6]

Zvi Gitelman cites a Russian peasant asking: "If our Tsar is at war with the German Kaiser, does that mean we ordinary people will have to fight?" The Jews asked: "What could the fight between 'Fonye the Ganev' and Kaiser Wilhelm have to do with us?"[7] The answer to both questions would soon become clear.

None in the crowds that gathered could have imagined how long the war would last or how many would die. There is no book comparable to that of Verhey about Germany, analyzing reactions of the Austro-Hungarian Empire to war;[8] however, it might be assumed that the situation was similar to Germany, and that whatever crowds there were, gathered mainly in the larger cities, amongst the *Bildungsbürgertum* (educated middle class).

Contemporary diarists describe parades, crowds lining the streets and railway stations, and intense grip of patriotism. However, if carefully analyzed, this enthusiasm was not uniform, and ambivalent; reactions depended on age, social status, cultural, and political orientation.[9] As in Germany, some academicians and intellectuals (especially journalists)—many involved in the prewar anarchist movement—were against the war from the start. Examples included Franz Kafka and members of radical Socialist movements. Friedrich Adler, a radical Socialist, passionate opponent of the war, close friend of fellow-pacifist Albert Einstein, assassinated Minister-President Karl von Stürgkh in 1916 to protest against harsh censorship and refusal to convoke parliament.[10]

It may be assumed that a proportion of Jews (and non-Jews) in Czech, Polish, Romanian, Southern Slav, and Italian portions of the empire saw the writing on the wall even before war began, and tried to embrace identity of one or other ethnic group. So the picture is by no means clear or uniform. That said, of all the empire's subjects Jews were amongst its most loyal, because they, more than other groups, understood the supranational underpinnings of the Monarchy. The fact that their enemy was Tsarist Russia, site of the Pale of Settlement, pogroms and oppression, made most Austro-Hungarian Jews of military age ready, eager and willing to fight in the empire's cause against what they called "the forces of darkness," the perpetrators of the recent Kishinev pogroms. This was especially true for Orthodox Jews of Galicia and Bukowina, and echoed from pulpits all over the empire.[11]

From what I could glean in memoirs, diaries, and newspaper articles, Jewish soldiers remained devoted to the Habsburg cause almost until the last (perhaps realizing intuitively that their fate outside the empire would be worse than under it).

Richard Arnold Bermann (also known as Arnold Höllriegel) reports that the outbreak of war created a watershed in his life: he walked around Vienna stunned, not participating in initial war enthusiasm.[12] In Zablotow, Galicia, nine-year-old Manès Sperber excitedly witnessed the trumpeter who had come to announce Galician mobilization.[13] Sperber's father was less hopeful, realizing that war would bring only disaster. Jewish women of his hometown ran to the cemetery to pray and weep. Sperber wrote:

> Young men were going off to war, brought to the station by mothers or wives, who did not conceal their fear for the future. Although muffled sobs could be heard, there was a mood of expectation, more hopeful than anxious. There wouldn't be a real war, and it certainly wouldn't last more than a few weeks. . . .

Kaiser Franz Joseph meant more for shtetl dwellers than for his other subjects. They saw in him their guarantor of civil rights, their protector against despotism and hate. Sperber continued:

> The mood in the shtetl during the first few weeks of war was manic-depressive: Hopeful expectation changed instantly to fear of Russian invasion, starvation, and epidemics. My father said: "Every war is a misfortune for us. No one knows how many of sitting in this room will survive this war."[14]

Arieh Leon Schmelzer describes the reaction he observed in the Jews of Bukowina:

> Tens of thousands of Jews filled the streets of Czernowitz and the provincial cities when the order for partial mobilization of July 26, 1914 appeared. Shouts of hurrah echoed and reechoed—the population was gripped with sixty years of pent-up patriotic upbringing, love for Kaiser and Fatherland, and faith in the military.[15]

It is probable that poorer Jews of the empire, especially in Galicia and Bukowina, responded with fear and dread when war was declared: little of their reaction is available in print. However, this fear was leavened by hatred of the Tsarist regime because of Jewish oppression. There is no evidence that these Jews fought less fiercely than their more well-off counterparts. Perhaps, the opposite was the case.

Arnold Hindls, who as reserve officer was called up as soon as the war began, remembered the words of his superior that "heavy clouds had appeared over the Fatherland."[16]

When war broke out, eighteen-year-old Viennese medical student Wolfgang von Weisl wanted to serve, "to fight a holy war against the Jew-murdering Tsarist regime." His father tried to volunteer at the age of fifty-seven; he later became deputy in the Imperial and Royal Judge Advocate's Office, ennobled during the last days of the war.[17] Similarly, Fritz Lieben, a Viennese reserve officer stationed in the capital, reported for duty on August 1, 1914: "Military service now appears very meaningful to me."[18]

Sigmund Freud declared August 1914 that "my entire libido is caught up in the war,"[19] and described how Jewish intellectuals in Vienna were filled with the "whirlpool of the time." He noted: "Perhaps for the first time in thirty years, I felt myself to be an Austrian and wanted to try to belong again to this less than hopeful Empire."[20]

However, within six months a disillusioned Freud wrote:

In wartime confusion that envelops us, relying as we must on one-sided information, standing too close to great changes that have already taken place or are beginning to, without a glimmering of the future that is being shaped, we are at a loss as to the significance of impressions that bear down upon us and the value of judgments which we form. We cannot but feel that no event has ever destroyed so much that is precious in common possessions of humanity, confused so many of the clearest intelligences, or so thoroughly debased what is highest. Science herself has lost her passionless impartiality; her deeply embittered servants seek for weapons with which to contribute towards the struggle with the enemy.[21]

Even a convinced pacifist like Stefan Zweig was initially caught up, when he saw the crowds that had gathered outside his Vienna office:

To be truthful, I must acknowledge that there was something majestic, rapturous, and even seductive in this first outbreak of the people from which one could escape only with difficulty. In spite of all my hatred and aversion for war, I should not like to have missed the memory of those first days. Each individual experienced an exaltation of his ego, he was no longer the isolated person of former times, he was now part of the people, and his hitherto unnoticed person had been given meaning. Even mothers with their grief and women with their fears were ashamed to manifest their quite natural emotions.[22]

The well-known Zionist illustrator and printmaker Ephraim Lilien (1874–1925), despite being nearly forty, volunteered enthusiastically as soon as war began, and eventually became a noted war correspondent.[23]

Egon Kisch from Prague described how, on July 31, 1914, after receipt of call-up papers, his mother wanted to pack more clothing for him. He asked her: "Do you believe that I am going into another thirty-years' war?"[24] During August 1–4, while he was being sworn in, equipped, and travelling by train to Vienna, troops were greeted with flowers, kisses, and pretty girls. Old women handed out copies of the Gospel of John and crossed themselves, with many parting tears. Kisch commented that the men tried their best to hide how moved they were under a veil of cynicism.[25] In Vienna, Arthur Schnitzler wrote simply on August 5: "World war. World ruin." Karl Kraus wished the Emperor a "good end of the world."[26]

Outside Vienna, where crowds were largest, critical voices could be heard: The war would win nothing good, and end up being a useless and destructive enterprise. From Prague, Franz Kafka wrote in his diary on August 6, that the emotional excitement in a patriotic parade evoked in him nothing but

> ... pettiness, decision inability, envy, and hate against those fighting. Laziness, weakness, and helplessness. A patriotic parade followed by a speech by the mayor. He disappears and then reappears. The German cry: "Long live our beloved Monarch!" I look on angrily. These processions are one of the most revolting manifestations of the war. Jewish merchants, who are part German, part Czech, are responsible for more noise now than they have ever made before. Naturally, they draw many off with them because they are well organized. The procession occurs daily, twice tomorrow on Sunday. ... There is an opportunism amongst Prague's Jews towards the German declaration of war, and their inconstancy in describing themselves as Germans or Czechs.[27]

The Czech Jews of Prague had traditionally been German in culture and language, with a hybrid sense of connection as "Czech-German Jews," and skepticism of a multiethnic identity.[28] In smaller Bohemian towns and villages, trust in Austria as protector of Jewish interests was even lower. In Vienna, Prague-born Hans Kohn joined an infantry regiment in early August with his friend Robert Weltsch. Kohn echoed common belief: "In 1914, many young men welcomed the war, viewing it as an exciting adventure. Few realized how mechanized warfare would soon become. There seemed ample time for the deeds of daring we had learned about."[29]

Avigdor Feuerstein (Hameiri), a Hungarian writer and journalist from Carpatho-Ruthenia, described apparent war enthusiasm of a crowd in the Budapest streets outside his nightclub and newspaper office: many opposed the war, but they were beaten bloody and silenced.

> The speaker grows ecstatic. The homeland is in danger. We must break the teeth of the Serbian dog, tear out the French serpent's tongue, cut off the British lion's head, shatter the skull of the Russian bear! "Bravo! Bravo!" We look at the crowd: the faces are all exultant, they are all in agreement! Finally: the anthem:

"To your homeland firm be,

As a rock in your loyalty, O Magyar!"

The editorial office is empty. How fearful is this emptiness.[30]

The above descriptions are limited to the Jewish *Bildungsbürgertum*. How did the Jewish elite react to the onset of the war? The Ephrussi family, titled and enormously wealthy Austrian bankers, originated in Russia and Russian Poland but moved to Vienna. There were members of the same family on both sides of the conflict. Viktor, son of Ignace von Ephrussi, was not as sanguine about the future of the war as the Jewish community of Vienna. He considered it a suicidal catastrophe, and sent his family to cousins in Bad Ischl. He moved into the Hotel Sacher, to see out the war with his history books, and run the Ephrussi banks. After six weeks, he realized that the war would not end quickly, and returned to live the in his palais with his family.[31]

From all corners of the empire came calls for Jewish unity, with hope for better future integration into society. All Jewish newspapers, Liberal, Zionist, Orthodox, combined in the same hope. Dr. Joseph Samuel Bloch from Galicia, editor-in-chief of the liberal *Dr. Blochs Österreichischer Wochenschrift*, began the July 31, 1914 issue of his newspaper with an editorial calling all Jews of the empire to follow the Kaiser's call and proudly serve the country that had been so good to them, with love, bravery, dedication, and confidence in rightness of their cause.[32] In the following week's issue, he published a second editorial, noting the confluence of war's beginning with the Jewish national mourning day, Tisha Be'av.[33] He admonished Austro-Hungarian Jews: "To work! Undaunted and hopeful! Everyone according to his strength! Let fulfilment of duty and conscience lead you on! We Jews cling to our traditional belief and hope, against the unsurpassed current peak of barbarism. These are the birth pangs of a new age."[34]

The first war issue of the *Monatschrift der Oesterreichisch-Israelitischen Union* expressed, apart from general feeling of Jewish patriotism, thanks to Kaiser Franz Joseph for having granted Jews full equality during his reign, which was not the case before:

> In this hour of danger, although we feel ourselves as co-equal citizens of this State, we bemoan the fact that, during long years of peace that preceded this war, we were treated as second-class cit-

izens. We Jews will happily carry any burdens which an unknown future fate will lay on us, in a spirit of innermost love for the Fatherland. We thank the Kaiser with our children's blood and all our earthly possessions for equality that he has granted us, demonstrating that we are his faithful and loyal servants, as good as any other ethnic group.[35]

The Galician writer Moritz Frühling invoked Tsarist Russia as an incarnation of Amalek, the age-old enemy of the Jewish people.[36] He stated that Jewish soldiers had a special reason to fight a "holy war of light over darkness" against enemies of their people, to take revenge for pogroms and their "raped and murdered sisters." Frühling wrote:

During the first days of August 1914, 126 years after Kaiser Joseph II allowed Habsburg Jews to serve in the army with an initial contingent of seventeen, an imposing number of 100,000 Jews have gone to war. Go forth, and emulate them![37]

In a plenary session the president of the Vienna IKG (*Israelitische Kultusgemeinde* declared that

Our sons go to war with greatest enthusiasm. . . . We ardently sacrifice blood and treasure to our dearly beloved Kaiser and Fatherland. Behind Russian ghetto walls, against which the best of our youth go forth bravely to battle, six million Jews suffer under inhuman oppression. We fight so that the government-inspired pogroms incited by hooligans are smothered.[38]

The July 31, 1914 issue of the Zionist *Jüdische Zeitung* began with an editorial emphasizing loyalty and patriotism of Austria's Jews and thankfulness for their good treatment:

We look across the border to Russia and Romania, where our Jewish brethren suffer fearfully. Whenever, in the past, we have experienced injustice in this country, we could always find redress with our Kaiser and his representatives. Happy the country that treats its Jews in this way! We join, with all other Jews, the many-voiced national chorus of our Austrian Empire![39]

The patriotic fervor of Austria's Zionists was perhaps stronger than that of the Liberals because of their strong connection to the Jews of Galicia. Galician Jews were depicted as patriotic and loyal Habsburg subjects, and "figures of light in the midst of dark treachery," who distinguished themselves by courage, and didn't correspond to the stereotypical *Kaftanjude*.[40] Austrian Zionists repeatedly made use of their positive depiction of Galician Jews, as active participants in the defense of the Monarchy, in efforts to crystallize the patriotism of all Austria's Jews. And in fact, Orthodox Jews of Galicia, Bukowina, and Northern Hungary proved to be fierce fighters, not averse to going into battle waving their tallitot, with phylacteries on their heads and left hands, shouting *Sh'ma Yisrael* (Hear O Israel), and firing with their right hands at a confused enemy.

The same warlike call was echoed in the July 30, 1914 issue of *Jüdische Volksstimme* from Moravia:

> War! The iron dice have fallen. All racial and religious differences have disappeared, and Austria's soldiers go off to battle as one man. We Jews have already sent many thousands of our sons to war: they are ready to serve Kaiser and Fatherland with Maccabean courage. May they all return home safely after having achieved victory![41]

From Vienna, *Die Wahrheit* echoed these sentiments:

> The solemn period that has dawned for our Monarchy requires highest dedication and sacrifice. As they have done in the past, our Jewish sons will go out to war and fight heroically, sealing their loyalty with blood, and, if necessary, their lives, to safeguard their Fatherland's honor. Never has there been a more righteous cause.[42]

The Orthodox newspaper *Jüdische Korrespondenz* only came into being on August 12, 1915, so we do not have their reaction to the start of the war.

As in Germany, rabbis hastened to join in patriotic manifestations. On August 4, two days before Austro-Hungary declared war on Russia, Dr. D. Herzog—Rabbi of Styria, Carinthia, and Krain[43]—published a sermon named *Das Gelöbnis der Treue* (The Pledge of Loyalty). Based upon Deuteronomy 4:32, he expounded treachery and lies of the "eastern barbarians" who threatened the empire, did not respect humanity, and wanted to destroy the hard-won progress of centuries of Habsburg peace, religiosity, and tranquility. He stated:

> It is the holy duty of every *Kulturvolk* [civilized nation] to go to war against these barbarians. Go out and fight against Amalek, so that every trace of them is destroyed utterly. Let us say with the Psalmist (Psalm 62:7–8): "On God my salvation and my glory rest; the rock of my strength, my refuge is in God. Trust in Him at all times, O people; Pour out your heart before Him; God is our refuge. Sela."[44]

Rabbi W. Reich from Baden expounded about a Jewish holy war in a series of articles published in *Dr. Bloch's Österreichische Wochenschrift* during August 1914. He declared Austria's hands to be free of blame for war, which was a punishment of Tsarist Russia for barbarisms and persecutions of the past ten years, especially the pogroms in Kishinev that had happened on April 6 and 7, 1903, followed by hundreds of smaller pogroms between 1905 and 1914. He urged Austria's Jews to "sacrifice life and possessions on the altar of the Fatherland and, if necessary, die a heroic death to preserve European morality and human rights." He compared and contrasted the manifold sins of antisemitic Russia, bloodthirsty France, and rapacious England (perfidious Albion) with the kindness and uprightness of Kaiser Franz Joseph, and called for unity with Germany, united for the first time after the Franco-Prussian War. The Tsar's manifesto, "To My Dear Jews," appeared to him like "hellish mocking laughter" in view of their treatment under his regime, and the height of hypocrisy, to which Rabbi Reich applied: "The One enthroned in heaven laughs; the Lord scoffs at them."[45]

Both Rabbi Reich and Rabbi (and future Chaplain) Rubin Färber of Mährisch-Ostrau depicted Franz Joseph as the agent of God, compared to the Tsar, agent of evil. He echoed general Jewish sentiment that the war was "a battle for good against the evil enemy Amalek, light against darkness, and law against lawlessness and barbarism."[46]

Was there a formal Austrian *Burgfrieden*?

Because the *Reichsrat* (Imperial Council or parliament) of Cisleithania had been adjourned by Graf Stürgkh in March 1914, and not been reconvoked when Austria declared war on Serbia four months later (it opened again only in May 1917),[47] Franz-Joseph could not proclaim his own *Burgfrieden* (civil peace) in the presence of parliamentary representatives, as Germany did.[48] Indeed the country was ruled by *Notverordnungsrecht* (emergency decree) even before the war started. Social Democrats found it easier to retreat from their former antiwar position, because Tsarist Russia was the main enemy.

When one saw a dagger at one's throat, Viktor Adler wrote, the first duty was to remove it. Hungary's parliament (which was still in session, and continued throughout the war) suspended internecine hostilities, and—at least on the surface and for a time—class struggle in Hungary ceased.[49] But this *Treuga dei* was only a parliamentary truce, not as spectacular and ideological as the German variant.[50] Bihari calls this the Hungarian *Sonderweg* (special path). The Hungarian government, led by Count Tisza, tried their best to rule out or minimize interference of the military and avoid the Austrian pattern. Thus, control and administration of the country remained in the hands of civilian politicians, which in practice meant Tisza himself.[51] McCagg asserts that the vast majority of Hungary's politicians entered a *Burgfrieden*-like moratorium on political conflict when war began, which enabled parliament to be kept open for the duration of the war.[52]

Because no formal *Burgfrieden* was proclaimed for Austria,[53] it is likely that it is was assumed, not formalized.[54] But, under the emergency decree, there was a wartime ban on inciting political, national, or religious animosity. As in Germany, however, antisemitism increased markedly during the last two years of the war (but without the noxious effects of the German *Judenzählung*) when a clear victory by the Central Powers became more and more unlikely.[55]

On July 31, 1914, an imperial decree proclaimed that, in large sections of the empire, political (but not autonomous district) administration be subordinated under the direction of Army High Command. In interests of military protection, this change was accompanied by transition from civil to military government, militarization of railways, a degree of dictatorship of the military over civilian population, diminution of civil in favor of military government, and an attempt (not always successful) to treat all nationalities as equally as possible. In practice, the spirit in wartime Austro-Hungary mirrored the German *Burgfrieden*.[56] Political parties acquiesced, but labor unions voiced their dissatisfaction with the Social Democratic Party for having these regulations forced upon them.[57]

At the outset of the war, Austrian Germans (nationalists and non-nationalists) were united behind the Monarchy, seeing the war as being between Teuton and Slav. Hungarians hailed the war proclamation with "at last." The Social Democratic Party, referring to the "suspension of class struggle," united trade unions in functioning and growth of the war economy. In August, *Népszava* wrote that a "truce" had been established between workers and capitalists for the duration of the war. Other newspapers such as *Typographia* and *Szakszervezeti Értesítő* wrote that "class conflicts had temporarily faded," "nobody is thinking of strikes," and "war has abolished class struggle. Rich and poor, employees and workers, are fighting together." Croats and Slovenes were equally wholehearted in supporting the war. Austrian Poles were more divided, but *Landtag* (state parliament) leaders decided that Russia was the main enemy. Initial reactions from Romania and Italy (both of whom would defect to the Entente) were positive. A typical reaction of the local population was reported in the Windischgraz region (now Slovenj Gradec in Slovenian Carinthia). A report of August 27, 1914 stated that "the local population has rendered proof of their loyalty to country, Fatherland and Kaiser in the past days, irrespective of nationality." Majority Slovenes viewed themselves as enthusiastic Austrians, despite accusations of disloyalty and espionage. Disapproving voices of the declaration of war came only from Serbs, Ruthenians, and Czechs.[58]

The initial refugee problem

In August 1914, Russia mobilized and attacked earlier than expected. Although checked by the German Army at Tannenberg, they initially conquered Galicia (including its capital, Lemberg), and most of Bukowina. Russian troops entered Galicia on August 18, 1914, and by November were closing in on the West Galician city of Cracow. In areas of densely concentrated Jewish settlement, arrival of the Russians meant start of violent anti-Jewish pogroms. Murder, rape, burning and looting of Jewish homes started in early August.

At this point, approximately 350,000 Jews were either expelled from their homes, or fled advancing Russians fearful of persecution because of their Austrian loyalty. By May 1915, at least one half (perhaps more) of the original 900,000 Jewish inhabitants of Galicia and Bukowina had fled.[59] *Ostjuden* who remained suffered under Russian occupation.[60] The Russian army, for the most part, maintained order.[61] However, pogroms regularly occurred in cities and countryside. Refugees were often destitute, hungry, and reliant on charity for food and shelter. The Russian army expelled large numbers of Jewish civilians, whose patriotism and loyalties were suspect, into the Russian hinterland. Refugees flooded into the rest of the empire, notably Vienna and Prague. By contrast, Hungary accepted few refugees from the Austrian portion of the empire.[62] Refugees began arriving late August 1914. By mid-September, *Dr. Bloch's Österreichische Wochenschrift* estimated that 50,000–70,000 refugees were already in Vienna, with smaller numbers in the rest of Cisleithanian Austria, and larger cities such as Budapest and Prague.[63] Sudden appearance of such large numbers of *Ostjuden*, concentrated in densely inhabited

Jewish areas of the VI, VII, and VIII districts, made the assimilated Viennese *Bildungsbürgertum* uncomfortable. These refugees also met a tacit rejection among the established, Neolog Jewry of Budapest. The editor of *Egyenlőség*, Lajos Szabolcsi—who reported 25,000 refugees—spoke of the growing "Galician flood."[64]

In an initial attempt to support the unexpected number of sometimes penniless refugees, authorities turned to the *Israelitische Allianz zu Wien* and the Vienna IKG for assistance. Both associations did not wish to declare this as a specifically Jewish problem, and requested that aid be shared between them and the government. The sudden influx of poor, uneducated, strangely clothed *Ostjuden* made assimilated, cosmopolitan Jews in large cities of the empire uncomfortable. Additionally, they spoke Yiddish (a descendant of *Mittelhochdeutsch*) instead of German, further differentiating them from their more Western-educated brethren. Amongst non-Jews, their sudden appearance led to increased antisemitism. As war progressed and fortunes of both sides changed, the number of refugees ebbed and flowed. Increasing shortages of food and other commodities as war progressed led to further resentment and alienation. This aspect will be dealt with in later portions of this book.

Unlike Germany, no precise statistics were kept on the number of Jewish soldiers who served in the Austro-Hungarian Army during World War I. Figures between 275,000 and 400,000 have been asserted: it is likely that 300,000-350,000 served. Of these, 30,000–40,000 died of wounds or illness. Approximately 25,000 Jews (c. 10% of all Jews who served) were professional or reserve officers, a much larger proportion than that in the German Army. More than 1,000 Jewish officers were killed in action, and at least 7% of all officers killed in action were Jews; however, it is likely that this number is much higher. At least 800 Honvéd officers were listed as killed.

According to Deák, proportional representation of Jews in the armed forces was lower than that in the general population. However, a great part of the Habsburg Jewish population resident in Galicia and Northern Hungary became refugees early in the war, and were thus less likely to be called up. Jews were as likely to be willing fighters out of loyalty to the empire or fear of Russians, as to avoid service due to pacifistic traditions, non-military lifestyle, or trading and other nonphysical occupations.[65] Half the Jewish career officers and 7.2% of Jewish reserve officers were decorated, some very highly. Out of a total of 275,000–400,000 Jewish soldiers, at least half of the Jewish professional officers received the Iron Crown Third Class or higher.[66]

Shirkers occur in every army and every ethnic group, but I could find no evidence of Jewish shirking (more than in the non-Jewish military population) in any of my sources.[67] The great majority of Jews were loyal soldiers of the empire. Antisemitism did occur and increased (especially on the home front), as it became clear that the war was lost and scapegoats were sought. However, unlike the German Army, strict censorship regime kept overt manifestations of antisemitism at bay.

Both Winter[68] and Ernst[69] have referred to the Eastern Front, and the Jewish civilian part played in it, as the "Unknown War." It is hoped that the contents of this book, together with my recent published English translation of the Bernhard Bardach diaries[70] and two recent books on the Jewish experiences of the World War I in Central Europe,[71] will help fill this gap.

Endnotes

1. W. Bihl, "Die Juden," in *Die Habsburgermonarchie 1848–1918*, vol. 3: *Die Völker des Reiches*, ed. A. Wandruszka and P. Urbanitsch (Vienna: Verlag der Österreichischen Akademie der Wissenschaften, 1980), 880–890; M. L. Rozenblit, *Reconstructing a National Identity. The Jews of Habsburg Austria during World War I* (Oxford and New York: Oxford University Press, 2004), 15. First published 2001. Lviv, Chernivtsi, Brody (all in Ukraine).
2. Rozenblit, *Reconstructing a National Identity*, 14–25; D. Rechter, *The Jews of Vienna and the First World War* (Oxford: The Littman Library of Jewish Civilization, 2001), 23–66; S. Panter, *Jüdische Erfahrungen und Loyalitätskonflikte im ersten Weltkrieg* (Göttingen: Vandenhoeck & Ruprecht, 1914), 53–55.
3. Rozenblit, *Reconstructing National Identity*, 43–45; J. B. Don, G. Magos, "A Magyarországi Zsidóság Demográfiai Fejlődése," *Történelmi Szemle* 27, no. 3 (1985): 437–469; K. Vörös, "A Budapesti Zsidóság Két Forradalom között, 1849–1918," *Magyar Írószövetség* 30, no. 12 (1986): 112–115.
4. P. C. Appelbaum, *Loyal Sons. Jewish Soldiers in the German Army in the Great War* (London and Portland, OR: Vallentine-Mitchell, 2014), 47–51.
5. Stefan Zweig (1881–1942), Austrian novelist, playwright, journalist, and biographer.
6. M. Rauchensteiner, *The First World War and the End of the Habsburg Monarchy, 1914–1918* (Vienna, Cologne, and Weimar: Böhlau Verlag, 2014), 136–141.
7. Z.Y. Gitelman, *A Century of Ambivalence. The Jews of Russia and the Soviet Union, 1881 to the Present* (New York: Schocken Publishers, 1988), 81. "Fonye the Ganev [thief]" was the Russian Jews' opprobrious name for Tsar Nicholas II.
8. J. Verhey, *The Spirit of 1914. Militarism, Myth, and Mobilization in Germany* (Cambridge: Cambridge University Press, 2000).
9. F.M. Schuster, *Zwischen allen Fronten. Osteuropäische Juden während des ersten Weltkrieges (1914–1919)* (Cologne, Weimar, and Vienna: Böhlau Verlag, 2004), 114–116.
10. Franz Kafka (1883–1924) was a German-speaking Bohemian Jewish novelist and short story writer, widely regarded as one of the major figures of twentieth century literature. Martin Buber (1878–1965) was an Austrian-born Israeli philosopher best known for his philosophy of dialogue, a form of existentialism centered on the distinction between the

I–Thou and I–It relationship. Friedrich Adler (1879–1960), son of Viktor Adler (1852–1918) was the prewar head of the Austrian Social Democratic Party.

11 M. L. Rozenblit, "The European Jewish World 1914–1919. What changed," in *World War I and the Jews. Conflict and Transformation in Europe, the Middle East, and America*, ed. M. L. Rozenblit, J. Karp (New York and Oxford: Berghahn Books, 2017), 36–37. Chișinău (Moldova).

12 R. A. Bermann, *Die Fahrt auf dem Katarakt (Autobiographie ohne einen Helden) 1883–1918* (New York: Archives of the Leo Baeck Institute [1918]), ME 322, 152.

13 Zabolotiv (Ukraine).

14 M. Sperber, *God's Water Carriers*, trans. J. Neogroschel (New York: Holmes and Meier, 1987), 69–72.

15 A. L. Schmelzer, "Die Juden in der Bukowina (1914–1919)," in *Geschichte der Juden in der Bukowina. Ein Sammelwerk*, ed. H. Gold, vol. 1 (Tel Aviv: Olamenu, 1958–1962), 67.

16 A. Hindls, *Aus meinem Leben* (New York: Archives of the Leo Baeck Institute, [1966]), 61.

17 W. von Weisl, *Die Juden in der Armee Österreich-Ungarns. Illegale Transporte* (Tel Aviv: Olamenu, 1971), 36.

18 F. Lieben, *Aus der Zeit meines Lebens: Erinnerungen* (New York: Archives of the Leo Baeck Institute. 1960), ME 207a, 104.

19 G. J. De Groot, *The First World War* (Basingstoke: Palgrave Macmillan, 2001), 20.

20 See Rauchensteiner, *The First World War*, 139.

21 S. Freud, "Zeitgemäßes über Krieg und Tod. I. Die Enttäuschung des Krieges," *Imago. Zeitschrift für Anwendung der Psychoanalyse auf die Gewissenschaftlichen. Herausgegeben von prof. Dr. Sigm. Freud* 4 (1915): 1–21.

22 S. Zweig, *The World of Yesterday* (London: Cassel and Co., Ltd., 1943), 173–174.

23 E. M. Lilien, *Briefe an seine Frau, 1905–1925*, ed. O. M. Lilien and E. Strauss (Köningstein/Ts: Jüdischer Verlag Athenäum, 1985), 9–13.

24 E. E. Kisch, *"Schreib das auf Kisch!" Das Kriegstagebuch von Egon Erwin Kisch* (Berlin: Erich Reiss Verlag, 1930), 12.

25 Ibid., 15–22.

26 E. De Waal, *The Hare with Amber Eyes. A Hidden Inheritance* (New York: Picador, Farrar, Straus & Giroux, 2010), 181. Arthur Schnitzler (1862–1931) was an Austrian playwright and dramatist. Karl Kraus (1874–1936) was an Austrian author and satirical journalist.

27 F. Kafka, "Eintrag 06.08.1914," in *Tagebücher 1910–1923* ed. M. Brod (Frankfurt am Main: Fischer Taschenbuch Verlag, 1976), 305–306.

28 D. Shumsky, "On Ethnocentrism and its Limits—Czecho-German Jewry in Fin-de-Siècle Prague and the Origins of Zionist Bi-Nationalism," *Jahrbuch des Simon Dubnow Instituts* 5 (2006): 173–188.

29 H. Kohn, *Living in a World Revolution. My Encounters with History* (New York: Pocket Books, Inc., 1965), 86. Originally published by Trident Press (1964).

30 A. Hameiri, *The Great Madness*, trans. Y. Lotan (Haifa: Or Ron Publishing House, Ltd., 1984), 12–14. First published in Hebrew by Joseph Sreberk as *Hashigaon Hagadol*, in 1929. Rev. and ed. P. C. Appelbaum (Middletown, RI: Stone Tower Press, and Boston, MA: Black Widow Press, 2021), 60–61.

31 De Waal, *The Hare with Amber Eyes*, 178–183.

32 Editorial, "Der Kaiser Ruft!," *Dr. Blochs Österreichische Wochenschrift*, July 31, 1914, 529.

33 The Ninth of Av, Jewish national day of mourning. Destruction of both Temples (587–582 BCE, 70 CE) and expulsion from Spain (1492) occurred on Tisha Be'Av.

34 Editorial, "Der Welt-Tischobeaw 5674," *Dr. Blochs Österreichische Wochenschrift*, August 7, 1914, 545–546.
35 "Der Krieg," *Monatschrift der Oesterreichisch-Israelitischen Union* 7/8 (July–August 1914): 2.
36 The Amalekites (Exodus 17:8–16) are the paradigm of antisemitism for the Jewish people; Jews are exhorted to "blot their memory out."
37 M. Frühling, "Gehet hin und tuet Desgleichen!," *Dr. Blochs Österreichische Wochenschrift*, August 7, 1914, 547–548.
38 Rede des Präsidenten, Plenarprotokoll, August 18, 1914, Central Archive for the History of the Jewish People, AW 71, 15. The number of six million would have terrible significance when the armies' roles were reversed two decades later
39 E. Zweig, "Oesterreich und wir Juden," *Jüdische Zeitung*, July 31, 1914, 1.
40 Editorial, "Unserer Aufruf," *Jüdische Zeitung*, September 18, 1914, 1.
41 Editorial, "Krieg!," *Jüdische Volksstimme*, July 30, 1914, 1.
42 Editorial, "Aus der Woche," *Die Wahrheit*, July 31, 1914, 3.
43 Kranj (Slovenia).
44 D. Herzog, *Kriegspredigten* (Frankfurt am Main: Verlag von J. Kauffmann, 1915), 14–18.
45 W. Reich, "Der Weltkrieg," *Dr. Blochs Österreichische Wochenschrift*, August 7, 1914, 546–547; idem, "Oesterreich's Zuversicht," *Dr. Blochs Österreichische Wochenschrift*, August 14 1914, 562–563; idem, "Oesterreichische Feinde," *Dr. Blochs Österreichische Wochenschrift*, August 21, 1914, 577–579; idem, "Zwei Manifeste," *Dr. Blochs Österreichische Wochenschrift*, August 28, 1914, 593–595. The biblical citation in the latter article (594) is from Psalm 2:4.
46 R. Färber, *Unser Kaiser, ein Sendbote Gottes. Predigten zum Allerhöchsten Geburtstage Sr. Maj. des Kaisers Franz Joseph I und aus anderen patriotischen Anlässen* (Mährisch Ostrau: Selbstverlag, 1915), 26–27; Rauchensteiner, *The First World War*, 317–354; Ostrava (Czech Republic).
47 C. A. Macartney, *The Habsburg Empire 1790–1918* (New York: Macmillan, 1969), 796; R. G. Ardelt, *Vom Kampf um Bürgerrechte zum "Burgfrieden." Studien zur Geschichte der österreichischen Sozialdemokratie 1888–1914* (Vienna: Verlag für Gesellschaftskritik, 1994), 54; M. Moll, *Die Steiermark im ersten Weltkrieg. Der Kampf des Hinterlandes ums Überleben 1914–1918* (Vienna, Graz, and Klagenfurt: Styria Premium, 2014), 39. Count Karl von Stürgkh (1859–1916) was Minister-President of Cisleithania during the 1914 July crisis.
48 Appelbaum, *Loyal Sons*, 51–54.
49 R. Okey, *The Habsburg Monarchy c. 1765–1918. From Enlightenment to Eclipse* (Basingstoke: Palgrave Macmillan, 2001), 379; A, Rachamimow, *POWs and the Great War. Captivity on the Eastern Front* (Oxford and New York: Berg, 2002), 137. Viktor Adler (1852–1918) was an Austrian neurologist, politician, and founder of the Social Democratic Workers Party (SDAP).
50 A Middle Ages movement led by the Catholic Church. The goal of both the *Pax Dei* and the *Treuga Dei* was to limit violence of feuding endemic to the western half of the former Carolingian Empire, following its collapse in the middle of the ninth century, with threats of spiritual sanctions; A. Watson, *Ring of Steel. Germany and Austria-Hungary in World War I* (New York: Basic Books, 2014), 93–94.
51 P. Bihari, *A Forgotten Home Front: The Middle Class and the "Jewish Question" in Hungary During the First World War* (PhD diss., Central European University, 2005), 49–51. Count István Tisza de Borosjenő et Szeged (1861–1918) was a politician, prime minister, and member of Hungarian Academy of Sciences. The prominent event in his life was Austria-Hungary's entry into World War I when he was prime minister for the second time

52 W. O. McCagg, Jr., *Jewish Nobles and Geniuses in Modern Hungary* (Boulder, CO: East European Monographs; distributed by New York: Columbia University Press, 1986), 179.
53 H. Petschar, F. Halas (Austrian National Library), and M. Rauchensteiner (University of Vienna), personal communications; Watson, *Ring of Steel*, 94–97.
54 Verordnung der Ministerien für Landesverteidigung und des Innern im Einvernehmen mit den übrigen beteiligten Ministerien zur Durchführung der Kaiserlichen Verordnung vom 4. Juli 1914, *Reichsgesetzblatt Nr. 141, betreffend das k.k. österreichische Kriegerkorps*: 869-875; "Kaiser Franz Josef an die Presse," *Neue Freie Presse*, August 9, 1914, 1.
55 Appelbaum, *Loyal Sons*, 239–283.
56 J. Redlich, Österreichische Regierung und Verwaltung im Weltkriege (Vienna: Hölder - Pichler-Tempsky AG, 1925), 113–146.
57 Ardelt, *Vom Kampf um Bürgerrechte*, 110.
58 A. J. May, *The Passing of the Habsburg Monarchy 1914–1918*, vol. 3 (Philadelphia, PA: University of Pennsylvania Press, 1966), 87–88; Macartney, *The Habsburg Empire*, 810–812; Moll, *Die Steiermark im ersten Weltkrieg*, 53; J. Galantái, *Hungary in the First World War* (Budapest: Akadémiai Kiadó, 1989), 65–66; Rauchensteiner, *The First World War*, 144.
59 Schuster, *Zwischen allen Fronten*, 125; R. Klein-Pejšová, "The Budapest Jewish Community's Galician October," in *World War I and the Jews. Conflict and Transformation in Europe, the Middle East, and America*, ed. M. L. Rozenblit, J. Karp (New York and Oxford: Berghahn Books, 2017), 113.
60 P. Ernst, "Der erste Weltkrieg in deutschsprachig-jüdischer Literatur und Publizistik in Österreich," in *Krieg. Erinnerung. Geschichtswissenschaft*, ed. S. Mattl, G. Botz, S. Karnern, and H. Konrad (Vienna, Cologne, and Weimar: Böhlau Verlag, 2009), 68–72.
61 This changed rapidly, and by early 1915 disorder in both military and the food supply had markedly increased; P. Holquist, *Making War, Forging Revolution. Russia's Continuum of Crisis, 1914–1921* (Cambridge, MA and London: Harvard University Press, 2002), 12–28.
62 Rauchensteiner, *The First World War*, 809.
63 Rechter, *The Jews of Vienna*, 67–74; Panter, *Jüdische Erfahrungen*, 60; Bihari, *A Forgotten Home Front*, 120.
64 L. Szabolcsi, *Két emberöltő. Az Egyenlőség évtizedei* (Budapest: MTA Judaisztikai Kutatócsoport, 1993), 172–173.
65 I. Deák, *Beyond Nationalism. A Social and Political History of the Habsburg Officers Corps, 1848–1918* (New York and Oxford: Oxford University Press, 1990), 196.
66 M. Paul-Schiff, "Teilnahme der österreichisch-ungarischen Juden am Weltkrieg," in *Mitteilungen zur jüdischen Volkskunde. Jahrbuch für jüdische Volkskunde*, new series, 26/27 (1924/1925): 153–154; E. A. Schmidl, *Juden in der k.(u.)k. Armee 1788–1918. Jews in the Habsburg Armed Forces* (Eisenstadt: Eisenstadt Jewish Museum, 1989), 144; M. Berger, *Eisernes Kreuz, Doppeladler, Davidstern. Juden in deutschen und österreichisch-ungarischen Armeen. Der Militärdienst jüdischer Soldaten durch zwei Jahrhunderte* (Berlin: Trafo Verlag, 2010), 113; E. A. Schmidl, *Habsburgs Jüdische Soldaten 1788–1918* (Vienna, Cologne, and Weimar: Böhlau Verlag, 2014), 115; idem, "Jüdische Soldaten in der k.u.k. Armee," in *Weltuntergang. Jüdisches Leben und Sterben im ersten Weltkrieg*, ed. M. G. Patka (Vienna, Graz, and Klagenfurt: Styria Premium, 2014), 46.
67 Bihari, *A Forgotten Home Front*, 118–119.
68 J. Winter, *Remembering War. The Great War between Memory and History in the Twentieth Century* (New Haven and London: Yale University Press, 2006), 80–83.
69 Ernst, "Der erste Weltkrieg," 47–72.

70 B. Bardach, *Carnage and Care on the Eastern Front. The War Diaries of Bernhard Bardach, 1914–1918*. Annotated and translated from the original hand-written German by P. C. Appelbaum (New York and Oxford: Berghahn Publishing, 2018).

71 J. Crouthamel, M. Geheran, T. Grady, and J. B. Köhne (eds.), *Beyond Inclusion and Exclusion. Jewish Experiences of the First World War in Central Europe* (New York and Oxford, Berghahn Books, 2018); G. Lamprecht, E. Lappin-Eppel, U. Wyrwa (eds.), *Jewish Soldiers in the Collective Memory of Central Europe. The Remembrance of World War I from a Jewish Perspective* (Vienna, Cologne, and Weimar: Böhlau Verlag, 2019).

CHAPTER 4

Snapshots from the Eastern Front: Diaries, Memoirs, Reports

The Austro-Hungarian Army served on the Eastern, Balkan, Italian, and Ottoman Fronts. Before World War I, approximately 2,200,000 Jews lived in all corners of the Habsburg Empire. Most, approximately three quarters, resided in the north-eastern provinces of Galicia and Bukowina, both of which would become major Eastern Front battlefields.[1]

Ostjuden, living in heavily Jewish section of the empire, rarely came into contact with worldly Cisleithanian Jews.[2] This would change when hostilities began. Information has been scarce on interaction between assimilated Austro-Hungarian Jews and their more Orthodox eastern counterparts (including those living in the Russian Pale of Settlement). To shed more light on this neglected aspect of the war, this chapter will explore diaries, memoirs, and other writings of Austro-Hungarian Jewish officers and men who served on the Eastern Front. Many writings document with brutal clarity the situation of helpless civilians—Jews and non-Jews alike—caught between two great armies.

In contrast to relative homogeneity of Jewish soldiers in the German army, the Austro-Hungarian army comprised soldiers from approximately twenty different nationalities, with different languages and traditions. Habsburg Jewish soldiers comprised two main groups: assimilated Jews from large cities such as Vienna, Budapest, and Prague, and Orthodox Jews primarily from Galicia, Bukowina, Northern Hungary. As stated previously, unlike the German army, Jewish faith was not a deterrent to promotion in the Habsburg army, before and. during the war (chapter 2).

Diaries and memoirs commonly report Czech disloyalty. As previously set out, the truth is more complex, related to bad leadership and other factors. In a letter dated February 19, 1917, Archduke Joseph recommended mixing nationalities inside k.u.k. regiments, to prevent minorities from having undue influence.³ The Czech Legion, founded in 1914, remained loyal to the Monarchy until closing months of the war, when, in their desire for independence, they switched support to the anti-Bolsheviks (chapter 1).

Were there differences in war experiences of Jewish soldiers from different regions of the empire? Did they feel similar patriotism about the war and loyalty to the empire? Was there more shirking in one national group than another? Did they differ in experiences with *Ostjuden* with whom they came in contact? This chapter attempts to shed light on these questions. Many Austro-Hungarian Jewish soldiers from Galicia, Bukowina, Northern Hungary differed from assimilated co-religionists in being strictly Orthodox (as far as exigencies of war allowed), but this did not prevent them from fighting just as courageously.

Many Habsburg Jewish families had two to eight sons serving simultaneously, with multiple casualties. Dr. Otto Strasser's two sons were both killed in one week, and by April 1916 Salomon Pollak had lost all three grandsons. The five Lichtenstein boys won seven decorations. Among five serving sons of Widow Herzog, one was awarded the Signum Laudis, another wounded three times by the end of 1916. Amongst eight Szántó sons, three won the Silver Medal of Bravery (First or Second Class). Widow Schaffer had eight sons in service, three already decorated with the Silver Medal for Bravery (First and Second Class) by 1917.⁴

As testified by diaries and memoirs, overt antisemitism was not as significant an issue in the Austro-Hungarian, as in the German army, where it existed from the outset of war—despite the *Burgfrieden*—and increased with time. The *Judenzählung* of October 1916—which did not occur in Austro-Hungary—led to a significant rise in antisemitism in civilian society, but its effects in the army were less clear.⁵ Antisemitism in the Habsburg army was not always overt, but did occur, especially when war news worsened in 1917 and 1918. However, strict censorship kept it in official check. Perhaps Jewish soldiers did not wish to see what was in front of them, let alone write it down, and personal documents are not always reliable indicators of what actually occurred.

I found several individual diary entries of antisemitism in the Austro-Hungarian army. Bernhard Bardach reports on it twice (chapter 1), and Teofil Reiss comments on it several times. Avigdor Hameiri singles out one Hungarian colonel as the unit's arch antisemite, in his book *The Great Madness* (see below). The Hungarian David Neumann (1894–1992), reported that, as the only Jew in his 1914 intake, he felt pressured because of existing prejudices to prove that he was as good a solder as the next man. When his captain excused him from punishment exercises because "as a Jew he exercises much better than any of you," he took it as an insult, and undertook a forty-kilometer march in the middle of winter with a 39°C fever, to prove that Jews were not shirkers. During the rest of his service, first in Italy and then on the Romanian Front, he encountered no antisemitism. This, despite that fact that due to illness he mostly served in a clerical ("shirker") position.[6]

The Austrian non-commissioned officer Eugen Hoeflich (later Mosheh Ya'akov ben Gavriel) (1891–1965) noted in his diary in July 1915: "one person says: Jews are cowards. Another says that he knows an exception to this rule, the first man contradicts him, and so it went on. I, the coward, must offer my life with these men!" Not long after, Hoeflich was seriously wounded, awarded the Bronze Medal for Bravery, and ended the war a lieutenant of the reserves.[7]

Far more often than antisemitism, soldiers commented, often scathingly, on inept leaders with little understanding of the arts of war, and, latterly, on deleterious effects of the blockade on home and fighting fronts. The longer war lasted, procurement of provisions became one the soldiers' overriding concerns, with catastrophic effect on civilian morale in the hinterland.

How did these expressions of antisemitism in Central Powers armies compare with that of their opponents? The Tsarist Army was, and remained, blatantly antisemitic.[8] German and Austro-Hungarian newspapers regularly mentioned bravery of Jewish soldiers, but this was forbidden by Russian censors. Only the Russian-Jewish periodical *Voina i Evrei* (War and the Jews) defied the ban. There were no Jews in the Russian officers' corps at the start of the Great War.[9]

Jews in the Pale of Settlement had been subjected to Nicholas I's 1827 Law on Conscription Duty, which obliged them, sometimes from age twelve, to serve for twenty-five years in the army without civil rights. Families, lacking breadwinners, were reduced to poverty, and required financial relief. Jews served in the Crimean War (1854–1855), and 500 Jewish soldiers died during defense of Sevastopol. Although the war ministry took steps toward establishment of a Jewish chaplaincy, nothing came of it. Soldiers took religious leadership on themselves, establishing soldiers' synagogues as far away as Irkutsk. Jews who retired from the army were permitted to settle outside the Pale.[10]

Only after Alexander II issued his "liberation" statute of 1874 did the army become the first Russian state institution to decide in favor of Jewish emancipation. Although Alexander agreed to give Jews non-commissioned rank, his government refused to allow Jews to become officers. From 1874 to 1914, only one Jew, Gertsel Yanklevich Tsam, was promoted officer through personal qualities alone. He was thus the Russian equivalent of Meno Burg (chapter 2), the only Jewish officer in the Prussian standing army. Despite revolutionary defections. Jews fought with distinction during the Russo-Japanese War of 1904–1905.[11]

Just before the war, in 1912, there was a heated debate in the Duma regarding drafting of Jews, who were accused of being draft-dodgers, while the opposite was, in reality, the case. The 1912 law was the last legal attempt to diminish what few rights Jewish soldiers had in the Russian army.[12]

Despite discrimination, approximately 180,000 Jews fought in the Russian army: a high percentage (given official antisemitism) were decorated, some highly. At least 1,957 Jews received the Russian Saint George Crosses of various degrees from 1914 through 1917. Russo-Jewish soldiers were forced to witness brutality and pogroms against their civilian coreligionists, and suffered at least twice as much from depression and other psychological conditions than their Christian counterparts. Not one Jewish officer was appointed between 1914 and 1917. As if to compensate, Jews were overrepresented in leadership positions in the post-revolutionary Red Army.[13]

Following the February revolution of 1917, the *Vserossiiskii Soiuz Evreev-Voinov* (VSEV, All-Russian Union of Jewish Soldiers) was formed in Kiev.[14] The organization claimed to be the official representative of all Jewish Russian soldiers, and also liaised with civilian Jewish organizations. The association provided assistance for Jewish soldiers while still in the field prior to the Treaty of Brest-Litovsk, and assisted in their integration into Russian society after years of war.[15] The Russian Civil War, which lasted through October 1922, threw everything into chaos, with Jews involved on both sides.[16]

Treatment of Jews in the Tsarist Army was thus the worst among all warring armies, and had not improved significantly in the century before the Great War. Of the three major warring parties on the Eastern Front, Russia was easily the most antisemitic, Austro-Hungary the least, with Germany in between.

In light of experiences of Jewish soldiers in Russia and Germany—the other protagonists on the Eastern Front—let us analyze the Austro-Hungarian Jewish military experience during the Great War, through the voices of men who were there. I have attempted to group diaries and memoirs by nationalities, to examine whether this difference could account for differing opinions and points of view.

This chapter asserts that bravery and resourcefulness of Austro-Hungarian Jewish soldiers was equivalent to that of their Christian comrades. Indeed, some of the bravest and most decorated of all soldiers were Orthodox *Peyesjuden* (side lock-wearing Jews) who adhered, as far as possible, to Orthodox rites including dietary laws. The sight and sound of fierce-looking, bearded soldiers storming into battle with tallit and tefillin yelling *Sh'ma Yisrael* (Hear, O Israel), must have terrified non-Jewish Russian soldiers. As stated previously, many Galician Jews did not serve because they were expelled from their homes early in the war, but there is ample evidence that a large number who remained served, and fought bravely.

The destructive effect of fighting on the Eastern Front on Jewish civilians in its path was enormous. Hundreds of thousands were expelled by Russian authorities on suspicion of espionage or collusion. This started immediately after hostilities began, with Russian occupation of Lemberg and Czernowitz.[17] The exact number of Jewish civilians killed as a direct result of war is unknown, but could have been as high as 200,000, or more.[18] Towns and villages changed hands, some many times. Each time, Jews bore the brunt of murder, rape, and pillage, mostly by Russian troops. It is instructive to note that the Central Powers were—despite large-scale requisition and sometimes pillage—regarded by Jewish civilian as liberators. This paradigm would be turned on its head two decades later. Jewish soldiers' reactions to these civilians were tinged by religious beliefs. As described by Bardach, assimilated Jews looked on *Ostjuden* as civilized observers would look on otherwordly beings, while Orthodox Yiddish-speaking soldiers must have been more comfortable in their world.[19]

Outbreak of war saw Austro-Hungarian Jews from all walks of life serving in the ill-prepared Habsburg armies. Unlike Germany, which had restructured and modernized its armies and railroads, Austro-Hungarian forces were often badly equipped and poorly led. However, Habsburg Jews were, like their German counterparts, united in love of their country and desire to defend it. In addition, Habsburg Jews were strongly motivated by Tsarist Jewish oppression, geographically nearer to them than to Germany.

Approximately 100,000 Jews served in the German army[20] and, as stated above, 180,000 in the Russian army.[21] It can therefore be seen that, with the 300,000–350,000 Habsburg Jewish soldiers, approximately 600,000 Jews served in all three armies. Apart from the Battles of Tannenberg, Masurian Lakes, and Courland (Western Latvia), where they fought alone, German troops were only sent east to bolster those of Austro-Hungary, as exigencies demanded, especially during the Brusilov Offensive.

Were many Austro-Hungarian Jews shirkers, as adduced by antisemites? There were (and are) shirkers in every nation and ethnic group, but there is ample evidence to prove significant Jewish participation in the war. The fact that many well-educated Jews—especially from large cities such as Vienna, Budapest, Prague—served in the rear (for example, as translators), does not diminish this fact. Even some dedicated leftists such as Béla Kun served from the beginning of the war, instead of working against the government. Lavoslav Kraus (see below), although realizing that the Habsburg Empire was disintegrating, and despite disparaging remarks about the Monarchy, fought bravely until the war ended. As late as 1918, most Jewish soldiers remained loyal to the Monarchy; only in the closing months of the war did this begin to fall apart. Bernhard Bardach's diary began to reflect the hopelessness of their situation only when Bulgaria sued for peace the end of September 1918; thereafter, things got progressively worse.[22]

Austria and Galicia

Arnold Höllriegel left a written account of his war service. Höllriegel (pseudonym R. A. Bermann, 1883–1939) was born in Vienna, grew up in Prague, and served as press correspondent throughout the war for the *Berliner Tageblatt, Prager Tagblatt,* and *Die Zeit* (Vienna). In Rzeszów, he had a chance to observe a typical Galician Jewish area, and heard the thunder of cannon. A sudden order came to evacuate the field hospital, and he left hastily. He was transferred back to Vienna, where he remained through spring 1915. He observed that, at the start of war, the blockade was not yet palpable: even white bread was available, but "it isn't healthy to eat white bread." In May 1915 he travelled to Slovakia. He felt "no trace of glory in the fighting, only loathing." He visited Lemberg after reoccupation, and commented on the good-natured stupidity of Austrian officialdom, frozen in old-fashioned ways. He visited the fighting in the Vladimir-Volynsky area, and was shot at by Cossacks.[23] He commented on an outbreak of cholera amongst the men: "even the regimental physician is ill."[24]

Italy declared war on Austro-Hungary in May 1915, and Höllriegel visited the Isonzo Front from his base in Trieste. He toured the karst plateau, where both sides had dug themselves in: each artillery barrage multiplied manifold, ricocheting off mountainsides.[25] Bermann opined that Austro-Hungary should have ceded the Trentino to Italy while Italy was still neutral, thus buying off Italy's neutrality. On one occasion, he was left alone in a trench: he had no revolver, so an ensign gave him a large axe. "No, I am not going to die alone like this." He climbed out, leaving the axe behind.[26]

Höllriegel could not avoid dangers of cholera, or sleeping in straw crawling with lice. In October 1918, he travelled from Belgrade through Bosnia Herzegovina, commenting on the beauty of multicultural, tolerant Sarajevo, with its Ladino-speaking Sephardic Jews and mixture of churches, mosques, and synagogues. He travelled through Novipazar and Montenegro, "with its tall, handsome men and beautiful women," arriving at the Dalmatian coast near Split.[27] But, in the end, "Austria's great cultural task of uniting the Balkans failed." Höllriegel paid a visit to the Russian Front in an observer balloon.

Travelling by train to Istanbul, he tried in vain to interview Enver Pasha.[28] Sultan Mehmet V agreed to an interview: "the fat, old man, bristling in scarlet, gold and jewels, limping with difficulty on a gammy leg, made gracious signs to us with a bejeweled fat hand while he shambled past. That was the entire audience." Höllriegel entered the main mosque, sitting through endless Moslem prayers. He was rewarded by meeting Enver Pasha, a "small, delicately built man in general's uniform," who was present at the prayers. Enver explained the situation of the Turkish army in the Dardanelles and Suez in excellent German. Höllriegel was the only one who got an interview with Enver: he sent it out of the country, against Enver's wishes. Two days later, the police came to his hotel to arrest him, but he had already left.[29]

Turkey during the war, nominally still a sultanate, was ruled by the triumvirate of Enver, Talaat, and Djemal Pasha, all three of whom were—singularly and collectively—responsible for the Armenian genocide, the first mass murder of the twentieth century. The results of this genocide were observed by Kaspar Blond in Aleppo (chapter 7).

Bravery amongst Jewish soldiers—irrespective of nationality—is well documented in memoirs and diaries. On December 15, 1914, acting Ulan Sergeant Aron Schapira, from Borszczow (Galicia), was tasked, with six riders, to spy out the surrounding area.[30] Leaving four men in the rear, he burst into the local marketplace, where he found 150 Cossacks, with their commanding officer, a major. The major galloped towards Schapira; when he arrived at sabre length, Schapira struck him such a violent blow that he was immediately rendered hors de combat. The 150 Cossacks raised their hands, and Schapira and his partner took them prisoner. Another Russian battery and a unit of Cossacks saw this and fled. Schapira locked the Cossacks in the district school, and awaited arrival of his troops. He was personally awarded the gold medal by Archduke Friedrich, a man previously accused of having antisemitic tendencies.[31]

Fritz Lieben, born in Vienna in 1890, was in the middle of his one-year volunteer service, when war began.[32] He was not impressed with the Austro-Hungarian army's preparations for war. After many delays, he arrived at the Russian Front. Nobody knew what to do, and there was no fixed quartermaster. They finally heard that the Russians had vacated Zamość (Poland), and his regiment marched into the town. No sooner had they arrived, when they were ordered to leave; they were subjected to heavy enemy fire, and retreated. They arrived in Jarosław but were soon beaten back by the Russians, and "regrouped"(in other words fled). They arrived in Tarnów, but Russians blew the bridge over the Dunajec River, so they had to retreat again, to Cracow and then on to Zolkiew.[33]

They crossed into Russian territory, passing through several torched villages: "The horizon is in flames." His regiment remained in the area through early 1916. They were stationed in the Volhynian swamps in March 1916, and were on the other side of the Styr River when the Brusilov Offensive began. A violent bombardment was followed by an enemy breakthrough, and the entire Fourth Army beat a hasty retreat to Vladimir-Volynsky. Lieben remarked on terrible poverty in small farmhouses. He spent his third winter of the war on the Eastern Front, and was in Romania in August 1917. He was transferred to the Italian Front in time for the Battle of Caporetto, and was on the Piave when war ended.[34]

Joseph Floch and Eric Fischer both illustrate the ossified, disorganized nature of Austro-Hungarian military leadership.

Joseph Floch, born 1895, studied at the Vienna Academy of Arts. In 1916, he enlisted, and was sent to the Eastern Front. His diary describes disorder, wastage of time and labor on unnecessary issues: Once officers found out that Floch was a painter, he was kept busy painting their portraits. The ninety-year-old Field Marshal von Seewitz was one of his first subjects. At first, Floch was naïve: when he told his assistant that he could care for his paints and brushes himself, the man was immediately called up to the front, and Floch was almost put into the stockade for pleading the man's case, asking for him to be sent home to help with harvesting. By 1918 he had been transferred to office duty, and was in his Vienna office when war ended:

> Hundreds of thousands of medals, distinctions, ribbons, shoes, weapons, other military equipment scattered over the floor. General plundering: Soldiers laden with knapsacks on their way home to Hungary, but Austrian soldiers robbed them at the station. The war ends in chaos.[35]

Eric Fischer was born 1898 in Vienna. His memoirs also detail the out-of-date, disorganized Habsburg army. He underwent officers' training under an elderly, ignorant major whose main interest was shiny buttons. His colonel was "well prepared for the previous war." After graduating from officers' training school, he was transferred to office duty. His colonel was obsessed, in the middle of a war, with out-of-date titles on office paper. The office was untidy and disorganized. Men were mixed up, transfers fell through cracks, and some deserters had two simultaneous names. One day in fall 1917, a Romanian prisoner of war was brought in; Fischer had no idea why he had been transferred from his prisoner of war camp. The man was imprisoned for over a year, until his papers arrived: there had been a mix-up whether he was a Romanian or Hungarian citizen. One of the draftees proved to be an Austrian archduke: the commanding colonel had a fit from worry of being accused of lèse majesté. The office physician was really a dentist.[36]

Teofil Tobias Reiss (plate 1), born 1889 in Lemberg, left a unique and extraordinary war diary, which has been translated into Hebrew, and recently into English, by his descendants.[37] One of sixteen children, he arrived in Vienna as a young man, and completed various trade courses until conscription. He served for nine years, before and throughout World War I. Reiss was a versatile, quick-thinking, enterprising, brave young man who served variously as medical orderly (Red Cross Bronze Medal of Honor), master artillery sergeant (Bronze Medal for Bravery), and non-commissioned kitchen provisions officer. His diary is unique: it deals with everyday life at the front, experiences as medical orderly at the front in the midst of bloody combat, death and wounded all around him, and as resourceful kitchen aide, who roots out stealing of rations, ready at any time to improvise good meals such as goulash and palatschinken in the field for his grateful comrades. He describes encounters with Jewish civilians, some of whom suffered terribly under Russian occupation, and helps them as a medical orderly whenever he can. Reiss has a panoply of young girls, sometimes more than one in the same town, at his disposal, even staying with their families. His diary is filled with acid comments on bad leadership, disorganized—sometimes scandalously bad—medical facilities, and supplies that do not arrive on time.

The diary (excerpted here in my own English translation) begins on January 1, 1915, in the firing line, Third Mortar Unit Battery, at Siemiechów (Poland).[38] Early on January 1, Russians started a murderous machine gun and artillery attack on Reiss's position, where he was serving as medical orderly and kitchen provisions officer. Reiss was quartered near the road to his position, where he had set up a medical clinic. He was soon knee-deep in wounded men, shells exploding around him. A wounded captain needed to be evacuated; because the other orderly and the physician were afraid, Reiss braved a murderous hail of machine guns and artillery fire, to give first aid to the man and other wounded on the line. "The front line is a terrible sight: blood, pieces of human flesh, hands, heads, feet, intestines." He bandaged a captain who appeared mortally wounded, sending him to a dressing station in the rear. The Russians continued their attack: Reiss had to look after fifty wounded men alone, because his cowardly comrades ran away. He wondered how he could cope, having to work in the kitchen as well.

The attack continued through January 3, and luckily reinforcements arrived. The regimental physician acted as if he were ill, and was conveniently transferred to the rear. "Thank God: a scoundrel who thinks that war is only for boozing and eating!" The other orderly disappeared, so Reiss was left on his own with sick and wounded. As he did throughout this diary, Reiss managed to meet young girls: "the farmer has two daughters, one dumb, and the other very dirty but pretty." Reiss was called to see an injured young Jewish girl. Russians had murdered her parents and raped their sixteen-year-old daughter so violently that her bowels spilled out. He gave her first aid, sent her to the field hospital, then buried her parents. The men received corn bread rations: "the devil take the person who invented this: it's so bad even the horses won't eat it!"

On January 7, a Russian night attack was fought off with heavy losses. Reiss requested a physician to help him. Fighting continued for the next several days: Russians fired in the street and no one could reach him to provide aid. There were no bandages for the wounded. The Russian attack failed, but stubborn fighting lasted for four days. Reiss sent sixteen wounded to hospital during the night. He finally received medicines and bandages from the senior regimental physician, who praised him for excellent treatment, and sent him cognac and cigarettes. One of the men appeared to have typhus: his face was black, and he refused food. It was cold, snowing, with no bread.

On January 12, Reiss had a violent argument with a physician's assistant, who ordered him to vacate the house where he was living and tried to make the wounded stand at attention. Reiss threw him out, reporting the matter to his superiors. There was little to eat, and it remained cold. A new, more sympathetic physician's assistant was appointed. By January 16, rain and fog had made fighting impossible. Reiss requested permission to travel to Cracow, but his captain refused because he believed Reiss would "make Jewish business." The Russians tried to break through, but were repulsed. After doing without for a long while, men again had cigarettes and wine. A day later, the second physician's assistant also conveniently disappeared, leaving Reiss alone again. In the following days, more Russian attacks were repulsed. Reiss developed a fever with nobody to look after him, but still had to help sick and wounded.

On January 30, the entire Austro-Hungarian army attacked in the Carpathians. With heavy fighting, they retook mountain passes, and Reiss had much to do tending wounded. He remained feverish and lost his appetite, but still had to work. All he could keep down were tea and rum. Finally, in the third week of February, he was diagnosed with a kidney infection, and transferred to hospital in a monastery in Zakliczyn (Poland). There was only one physician for the many sick and wounded.[39]

On February 26, Reiss was transferred to hospital in Żywiec. His fever was still high and his feet swollen: a physician made a superficial examination, diagnosing nephritis. He was given tea, but no further care, while the physician disported himself with whores. On March 3, Reiss escaped from an open window in shirt and underpants, reporting his scandalous treatment to command in town. A day later, a thorough investigation was performed, "the scoundrel doctor and two nurses removed," and Reiss examined by an American physician. Proper medicines were prescribed, and for the first time since he became ill he finally received some soup. All patients were grateful for his intervention. He was transferred to a hospital in St. Polten, where he was properly treated, and transferred back to a hospital in Vienna, where he recovered. By the middle of March, he could eat meat again, and by March 25 he could get out of bed. Pesach fell on April 2. His family did not visit, and he ate in the Jewish communal kitchen. Food in the hospital was bad, and, on April 8, he returned to duty.

On April 11, he was back with his unit, now in Gyulafirátót (Hungary), where he was ordered to open a sickbay. Corruption was rife: those who bribed remained in the rear. He received thirty crowns from his parents, but no letter with it, and stayed in the local inn. On April 16, he was called to see a farmer's daughter who had become ill. There was no physician, so he had to care for her. Reiss diagnosed life-threatening pneumonia.[40] Her condition worsened, but the farmer refused to call in a doctor. He nursed the young girl as best he could, but she died in agony two weeks later. Reiss felt helpless: there was nothing he could do. He and his unit attended her funeral. He received no mail, and was lonely. "No one writes to me, so I will write to a few girls, so that I also get some mail." On May 31, he requested to be transferred to the front, because "the rear is only for slackers." His transfer was approved, and on June 21 he was sent to the front via Mährisch-Ostrau.[41]

On June 25, he arrived in Tarnów, "a dirty, typically Jewish town." Even the uneducated Reiss looked disapprovingly at the poor *Ostjuden*. Russians had destroyed most of the town during their occupation. On June 27, he arrived at Przeworsk (Poland). Everything had been shot up: no houses standing. He slept under an empty wagon.[42]

While Reiss was sleeping, Russian planes bombed the railway station. When he awoke, the wagon was already burning, so he ran for cover. Dead and wounded were everywhere; screams of pain and misery were heard. Twenty-four ammunition wagons had exploded. Reiss helped with first aid as much as he could, but all his things were gone. He was lightly wounded in the left thigh, and lucky to be alive, because there was ammunition in the wagon under which he slept.

Newly fitted out, he was sent to Tarnogród (Poland), where he rejoined his battery on June 29; everyone was pleased to see him. He met up with his brother Ignaz and wept for joy: "Lord, how dirty he looks! He is a cook. I asked his sergeant to give him a few hours off, so that I could give him fresh linen and uniform, food, and ten crowns."

Reiss and his unit were force-marched into a nearby forest, where they spent July 1 and 2. There was a battle in the forest: no water, sweltering heat, the men collapsed from hunger, thirst, and heat; many fainted. There were many wounded and dead, and Reiss worked non-stop for two days. On July 3 he came out of the forest lucky to be alive. Bodies lay in the street, no time to bury them. Two days later after another forced march, there was another large infantry and artillery battle, which lasted for a week. There were many dead and wounded, and his unit was pushed back. There was no water, men were dying of thirst, and reserve supplies used up. He made a goulash out of one of the horses. Repeated forced marches under heavy enemy fire, no food or water, had become unendurable. An infantry bullet shot off Reiss's cap.

On July 11, they arrived in Zakrzów, "a Russo-Jewish town with only a few Jews." There was nothing to buy there but fighting quieted down and troops received food and water. Reiss brought the officers tomatoes and potatoes: "they wanted to kiss me." Finally, men were able to bathe again. A few days later, he drank cocoa with one of his female friends, Rachel Bronner. She had suffered a great deal with all the fighting, also from the Russian soldiers, who instigated a pogrom, hacked off the heads of most of the men, and raped the women.

By Thursday, July 15, food was finally plentiful. But Reiss and his unit were now in enemy territory. With rest and proper rations, men recovered quickly. On July 18, the Austro-Hungarians launched an offensive: the Russians defended themselves like madmen. Despite heat, fleas, mice, and lice, the Russians were "chased like dogs, and are to be pitied. Many remain behind: I give them what I can; I have no bread, but I give each Russian rum and cigarettes." By July 25, Reiss and his unit were in Bełżyce (Poland). After the latest battles, he was feeling sick and exhausted. In the sickbay, he was diagnosed with a "heart condition," and, on August 1, admitted to a Lublin field hospital. He was transferred to another hospital, but his condition worsened, and there were no physicians to treat many hundreds of wounded, only overworked nurses. He was again transferred by "a railway car fit for pigs" via Krasnik and Rzeszów, arriving in Łańcut on August 5,[43] where hospital conditions were primitive. A local school was used as hospital, there was nobody to cook food, one physician for 800 patients. Reiss lay on straw, weak and hungry because he had no money to buy food. There was no treatment: anybody who could not help himself died, especially those with no money and no acquaintances to assist them.

Nothing daunted, and despite his heart condition (no details given), Reiss went into town and "got acquainted with Miss Sabine Sauer," whose parents, conveniently, were well-off butchers, so that food was plentiful. The hospital physician could not care less, so Reiss was a daily guest at the Sauers. "Sabine appears to have fallen in love with me." His condition improved, with rest and proper food. Sabine declared her love for him. The doctor in the hospital told Reiss that he must find a place to stay because he had only space for the wounded, so Reiss found a place with the Sauers:

> Sabine is a classy young lady, who looks after me and gives me the best to eat, I spend the days "like a god in France." I must report to hospital daily. I must take care with Sabine because she is in love with me, and I must not turn her head.

On September 5, Reiss received an order from the hospital to travel to Mährisch-Ostrau. He parted from Sabine and her parents, arriving in Ostrau that evening. He spent several days in the hospital amongst sixty patients with "a high degree of neurasthenia."[44] Because he was a Jew in a field hospital with German wounded, he was transferred to a local hospital barracks, about 200 men in each barrack. Treatment was the worst imaginable, and food terrible. He requested a transfer and was scheduled to arrive in Prague on Yom Kippur, September 10. He obtained a permit to attend synagogue (no details given).

Before he departed for Prague, he made a side-trip to Łańcut to visit Sabine. He stayed with the Sauers through October 2. "Sabine loves me, but I cannot get involved in a complicated love relationship." He left for Prague on October 3, where he remained in a quarantine hospital through October 8, and was then transferred to a monastery hospital where treatment was good. He stayed there for ten days until he recovered. He requested leave in Vienna, where he arrived on October 19. Reiss gives no details of his illness, but it seems strange that he moved so easily from hospital to the Sauers—where he indulged his appetites with gusto—and back again; he was no malingerer. Home in Vienna, his parents did not care where he was; they had so many other children, and his mother had to stand in line for days to purchase provisions. In Vienna he met his future wife Pepi Kamiel for the first time: "She is a very dear young girl."

After a boring week in a Bosnian infantry convalescence home, he was declared fit for duty on October 27. He spent time between October 28 and the end of December in the area of Gyulafirátót/Enying (Hungary), where he again visited the Sauers, and found time to visit Cracow and Vienna (where he met the Aufgebauers, who had daughters). From December 13 through 28 he was stationed in Enying, where, while on patrol, he arrested an artilleryman with a prostitute and brought him back to the unit. On December 23, he was transferred into the field, but his captain liked him and wanted him to stay in the rear. On December 29, Reiss was sent to Lemberg as escort for artilleryman Katowicz and three other men. A day later, on the way, Katowicz deserted. Reiss looked for him all night and arrested him in a brothel. He became so wild that he was manacled and jailed. They arrived in Lemberg on New Year's Eve. Katowicz tried to run away, but he was caught again.[45]

On January 1 1916, Reiss handed Katowicz to the authorities in the citadel. He himself was arrested for attempted desertion, but released quickly after he submitted written documentation of why he had been delayed. He spent the rest of the night, and the following day, with Chania Neumann, "an excellent young lady." On January 3, Reiss was ordered to take Katowicz back to the front; if he remained alive, he would obtain leave, as a reward. They arrived in Zamość the evening of January 6. During the evening, fighting lessened. They marched away, and at 6.00 am next morning he handed Katowicz over to court martial in Zamość. Reiss was interrogated and imprisoned, but released after the officials opened his sealed letter from the commandant of the Lemberg citadel. As a reward for properly escorting Katowicz, he received ten crowns, and food for the way back. After having been shot at by the Russians, and waiting most of the night in an empty train, he arrived in Krasne (Poland) on January 7. "Only German soldiers can travel in carriages; I have to travel in a cattle car."

Reiss travelled to Lemberg for written leave approval, and spent January 9 through 18 at the Sauers. Reiss explained to Sabine that marriage was impossible: he loved her platonically but any effort for a closer relationship was pointless. He left, travelling via Cracow to Vienna, where he felt like a burden. He was welcomed warmly by the Aufgebauers, and slept at their home. "I'm lucky that I have such good acquaintances." On January 23, he left "Vienna city of my dreams. . . . It's hard for me: I have parents and siblings, but am alone in the world." Yet another young lady, Anna Uhl, accompanied him to the station.

On the way back to Enying, Reiss developed toothache. The local veterinarian, who also pulled human teeth, broke the tooth, exacerbating the toothache. He had the tooth extracted by a dentist, but it cost him six crowns. He arrived in Enying on January 27, and immediately took up his duties. That evening, Reiss was informed that he had been sentenced to fourteen days' imprisonment, strict regime. The unfair reason for this was "a recent incident" of January 12, 1915, when he did not allow an ensign to throw the sick and the wounded out of their quarters in an inn. Reiss did not protest, and began his sentence on January 30. His only complaint was that his room was cold, and wood for heating was not brought in. He was released early "because of my kind heart and faithful comradeship: perhaps my actions saved the life of this comrade or that. In this way I have atoned for my punishment with a clear conscience." On the way back to his unit, he was ordered to take a deserter to Lugusz via Budapest and Temesvár.[46] In Temesvár, he spent time with a beautiful gypsy girl, Gundina Maria. Back at his unit in Enying on February 16, he demonstrated to his captain how mens' food was being stolen and sold. Culprits were punished, and Reiss took over the soldiers' mess:

> I will now make order without mercy. Woe to those who steal food!
> The men should eat as much as they want, and remember me for it.
> Those who work should eat their fill: let the others peg out![47]

When he took over the mess, Reiss found everything dirty: kitchen personnel filthy, utensils rusty and mildew-covered, mice ran over provisions. He was not surprised that all the men had belly aches. He made sure that the kitchen was washed, cleaned, and properly outfitted. Personnel were changed: two men were locked up for theft, new utensils received. Men were overjoyed at increased meat portions. There was enough for everybody, some men even went back for seconds. For upcoming Pesach holiday, Reiss was granted permission to cook separately for Jewish soldiers. His captain praised him saying that he was a "different Jew from the others." On March 24, he left for Vienna to purchase kosher provisions and matzot with money that his captain had given him. "Anna Uhl is a good young woman and her father is very friendly. She wants me to stay there until I leave." He visited his parents, but felt estranged from them. He spent the rest of the time with Anna, and left with provisions three days later.

The men were very pleased to see him, decorating the kitchen with flowers and placing a five-liter bottle of wine on the table. He himself brought a ten-liter bottle of wine to celebrate his return. The officers brought fifteen more liters as well as sausage for the feast, and were of course invited to participate, so they brought even more wine. Celebrations, with music, went on until midnight. Reiss was promoted master artillery sergeant, and another party was held in his honor: boozing went on until 1.00 am.

The period from April 12 to 17 was Pesach. The hall was festively decorated, everyone was invited. Men sat together at a large table, officers on a platform of honor, and there was a separate table for the men. First they read the evening service and then recited *kiddush* (blessing) with best kosher wine, donated by the Enying Jewish community. Each participant received one cup of wine and two matzot, courtesy of Magdeburg and Budapest Jewish communities. Afterwards, he thanked non-Jewish officers and men for their participation, then heads of the Magdeburg, Budapest, and Enying Jewish communities for generous donations; the priest and mayor were both present. Reiss explained the Jews' bondage and Exodus from Egypt, spoke about the current conditions of the Jews, and asked them all to join in swearing fealty to God, Kaiser, and Fatherland. All rose and swore: "We swear by God the Holy that we will defend the Kaiser, Fatherland and all its elected officials with our blood." Then they all sang *Gott erhalte*.[48] "It was so solemn that all present were moved to tears." The meal consisted of turnip soup, lamb purée, and apple sauce, all prepared by Jewish cooks.

On May 11, Reiss obtained leave again, arriving in Vienna a day later. He spent time with Rosa and Mina (one of the Aufgebauers' daughters), visited his parents and other friends, returning to Enying on May 19. "No one accompanied me: if it were not for my acquaintances, I would be alone like a dog." On return, Reiss found that non-commissioned officers, even those whom he had called friends, were conducting "taste tests," taking more food than was due, short-changing ordinary soldiers, who did not receive an additional food allowance. They tried to get Reiss into trouble, but his captain understood, and the matter was dropped. June 1 was Reiss's twenty-seventh birthday: "Will I live another twenty-seven years?"

In Enying, Reiss discovered the Dreifinger family. "Dreifinger has two daughters and wants to marry one off to me. I will stop visiting there: despite loneliness, I cannot yet think of marriage." Reiss remained in Enying through June 15. On June 16, he was commanded to take artilleryman Melnicki, who had gone crazy and had to be straight-jacketed, to Vienna.[49]

As soon as he arrived in Vienna, "I just got to know Miss Lina Kohl and she has already made me a marriage proposal! It's terrible, this business with the women!" He left Vienna on June 18, spending time with Lina Virga at the station waiting for the train. "I cannot speak to any girl because they immediately want to get married. I don't like any of them, and prefer Pepi Kamiel."

The entry for June 23, made in Enying, sounds worried:

> Now everything is finished! The corporal comes to me while I'm working in the kitchen and tells me that my wife has arrived. I tell him to stop joking, but he says that he wouldn't do such a thing to me while on duty. I go out, and before me stands Sabine Sauer. I thought that I was going to have a stroke! I naturally brought her to my room and told her that it isn't nice and doesn't suit me at all that she came to visit me, and that she should depart the next day. Naturally, she started to cry.

Reiss arranged for Sabine to dine with the Dreifingers, so that Dreifinger would not leave him alone with his daughter, whom Reiss also did not like much. On June 26, Sabine finally got the message and left. Reiss was cooking full-time, for as many as 300 men, in Enying and Hajmáskér (a short distance away).[50] He spent August 2 and 3 on leave in Vienna, returning to Hajmáskér a day later. In Vienna he "talked to Lina all night." He returned to Hajmáskér, where he remained through the end of August, feeling lonely and lousy, without his family, and undecided which woman to choose.[51] A transport was being sent to the field. Reiss volunteered, was declared healthy, and left for the front as first artillery sergeant. The kitchen staff donated a barrel of beer for his parting, and he left "this boring life, and the issue of slackers" on September 12. He travelled through Vienna, where he spent a few days and met diverse girls—including Amalia Lanik—who plied him with food and whatever else he needed. He did not spend much time with his parents, "because they are struggling to make ends meet and I'm an additional burden." He spent Rosh Hashanah on September 28 and 29 in Vienna, travelling back when the festival ended. Only Amalia accompanied him to the station: "I'm sorry she thinks she will marry me, but I will not." He travelled by train across Hungary to the Carpathians, arriving in Brzezany on October 5.[52] The Russians had broken through, and Brzezany was under fire: houses were burning, many were wounded. Reiss was kept busy. Fighting lasted through midnight and the Russians were repulsed.

On October 6: "Fighting is scheduled to start again at 4.00 am. Today is Yom Kippur. May God forgive me, but I cannot go and pray." On October 7, Reiss was relocated to Chadky.[53] Fighting began again, with many wounded, particularly telephonists. One man had a bullet wound, with fatal brain prolapse: he had been serving since war began, and was a father of four children.

It was very cold and, to prevent men from developing pneumonia, Reiss used a local chapel as sickbay. He warmed the room, preparing goulash with dumplings and potato soup for officers and patients. Men were so overjoyed that they kissed him. In absence of a physician, he again treated patients, and prepared chicken goulash, barley soup, roast beef, and palatschinken for officers and men. One officer complained that men should not eat the officers' food and that he was a "cheeky Jew." Reiss reported this, and his captain sided with him. On October 13 he returned to Brzezany, where he organized a "fine sickbay." He alternated between the two towns, looking after both the sick and the kitchen. He commented on the number of prostitutes in the towns. Four days later, temporary cessation of hostilities allowed the mess kitchen to be moved into town. He met a plump dark-haired Jewish girl, "but I couldn't sleep because she wanted to have a good time. She nauseated me, because a woman who puts out too much is a whore."

Reiss remained in Brzezany through November, serving as kitchen head. He was enterprising in obtaining extra food. He procured a barrel of herring, which pleased men greatly. Lunch was usually soup with rice, a herring, with half a liter of rum and tea. At 11.00 am on November 6, a heavy Russian attack began. The house in which Reiss stayed took a direct hit. Miraculously, he was not harmed, and, with fourteen dead and thirty-four wounded, reverted to working as medical orderly. The civilian population fled. The Russian attack was unsuccessful, and things quietened down. Reiss was upset about the antisemitism he saw around him: "when a Jew is relieved everyone gets excited, but when ten Christian Austrians are relieved, it's accepted as natural. A Jew is good enough to fight, but why should he have rights?"[54]

On November 22, Reiss noted:

Kaiser Franz Joseph has died. A day of mourning, also in town. Jews especially are weeping: in the synagogue it is like Tisha Be'av, the Jewish day of national mourning. This afternoon we swore allegiance to Kaiser Karl: it's his birthday today: strange coincidence![55] The Jews say that Kaiser Karl is a good man and the soldiers are for him, too. The Ukrainians and the Czechs say he can remain Kaiser if he gives them independence, otherwise Masaryk will remove him and declare a republic.[56] I don't want to hear anything about this: The Ukrainians and the Czechs are disloyal.

On November 23, a townswoman was killed by shrapnel, and Reiss could do nothing about it. On December 2, he was invited for a Sabbath lunch with a recently married Jewish family, who were religious and well off. "I would like such a Jewish girl who observes Shabbat. What an ideal life—maybe Pepi Kamiel?" During the past weeks, Reiss had been feeling poorly, but on December 3 he really became ill, lonely, and physically broken. His soul was sick, and he felt abandoned. "If I am killed, no one will weep for me." Despite six aspirins and half a liter of rum, he could not sleep. On December 4, ill with a 39.4°C fever, Reiss slept in a stable before marching off the next day.

They departed for Lipica Dolna (Ukraine), arriving two days later. Reiss collapsed from exhaustion, sharing a hospital with sick and wounded Turks, who did not eat pork as well. On December 9, 153 sick and wounded soldiers departed in a stinking cattle car, fed like pigs. They arrived in a hospital in Stryj.[57] All the men were housed in one cold lice-infested barrack. "Infamous disgrace that a government treats its soldiers in this way. A pox on them! May all government ministers be patients here as well!" Reiss complained: "Herr Senior Physician: steal less and take care of the sick and wounded! If you were with me on the line I would shoot you dead." He was transported out, arriving in Drohowszyne on December 11.[58] Here, finally, the field hospital (housed in an orphanage) was clean, well-heated, with excellent food, physicians, and nurses. Reiss made his last entry for 1916 with the hope that the new year would bring peace.[59]

Reiss gradually recovered (his disease is not specified), but felt abandoned because no one wrote to him. On February 6, 1917, he wrote:

> I am healthy again. Good food, exemplary treatment, conscientious physicians. If everyone acted like this, nothing bad could happen to us, and we must win the war. I leave hospital tomorrow.

On February 7, Reiss travelled back to the front near Lipica Dolna. While he did so, a Russian gas attack drove him into a well. Lacking a gas mask, he covered himself with wet blankets, which became covered with ice. He was transferred to work under a Prussian physician, who warned him to differentiate between sick patients and malingerers. Reiss was in the line of fire. On February 14, a shell exploded ten meters from where he was working; German soldiers ran away instead of helping him. Around 5.00 am on February 18, the Russians began a violent artillery bombardment, with terrible casualties, and Reiss spent February 20 and 21 taking care of wounded.

By February 22, following his newspaper announcement, Reiss had received 106 marriage offers from beautiful girls, at least according to their pictures. "But these are nothing to me, I will write to Pepi Kamiel." On February 23–28, the fighting lessened, and men could wash and relax; Reiss roasted some potatoes, which he found in a ditch, and fed the Germans and his own men.

On March 1, Reiss was ordered to the forward lines to help with wounded. His journey was two awful hours through a forest, barbed wire, mud, and corpses. Fighting was terrible: it came to hand-to-hand combat, and there were many dead on both sides, mixed up with each other. Reiss brought the Austrian dead and wounded behind the lines, and helped with bandaging. He was, miraculously, unharmed. At first, the Russians fired at the house where he was tending the wounded despite the Red Cross flag, but he soon came to an understanding with them, and they helped each other with the dead and wounded.

The fighting was renewed on March 12. There was an infantry battle with mortars, hand grenades, and gas. One of Reiss's men had his arm shattered by a dumdum bullet. Reiss was lucky again, and given a bottle of cognac as recognition for bravery and hard work, which he and his comrades quickly demolished. He was called to help a pretty eighteen-year-old girl who had been shot through the abdomen: he could do nothing for her.[60] Reiss tried to take care of civilians and soldiers alike. "May God protect us!" He helped vaccinate troops, and received a Talmud from one of his sisters, which he started to read.[61]

At 9.00 am on March 17 in Lipica Dolna, the Russians started firing again. A young girl was seriously wounded by five bullets; she didn't survive, even though Reiss spent three hours trying to treat her. The Russians fired at the house he was using as sickbay. A German soldier was hit: his head flew into the air like a football. Reiss had a new shelter with room for nineteen people built in the forest, safe from shelling. The fighting died down, the sun came out, and the men washed themselves. Reis had a mass grave dug, with all the men's addresses noted. He hoped that a mass for the dead would be held there later.

On April 5, Reiss's lieutenant gave him 200 crowns for seder celebrations.[62] He chose a nice location, cooked himself, and saw to the availability of matzot, but both seders were cancelled because of gas attacks. The morning after, men finished two-days food. Reiss was put up for the Merit Cross. On April 8 in Lipica Dolna, Reiss prepared food for Easter, enjoyed by all. On April 21, he was awarded the Red Cross Bronze Medal of Honor. On May 2, for recuperation and to reward his brave conduct at the front, Reiss received an extraordinary fourteen days of leave. He spent May 3 to 19 in Vienna, with Pepi Kamiel. "An excellent young lady, much liked by my sisters. She isn't particularly pretty, but very friendly and clever. She can sew, and live independently during hard times. If I return healthy from the war, I will marry her."

From May 20 through 29, there was static warfare with sporadic firing in Lipica Dolna. Reiss began to feel ill, he developed fever and vomiting, and was sent to a series of field hospitals in towns on the Eastern Front. A few were clean and decent, most filthy, with treatment "beyond criticism." Eventually, he landed in a field hospital in Kragujevac (Serbia), where he stayed from June 27 to July 22. On July 28, Reiss left Serbia, travelling via Budapest to Vienna.

> I stay here through July 27. A nice town. But I must take care because the Serbs are selling poisoned food. Everything is poisoned: fruit, wine, raki, meat. Before one eats, Serbs must eat it first: if they refuse, they are immediately imprisoned.[63]

During his stay in Vienna he proposed to Pepi, and she accepted. He returned to Serbia on August 19, where he convalesced in Kragujevac through September 12. "During this time all I did was eat and sleep. They fattened me up because I was so thin."

The period from September 13 to October 1 was spent in Vienna. "On Sunday September 23, I go for a trip to Severing with Pepi, Lotte, and Miss Schnauzer. Lotte is conceited: I'm not sure how to interpret this: in any case, I prefer Pepi." He found lodging with friends, to save money and not burden his parents. He spent Yom Kippur day with his father in synagogue. Reiss's father wanted him to marry a girl with money, but he told him that he already had a girl, and his father agreed. After Yom Kippur, Reiss and Pepi announced their engagement, and celebrated with a party. However, he noted in his diary that "Pepi has a very cold disposition."

During his return trip, Reiss reflected on his future, deciding to report as healthy back to his unit. He reported to the convalescent home in Kragujevac one final time, then to his unit in Čačak (Serbia), where he requested transfer to the front. He did not approve of some officers, who were "rascals and slackers." His transfer was approved, and he departed on October 15, via Belgrade, Przemyśl, Lemberg, Stanislau, and Chortkow, where he arrived on October 21 and awaited orders.[64] He spent nights in an empty carriage, in the railway station, or in a local prayer house, and arrived, after walking a great distance in snow and freezing temperatures, at the front in Burdiakowce two days later.[65] He ate turnips and potatoes from the field: there was nowhere to buy food or even beg from. Officers and men were pleased that he returned. The front was quiet, and men hunted wild boar. Reiss sometimes visited the Russians, exchanging rum for tobacco, which he brought back. He cooked for the officers, and had a good time with the girls, who called him "Pan Doktor"—all came to him for "treatment." Castor oil and aspirin were sovereign remedies. On December 24 he marched off, travelling through Cyganów (Poland), where he finally received a letter from Pepi, and got drunk with his comrades, and Borszczow, a dirty town where he quartered with Magdalena Czeplinek, "a very pretty girl," to Germanowka.[66] Reiss was awarded the Bronze Medal for Bravery. He celebrated New Year's Eve in Germanowka with rum, wine, goulash, and a sincere prayer for peace.

Reiss sent Pepi 150 crowns on January 2, 1918, but she did not respond immediately. "Out of sight out of mind, it seems." He spent January 2–14 walking in the woods, exchanging rum for tobacco with the Russians, and playing cards. Because the front was so quiet, he applied for (and was given) leave. He arrived in Vienna on January 18 via Lemberg on a freezing train, feeling sick again. He spent January 18 through 26 in Vienna, bringing provisions for Pepi, spending much time with her. He visited his parents. Parting from Pepi at the railway station was difficult: "I love her." On January 27, Reiss travelled via Lemberg and Czernowitz to Rarancze, where he joined field artillery 18/5, and took up medical duty on January 31.[67] By February 1, Reiss had established a sickbay. He led Russian women to the border because there was nothing for them to eat, and arranged their return with the Red Cross.

On February 4, permission to marry arrived. Reiss wrote to Pepi to prepare for the ceremony. Two days later, a woman doing washing at the stream gave birth and fainted. Reiss was called: he administered aid, tied the umbilical cord off, helped with the birth, and looked after the mother. All officers present praised him for this good deed. The civil population brought him flowers and small gifts, and called him *Oberarzt*. On February 7, Reiss was informed that his leave to get married was cancelled until further notice. On February 9, a separate peace between Ukraine and the Central Powers was declared. Reiss waited impatiently for marriage leave.[68] On February 15, the Polish Legion (see below) mutinied.[69] After heavy fighting with many casualties, the legion was disarmed and every eighteenth soldier shot, the rest led off under guard.

Finally, on February 17, having given up all hope, Reiss received his travel permit, and travelled to Vienna. He organized the ceremony in the Rossauerkaserne. On February 23 Reiss was called up in his temple and the day after they visited Pepi's mother's grave. The marriage was solemnized on February 26.

> Marriage in the barracks, in a nice synagogue. Everything in blue, soldiers held the *chuppah* (marriage canopy) up, a military delegation from private to major. Service by Dr. Frankfurter, who gave a short but beautiful sermon.[70] Pepi realizes that she is marrying a soldier. The table is simple but charming.

Reiss was given extended leave, so they could have a real honeymoon. He returned to the front on March 23. He travelled through Czernowitz (by this time completely destroyed by repeated reoccupations), Hungary, Salzburg, and Innsbruck, on his way to the new assignment on the South Tyrol, and departed for Bozen on May 5.[71]

The next section of his diary, recording the experiences on the Italian front, is included in chapter 5.[72]

Reiss was evacuated from the Italian front on June 20, with no feeling in his feet. After neurological and other treatment in Vienna and Cracow, Reiss was diagnosed with "traumatic neurosis."[73] He gradually recovered, spending time with Pepi who helped nurse him back to health. By September 28, he was well enough to be transferred back to the front. On September 30, Reiss travelled to the rear echelon in Tarnów. He became ill again and was sent to a convalescent home.[74] His diary ends on October 2:

> Bielitz. Great disorder in the home. It's raining. Everything is very expensive: from yesterday to today has cost me 100 crowns. Life has become difficult, and I need Pepi in Vienna. I miss my position in the field and will report to the front.[75]

Teofil Reiss's Eastern Front diary reflects a simple man whose secular education level is not high (reflected by many syntax and spelling errors in his

German). He is brave and resourceful, ready to plunge into the bloody fray when needed, devoted to the Monarchy, a staunch supporter of war against Russia. When the Kaiser dies in November 1916, he is appalled that Ukrainians and Czechs do not share in the general mourning, but want their own country. Whenever he spends time behind the lines because of illness or wounds, he is eager to return. When hospital care is poor, he tries to improve it. Life has given him little and he expects little in return, but rejoices when good things happen. He rails against inadequate provisions, corruption in the officers' corps, and poor leadership. He does not think deeply about the futility the war; he is practical and proud of service to his comrades, of his help as medical orderly to soldiers and civilians, and of improving mess facilities and provisions. Goulash and palatschinken instead of army bread and stew at the front must have been a godsend to the rank and file. His escapades with ladies, who pop up everywhere during his service, give his diary a light-hearted insouciance in the midst of war, bloodshed, and suffering. Reiss is not religious and looks on *Ostjuden* with an air of indifference tinged with superiority.

Marsha Rozenblit has used the example of Teofil Reiss to explain how the ordinary Viennese chose their marriage partners during the war. Although he was very attractive for women (many wanted to marry him), Reiss chose, against the first decision of his father, Pepi Kamiel, who was neither pretty nor rich, but a "very dear girl"—loyal, intelligent, a devoted daughter, and a hard worker. Money, physical appearance, love, passion—none played a role, although Teofil and Pepi later grew to love each other.[76]

Hungary and Bukowina

We have already encountered Avigdor Feuerstein (Hameiri, see plate 2) in chapter 2 with his comment on "war enthusiasm." He will also appear later in chapter 7 as a Russian prisoner of war. Hameiri is a unique example of a Hungarian Jew who wrote of his war experiences in Hebrew. He was born in 1890 in Ó-Dávidháza, Carpatho-Ruthenia, and was a rising young poet, theater critic, and newspaper editor in Budapest when the war broke out and he volunteered.[77] He set down his war experiences in the k.u. army from 1914, until he was captured in the 1916 Brusilov Offensive, in his book *The Great Madness*, which is excerpted here.[78] Both this, and his second book describing his captivity in Russia and Central Asia (chapter 7) have been described by Abramson and Holtzman as "auto-fiction," or "non-fiction novels," in which the author attempts to distance himself from cruel reality. As is often the case in war literature, fiction is probably the most effective vehicle with which to describe life at the front vividly and in greatest detail. Both books provide unique insight into war experiences of Jewish soldiers in a Hungarian regiment on the Eastern Front.[79]

As soon as war was declared, Hameiri was ordered to pack and report to the local commandant. He was taken, in evening clothes, to the army barracks where he was immediately pounced upon by a sergeant who smacked a cigarette out of his hands: "Where do you think you are—in a beer hall?" Budapest was in ferment: voices shouting orders, artillery, cavalry, tears, singing, the national anthem, farewells, and flowers.

No sooner had Hameiri reported back to the sergeant, than eighteen women, amongst them his girlfriend Mansie, rushed in crying, embracing their men, begging them not to go. All women were whores: Mansie was a cabaret singer and dancer. Accompanied by "a parade of whores"—each woman marching alongside her man—the men were ordered to march to the railway station. For Hameiri, it was a symbol of the madness to come. Men were crowded like sardines into the train. Hameiri found himself in the same coach as a Hungarian nobleman: "What a democratic jaunt!"[80]

The train left in a cacophony of drunken singing, yelling, wailing, and whistles. One smart aleck climbed on top of the train to wave goodbye to his favorite city, and was decapitated by a sharp bridge arch. The first war casualty! On the third day they got off in a small town and were ordered onto a large wagon pulled by German horses. After a few hours, a sergeant yelled at them to disembark: they jumped out into doughy waist-high mud, and fell asleep in the rain, exhausted.

When he awoke, Hameiri took stock of what he saw. Men were attempting to adapt to their new situation in comical ways: He was reminded of the Latin idiom: *sunt lacrimae rerum*.[81] "Yes, things can really shed tears: the dinner jacket is crying." It was as if his discarded civilian dinner jacket—the sign of his social position, culture, and freedom—was weeping, while the blood-stained tunic laughed at him mockingly.[82] He imagined Hamlet wondering about how "imperious Caesar, dead and turned to clay" might have "stopped a hole to keep the wind away,"[83] and about the true purpose of war. Was there nothing but war, sergeants, and officers? No culture, literature, poetry, theater—only endless war?

More than a month passed: they were transported directly to the front, without proper training: "Russian dogs must be driven out of the homeland immediately." The Russians approached: dead bodies filled the space between the lines, and medical orderlies fell like flies. Rain poured down, gun barrels were clogged with mud, exploding and killing those who fired them. Someone yelled: "The Russians are fighting but have no rifles!" By evening, soaked to the bone, Hameiri and his comrades had driven the Russians off. A Jewish soldier died near Hameiri. They dug a grave, and the new sergeant recited Jewish prayers that Hameiri had taught him "with mispronounciations of a non-Jew." Fierce fighting continued into the night; men were screaming, falling all around. Hameiri was shot in the right leg above the knee, bandaged, and carried off to the hospital train. "Click-clack. What has happened?"[84]

From the field hospital, Hameiri was transferred to a drill school, to teach him discipline and how to use a rifle properly. He had his first opportunity to observe an Austrian officer up close, and did not like what he saw:

> Who sits beside an officer? A whore: worse still, another officer. . . . The army officer, if I thought of him at all, had always appeared to me to be a useless and superfluous creature in God's great world. A sleek creature, strutting about like a clockwork doll, its bones, from head to foot, dry as sticks. . . . I asked myself what was the actual purpose of creating, say, the grasshopper, the frog, the officer? . . . This character in a stiff collar, with a whip under his arm, ready at all times to avenge his poor wife's honor?

Hameiri's first lieutenant was a pompous, self-opinionated idiot: Yet, after a while, Hameiri started to respect this man with "His Majesty's polished buttons." He could not share this feeling with anyone and felt ashamed of himself for having stooped so low as to regard this pompous caricature in the same breath as the Jewish sages of old.[85]

Hameiri took his "final test in the soldier's academy." He had a conversation with the first lieutenant about merits and demerits of contemporary Hungarian poetry, debating whether a poet who is opposed to the war could be called "great." He was questioned about his concept of "absolute honesty and justice."

> Beg to report, there is no absolute honesty and justice in the world, sir. "And never will be?" Beg to report, only when there will be no more wars in the world, sir. "You should add, when we emerge victorious from all wars!" Beg to report, yes, sir, we will *all* emerge victorious in *all* wars.

The first lieutenant was unimpressed: all Hameiri's comrades were promoted to non-commissioned officers except himself.

At the end of the officers' course, a ball was announced in which all men had to take part. His lieutenant took Hameiri aside and told him that he must help: he could not do so himself, because he was a Jew. Hameiri was tasked to write a poem and read it at the ball. This poem, seemingly insignificant in itself, plays a pivotal role in the novel's development. Hameiri sat in a café, contemplating how he could use this poem as revenge against his superior. Hameiri entitled his poem "A Letter to the Colonel." Its subject was a scrawny misshapen Jewish corporal, who lay mortally wounded in a field hospital, writing a letter to his colonel. About to die, his last wish was that the colonel come and say to him: "You are a brave fellow!" Hameiri read the poem to the lieutenant, who was moved to tears. "The colonel must hear of this!" The next evening, on Hameiri's arrival at the lieutenant's quarters to meet the colonel, he was met by the colonel's wife, who was deeply moved when he read it. She did not object to the fact that the subject of the poem was a Jew, and asked that Hameiri be promoted to lance-corporal. The next evening, he read the poem to the colonel's younger son, who insisted that Hameiri be promoted corporal. When the colonel heard the poem, Hameiri was promoted sergeant. Against stupidity, even the gods fight in vain!

The well-attended ball concluded with reading of Hameiri's poem, with stormy applause. Hameiri was called to report to his commanding officer, who recommended that he convert, "because he was good officer material." Hameiri responded that he did not believe in organized religion: "a man can't convert a coin that he doesn't have." The commander roared with anger, and dismissed Hameiri, who was sent off to the front as non-commissioned officer.[86]

Hameiri was given a few recruits to train in drill, marching, rifle-carrying, and saluting. He was regarded as a failure because all his comrades were now officers. His commanding officer took a dim view of good relations between his soldiers and himself, and commanded him to spit in their faces. Hameiri refused, and was rewarded by a court-martial and a day's solitary confinement in a dark cell, on bread and water, lying on the floor. Upon release, he was approached by one of his recruits: an eighteen-year-old handsome Magyar lad named Pály, who wanted to become his batman (even though Hameiri was only a sergeant). Hameiri liked what he saw: outwardly, Pály always behaved properly, but inside him Hameiri sensed great strength of character. Pály called the commanding colonel "his piggishness." Hameiri learned the need to use foul language in his day-to-day dealing with his men. He did not like it, but understood its necessity.

A skinny, swarthy, small, pigeon-chested former *yeshiva* student named Jacob Margolis, who spoke excellent Hungarian, agonized with his initial inability to adjust to filthy language. He had a natural sense of humor, but his face remained grave while telling jokes, which made people roar with laughter. He adapted to crudity around him by carrying it to the point of absurdity, and became popular throughout the regiment.

> "What were you in civilian life?" the commander asks Margolis.
> "Beg to report, a *mamzer*, sir."[87]
> "What's a *mamzer*?"
> "Beg to report, an ass-licker, sir!"
> "What?" the commander thunders: "Do you know what you are saying?"
> "Beg to report, I don't know, sir. The lieutenant says a piece of garbage like myself isn't supposed to ask questions!"

Each man received a small metal bookcover; inside was a slip of paper with name, rank, dates of birth and mobilization. These early dog tags were to inform next of kin in case of death, which suddenly appeared near. Margolis stated that there was nobody to say *kaddish* (prayer for the dead) for him, so he would throw his dog tag away. Uncle Osterreicher, a pious Orthodox Jew of about fifty—a soldier before war who had been mobilized again—said that he would recite *kaddish* if need be. His two sons were killed last week, and all he had left were two daughters and a grandson.

The men marched off to Galicia, approaching the front. In the distance, they could hear guns roaring. Towns and villages through which they passed were almost abandoned, except for pale, exhausted, starving people who begged for a crust of bread. Most houses were destroyed. Black cloying Galician mud reached to their ankles. The closer they got to the front, the more skeletons of horses, broken carts, and bicycles they saw. Hameiri asked a Ruthenian peasant why he was not fighting, and was told: "The Jews made this war: isn't it enough that they took my only son to get killed?" "I am a Jew too, uncle." "Go with God, then!"

They travelled in the direction of Buczacz through destroyed villages, and were billeted in a village in which every family had at least one badly wounded person.[88] All women, young and old, had a gaping tear in their tattered clothes—right over their genitalia. They had done this to themselves, to attract men. One said: "What can be worse than hunger? Death? We'll all soon starve to death anyway." The next day's order stated that the women were all rotten with syphilis, and that the entire village was to be burned to the ground. An old Polish peasant said: "It's the damn Jewesses who started it. They taught our women to become whores, damn them to hell!" Margolis replied: "Ever since we got here, I've been looking for a Jewish home in which to spend a Sabbath evening. There isn't a single Jew in the whole village! A plague village—a real plague village!" The Jews, as always, were responsible for everything.[89]

A few Jews were sitting studying in the partially destroyed synagogue when shells started falling in the town. To Hameiri's surprise, there was no panic and people kept walking in the street, ducking slightly when they heard a shell whining overhead. For the first time, men saw the observant uncle Osterreicher praying with tallit and tefillin. Even on the march, he prayed solemnly, wind blowing his tallit and tefillin. Hameiri asked him what he would do on the front: "Our blessed sages commanded that we put tefillin on the left hand: the right hand is for shooting!" Uncle Osterreicher was the living antithesis of the antisemitic caricature of the cowardly Orthodox Jew who refused to fight. This chapter records other examples of Orthodox Jews fighting fiercely.

A forced march began, spurred on by the merciless Colonel Figer—a handsome, tall, blond, cruel martinet, "with the face of a boulevard pimp," on his horse: "Hey, Margolis! You think you're looking at your beautiful mother wanting to fuck her, to sow her with your Jewish syphilitic seed, huh?" He was partially lame in one leg, having shot himself in the foot to get leave and obtain less dangerous duty. Uncle Osterreicher was a special target for Figer's cruelty. His constant praying attracted Figer's attention and, during the forced march, he ordered the old soldier to run through the mud in front of his horse in full pack, until he almost collapsed. "Run, Jew, run!" Figer found this amusing. Another officer who gave the men a hard time was their immediate superior, Lieutenant Stubniak, a Hungarian Slovak. Stubniak made the lives of Hameiri and his men miserable for months with stupid disciplinary rules, even though they were so near the front that fighting could break out at any moment. One man was ordered to drink the contents of his spittoon as punishment for spitting on the floor in his quarters.

Pály attached himself to Hameiri as batman, but Stubniak forbade him to have a batman at all: "If he so much as polishes one of your boots, it's solitary confinement for you!" Despite this, Pály would not leave, and, in any event, the next day they had to leave for the front, so Stubniak's order was ignored.

A violent Russian bombardment began again. "God damn it!" said one man. "They won't even let a man stare at the stars in peace!" At 3.00 am next morning, they departed for the front. They entered a covered bunker with slits facing the enemy trenches. Hameiri's men, apart from Pály and Margolis, comprised an interesting variety: a Magyar; a half-Serb with face full of scars from old wounds; a Croatian giant with a gold medal on his chest who spoke broken Hungarian; a lanky Tyrolean; a tubby Jewish corporal named Rosenberger, with a joke for every occasion; a former Hungarian actor; an Italian from Fiume;[90] a sculptor; a dandified student who had failed even to become a corporal.

The battle raged: six were killed, and two seriously wounded. Margolis, the scrawny student, adapted well. He rushed bravely through the tumult like an enraged bee, and attacked Russians single-handed. Uncle Osterreicher, his tefillin still on, fought on fearlessly. When the men were relieved, they sat and talked of home. Nobody liked Figer and Stubniak. Uncle Osterreicher told the men that his beloved grandson in Warsaw was celebrating his bar mitzvah soon, and he looked forward to being there.[91]

As non-commissioned officer and quartermaster, Hameiri was kind and distributed his own gifts from home among his men. He was well-liked among the soldiers. For the selfish and self-absorbed officers, this only became a reason to hate him. The battle around Częstochowa (Poland) raged for ten hellish days, costing many lives. Almost all Jewish officers and men distinguished themselves by acts of bravery; this maddened non-Jewish officers, causing hitherto suppressed antisemitism to break into the open.

Hameiri got a new commanding lieutenant: a devout, formidably honest, Calvinist Magyar. Margolis was promoted again, and Uncle Osterreicher awarded a gold medal and financial reward. He recommended that Hameiri be promoted ensign. Hameiri was called before Figer and accused of stealing the soldiers' money and rations. Because of his crime, his promotion was delayed. As punishment, he was bound and placed inside a hut for two hours. The Russians started firing again. A shell shrieked over Hameiri's head, slicing off the right-hand corner of his hut. Hand grenades flew, and two other corners of the hut were torn off, but Hameiri obstinately did not try to escape. He was joined by Pály. The sergeant found them in the hut and bawled at them to get out immediately. Hameiri reported the affair to his new lieutenant, who fumed with rage about this idiocy. He drank a toast to Hameiri's bravery, and ordered him to sew on his ensign pips immediately.

Against his better judgment and despite having been labelled a thief, Hameiri was satisfied with the benefits of his new office: no more crawling on his belly through mud and excrement; a light revolver instead of a heavy rifle and a backpack; better rations; Pály as permanent batman. The young Magyar was devoted to him and looked after his every need, even forcing him to overeat.

As a newly minted officer, Hameiri was tasked with guarding a nearby hilltop with his company. This hilltop had caused terrible casualties, changing hands eight times in one day, but was finally in Austrian hands. Hameiri received permission to choose thirty men, half a company: artists, Gypsies, *yeshiva* students, veteran horse thieves, gamblers, pickpockets. Margolis came along as telephonist. Where had he learned this? Before the war he hadn't even spoken on the telephone! Word reached Hameiri that the Hungarian actor who was part of his troop had been court-martialed and sentenced to death for desertion. Hameiri and his company had to execute the sentence. It was ironic, because the man was a rabid antisemite. While standing at his place of execution, the man confessed to being a converted Jew, bequeathed his clothes and boots to his comrades, and faced death bravely. Thirteen shots to the head finished the grisly business, and Hameiri collapsed, vomiting. "It's very hard to die, but a thousand times harder to kill consciously and deliberately."[92]

The dead man's religion sparked debate. The converted Jew died with his prior faith intact! Why did he not cross himself and recite the Christian credo, as he did so often while alive? "Holy Virgin! Holy Virgin!" But at the hour of his death he reverted to Judaism! Uncle Osterreicher was outraged by the business. During the execution, Hameiri saw that two men in the firing squad each shot at the clothes that the victim had promised to the other. Religious conflict and greed made an ugly mixture.

The night before the next attack, the men wrote letters home. Lieutenant Stubniak, who already had a reputation of cowardice in the face of the enemy, was crazy with fear. He was being examined by the doctor, when Margolis came in and made a joke. Everyone, including Stubniak, laughed, and the doctor could see that Stubniak was malingering. He was court-martialed and degraded one rank to second lieutenant. "Stubniak is not crazy after all!"

Hameiri and his men approached their goal in the middle of a snowy night. They had to dig a path through the snow, and it took them over four hours to reach the trench on the other side of the hill. Snow stopped the attack, so they sat around reciting poetry and telling stories to pass the time. After a few days sitting around being bored, Hameiri took Pály, Margolis, and two other men to make a sortie through no-man's land and see what the enemy were doing. After about two hours, they heard whispering behind them, and hurried back to their positions. After a good meal, Hameiri took Pály, Margolis, and three other soldiers drawn by lot (two Jewish), and they went out again. Margolis had to lay a telephone line down the trench. Suddenly, they encountered a Russian patrol who bayoneted one man and captured all the others except Margolis, who escaped.

Russian soldiers appeared friendly, shared cigarettes with their captives, and embraced them. Hameiri and his men were led to the disordered front-line Russian dugouts. The Russians, apparently good, simple men, led their prisoners to a Galician farmhouse, full of Cossacks. The scene that greeted them was straight out of Grand Guignol. A drunken group of Cossacks were sitting around a table full of liquor bottles, celebrating the Orthodox Christmas. A severed Jewish-looking head lay in the middle of the table, with the body underneath. A Jewish prisoner was forced to drink the blood mixed with alcohol. They forced his mouth open with a bayonet, and poured the liquid down. He vomited, and dropped down dead. Another Jewish man was crucified on the wooden wall: while nails were being hammered in, he went mad and started to kick the Cossacks, whereupon they shot him dead. Hameiri, Pály, and his remaining men were led outside: An order was given to dig a grave and bury them alive. While waiting to die, they were rescued by their company. Hameiri saw that the eighteen-year-old Pály's hair had turned white, and that his own hair had turned grey. Margolis recited *kaddish* for the dead who were buried at the foot of the hill.[93]

Snow continued to hold up the expected Russian offensive. Hameiri decided not to take any more "strolls." "Another stroll like that one will make me eighty years old!" Finally, a thaw began, and the great offensive began along the entire front, from Czernowitz to Riga.[94] Hameiri looked and listened to fighting, firing, and bombardments, and decided that this was lunacy. Not one of the men on either side hated each other, but they were still ready to kill, wound, maim. Why not, instead of an orgy of killing, hug and embrace each other? Surely that would be more sensible? On the fourth day of the battle, Chortkow was taken. Hameiri's motley platoon of *yeshiva* students, actors, pickpockets, and assorted rascals had done wonders. Six of his men were dead, fourteen lightly wounded, one seriously. The dead, dying, medals, swaggering sergeants, "a company wins a tremendous victory but all men are dead." All sorts of posthumous medals. The whole thing was one great mockery.

After the hard-won victory, there was a lull in fighting. Figer pinned the gold medal on Hameiri who made the mistake of pointing out to the antisemitic colonel that his blood was of Maccabean, not Magyar origin. Figer resolved to block any further promotions for Hameiri. Uncle Osterreicher was sentenced to a day's fast for saying a prayer for a dead Russian Jewish soldier. It was near a Jewish fast day anyway. Figer was now on the warpath against all Jewish soldiers.[95]

The calendar said spring, but it could not be discerned yet in the gray Galician sky and gloomy black fields. The men got used to suffering and privation, but absence of women was hard to bear: the slightest whiff of spring made their juices run. The giant Croatian suffered terribly. Stubniak went crazy: he was court-martialed for sneaking into the nearby town and raping an old woman, and sentenced to twenty-five strokes on his heels. Another man was court-martialed for a similar offence, degraded from corporal to private. The order went out that punishment for rape and unauthorized entry into a town would be death by hanging. Hameiri tried his best to control the giant Croatian.

Command found the answer to the spring fever: assault the enemy everywhere! "Here is the reason for banning women from the front! Sex consumes the men's fighting spirit!" The giant Croatian rushed into the enemy camp like a wild beast, using his rifle butt to strike at the enemy; an unscheduled bayonet fight ensued. After the battle, the Croatian became abnormally subdued, he had lost his sense of humor and his appetite.

They stopped to rest in a local village. Pály brought the news that he had found one single Jewish girl, but that she was insane. She was beautiful, and sat by the window staring into the forest; her face looked dead. Hameiri visited her: the house in which she lived was in disarray, furniture broken. She looked at Hameiri with empty eyes and did not react when he offered her food and drink. She was thin and wasted, like a consumptive. Pály found an ancient crone of ninety-three left in the village, who told them what happened. Cossacks entered the village and almost destroyed it. One of them killed the girl's parents in front of her; she pleaded with him, and he spared her. A few days later the two were seen in the village arm in arm like lovers: she looked normal. When the Cossacks were driven out, she was left behind.

The Russians opened a fierce bombardment, and a twenty-eight-caliber shell landed on her house. When the ruins were searched, they found her dead together with the giant Croatian: he had ejaculated into the half-dead girl before dying himself. In the same bombardment, Stubniak was castrated by a piece of shrapnel. "That is your second degradation: from man to eunuch."[96]

In August, there was "beautiful weather, enough to make a man mad." It was peace and quiet all round. Less than an hour later, the Russians opened fire. The telephone rang; Hameiri and six other men lined up. Hardly had they departed, when Hameiri heard a whistle and a terrible blow knocked him flat. When he came to, an army doctor was yelling that he must be evacuated immediately. He passed out again, and awoke in the high command field hospital. His wound was large and dangerous: a piece of shrapnel, about half the diameter of an egg, had pierced his chest an inch or so above his heart, between the two great arteries. If it had hit one, he would have been long dead. After the metal was removed, it took a few weeks for his condition to stabilize. His fever rose: the wound was probably infected, but gradually healed. He was transferred to a hospital in Budapest for convalescence.

Hameiri was disgusted by dandified doctors, who treated patients like subjects of observation, not real people. Nurses were usually from aristocratic families: for them, nursing was a form of amusement or career enhancement. Only one nurse, a former prostitute, treated the wounded with compassion. Former nightclub entertainers and dancers like Mansie remained faithful to their lovers. They volunteered for hospital work when the war began, working with diligence and devotion. By contrast, wives became whores, cheating on their husbands, especially with Russian prisoners. The war brought out people's real character.

He visited Mansie, who fainted on seeing him. The doctors spoke highly of her devoted work: she had even sworn off alcohol for the duration of the war. Hameiri also visited the wife of one of his comrades, Ensign Krak, at the front. She threw herself at him, and he left in disgust. He saw a young woman on a tram, whose husband was also at the front: she was shacked up with a wounded soldier, Ensign Szegedy—her husband's best friend—who was convalescing at home. Disgusted, Hameiri requested immediate transfer back to the front.

Back at the front, Ensign Krak came to see Hameiri, pleased that he had met his young wife. Hameiri met with Krak and his other comrades, and they summarily sentenced Ensign Szegedy to death. Krak wanted to carry out the sentence himself, but a fierce battle between the lines saved him the trouble. Ensign Szegedy was killed, and "the evil in their midst was purged."[97]

They crossed the Dniester and were deep in Ukraine. It became clearer and clearer, even to those who did not wish to see it, that Jews were as brave in battle as the purest Calvinist Magyar. Scrawny Corporal Margolis linked up with the enemy's telephone line, crawling on his belly 400 paces under the enemy's nose to complete his mission. The excellence of Jewish soldiers was particularly galling to "pure races" of the empire—Italians, Romanians, and especially Austrians. As if there was such a thing as pure races![98]

Hameiri lost several men in the last attack: Krak was killed almost immediately, and the scarred Serbian and fat Corporal Rosenberger, the eternal joker, were also killed. Hameiri mused about the loss of so many men for so small a gain. Winter would not depart, and a fierce snowstorm covered everything in sight. The colonel invited Hameiri for a drink. The regiment artisans had built him a noble dwelling, with hangings, pictures, and books. Hameiri returned to his own primitive dugout, where he had been living for the past two months. The men waited in their "nest," warming themselves at the stove, waiting for death. The officers did the rounds, requisitioning any comfortable quarters held by those of lower rank.

Idleness and boredom gave rise to revolting officer behavior: boozing, overeating, smoking, cursing, playing tasteless practical jokes. Lack of women gave rise to drunkenness and viciousness towards the enlisted men. Colonel Figer specialized in punishments combining mental with physical suffering, each an occasion for drunken celebration. A carpenter was made to eat wood shavings, a locksmith to swallow nails, a shoemaker to eat glue. Hameiri wondered about millions of ordinary men from all walks of life who danced like puppets on a string at the behest of a small coterie.

Snow began to melt, and another general offensive was about to begin. But after two years, where were the additional men and equipment going to come from? Men were out of strength and patience. God must be a stupendous beast: not merciful and kind, but cruel, murderous, sadistic, contemptuous of his victims. While the men waited for the offensive, someone inscribed the words "Mene, mene, tekel ufarsin" on the wall of the officers' lodgings during an orgy of drinking, and scared them half to death. Each man felt that his end was surely coming. Hameiri suspected Margolis.[99]

It was April 1916, and spring had arrived in Galicia: the sun shone, birds sang, everything was green. This year the change in season was greeted with profound sadness, not like the hope of the previous year. Uncle Osterreicher received a new pair of tefillin from Lemberg, to replace ones that had been damaged by a bullet and rendered not kosher. He donned his tallit and his new tefillin, and made a solemn vow that he would not depart from this world until he had prayed in a *minyan* with "them over there" in peace.[100] Hameiri led seven of his men in a sortie before the upcoming spring offensive; Uncle Osterreicher and Margolis were part of the group. Suddenly, they came upon a group of eleven Russians. The two rows of men stood, looking at each other. They proposed a prisoner exchange, and decided to send Uncle Osterreicher along with the Russians, to rest a little. Why should this pious old soldier, on whom a family depended, get killed? Let him wait for peace in captivity. The two sides exchanged a few of their number, embraced, and returned to their respective camps. Word came later that Uncle Osterreicher died of typhus on the way to prison camp.

The long-awaited offensive began, at the beginning of a beautiful June.[101] The Russians opened a violent bombardment, and men took shelter in a concrete bunker.[102] Colonel Figer ordered patrols. Sixteen men volunteered, and Hameiri chose three more to go with them. He crawled forward at the head of his men, through murderous artillery and rifle fire. Pály appeared, despite being ordered back. After three days of continuous shelling, there was sudden silence. Margolis fixed the torn telephone lines without telling anybody. Hameiri and his men were desperately short of ammunition. He cursed at the cowardly Figer, and went out to get some. When he returned, his platoon was spread over 150 paces; most had been taken captive. The Russians were advancing by the thousands. Where did they all come from? Hameiri and his men were surrounded, and all taken prisoner.

The book ends with Margolis saying:

> Well, then, tell me, sir: what was all this game about? Couldn"t I have simply bought a ticket to tour Russia by train? Was it necessary to make all this *tararam* for this? Was it, sir? . . .[103]

The Great Madness and *All Quiet on the Western Front* were published as novels around the same time. Hameiri's colorful cast of characters is broader than Remarque's, exemplifying the polyglot Habsburg army. He describes simple Magyar peasants, sophisticated Budapest artists, shady underworld characters, Serbs, Croats, and Italians, Talmud scholars, haughty Austrians, nationalistic Czechs, a Gypsy or two, and some spicy Hungarian cabaret girls. Hameiri mixes war memoirs with his musings about Zionism, literature, and other issues. His comments on Austro-Hungarian officers are pungent, and he never forgets his religion or his deep Hungarian roots. In his unique voice, Hameiri mixes suffering and cruelty with gentleness and piety, thoughts on Zionism, bawdy humor, common humanity on both sides, pacifism, and the futility of war. *The Great Madness* is the only Hebrew novel about Jewish soldiers fighting in World War I. It is a unique antiwar novel of the highest caliber, and deserves to be more widely known.

Fueled by their patriotism, Jews of all ages volunteered to serve in the army. An anonymous letter from Budapest, published in *Dr. Bloch's Östereichische*

Wochenschrift (April 30, 1915), reports the patriotism of a fifty-eight-year-old Hungarian volunteer soldier. As the letter states, in the Budapest synagogue, a tall, powerful, white-haired, grey-bearded old man made a deep impression. When he heard of the outbreak of war, he volunteered immediately. He travelled to Pressburg and reported to his regiment, appealing to the fact that he had served in that same regiment thirty-four years ago and requesting readmission as a volunteer.[104] His request was accepted. He was sent to the Carpathians, where he fought in early September against the Russians. Always in the front line, he encouraged the younger soldiers to stand fast. When the severe Carpathian winter began, he was assigned to a ski troop and trained in Semmering.

A month and a half before the letter was written, he and a comrade volunteered to spy out Russian positions on the other side of the San River. In February cold, they swam to the other bank and, crawling on their bellies, spied out enemy positions. They had almost reached the Russian positions, when they were detected and assailed by a hail of bullets, forcing them into the water again. Only the fact that they were underwater saved them from certain death. Their information allowed the Austro-Hungarian artillery to shoot the Russian-occupied town on the other side of the San to pieces within an hour. The ice-cold water made him seriously ill; he was evacuated, promoted, and put in for a medal. After his recovery, he returned to the Carpathian Front.[105]

The Brusilov Offensive (June through September 1916) was the Russian army's greatest feat of arms during World War I. It broke the back of the Austro-Hungarian army, inflicting massive casualties. The lethal accuracy of overwhelming artillery barrages, combined with the new strategy of the Russian shock troops who attacked through the enveloping smoke caused by the shelling, was a terrifying experience, which no Austrian soldier would forget.[106] Bernhard Bardach was in the middle of this offensive, reporting it in detail.[107] As a physician, he had experienced war and destruction. However, young men like Adolf Mechner had never before seen death and destruction, especially on so massive a scale.

Adolf Mechner was born in 1897 in Czernowitz. He wanted to volunteer as soon as war broke out, but was not yet eighteen and at school, so his mother forbade it. Czernowitz was near the Russian border, and fighting there started almost immediately. Russians entered the city on September 15.[108] At first, the Russian troops were well disciplined, but they demanded a great deal of money. Most of the rich had left, and the banks were emptied, so the Russians demanded silver and jewelry instead of money. Mechner escaped to Vienna, where he saw shortages develop and go from bad to worse.[109]

At age eighteen he enlisted, was accepted as a one-year volunteer, and sent to officers' school. Mechner's initial war enthusiasm was dampened by his family's flight from Bukowina for fear of the advancing Russians. His first day as a soldier was October 15, 1915. After the usual harsh basic training, he was sent to the Eastern Front on January 27, 1916. Even near the front, punishments for petty offenses were severe. Mechner and his comrades were punished by a week's incarceration for "undisciplined behavior." They left for the Russian Front on May 7, travelling through the Carpathians. The colonel in charge was sixty years old, and "not well informed."

At first, the line was quiet. Trenches had to be constantly repaired, especially when it rained. Mechner learned to recognize each type of bombardment by noise and explosion pattern. One day, his regiment was suddenly ordered to retreat as rapidly as possible. Mechner found out later that this was because of the Brusilov Offensive. They dug in in front of Brody (Ukraine), which was aflame. At midnight, Russians opened up a violent artillery bombardment. "It was the first day in my life that my knees shook." Russian infantry moved in up to sixteen lines, one after the other—the so-called "Russian steamroller." Mechner, a sharpshooter, killed many Russians: he was advised not to take prisoners, but rather shoot them, even if they had their hands up. He refused. The Russians broke through, but retreated, and the line was restored.

> When daylight started, we saw a terrible picture. Hundreds of dead and wounded in front of our line. We and our Red Cross men went out with stretchers, under a white flag. What we saw is hard to describe. Besides many dead, there were many severely wounded. Men lying in front of my foxhole all had head wounds. The worst damage was done by our artillery. One wounded officer made me cry like a child. He had his lower leg hanging on a tendon, and also a big hole in his abdomen. Many wounded stood with their hands up. They were hiding and waiting for the right moment to be taken prisoner.

On August 2, everyone dug in. Russian artillery opened up and hit the house in which a soldier had been playing the piano a short time earlier. There was so much artillery fire that the Austrians remained in their trenches. It became dark, and all hell broke loose. Another retreat was ordered, but Mechner and a few other men were ordered to stay behind. They refused, and he and his friends ran back to join their retreating regiment. They crossed the bridge over a river, arriving in a village where they found some members of their regiment. Mechner stated that running away was one of the smartest things he ever did, because to remain behind would surely have meant Russian captivity in Siberia until the war's end. He hurt his back and knee during escape, and was hospitalized. During his stay in the hospital, Mechner was plagued by bad dreams of Russian attacks: the doctor who treated him called it a "neurosis."[110]

In early January 1917, Mechner was sent to officer's training school. Training was severe, his feet swelled and became very painful. He was transferred to a regiment in Eastern Croatia, then to the Italian Front. His service in the Isonzo is described in chapter 5. On September 17, 1917 he received the Bronze Medal for Bravery for service on the Russian Front, followed by many other decorations. In January 1918 he was promoted ensign. He was in Vienna when the war ended.[111]

Mechner's comments on lack of cohesive leadership, highlighted by the carnage and confusion of the Brusilov Offensive, are echoed in writings of many other soldiers and officers. Soldiers fought well when properly led, but this was often not the case, especially in the Eastern Front, where help from the German army was necessary to stabilize the situation.

Max Reiner, also from Bukowina, served from 1914 to 1918, both as decorated front-line officer, and, during the latter part of the war, as military advisor on political and journalistic issues. A committed Germanophile, his observations regarding attitudes amongst German troops and civilians as the war progressed were unique. Born in Czernowitz in 1883, he worked as a journalist and theater critic for the *Vossische Zeitung*. He joined his regiment when war was declared, and was sent to Lemberg at the end of August. His regiment was a mixture of Austrians, Germans, Ruthenians, Poles, and Jews, and his comrades did not share his enthusiasm for Germans.[112] He was awarded his first medal in November 1914, and hospitalized around Christmas with severe articular rheumatism, apparently contracted in the Carpathians. After recovery, he served on the Russian Front in 1915, and during the 1916 Italian offensive. After leave in Berlin, he returned to the front and heard rumblings of mutiny amongst a group of German soldiers: "if the authorities don't do it, we ourselves will end this war." Granted leave in 1917, he witnessed the havoc wrought in Berlin by food and fuel shortages and, for the first time during the war, felt a strong antisemitic undercurrent, with stories of Jewish shirkers and war profiteers.

In April 1918, he was transferred to Ukraine, where he heard stories of soldiers who were murdered while travelling alone, and about some cases of stealing of grain and livestock from the farmers. In July he was ordered to report to command, to advise on political and journalistic issues. Back in Berlin, he observed that, after news arrived of the surrender of 16,000 troops at Amiens on August 8, morale on the home front deteriorated.[113] Sent back to Ukraine, Reiner was in Lemberg on October 26 when the Central Powers began to collapse. On October 31, a battle for the city broke out. The Ukrainian legions occupied the city, and the Austro-Hungarians fled, taking refuge with the German army. Soldiers' councils took over Germany, and the war ended.[114]

Reiner's comment on rising antsemitism in Berlin was, at least partially, the result of the *Judenzählung* of October 1916, which was rejected by Austro-Hungary (chapter 1). As the war situation deteriorated, scapegoats were sought, and Jews made a convenient target. The Russian general staff also asked regimental commanders for extensive data on Jewish soldiers who had been killed, wounded, or lost in action, and those who had earned medals or deserted. However, results were treated pragmatically by commanding officers.[115] General Aleksei Brusilov wrote that, despite his negative overall opinion of Jewish soldiers, there were cases of Jewish bravery and fighting prowess. Because they were treated with so much prejudice, he did not blame the Jews if some of them made poor soldiers.[116]

Czechia and Slovakia

Lieutenant Fritz Mändl, a Jew from Prague, left a diary with photographs dating from February 2 to July 20, 1916, written in conjunction with his comrades in the Seventy-Third Infantry Reserve. It details field exercises, maneuvers, patrols, and training in the Austrian countryside, far from the front. On July 2, Mändl and his unit were transferred to Italy, where training and exercises continued. There are no indications of how he and his comrades felt about the war, nor about the presence or absence of antisemitism.[117]

Corporal Siegfried Spitzer from Schaffa served for thirteen months on the Russian front.[118] In two letters to his parents, he described how he won the Silver Bravery Medal Second Class. His regiment had to storm an enemy redoubt, and he was one of the first to attack. Suddenly he found himself surrounded, and had to fight back:

I didn't have time to strike anyone more than once because the enemy were many and I had to stir my stumps. Meanwhile, our own troops penetrated everywhere. The enemy were Circassians, who didn't move one inch.[119] Everyone, including the officers, fell where they stood.

Another letter home described a patrol tasked to search a village for Russians. Despite precautions, Spitzer and his men were encircled. His leader and ensign were wounded, and Spitzer left alone. Because the road had been cut off, he acted as vanguard to protect the back of his patrol, He found the ensign lying on the bank of the River Dniester, seriously wounded. Spitzer stayed behind to protect him, and was lucky that rapid fire from their positions on the heights caused Russians to flee and take cover. Eventually, a few men returned to help him and recover the ensign. The ensign was still alive when brought back to his position, but died soon after.[120]

Croatia

Lavoslav (Leo) Kraus published a memoir of his World War I activities in 1973.[121] As with all retrospective memoirs, the passage of over fifty years may have colored his impressions and descriptions. Born in 1897 to working-class parents in Osijek (Croatia), Kraus graduated from grammar school in 1915, and served in the Austro-Hungarian army through the end of the war.

Kraus was drafted soon after graduating high school, and spent the second half of 1915 as one-year reserve officer in training in the Seventy-Eighth k.u.k. Regiment, in which he remained throughout the war in Ogulin and Rijeka (Croatia). His comrades came from all over the empire—Czech, Hungarian, Italian, Austrians, Poles, and Slovaks. Stirrings of Slav nationalism were noted.[122]

In spring 1916, Kraus was transferred to the Eastern Front. He had a "short session with Brusilov" while serving on the front in Eastern Galicia at Stanislaw.

> I heard a horrible and powerful roar of cannons. The Russians, under General Aleksei Alekseevich Brusilov's command, sent, as a sign of welcome, a thick blanket of shrapnel fire towards our troops.

Under constant Russian pressure, Kraus and his regiment retreated rapidly. Despite threats of severe punishment, men threw bullets and bombs away into the nearby wheat field. Kraus was commanded to create order out of chaos. A Gypsy was executed for firing into his leg through army bread, to escape front-line duty.[123]

During the Brusilov Offensive, Kraus reported acts of terror committed against local Ukrainians in East Galicia by Austro-Hungarian soldiers. In reprisal for signs given to the enemy from the local church steeple, five peasants were hanged in the town square. Kraus states: "There is less harm in killing five innocent people than in putting the whole unit in danger."[124]

During the course of service on the Eastern Front. Kraus was awarded the Large Silver Medal for bravery under fire, and silencing three cannons and emptying the Russian outposts. "I personally killed <u>one man</u>—I wonder: <u>why</u>?"[125] A few weeks later, he was wounded in the thigh during an attack. When the firing ceased, he and his men dragged themselves to the nearest dressing station. During his time at the dressing station, Kraus came to understand the great truth: "We are all together in this Monarchy—just like Russians in their own Empire or French in their Republic."[126] With his "thousand-gulden wound," Kraus was hospitalized behind the front in the Carpathians, and sent back to Osijek in October 1916. After recovery, he returned to his old unit, now stationed near Munkács.[127] There, he heard of the death of Kaiser Franz Joseph, and the soldiers swore an oath to Kaiser Charles.[128]

Winter 1916–1917 passed quietly. Signs of fraternization with the Russians began to appear, which were put down by Kraus's captain. In private, however, he told Kraus that, being a Polish nationalist, he was sympathetic towards the Russians and would not punish anyone. The Kerensky Offensive in July 1917 started formidably with fierce attacks by Cossack units, but soon petered out.[129] In fall 1917, his unit was fighting in the vicinity of Czernowitz. Kraus commented on the Polish Legion:

> I remember seeing some units whose members wore an unknown uniform. These were volunteer units of the Polish Legion under command of Piłsudski fighting against Russians with the Central Powers. I wonder until today: if Germany had won, what freedom would Poland have?

During morning hour, the Russians broke through the Austro-Hungarian line, forcing them to retreat. Kraus rallied his men, stabilized the line, and forced the Russians to retreat and finally withdraw (partially because their will to fight had evaporated). For this act, Kraus was awarded the Gold Medal for Bravery.[130]

In early December 1917, after the Bolshevik Revolution, Kraus found himself in the snows of the Western Ukrainian forests. A Russian military delegation waving a white flag and bearing gifts asked an Austrian delegation to visit them. Kraus and his regimental delegation were welcomed by the red flag, hearing the name of Lenin and the Internationale for the first time. "I liked the revolutionary relations very much, but I knew that these would quickly disappear, replaced by harsh discipline."[131]

In August 1918, Kraus was transferred to the Piave. There, he discovered the existence of brothels as military institutions. Influenza raged amongst his regiment. After the Armistice, Kraus escaped from the Italians, and returned home.[132]

Kraus is cryptic about his Jewish origins, and his attitude to the Habsburg Empire. As his memoirs state, during the course of his service he gradually came to doubt the ethical underpinnings of the war, and by 1917 Kraus stopped believing in a Central Powers victory. Despite this, he fought courageously, was awarded the Silver and Golden Medals for Bravery, and eventually promoted lieutenant. During the Russian armistice, he became friendly with Russian officers, became an atheist, and would later become an active member of Tito's Communist Party of Yugoslavia. His is the only known example of a published World War I battlefield memoir of a Croatian Jew.

Poles and the Polish Legion

Polish-speaking soldiers fought for the Habsburg army in large numbers (chapter 1). Additionally, on August 22, 1914 Józef Piłsudski ordered the formation of two volunteer Polish Legions. The Austrian government, who had the jurisdiction over the area, officially agreed to their formation on August 27, 1914. These legions became an independent formation of the Austro-Hungarian army, thanks to efforts of the Temporary Commission of Confederated Independence Parties and Polish members of the Austrian parliament. Their personnel came mostly from former members of scouting organizations, including *Drużyny Strzeleckie* and *Związek Strzelecki* (rifle and shooting association teams), as well from as mostly young Polish volunteers (between nineteen and twenty-four years of age) from around the empire. Legionnaires swore an oath to the Emperor and were placed under Habsburg military command structure, but they were not sensu stricto a part of the Central Powers armies. Initially, there were two Polish legions: the Eastern and the Western Legions, both formed on August 27. After a Russian victory in the Battle of Galicia (August–September 1914), the Eastern Polish Legion refused to fight on behalf of Austro-Hungary against Russia, and was disbanded on September 21. The Western Legion, transformed into three brigades, fought against Tsarist Russia until 1916, including the Brusilov Offensive. Indeed, the Legion was one of the only units to emerge from the latter offensive with credit. After the Act of November 5, 1916, which pronounced the creation of the puppet Kingdom of Poland of 1916–1918, Polish Legions were transferred under German command. However, most members refused to swear allegiance to the German Kaiser and "loyal comradeship in arms with the armies of Germany and Austro-Hungary." Their leader, Piłsudski, was imprisoned, and recalcitrant legionnaires interned.[133] As Teofil Reiss documented, Polish Legions mutinied towards the end of the war when all was lost and their goal was an independent postwar Poland.

Marek Gałęzowski has documented 649 Jewish members of the Polish Legion. However, he correctly insists that they were not sensu stricto members of the Austro-Hungarian (or German) army. With a maximal strength of up to 25,000 by 1917, approximately 2.5% of the Legion was thus made up of Jews.[134] Stanislaw Albin (Apfel-Czaska, 1985–1968) joined the Legion in September 1914, and was promoted sergeant in February 1915. He was awarded the Virtuti Militari (Poland's highest military decoration) for bravery during the Battle of Jastków on July 31, 1915, when he volunteered to enter enemy trenches alone to tend to wounded soldiers under fire.[135] Albert Izydor Bores (1896–?) demonstrates the complex relationship between the Polish Legion and the Austro-Hungarian army. Bores joined the Third Brigade of the Polish Legion in July 1915, and served in Volhynia for the next two years. Starting in May 1917, he served in the Polish Auxiliary Core, the Polish military formation in the Austro-Hungarian army. He was taken prisoner and interned in Western Ukraine before being incorporated into the Austro-Hungarian army. In July 1918, he volunteered for the Polish army, Thirty-Ninth Regiment, in which he fought against the Ukrainians and the Bolsheviks between 1918 and 1920.[136] Władysław Steinhaus, the nineteen-year-old son of *Reichsrat* Representative Dr. Ignacy Steinhaus, served as ensign in the Third Brigade of the Polish Legion. He died on October 31, 1915 from a wound received in an attack on Kukle, east of Lublin.[137]

Pilots and observers

Jews served as pilots and observers in the Austro-Hungarian air force, but there is no published material on their service comparable to Jews in the German Air Force,[138] and we are left with anecdotal accounts. Two of the three pilots reported here were Hungarian Jews.

An editorial in the October 30, 1914 *Neue National Zeitung* reported that the Hungarian pilot First Lieutenant (later Captain) Aladar Tauss(z)ig landed on October 1, 1914 in the besieged fortress of Przemyśl, to exchange information and intelligence. Taussig volunteered, despite unfavorable weather. Under pouring rain, low clouds, Russian artillery, and bullets, some of which hit the airplane's wings, he landed safely in Przemyśl. The airplane was soaked and had to be dried out. Five days later, laden with mail and other necessities, the airplane set off. Russian artillery was waiting, and the plane made wide turns to avoid shrapnel. Inaccurate Russian fire meant for the airplane landed in the city. The plane ascended even higher; suddenly the compass stopped working and the plane, covered in snow, could not be brought into a horizontal position. The pressure pipe that Taussig obtained in Przemyśl burst, and the pilot had to hand pump the machine. The plane descended to 600 meters, and a bullet almost hit Taussig's upper leg. By the time he landed safely, the plane had been shot in many places in the wings and body.[139]

An article in the April 2, 1915 issue of *Dr. Bloch's Östereichische Wochenschrift* describes the death of pilot Friedrich Rosenthal. This story originally appeared in a Lemberg newspaper under Russian censorship.

During an observation flight, Rosenthal flew over Zolkiew, noticing that a Russian pilot was quartered in one of the houses. He started to bomb the house, but did no damage. When the Russian pilot saw this, he got into his plane, rose up to attack, and a bitter revolver air duel developed. The Russian pilot was severely wounded. While his plane descended, it tore into Rosenthal's aircraft. The Russian plane landed almost undamaged. By contrast, the Austrian plane was destroyed. Rosenthal, seriously wounded but alive, was pulled out from under it, but died of a vertebral fracture after a few minutes. Even the Russian newspaper recognized his bravery.[140]

Another article from *Dr. Bloch's Östereichische Wochenschrift* (December 29, 1916) describes exploits of Pilot-Sergeant Robert Fried. Fried, a well-known Budapest motor car driver and cyclist, enlisted in a Vienna flying regiment when war started. He rendered valuable observation service in Serbia, and was transferred to the Italian front, where he bombarded Italian towns.

He also performed valuable observation work on the Russian Front, for which he was awarded the Iron Cross Second Class by the German Kaiser. The article states that Fried was put up for promotion and further awards. He had three brothers, all in service at different fronts; all distinguished themselves.[141]

Orthodox soldiers

Orthodox soldiers became some of the unlikeliest heroes on the Eastern Front. Their desire to fight against the Russians was fueled by prewar Tsarist pogroms, Jewish restriction to the Pale of Settlement, and knowledge that Russian soldiers had looted, driven out, and murdered helpless Jewish civilians in many parts of occupied Galicia and Bukowina early in the war. The sight of religious Jews charging into battle yelling *Sh'ma Yisrael* must have been unnerving. In a letter to his wife in early 1915, a Russian Orthodox Ruthenian in the Austrian army wrote:

> Please go to Chaim-Juden and ask him what *Sh'ma Yisrael* means. Jews yell this during the worst attacks of rifle and machine gun fire, and it looks like bullets avoid them. Many of us, but relatively few of them, fall. Please ask Chaim-Juden what this incantation means, so I can also use it in an emergency.[142]

Similarly, an article in a September 1915 issue of *Jüdische Volksstimme* reports on the role of Orthodox Jewish soldiers in the battle for the recapture of Lemberg:

> Elite troops were chosen to attack the main thoroughfare of Lemberg, including 400 Jewish *Landwehr*, with long beards and side locks. A command was given not to force Polish Jews into battle, if they did not wish to attack. But they did, and our troops assailed the Russians with extraordinary violence. They fought with firearms and rifle butts, despite Russians trying to keep them away with terrible fire. All Polish Jews, without exception, took part enthusiastically in the attack. They wound their tefillin around their heads, and while attacking, sounded the Old Testament war cry of *Sh'ma Yisroel*. In this fierce battle, all the hate of Polish Jews against their Russian oppressors came to the fore. The exceptionally brave behavior of

these Polish Jews, admired by all, had a significant effect: after a violent, bloody battle lasting only an hour, the front was broken and the main thoroughfare of Lemberg taken.[143]

Physicans

A significant number of Austro-Hungarian military physicians serving on the Eastern Front were Jewish. Amongst the most notable, was the Austrian Dr. Alfred Adler, one of the founders of psychotherapy. Drafted in 1916, Adler saw service on the Russian front, first in Cracow, then in Brünn.[144] He was transferred to the village of Petzenkirchen, where he was in charge of Russian typhus prisoners. Adler saw firsthand the deep physical and psychological trauma that war inflicted on soldiers. His observations led to postwar lectures and articles on what he diagnosed as "war neurosis," known today as post-traumatic stress disorder.[145]

Aside from Dr. Bernhard Bardach (chapter 1), there is little published on Jewish physicians in the Austro-Hungarian Medical Corps.[146] The following excerpted feuilleton describes the front line service by Assistant Physician of the Infantry Reserve Dr. Isidore Segall (nationality not mentioned).

During late autumn 1915, in the fighting around Trawniki (Poland), he erected his dressing station just behind the lines. Fighting was bitter, and wounded came in droves from all regiments. Segall worked uninterruptedly for forty-eight hours. Eventually, the position could not be held, and the order came to retreat. He remained at his post, operating, cleaning, bandaging wounds. Only when the last man had been taken care of did he allow himself to be withdrawn to safety.

The next night, the order came down to search the battlefield for dead and wounded. Dr. Segall, at the head of his medical staff, went onto the field where the enemy was still firing. His stretcher-bearers advanced into a hail of bullets and did their duty, exemplified by their leader. In doing so, they saved many men and much material. Dr. Segall then guided his personnel back to the safety of their positions.

A short time later, during an attack on his own Third Battalion, Dr. Segall erected another dressing station just behind the firing line. The Russian attack was overwhelming. Officers fell, men lay powerless, and an entire unit began to totter. The doctor jumped into the breach. He spurred the men on to hold out, took over command, refused to give up, pulled men together, and gave them hope. The situation improved, and, with Segall's moral help, the position was reoccupied. Segall did not leave his men in the lurch: he obeyed orders only at the last minute, and was one of the last to retreat to safety.

On October 20, during fighting around Wolina (Poland), Segall's dressing station was located in the middle of the firing line, on a railroad embankment. Thus, he could provide assistance to hundreds of wounded where they lay. When both sides were exhausted, and a pause in the fighting allowed, Dr. Segall saw to it that large quantities of potatoes were cooked, tea prepared, and handed out by his medical team to exhausted, numbed soldiers, who had been in the firing line for days.

For his bravery under fire, Segall was awarded the Knights Cross of the Order of Franz Joseph on the ribbon of his Military Service Medal.[147]

Miscellaneous snapshots: boat attack on the Pripiat' marshes

An anonymous feuilleton describes exploits of a Jewish soldier in October 1915, on a boat on one of the rivers on the Eastern Front, probably part of the Pripiat' marshes in modern-day Belarus. The soldier volunteered to reconnoiter the enemy, passing by boat through a swamp. After trying several times to find the right way, he landed in the cold and rain on the far shore and spied out the Russian position. He had to turn back, because he and his three men were shot at by friendly fire. He tried again the next day, with more men. Following an all-night trench watch, he awakened his men at 4.00 am. After a difficult journey through reeds, they arrived at 5.45 am where boats were hidden. Most men could not paddle and there were no regular oars, so they used wooden paddles. During the journey, they were shot at by the enemy from both sides. They hid the boats, crept on their stomachs, catching the left flank off guard, crawling through fields of weeds a further 300–400 meters to the trench, hidden on the ruins of a shot-up estate. They crept nearer in single file through a hole, then through a gully in a field of weeds.

After about thirty minutes, the moment came, they jumped up, and with a loud "hurrah" stormed the surprised Russians. When the Russians saw them, they emerged from their holes, hands in the air. The Russians' rifles were gathered, ten prisoners led back to the boats, and taken back; they arrived on the other river bank at 7.45 am. The attack was mentioned in dispatches.[148]

Vagaries of war

Battalion adjutant ensign Jack Löwenstein described vagaries of war during an attack in December 1915.

In the field, fighting raged. Löwenstein sat in his dugout, next to a telephone, with which he relayed orders from command into the trenches. It began to get dark, and everyone got ready for bed, when suddenly, a short ring from the telephone announced: "Be ready to march in an hour!" Everything was readied, and the column marched off into the dawn. Soon the battle line was at the forest edge, and Löwenstein and his men attacked the enemy, who had established themselves in a village. Artillery fire poured into the village. Löwenstein and his men arrived at their positions, almost every hand gripping a rifle, waiting for the appointed time. An oppressive silence was followed by a thousand-voiced "hurrah" from the attackers. "No thoughts, no feelings, only: attack! Everyone jumped forward." One man fell, then another: no one noticed. The wild chase led through a swamp, men waded hip-deep through water—forward, no stopping, rifles overhead, officers in front.

They came up against obstacles, and enemy fire was terrible, but men did not waver. The enemy retreated: those who did not reach their goal, or did not give up, were shot down. They fled across the river, and were pursued, but demolished the bridge, reassembling on the other side of the river. Someone grabbed Löwenstein's arm, pointing to the enemy: he could not speak anymore, but sank into the mud, a red mark on his forehead. Löwenstein cried loudly: "Down!" but then noticed a hard, dull thud in his chest. He lay motionless, knowing that he had been severely wounded. He could not move before nightfall for the fear of being shot down. Shooting continued. Löwenstein was struck again, this time in the hip. He lay motionless and thought of his life at home. He fell half-asleep, and by the time he awoke it was dark. He wriggled onto the road, got up, and ran to his shelter. His men carefully brought him to a doctor. A bullet had penetrated his cigarette box and only wounded him superficially; a second bullet shot through his notebook, making a hole through plans, maps, and photographs, and hardly penetrated his body. The physician kissed him, averted his eyes, and wept for those who had not been so fortunate.[149]

A Jewish soldier-poet

Hugo Zuckermann was born in Cheb, Royal Bohemia, in 1881. Before becoming a lawyer in Meran, he helped found a Jewish theater group to play modern Yiddish dramas in German.[150] Before succumbing to battle wounds in December 1914 on the Carpathian front, he wrote nine war poems, the first of which, "Österreichischer Reiterlied" (Austrian Cavalry Anthem), became famous throughout the army. I include one of his poems, in my own translation:

> Soldiers Grave
>
> A simple cross
> Between two folded fields.
> Snow is coming,
> Erasing the last mortal trace
> Of someone who kept faith
> To his flag's oath.
> Rain has washed his name away—
> Lost and forgotten.
> Oh soldiers grave, soldier's grave,
> Wet by no tears of mourning![151]

Contact with Jewish civilians

Throughout Eastern Front service, Jews serving in armies of the Central Powers, especially Austro-Hungary, came into frequent contact with Jewish civilians, caught between two great armies. These civilians suffered greatly, especially under the hands of Russian troops who often treated them brutally.

A January 1915 issue of *Jüdische Zeitung* contains a letter from a Jewish athlete from Vienna describing havoc wrought by the Russians. On November 16, he almost fell into the Russian hands in the Hungarian and Galician Carpathians. In all his wanderings, there were no more pitiable people than the Jews. No house had been spared. He would never forget the sight of some erstwhile Jewish homes: nothing but blackened piles of rubble. Because even walls were made of wood, only doorposts with the mezuzot remained. The Aryans marked their houses with white or blue crosses, to protect them. The Jews had mezuzot, which they did not remove despite all dangers. "In the current language of the Russians, 'cross' means 'pardon,' but 'mezuza' means 'plunder, and then when empty, burn down.'"

The Jewish temple in which he had worshipped was not spared, now serving as a stable. Collection boxes were broken into, Torah scrolls torn. Families who remained behind were not able to defend their property. If they did not give it up willingly, they were forced:

> The poor women! In one occupied town there was a hunt for Jewish women. They were taken from their homes, wrenched from arms of their fighting men. One woman, who had fled there from a neighboring town, was raped in front of her mother and four children. The black and blue bruises on their faces were their trophies of war. My thoughts are much occupied with the future of these Jews.[152]

Two letters from the field from an unnamed Viennese reserve officer published in *Dr. Bloch's Österreichische Wochenschrift* (January 1916) described meetings between cosmopolitan Viennese Jews and Galician *Ostjuden*.

The first letter came from Vladimir-Volynsky: The regimental quartermaster referred the writer to a Jew, better said a "little Jew," small and Jewish-looking, with his pale, narrow, sparsely bearded face, little black cap, and caftan. His Yiddish was almost incomprehensible, spoken in breathless haste as though Cossacks were behind him. But Jewishness was his destiny. He grew up a poor orphan boy. In Warsaw he attended a private Jewish gymnasium, but could not complete more than four classes and then had to leave and earn a living. His deepest sorrow was that he had not learned more. He served as an expert in writing, speaking, and as spiritual pettifogger, assisting farmers in relations with authorities. This had allowed him to buy a decent house before the war began. Since Austrian troops arrived, all businesses had stagnated, his included. He chided himself: "war is war, things will improve when it ends," and was pleased to welcome Austrians. At any rate, he would earn his daily bread. His little one would learn as well: "He has to learn; he is learning Hebrew, and can already read Russian." Since the Austrians arrived, he chose to teach his son to read German, with aid of a grammar primer, which he had used many years before as a Warsaw schoolboy. The boy read sentences from the old book with exaggerated fluency. He could also recite some poems in it from memory. He spoke the first lines of Schiller's poem "Der Taucher" with horrible pronunciation and grammar. But it was still Schiller, and it filled the boy with "Schiller-enthusiasm."[153]

> What is the ideal of all Jews? Reading and studying! And the Germans? When one joins in the chorus of their haters, one must

not forget that this powerful, warlike nation is also a nation of writers and poets.

In a second letter, Jewish civilians in an unnamed town had ample time to compare Russian and Austrian domination; they preferred the Austrians. As in Lemberg, they showed their patriotic feeling and, without fear of sacrifice or danger, helped prisoners escape without detection by enemy spies. The writer's batman, escaped from Russian captivity, was hidden in Lemberg for six weeks: their arrival in Lemberg had given him a welcome opportunity to introduce his superiors to his patroness. Arriving at about 8.00 am, they saw a typical middle-European reception room. While entertained by the small, rotund *Hausfrau*, they were treated to tea and cake by her grown daughters. When endless columns of Austrian prisoners were led past, she sneaked gifts to them. Several times she was rewarded for this with a blow from a Cossack *nagaika* (whip). She was not afraid of such blows, and not sparing with her money to soothe the pain of Austrian prisoners, or help them escape. She made it clear that, in Holy Russia, everything could be obtained with money, except by the Tsar, who had everything already, and described the murder of local Jews in the town square by a group of Cossacks.[154]

A letter to his children from an unnamed *Landwehr* soldier in June 1917 described suffering of Jewish civilians on the Eastern Front. It is also an example of good will of the Jewish population towards Central Powers soldiers:

> We arrived in a little East Galician shtetl at 11.00 pm on a cold night, tired, hungry, and soaked. There were no paved streets, and rain makes roads bumpy and muddy, so we sank knee deep in mud. Our quarters were an empty farmhouse. Our stomachs were grumbling, and I was deputized to buy provisions. Rain poured down: suddenly someone pulled at my coattail. Before me stood a nine- or ten-year-old Jewish boy. He spoke quite a good German, and offered me help. He said that he was Jewish, and German soldiers helped Jews. I should go with him to his mother's cottage: I went to his mother, a poor widow: she dried my clothes, giving me coffee, bread, and eggs. I asked her whether I could also obtain some eggs for my comrades. She said that her son would bring some.
>
> She told me about her tribulations when Russians had broken

in. They took everything, beating her and her children bloody. Her husband, a watchmaker and goldsmith, had been hanged. Half-naked, she and her children had to flee into the woods: they froze and starved there for more than eight days. Then the Germans came, and brought her and her children back home.

Next morning, the boy asked me to come to his mother again. She told me that, before the Russians came, she had been well off. Her boy, who was good and hard-working, had learned to make rings from his father. He was now making aluminum rings from pieces of shrapnel, which he sold to lovers, to support his family. He offered me two rings to send to you and asked me to tell you that a small Jewish boy had made them. And so, every time you look at the rings, you should think of a small boy who bears deprivation cheerfully and is happy to work, to help his mother. A few hours later, we had to depart; we marched out cheerfully, to meet the Russians. I remained in good spirits through the storm, because I knew that a small, brave boy was praying for me.[155]

This picture was not one-sided. German and Austro-Hungarian soldiers robbed and pillaged civilians of all faiths caught in the war. Provisions were requisitioned for personal use or for the army, often leaving civilians with little to nothing. But widespread barbarity, rape, and murder, as was seen with the Russians, was not the norm.

This chapter closes with an anonymous article in *Jüdische Volksstimme*, which movingly describes a 1916 *yahrzeit* (annual memorial for the dead) service in the Galician trenches:

During a period of fighting, a comrade came, rifle on shoulder, and asked: "Are you a Jew?" "Yes, why do you ask?" "I have a candle, and want to say *kaddish* for my father. I still need a few men for the *minyan*." The author went to his section leader, requesting permission to attend the *minyan*. Four soldiers from his company accompanied him. They crept behind the line to join the *minyan*. Three men were waiting. They lit a candle, placed it in a damp hole in the ground; and started to pray. This prayer was not only for the soul of a dead father, but also for many thousands, whose souls are floating around in the heavens, looking for someone reciting *kaddish*.

The enemy must have sensed something, because bullets and shrapnel started to explode around them. When they were almost finished, the captain of a nearby battalion approached. His father was a Jew, but he had left the faith years ago. He did not realize what was going on, but took out a cigarette case, to light a cigarette from the burning candle. "Herr Captain," a comrade dared to say, "Please don't light it. This candle serves another purpose."

"What purpose?"

The captain stood as if frozen, his face became pale. Old memories came over him. He took the cigarette from his mouth, put it back in the box and, after some moments of silence, said to us: "I want to pray with you. I too want to be a Jew, comrades. I am a Jew..."[156]

Conclusions.

Despite trials and tribulations, Austro-Hungarian Jewish soldiers retained their courage, humor, quick-wittedness, and compassion. Orthodox and assimilated Jews alike fought bravely despite poor leadership. Jews enjoyed promotion privileges similar to non-Jews, and were similarly loyal to the supranational Habsburg Empire. Jews and non-Jews complained equally about bad leadership. Although antisemitism existed in the army, and increased during the war, it was kept under official control. I could find no significant differences in the attitudes of Jews from the different Habsburg nationalities. Patriotism of Hungarian Jews was second to none. Czechs were, as far as diaries, memoirs, and second-hand reports are concerned, just as patriotic as Jews from other nationalities. This is addressed in more detail in the next chapter, in the report by Egon Erwin Kisch from the 1914 Serbian campaign.

Endnotes

1 M. L. Rozenblit, *Reconstructing National Identity: The Jews of Habsburg Austria during World War I* (Oxford & New York: Oxford University Press, 2004), 15. First published 2001. The old Austro-Hungarian province of Bukowina is located on the northern slopes of the Central-Eastern Carpathians and adjoining plains. It is today divided between Romania and Ukraine.

2 P. Ernst, "Der erste Weltkrieg in deutschsprachig-jüdischer Literatur und Publizistik in Österreich," in *Krieg. Erinnerung. Geschichtswissenschaft*, ed. S. Mattl, G. Botz, S. Karner, and H. Konrad (Vienna, Cologne, ande Weimar: Böhlau Verlag, 2009), 68-72.

3 Österreichisches Staatsarchiv/Kriegsarchiv/FA/NFA HHK-HFK/HGK Erzherzog Karl Akten 50, 656–658.

4 "Acht Söhne Soldaten," *Dr. Blochs Österreichische Wochenschrift*, May 5, 1916, 297; "Die Tragödie dreier Brüder," ibid., May 19, 1916, 345–346; "In einer Woche zwei Söhne verloren," ibid., October 6, 1916, 662; "Fünf Söhne," ibid., December 22, 1916, 829; "Acht Söhne," ibid., January 19, 1917, 38; "Fünf Brüder," ibid., February 16, 1917, 103; "Fünf Söhne, sieben Auszeichnungen," ibid., March 16, 1917, 166–167; "Acht Söhne im Felde," ibid., April 12, 1918, 215.

5 M. Grünwald, "Antisemitismus im Deutschen Heer und Judenzählung," in *Jüdische Soldatsen—Jüdischer Widerstand in Deutschland und Frankreich*, ed. M. Berger and G. Römer-Hillebrecht (Paderborn and Munich: Ferdinand Schöningh, 2012), 143–144; P. C. Appelbaum, *Loyal Sons: Jews in the German Army in the Great War* (London and Portland, OR: Vallentine Mtchell, 2014), 239–283.

6 E. Schmidl, *Habsburgs jüdische Soldaten 1788-1918* (Vienna, Cologne, and Weimar: Böhlau Verlag, 2014), 117, 181–184.

7 E. Hoeflich (M. Y. Ben Gavriel), *Tagebücher 1915 bis 1927*, ed. A. A. Wallas (Vienna, Cologne, Weimar: Böhlau Verlag, 1999), 5.

8 Y. Petrovsky Shtern, *Jews in the Russian Army, 1827–1917: Drafted into Modernity* (New York & Cambridge: Cambridge University Press, 2014). First published 2009.

9 Ibid., 242–268.

10 Ibid., 1–128. A statue to 500 Jewish soldiers who died defending Sevastopol appears in ibid., 159.

11 Ibid., 167–227. On Gertsel Tsam, see ibid., 134–136.

12 Ibid., 242–248.

13 Ibid., 248–268. The number of 180,000, which is lower than most estimates, is courtesy of Yohanan Petrovsky Shtern (personal communication), an acknowledged expert in this field.

14 Kyiv (Ukraine).

15 M. Kálmán, "The Union of Jewish Soldiers under Soviet Rule," in *World War I and the Jews. Conflict and Transformation in Europe, the Middle East, and America*, ed. M. L. Rozenblit and J. Karp (New York and Oxford: Berghahn Books, 2017), 151–174.

16 O. Budnitsky, *Russian Jews between the Reds and the Whites, 1917–1920*, trans. T. J. Portice (Philadelphia, PA: University of Pennsylvania Press, 2011).

17 Lviv, Chernivtsi (both in Ukraine). Czernowitz was capital of the Austro-Hungarian province Bukowina.

18 S. An-sky, *The Enemy at His Pleasure: A Journey through the Jewish Pales of Settlement during World War I* (New York: Henry Holt and Co., Metropolitan Books, 2003), ix–x; D. Rechter,

The Jews of Vienna and the First World War (Oxford and Portland, OR: Littman Library of Jewish Civilization, 2008), 67–100. First published 2001.

19 B. Bardach, *Carnage and Care on the Eastern Front. The War Diaries of Bernhard Bardach 1914-1918*, trans. P. C. Appelbaum (New York and Oxford: Berghahn Books, 2018), xiii.

20 Appelbaum, *Loyal Sons*, 273.

21 Petrovsky Stern, *Jews in the Russian Army*, 252–254.

22 Bardach, *Carnage and Care*, 277 et seq.

23 Volodymyr-Volynskyi (Ukraine).

24 R. A. Höllriegel, *Die Fahrt auf dem Katarakt. Autobiographie ohne einen Helden* (New York: Archives of the Leo Baeck Institute, [1918]), ME 322, 153–201.

25 Karst topography is a landscape formed from dissolution of soluble rocks such as limestone, dolomite, and gypsum. It is characterized by underground drainage systems with sinkholes and caves.

26 Höllriegel, *Die Fahrt auf dem Katarakt*, 201–216.

27 Novi Pazar was an Ottoman *sanjak* (second-level administrative unit) created in 1865. Ottoman rule lasted until the First Balkan War (1912). The area included territories of present-day North Eastern Montenegro, South Western Serbia, and Northern Kosovo. The region now known as Raška was also called Sandžak.

28 Ismail Enver Pasha (1881–1922) was one of the three de facto leaders of the Ottoman Empire during World War I, a prime instigator of the Armenian genocide.

29 Höllriegel, *Die Fahrt auf dem Katarakt*, 217–245.

30 Borshchiv (Ukraine).

31 "Ulanenwachtmeister Aron Schapira mit der großen silberen und der goldenen Tapferkeitsmedaille ausgezeichnet," *Dr. Bloch's Österreichische Wochenschrift*, April 9, 1915, 275; E. R. von Rutkowski, "Aron Schapira: ein Unteroffizier im Weltkrieg 1914–1918, Träger der goldenen Tapferkeitsmedaille," *Zeitschrift für die Geschichte der Juden* 9 (1972): 53-64; Schmidl, *Habsburgs jüdische Soldaten*, 119–120.

32 F. Lieben, *Aus der Zeit meines Lebens: Erinnerungen* (New York: Leo Baeck Institute, 1960), ME 207a.

33 All towns in Poland except Zolkiew (Zhovkva, Ukraine).

34 Lieben, *Aus der Zeit meines Lebens*, 103–123. Volhynia is a historic region in Central and Eastern Europe, situated between South-Eastern Poland, South-Western Belarus, and Western Ukraine.

35 J. Floch, *Memoirs by Joseph Floch* (New York: Archives of the Leo Baeck Institute, [1946]), ME 761, 25–32.

36 E. Fischer, *Memoirs and Reminiscences* (New York: Archives of the Leo Baeck Institute, [1984]), ME 348, chapter 3, 1–17.

37 T. Reiss, *Tagebuch eines jüdischen Soldaten* (New York: Archives of the Leo Baeck Institute, [1919]), DS 135 A93 R45. Hebrew translation published in 1995 by Reiss's son and other relatives; T. T. Reiss, *In the Line of Fire: A Soldier's Diary 1914–1918*, trans. T. Erez (n.p.: Createspace Independent Publishing Platform, 2016).

38 Reiss, *Tagebuch*, 6. Page numbers are given for the German original, not the concomitant Hebrew translation.

39 Ibid., 8–42.

40 Three decades later, bacterial pneumonia could be cured with penicillin.

41 Ostrava (Czech Republic).

42 Reiss, *Tagebuch*, 46–72.

43 All in Poland.

44 A dubious diagnosis, probably malingering.
45 Reiss, *Tagebuch*, 74–112.
46 Lugoj (?), Timişoara (Romania).
47 Reiss, *Tagebuch*, 114–134.
48 *Gott erhalte Franz den Kaiser*, the old Austro-Hungarian national anthem, melody by Franz Josef Haydn.
49 Reiss, *Tagebuch*, 136–160.
50 Both in Hungary.
51 *Mies*, Austrian dialect.
52 Berezhany (Ukraine).
53 Not found.
54 Reiss, *Tagebuch*, 162–202.
55 Kaiser Charles's birthday was August 17.
56 Tomáš Masaryk (1850–1937); Czech nationalist, first president of the Czechoslovak Republic.
57 Stryi (Ukraine).
58 Not found.
59 Reiss, *Tagebuch*, 204–214.
60 Because of inevitable development of peritonitis, untreatable in the preantibiotic era.
61 His religious education must have been good, if he was able to do this.
62 Ceremonial meal the first two nights of Pesach.
63 Reiss, *Tagebuch*, 216–256. Serbia was invaded and occupied by the Central Powers in October–November 1916.
64 Ivano-Frankivsk, Chortkiv (Ukraine).
65 Burdiakivtsy (Ukraine).
66 Borshchiv, Hermanivka (Ukraine).
67 Ridkivtsy (Ukraine).
68 Reiss, *Tagebuch*, 256–296. A peace agreement with Ukraine was signed on February 9, 1917, a month before the Treaty of Brest-Litovsk. It enabled Germans to enter Ukraine and utilize its grain, coal, and other natural resources.
69 The Battle of Rarańcza, fought between Polish Legionnaires and Austria-Hungary, from February 15 to 16, 1918, near Rarańcza in Bukowina. It ended with a Polish victory.
70 Rabbi Arnold Frankfurter, the head Vienna garrison chaplain (chapter 6).
71 Reiss, *Tagebuch*, 298–310. Bozen: Bolzano (Italy).
72 Ibid., 310–324.
73 A form of post-traumatic stress disorder. Psychiatry was in its infancy during the World War I.
74 Reiss's lack of enthusiasm for serving again on the Italian Front probably made him report sick again.
75 Reiss, *Tagebuch*, 324–334. Bielitz: Bielsko-Biała (Poland).
76 M. L. Rozenblit, "Jewish Courtship and Marriage in 1920s Vienna," in *Gender and Jewish History*, ed. M. A. Kaplan and D. D. Moore (Bloomington and Indianapolis: Indiana University Press, 2011), 89–93.
77 Stary Davidko, a village near Munkács (Mukachevo, Ukraine).
78 A. Hameiri, *The Great Madness*, trans. Y. Lotan (Haifa: Or-Ron Publishers, 1984). First published in Hebrew as *Hashiga'on Hagadol* (Tel Aviv: Joseph Sreberk, 1929). Revised edition: ed. and trans. P. C. Appelbaum (Middletown, RI: Stone Tower Press, and Boston, MA: Black Widow Press, 2021). The page numbers are from the Appelbaum translation.

79　G. Abramson, *Hebrew Writing of the First World War* (London and Portland, OR: Vallentine-Mitchell, 2008), 22–67.
80　Hameiri, *The Great Madness*, 64–90.
81　"These are the tears of things." Virgil, *Aeneid*, book 1, line 462.
82　Abramson, *Hebrew Writing*, 52.
83　Shakespeare, *Hamlet*, act 5, scene 1.
84　Hameiri, *The Great Madness*, 91–106.
85　Ibid., 107–122.
86　Ibid., 123–142.
87　Bastard/illegitimate son (Hebrew).
88　Buchach (Ukraine).
89　Hameiri, *The Great Madness*, 143–160.
90　Rijeka (Croatia).
91　Hameiri, *The Great Madness*, 161-186.
92　Ibid., 187–212.
93　Ibid., 213–238.
94　The Gorlice–Tarnów Offensive was the Central Powers' chief offensive effort of 1915, causing collapse of Russian lines, and surrender of Russian Poland. The continued series of actions lasted most of the 1915 campaigning season, starting in early May and ending due to bad weather in October.
95　Hameiri, *The Great Madness*, 239–256.
96　Ibid., 257–269.
97　Ibid., 270–301.
98　Ibid., 302–324.
99　Ibid., 325--355. "God has numbered your reign, he has weighed you, and found you lacking" (Daniel 5:25).
100　Quorum of ten adult men.
101　The Brusilov Offensive, launched on June 4, 1916, and ending in late September, was the Russian Army's greatest feat of arms of the war. It broke the back of the Austro-Hungarian Army, which suffered about 750,000 total casualties and losses. It also exhausted the Russian Army, leading to dissatisfaction and privations at home, proximate causes of the Russian Revolution.
102　Hameiri and his men were captured at the beginning of the Brusilov Offensive.
103　Hameiri, *The Great Madness*, 356-381.
104　Bratislava (Slovak Republic).
105　"Ein 58 Jähriger freiwilliger Kriegsheld," *Dr. Blochs Österreichische Wochenschrift*, April 30, 1915, 330.
106　G. A. Tunstall, "Austro-Hungary and the Brusilov Offensive of 1916," *The Historian* 70 (2008): 31–53. Ludendorff was to adopt the use of shock troops, first used during the Brusilov Offensive, during his March 1918 Spring Offensive.
107　Bardach, *Carnage and Care*, 127–155.
108　Part of the Russian advance into Eastern Galicia in August 1914.
109　A. Mechner, *My Family Biography, 1897–1984* (New York: Leo Baeck Institute, 1981), ME 822, 74–87.
110　Almost certainly a form of post-traumatic stress disorder. Psychiatry was in its infancy during World War I.
111　Mechner, *My Family Biography*, 87–128.
112　In the Austro-Hungarian context, Ruthenians are Ukrainians.

113 Ludendorff referred to August 8, 1918 as the "black day of the German Army." It became clear that the German Spring Offensive had failed, and that the Central Powers would lose the war.
114 M. Reiner, *Mein Leben in Deutschland vor und nach dem Jahre 1933* (New York: Leo Baeck Institute, 1940), ME 517, 44–60.
115 Petrovsky Stern, *Jews in the Russian Army*, 254.
116 A. A. Brusilov, *A Soldier's Notebook 1914–1918* (Westport, CT: Greenwood Press, 1971), 163–166. First published: London: Macmillan, 1930.
117 F. Mändl, *Und wenn die Welt voll Teufel wär*, Archives of the Prague Jewish Museum, Collection of Visual Arts, inventory number 091.720.
118 Šafov (Czech Republic).
119 Mostly Muslim Caucasian nation native to Circassia, many of whom were displaced in the course of Russian conquest of the Caucasus in the nineteenth century.
120 M. Halberstam, "Aus den Feldpostbriefen eines tapferen Juden," *Dr. Blochs Österreichische Wochenschrift*, May 26, 1916, 352–353.
121 L. Kraus, *Susreti i Sudbine: Sjećanja iz Jednog Aktivna Života* (Osijek: Glas Slavonije, 1973).
122 Ibid., 69–73; F. Hameršak and L. Dobrovšac, "Croatian-Slavonian Jews in the First World War," in *Quest. Issues in Contemporary Jewish History, Journal of Fondazione CDEC* 9 (October 2016): *The Great War, Reflections, Experiences and Memories of German and Habsburg Jews 1914-1918*, ed. P. Ernst, J. Grossman, and U. Wyrwa, 94–121, www.quest-cdecjournal.it/focus.php?id=378, accessed April 6, 2021.
123 Kraus, *Susreti i Sudbine*, 75–77.
124 Ibid., 78.
125 Ibid., 79.
126 Ibid., 80–81.
127 Mukachevo (Ukraine).
128 November 21, 1916.
129 The Kerensky Offensive (July 1–19, 1917), named after Alexander Fyodorovich Kerensky (1881–1970), head of the Provisional Government, was the last Russian offensive of the war. Initial gains were quickly neutralized, and the Russian Army rapidly became a spent force due to widespread mutinies.
130 Kraus, *Susreti i Sudbine*, 85–96.
131 Ibid, 100.
132 Ibid., 109–111. The 1918–1920 H1N1 "Spanish" influenza outbreak resulted in the death of 50–100 million people worldwide.
133 M. B. B. Biskupski, *Independence Day: Myth, Symbol, and the Creation of Modern Poland* (Oxford: Oxford University Press, 2012), 9–11; A. Watson, *Ring of Steel. Germany and Austro-Hungary at War, 1914–1918* (New York: Basic Books, 2014), 97–99, 412, 499. Józef Klemens Piłsudski (1867–1935) was a Polish statesman who served as the Chief of Polish State (1918–1922), First Marshal of Poland (from 1920), and *de facto* leader (1926–1935) of the Second Polish Republic.
134 M. Gałęzowski, *Na Wzór Berka Joselewicza: Żołnierze i Oficerowie Pochodzenia Żydowskiego w Legionach Polskich* (Warsaw: Instytut Pamięci Narodowej, Komisja Ścigania Zbrodni przeciwko Narodowi Polskiemu, 2010); Watson, *Ring of Steel*, 99.
135 Gałęzowski, *Na Wzór Berka Joselewicza*, 134–137.
136 Ibid., 182.
137 Schmidl, *Habsburgs jüdische Soldaten*, 121.
138 P. C. Appelbaum, *Loyal Sons*, 207–237.

139 "Die Heldentat eines jüdischen Fliegeroffiziers," *Neue National Zeitung*, October 30, 1914, 1–2; W. von Weisl, *Die Juden in der Armee Österreich Ungarn. Illegale Transporte* (Tel Aviv: Olamenu, 1971), 20.

140 "Der Tod des österreichischen Fliegers Rosenthal," *Dr. Blochs Österreichische Wochenschrift*, April 2, 1915, 255; von Weisl, *Die Juden in der Armee*, 20.

141 "Flieger-Gefreiter Robert Fried," *Dr. Blochs Österreichische Wochenschrift*, December 29, 1916, 846.

142 Spiegl, "Der Sch'ma Ruf im Feuer," *Dr. Blochs Österreichische Wochenschrift*, January 15, 1915, 45.

143 "Die polnische Juden bein Stürmen," *Jüdische Volksstimme*, September 7, 1915, 3.

144 Brno (Czech Republic).

145 P. Bottome, *Alfred Adler. A Portrait from Life* (New York: Vanguard, 1957), 117–119.

146 Bardach, *Carnage and Care*. After this book had been completed, I was made aware of the war diaries of Dr Isaak Barasch. Barasch was born into a Jewish family 1885 in Zloczow – now Zolochiv – in the Ukraine, in what was then Galicia. He studied to become a doctor in Lwow (Lviv, Ukraine) and Vienna and served with the Austro-Hungarian army on the Italian front from 1916 to 1918. He died of influenza during the 1918 pandemic. (Barnsley, South Yorkshire: Penn and Sword, In preparation).

147 "Ein mutiger Arzt," *Dr. Blochs Österreichische Wochenschrift*, May 12, 1916, 330-331.

148 "Ein Feldpostbrief," *Dr. Blochs Österreichische Wochenschrift*, November 12, 1915, 842–843.

149 "Sturmangriff," *Dr. Blochs Österrichische Wochenschrift*, December 10, 1915, 898.

150 Eger (Czech Republic); Merano (Italy).

151 H. Zuckermann, *H. Zuckermann. Gedichte* (Vienna and Berlin: R. Löwit Verlag, 1919), 7–12, 107.

152 "Aus dem Feldpostbriefe eines Wiener jüdischen Turners," *Jüdische Zeitung*, January 29, 1915, 2.

153 Friederich von Schiller (1759–1805) was a German poet, philosopher, physician, historian, and playwright.

154 "Aus zwei Feldpostbriefen eines Wiener Reserveoffiziers," *Dr. Blochs Österreichische Wochenschrift*, January 7, 1916, 27–28.

155 "Von einem Judenknaben in Galizien," *Dr. Blochs Österreichische Wochenschrift*, June 15, 1917, 380.

156 "Jahrzeit im Schützengraben," *Jüdische Volksstimme*, July 8, 1915, 6.

CHAPTER 5

Snapshots from Other Fronts: The Balkans, Italy, and Palestine

The Austro-Hungarian army also fought in theaters of war other than the Russian Front. Serbia was invaded twice: once unsuccessfully in 1914, the second time successfully, with the aid of Germany and Bulgaria, which joined the Central Powers in 1915. As soon as Italy joined the Entente (May 1915), fighting in the mountains in the Tyrol and Isonzo began, and went on uninterruptedly through the end of the war. The Tyrol and Isonzo were perhaps the most dangerous of all fronts: freezing winter temperatures with snow and avalanches, vertical combat, tunneling inside mountains in all weathers, shards of mountain rock ricocheting after being hit by shells and shrapnel. Austro-Hungarians also fought in Palestine with the Ottoman Turks against British and Australians. This chapter describes Habsburg Jewish soldiers' experience on these other fronts.

I posit that Austro-Hungarian Jewish soldiers' experiences in Italy, Serbia, and Palestine did not differ from those on the Eastern Front. There was, however, the important distinction that there were very few *Ostjuden* in Italy and the Balkans. Either there were no Jewish civilians in areas of Italy where the fighting was fiercest, or communities were small. By contrast, Jewish soldiers encountered in the Balkans (many for the first time) large numbers of Sephardic Jews who spoke Ladino, and had different clothes, customs, degrees of religious observance, and appearance than Ashkenazi Jews.[1]

Secondly, it is posited that failings in the Austro-Hungarian Army—poor leadership and unsatisfactory equipment and provisions—were identical on all fronts. Nowhere was lack of organization and training more marked than during the initial 1914 Serbian campaign. The Austrians assumed that they would walk easily through tiny Serbia, forgetting that the Serbs had been fighting a guerilla war against Turks for hundreds of years, were renowned as brave fighters, fiercely patriotic, and fighting for their homeland. The Austro-Hungarians were bloodily repulsed and only dared enter Serbia again in 1915, bolstered by German and Bulgarians forces, which, together, forced the Serbian army out of the country. In the Tyrol and Isonzo, Austro-Hungarians fought bravely under impossible conditions and, bringing their mountain skills to bear, were more than a match for anything the Italians (who also fought bravely) could throw at them. But throughout the war and on all fronts, the Austro-Hungarian army was plagued by inadequate leadership and bad organization.

Austrians, Hungarians, Czechs, and soldiers from other provinces fought together. The patriotism of Hungarian Jews during the war was second to none. Especially after the Kossuth Rebellion (chapter 2), they felt themselves true Magyars, loyal to the supranational state. Similarly, Czech Jews like Egon Kisch fought courageously during the 1914 Serbian campaign.

Balkan Front

Otto von Bismarck remarked that "some damned foolish thing in the Balkans will set the explosion off." A river of ink has been spilled on how and why Europe went to war in 1914. Notable works include Sir Christopher Clark's *The Sleepwalkers*.[2] Bismarck proved correct, and a spark in the Balkans on June 28, 1914 set Europe and the world ablaze a month later.

Austro-Hungary went to war in late July 1914, confident that it could conquer Serbia and knock it rapidly out of the war. Overall, the Fifth and Sixth Austro-Hungarian armies comprised about 270,000 men, better equipped than the Serbs. However, the Serbs—an intensely patriotic people—were fighting in and for their homeland. After a fierce four-day battle, the Serbs beat off the Austro-Hungarians on Cer Mountain (August 15–24, 1914). Serbia then went on the offensive and attacked the Hungarian region of Syrmia (now Serbia). To counter this, Austro-Hungary launched their own offensive against Serbia in hopes of forcing the Serbian contingent back to protect their homeland. This time the Austro-Hungarian army gained the upper hand, occupying Belgrade, although both sides suffered comparable losses. The Serbs drove the Austrians off at the Battle of Kolubara (November 16 to December 15, 1914) and retook the capital.[3] A deadly typhus epidemic killed thousands of Serb civilians during winter 1914–1915, and may have been an important reason why the Austro-Hungarians did not attempt to reenter Serbia that winter.[4]

As already pointed out, Balkan Jews (living in Greece, Croatia, Serbia, Macedonia, Bulgaria, and Bosnia-Herzegovina) were mostly "Spaniols," Jews of Sephardic descent who traced their origin from the 1492 Spanish exile. Because Bosnia-Herzegovina had fallen under Austro-Hungarian rule in 1878, they were already a known quantity, and their mother-tongue Ladino had been heard before.

Serbia 1914

Egon Erwin Kisch (plate 3) published a unique book of memoirs of the ill-fated 1914 Serb campaign. Although it appeared about fifteen years after the campaign, it was constructed from notes made on the spot, or a maximum of twenty-four hours thereafter.[5] Kisch was born in Prague and, as a Czech Jew, he shows no signs of disloyalty (see chapter 1), only disgust at bad army organization. His book demonstrates the quick disillusionment of the Austro-Hungarians after an initial confident entry into Serbia in face of unexpectedly brave, organized opposition. After brief initial occupation, troops rapidly withdrew from Belgrade, and then Serbia proper. Kisch was outraged at the incorrect, misleading war news appearing in home newspapers: people had no clue of what was actually occurring. Interspersed with chaotic battle scenes, Kisch's reflections provide a unique glimpse into Serbia and Bosnia-Herzegovina at the start of the war, describing chaos, lack of preparedness, confusion, and bad leadership (including bribery and corruption) of the Austro-Hungarian army. A narrator positioned right in the middle of fighting, he compellingly describes the carnage of battle. His Serbian opponents are well-led, brave, resolute, if sometimes dishonorable, fighters, who continue firing after waving a white flag. Civilians, including Orthodox priests, are content to be shot as martyrs, making Kisch doubt how easily Serbia can be conquered. The chaotic first two months of the campaign are described in excruciating detail including ferocious battles, terrible weather, corrupt leadership, incompetent provisioning, and failure to prevent a cholera outbreak in winter 1914. Kisch is conscious that he is Jewish and fasts on Yom Kippur. Apart from an indication of antisemitism in Prague, the subject is not mentioned in a military context.

Egon Kisch's war diary is an accurate description of the 1914 Serbian campaign. The Austrian army advanced, confident of early victory against what they thought would be a minor enemy. The Serbs proved to be fierce fighters, and soon disabused the Austrians of these ideas. Kisch does not seem to have been present at the Battle of Cer Mountain,[6] but he was in the thick of the disastrous river crossings and temporary occupation of Belgrade. Soldiers had little idea where they were going and why, there were insufficient boats to cross the wide, deep rivers, and provisions were irregular and often inadequate. Sappers did their best to construct pontoon bridges to compensate for bridges destroyed by the Serbs, whose fortified positions were often better constructed than those of the Austro-Hungarians. The wounded streamed back to an unprepared medical corps. Thought was not given to provision of changes of clean dry clothing, and men suffered from mud, lice, hunger, and—during the winter of 1914–1915—frostbite and cholera. They were driven out of Serbia with bloody noses. Kisch was infuriated at newspaper propaganda and statements by senior army leadership that this had been a successful campaign: he and his comrades knew better.

Egon Erwin Kisch was born in Prague in 1885; he was called up for military service in 1914 and became a corporal in the Austrian army. He fought on the front line in Serbia and the Carpathians, and was briefly imprisoned in 1916 for publishing reports from the front critical of the Austrian military's conduct of the war. Nonetheless, he later served in the army's press corps along with fellow writers Franz Werfel and Robert Musil.[7]

On the way to the Serbian Front, Kisch's squeamish stomach, jerking train movements, a head cold, and inconveniences like not being able to change clothes caused his comrades to say: "He will die even before we reach Serbia." On August 6, they reached the bridge across the Danube on the Croatian border. They marched through Slavonia (Eastern Croatia) into Bosnia Herzegovina in the blistering summer heat. In Bijeljina (Bosnia), they saw a student and a Serbian Orthodox bishop hanging together from gallows.

In town, Kisch observed a mixture of young girls in Turkish trousers, men with different colored fezzes and turbans, and people elegantly clothed in western style. He heard a muezzin wail "a *kol nidrei*-like melody," and attended a service in the local mosque, where the imam told Moslem soldiers that they were absolved from fasting according to rite. Kisch saw a Serb go calmly to his death, and realized: "It will not be easy fighting against a people who have decided to die rather than submit to us!"[8]

On August 9, during a field mass, men were informed that Pope Pius X had granted the soldiers absolution of all their sins (presumably making it permissible for Catholics to kill the Eastern Orthodox). Serbian hostages, including Orthodox archbishops, were executed for supposed espionage. One priest had long black hair and piercing eyes; he was perforated with bullets and soaked with blood. Hostages went to their death without complaint.

"The price for one visit to the local bordello was one crown. Most prostitutes were Hungarians, with a few pretty Croats." On August 11, Kisch and his regiment left Bijeljina, and marched to the Drina River, on the Serbian border. Men were plagued by swarms of what at first resembled flies or mosquitos, but were really bullets. During the night, the Serbs attempted to hinder the Austrian engineers from building a bridge across the river, and the Austrian artillery opened fire on them. The Austrian fire was inaccurate; many shells exploded on the other side of the river.

At 1.00 pm on August 12, they crossed the Drina River into Serbian territory, where Kisch experienced his baptism of fire. They advanced in the direction of Lešnica (Serbia), where they were attacked by the Serbian artillery, neutralized by the Austrians. They scaled hill 404; fighting erupted again. Kisch sent an urgent message: "Five men lost in five minutes. Position dangerous." Reinforcements arrived, and the Austrians broke through. Kisch and his men suffered terribly from thirst, and Kisch was concerned that cholera might break out. They found six dead Serbian soldiers armed with dumdum bullets. Kisch remarked on how stupid and careless many high ranked officers were: they did not have a clue where they were going.

After resting on the hill, they stormed Lešnica. Soon, white flags hung out of the windows. The local population was astonished that many Austro-Hungarian soldiers were loyal Czechs, fighting against fellow Slavs. A violent thunderstorm began, lasting for hours; soon men were ankle-deep in water. Advancing became impossible until the storm abated.

On August 16, after ingesting "a mud suspension that is called coffee," men advanced again. Provisions were terrible: there was so little water that one man gargled with his own urine. There were no water casks in Kisch's unit. Fighting broke out again, and Kisch observed the grisly image of countless horribly wounded men carried on stretchers. Some men appeared psychologically disturbed. Kisch and his men were ordered to Milina Dolna (Bosnia) to fetch provisions: easier said than done, because narrow mountain roads were clogged with the wounded. Horses also badly needed fodder. On the way back with provisions, Kisch saw many Austrian corpses. They were attacked again, a hail of shrapnel whistled over their heads, and chaotic confusion of wounded transports clogged up roads. Finally, they arrived back with provisions, which had to be unloaded and carried to men in the front line.

Kisch passed a local brickworks turned into a field hospital. There was a hustle and bustle of soldiers, medical orderlies, and physicians of all ranks, assistant physicians, and medical students, all working in difficult conditions. There was no straw, the wounded lay unprotected on the bare barn floor looking at their crushed hands, or screaming if someone trod on a wounded leg.

Surgery was done on tables and cabinets requisitioned from somewhere else. A fully clothed anesthetized infantryman from Kisch's regiment lay on the table, trousers slit open to the hip: one of his legs was being amputated above the knee. On the small table next door lay another anesthetized man, shot through the belly. More and more wounded arrived; blood streamed down the corridors into the sticky dust. The air smelled of mud, blood, sweat, and intestinal content. Outside were piles of clothes, weapons, ammunition, implements of all kinds, and food taken from the wounded. Behind the brickworks lay a hundred dead bodies; ambulances and horse-drawn wagons travelled back and forth on their weary way. Men drank and filled their water bottles from the nearby stream, which had become paste-like and chocolate brown.[9] On the way back to their company, more shells exploded around them. Hundreds of soldiers rushed—wounded, panicked, terrified—out of the forest. Horses ran around. Back at their positions, meteors of light flew out of the flare guns. The artillery gradually lessened, the crickets' cheeps stopped. "Where does peaceful nature begin, and man-made war end?"[10]

On August 18, the Serbs attacked the Austrian flanks with mercilessly accurate artillery fire: Kisch saw hundreds of wounded passing by on foot or in vehicles. The Serbs knew every nook and cranny of their own terrain—exactly where to conceal their artillery, and how to use it. The Austrians had landed in the middle of the Serbian firing range. Their orders were confused: two companies retreated to a nearby village. Night patrols found enemy artillery and infantry in the woods. Kisch's men advanced, finding bloody signs of yesterday's battle. The Serbs opened fire on them again: a hellish rain of fire came from positions they could not see. As soon as the Serbs became visible, the Austrians attacked, occupied their trenches, and the Serbs put their hands up. But this was just a trick to lure the Austrians forward: they advanced, seeing no opposition, but the Serbs fired through holes in a nearby garden wall, which the Austrians could not see. They used hand grenades, new to the Austrians. The wounded fell left and right. In the process of flinging themselves behind tree trunks or any other possible protection, the Austrians were decimated. Suddenly a Serbian horn signal was heard: the firing stopped, and someone came out from behind their wall waving a white handkerchief and calling in German, "officer to the front."

An Austrian officer jumped forward but was immediately shot, whereupon a volcano of Serbian artillery, hand grenades, and rifle fire exploded from the wall. The Austrians panicked, and fled as if the devil was behind them. It started to rain, and darkness fell. Kisch's captain encouraged his troops; again, they advanced into the jaws of death. The wounded were loaded onto improvised stretchers; men tried to climb down the hill with them in the dark. A violent storm broke, with thunder, lightning, hail. The march back took many hours: the road was full of puddles of blood. Kisch's men stopped at the field hospital in Milina: over 2,000 wounded in three days, with many dead.

By August 19: "The army is beaten, in wild, uncontrolled flight." From Kisch's company alone, thirty officers and hundreds of men were dead or wounded, two machine guns lost, men were without weapons. In the brick house, physicians amputated arms and legs, trepanned skulls, reset fractured jaws, removed bullets from temples or intestines; but more and more wounded arrived. Doctors worked day and night. Except for the doctors, who remained with the wounded that were too sick to move, everything and everyone—baggage trains, ambulances, men—retreated, to avoid being captured.

This was not a beaten army—it was an uncontrolled rabble. Horses, carts, and artillery pieces, mixed up with officers, men, sappers, *Landwehr* men, artillerymen, and medical orderlies clogged the roads. No one listened to orders. Men were run over, wagons crashed into each other, horses bit one another, driven insane by whipping. The army was incapable of moving. Serbian artillery rained down ceaselessly, wounding and killing men and beast, destroying munitions, supplies, and wagons. Dead and wounded horses lay everywhere; wounded horses were not put out of their misery.

The terrain was flat, with no protection against flying shrapnel. Fleeing troops were treated with scorn by the local population. Men were thirsty, and drank raki as though it were water, falling over, dead drunk. After about half an hour, an infantry staff officer tried to restore order and cover the retreating men. Towards evening, a better effort at resistance was made in front of Lešnica. Almost all Austro-Hungarian officers either were wounded, or fled by car.

On August 20, they were ordered back to the other side of the Drina River, and hold fast there to the last man. Kisch heard that thousands had fled the fighting into Bosnia. The mood was depressed: "our generals are incompetent donkeys: the fate of hundreds of thousands is entrusted only to those with influence. The Serbs certainly know how to defend their own country."

Men took up new positions in Janja (Bosnia), and finally got something decent to eat: good soup, Hungarian salami, bread, and coffee with rum. The town had a Muslim appearance, with pictures of the Turkish Sultan in the windows.[11] On August 22, many soldiers were sick with nausea and diarrhea: perhaps from the coffee, overeating, bad food and water, or cold Bosnian nights in tents on wet grass. The doctors diagnosed dysentery, but all they had to treat it was opium, available only for officers. Eventually, the outbreak spread, and all Kisch's comrades were "shitting blood."[12] Rain poured at night. They received the initial casualty lists for the first few weeks of the Serbian campaign, which were terrible: 71% of officers and officer aspirants, more than 25% of the men lost. Had Kisch's regiment been destroyed already? Kisch stood guard duty on the Drina, while men dug trenches to protect themselves from artillery fire on the other side. It was only August 25, but they froze in their tents at night.

On August 26, their few days of rest were interrupted by arrival of a breathless, naked man, part of a patrol on the Serbian side of the river. He had to swim back to escape murderous Serbian fire. Another member of the patrol arrived with a shattered arm and shrapnel splinter in his face. The Serbian bombardment continued the next day. Airplanes from both sides circled around. In the afternoon, a major visited:

> . . . an old geezer has arrived with stiff collar and pathetically funny recommendations, to solve the Balkan question. He yells so loudly that the Serbian Command can hear everything, and note down all our installations.

At 4.00 pm, reinforcements arrived by boat: men tried not to tell the new arrivals how bad things had been. Serbian patrols slipped through the Austrian advance lines, hurling hand grenades at baggage trains and artillery columns.

The old major continued his stupidity, with ridiculous orders for strict military discipline in a war zone. Kisch was infuriated to read lies and half-truths about the recent Serbian campaign in Austrian newspapers. According to the newspapers, the invasion of Serbia was planned to be a short-lived punitive expedition, followed by immediate retreat, and had been successful. The main Austro-Hungarian force had to be concentrated in the north-east, against the Russians; the entire Serbian army was active in this campaign, not just a small part. "Surely nobody will believe the rubbish they are printing!" On August 31, Kisch noted that he had now been away from home for an entire month. Newspaper articles became more and more ridiculous.[13]

On September 1, Kisch's unit was relieved by a Honvéd battalion. He complained of extremes of temperature: unendurable heat during the day, frosty cold at night. They arrived in Donji Brodac (Bosnia), without any idea where they would proceed from there. Perhaps to the Russian Front? Even the officers did not know. Kisch's right foot was blistered and torn open by constant walking in the heat: a physician cut the dead skin away, but could not spare a bandage because "bandages are only for serious bullet or artillery wounds." Kisch made do with footcloths. Men were hungry and cold, and sleep was difficult inside cold tents. Kisch's spoon (his only remaining eating utensil) was stolen from his provisions bag. "So now I will have to eat soup by hand."

Men were kept busy with useless exercising for six or eight hours a day. Nonsensical rumors did the rounds. Graf Tisza stated that "not a single Austrian soldier or artillery piece has been captured by the Serbs." "What ridiculous propaganda!"[14] On September 7, Kisch finally received a package from home, containing winter clothing, chocolate, sardines, and biscuits. At 6.00 pm, men were told they would attack the Serbs again tomorrow morning. The thought did not fill them with joy.

At 4.30 am on September 8, Kisch and his comrades marched off. Within ten minutes, they began to encounter Serbian fire, and took up position in Velino Selo (Bosnia). As before, the wounded streamed past. Their broken bones hung from torn flesh, pieces of skin from hung wounded faces and head wounds, everything was drenched with blood. Groans of wounded were heard everywhere. The dance of death got worse by the minute. At the bandaging station, the dead lay in heaps. One man clutched a photograph of his young wife and children in his stiffening hands.

Kisch did not know where to begin to describe the horrors he saw that day. "I am writing while pieces of the dead and pieces of shrapnel fall around me." That evening, they reached the Drina River, the same islands that they occupied and were driven out of before. They knew that they had to cross the river again; also that losses would be heavy.

The attack began the night of September 9. In no time, Kisch's provision bag and package of winter clothes were full of holes. A shell whizzed over his head, hitting a nearby tree trunk. His company tried to cross the river in pontoon boats. Kisch saw hundreds of Austrian soldiers, many wounded, wading sometimes waist-deep in the river, with their hands up. The wounded screamed for medical assistance. The orderlies helped with evacuation. During ten minutes of rowing, they scarcely travelled twenty meters. Oarsmen were afraid to row, and had to be threatened by a lieutenant's revolver before they got going. Pontoons finally reached the Serbian side of the river, and they marched through the nearby forest. Bullets whizzed around, striking men and trees: all about Kisch saw pieces of torn clothes, boots, flesh, bandages, discarded rifles, and rucksacks. They reached the Sava River. Kisch saw that they had marched into a mousetrap, surrounded by the Drina and Sava rivers on three sides, and a high cornfield full of Serbs on the fourth side.[15]

Kisch's unit was ordered to advance into the cornfield: his comrades fled back, terrified. They took up position on a low hill covered with corn, which the Serbian artillery couldn't reach easily. The artillery fire around them was violent. Kisch lay on the ground and dug a small hole with his hands. Near the Austrian position, there were abandoned Serb trenches, well built with concrete and firing slits, almost impossible to take. Over 10,000 men remained at their positions until evening. The artillery and machine gun fire from both sides was apocalyptic. The men were thirsty, but there was nothing to drink.

At 2.00 am, the order came for all troops to retreat to the Bosnian side of the river. How was this possible without a bridge? There were thousands of men, and at most twelve small pontoon boats, each of which could take at most forty men, including the many wounded. How could they escape this mousetrap? The Fifteenth Company moved back to the forest on the banks of the Drina. At first they thought they had lost their way because they had no proper directions, but they eventually reached the river. Crossing was chaotic, and pontoons were overloaded. Some men tried to swim, up to their neck in water, but had to stop in the middle because the river was too deep to wade through with knapsack and rifle.

Suddenly: "The Serbs are at the river bank!" Artillery and machine gun fire swept the river, which filled with drowning, screaming men, gasping for air. Some sank, others ran back to the river bank. Kisch grabbed hold of the side of a packed pontoon with sixty men trying to get on. He lost his hold on the boat, and tried to swim. Serbian bullets hit the boat. Terrified men screamed. The men tried to stop the holes in the boat, which was driven by the current in a northerly direction. Kisch did not know exactly how, but he reached the Bosnian side and was pulled out of the river.

A column of wretched soldiers, some in underclothing, others in full uniforms, trotted apathetically in single file. They looked for, but could not find, the nearest dressing station. Finally, Kisch and his comrades found the road back to Velino Selo, and marched back to their previous position. Men called out the names of their fallen comrades. Kisch wept like a child, and couldn't fall asleep. The attack had been a complete failure: the Thirty-Sixth Infantry Division could not even cross the river: the attack had been an unmitigated disaster for the Austro-Hungarian Army.[16]

On September 11, men marched away into Slavonia (Eastern Croatia), and took up positions on the Raca Peninsula, where the attack began.[17] The river bank was protected with barbed wire, and the bridge guarded by Croatian *Landwehr*. Civilians were hanged on suspicion of having helped Serbs. It started to pour with rain, but men were ordered to march off, to help a division cross the river. "What is this all for? In this awful weather?" Kisch had to wear footcloths instead of stockings, and each man was given only 180 rounds of ammunition. They occupied the Austrian portion of the Sava River bank.

Press rumors that Austrians were advancing into Serbia proved wrong. In fact, Serbs were bombarding Raca. Kisch's unit took cover at the railway station, and tried for the third time to cross the river. They saw blackened, rotting, burnt bodies from the last few days of fighting; the stench of rotting corpses was terrible. Their advance was complicated by hordes of *Landwehr* soldiers fleeing from the firing line. Finally they reached the bridge, where a dressing station was set up, but it had to be moved because of bombardment. They met about 100 soldiers with obvious self-mutilations in the hands or feet: powder-burns on their wounds gave them away.

Finally, they crossed the Sava. The river bank was full of rotting corpses from previous battles. The Serbs were in the forest, only thirty paces away. The Austrians tried to attack, but were violently beaten back. They attacked again, realizing that most were going to die. Fighting was terrible; many were killed but the Serbian position was taken. However, the Serbs dug in again, thirty paces from the new position. Kisch's unit lost most of its officers.

On September 19, men underwent sickbay examination for colic, diarrhea, joint pain, sprains, and so forth. There were no medicines, no opium, very little cotton wool, almost no bandages no nursing possibilities. Kisch had an infected bayonet wound from a few days ago examined and cleaned as well as possible, but there was danger of spreading infection. The Austrians advanced again at 3.00 pm. The Serbian shelters were not as good as they were on the river bank; but, from piles of bodies, Kisch could see that they were defended fiercely. The air stank with Serbian corpses. The Austrians dug in for the night, building fortifications as best they could. Some men dared return to the nearest town to fill their bottles with raki, others drank from fountains, even though they might be poisoned or contaminated. "Thirst is stronger than fear of death."

Rain poured the night of September 20; Serbs fired on Kisch's position. He was nauseous, suffering from dysentery. The mobile kitchen did not visit, and he was famished. He remained in the shelter for two days. On September 22 Kisch's regiment joined a battle that had been going on for nine days near Vasiljevica Koliba (Serbia). If they could break through, the fertile northwest of Serbia would lie open. Serbian forces were stronger than Austrians, with artillery and machine guns, well protected with barbed wire. Kisch was impressed with Serbian fortifications.

To complete Kisch's happiness, a miserable windy rain howled, mixed with roar of cannons, howitzers, and shotgun fire. The ground was covered with frost. Everywhere Austrians penetrated, Serbs put up desperate resistance. As usual, newspapers exaggerated their successes, minimizing their losses.[18]

Fighting continued on September 24. "Suddenly the earth shook, the air whistled." Kisch's cap flew off, and clumps of earth hit him in the face. An infantryman lay at his feet, head blown off. A hand grenade had gone off by mistake. Kisch's local newspaper alternated soulful reports of a romantic play, lottery results, and the price of sugar, silver, and cotton, with the latest casualty figures. A Berliner remarked: *zum Kotzen* ("it makes me vomit"). Newspaper propaganda, compared to Austro-Hungary's failures in Serbia, was humiliating and infuriating. It had become very cold, and Kisch was freezing without winter clothing: his winter clothes had been ruined or lost in the fighting, and no replacements had yet been provided.

Fighting on September 25 beggared description. It began at 7.30 am with a feeble Austrian attack: scarcely one third of the soldiers attacked, and those that did so were easily repelled or killed. It was not the soldiers' fault: the distance between them and the enemy was too long, and the terrain open: a single Serb company could destroy an entire regiment with machine gun fire. The Austrian attack had, as before, been badly planned. Again, a small army of the dead and wounded with every kind of mutilation accumulated. The Serbs shot at the retreating Austrians. The day after, reinforcements arrived, but green recruits were thrown into battle, and many were killed almost immediately. Despite failures, however, two bridges had by now been constructed over the Drina River, so that the Austro-Hungarians were connected with Austria on two sides.

The cook made Kisch a small cake with plum mousse. Kisch was beside himself with joy: it was a real change from the same old awful food every day. When the cake arrived, nicely wrapped in paper just like home, Kisch started to cry and got drunk. Strain had overcome him.[19]

During the past nine days, men had made themselves relatively comfortable in their shelters, but now they were ordered to leave. Where were they going? Rumors abounded. The Sava and Drina Rivers flooded the nearby meadows. The main bridge had been destroyed, but a small pontoon bridge replaced it.

On September 30, Kisch spent Yom Kippur in Velka Brana.[20] He fasted, also out of need: they had not received rations for two days. There were many new wounded to treat, but the physician-in-chief declared himself ill, and left. Kisch felt that his senses had been dulled from all the suffering. All his regimental friends were dead. Would they have to fight to the last man? On October 5, a Serbian shell exploded in the middle of the garden where the officers' corps were eating dinner; many were wounded.[21]

On October 8, a major was shot in chin and shoulder, and bandaged as Kisch watched from a distance. A Serbo-Croatian Austrian infantryman cried out that his group wished to cooperate in burial of the dead, and not to shoot. This had to be translated three times: even then the Serbs refused, because corpses lay eight to ten steps from their positions, despite their stench. "What do the Serbs care about 'humanitarian issues'?!"

On October 9, Kisch and his men dug more shelters. Provisions remained awful. The day after, a twenty-four-centimeter artillery piece joined the concert of Austrian artillery pieces; shells flew through the air like ships. On October 11, the word of the day was mud. It poured all night: the roads and shell holes overflowed with water. Men could not take one step out of their huts without bringing back a mountain of mud into bed, and water in the trenches was waist-deep. Kisch felt that he had become like a dead man walking, with no desire to live anymore.

After the direct hit of a few days before, the division command moved rapidly to the Bosnian side of the river. Kisch saw five corpses that had been lying in the river for a month: skin came off their hands like gloves. On October 13, Kisch heard that the second bridge over the Drina had been destroyed by Serbs: they were now completely cut off, and, in case of a Serbian attack, it would be best to be captured. The bridge over the Sava was also severely damaged, although sappers were trying to repair it. One of his regimental officers invited him to share his quarters. Kisch was struck by how much better officers lived than enlisted men.

On October 14, Kisch was tasked with finding a new source of drinking water. Both bridges were now destroyed, and the only way supplies could get in was by a small river steamer. When the Serbs found out that the Austrians were cut off, they attacked unsuccessfully with a sea of rifle, artillery fire, and grapeshot. The day after, the last two active officers in Kisch's original battalion were taken to field hospital. Rivers remained in flood; the Serbs had diverted two streams from the Drina River, to flood Austrian communication trenches. On October 20, Kisch and his men built a new subterranean blockhouse, better equipped and roomier. Unfortunately, their quarters lay in a side branch of a communications trench between regimental command and the officer's latrine, and their neighbors were five dead Serbs, buried in the roof.

On October 24, engineers from both sides worked on trenches. In some places they were only fifteen paces from one another, and could clearly see each other. In the evening, the Austrians heard a Serbian band celebrating a recent victory. Kisch reported that the mood at home in Prague was antiwar: no one believed reports of victories. On the contrary: news of lost battles, terrible losses of men and material filtered in. There were hidden negative comments and gallows jokes about the government, and an unfair antisemitic mood. When Kisch saw how many Jewish soldiers were serving with him, his blood boiled. Lies spread by Field Marshal Potiorek (1853–1933), commander-in-chief of the Balkan armies, about fictitious Austrian victories, also upset Kisch greatly.

On October 26, preparations were made for a new offensive, which began the next day. Engineers cleared away the Serbian barbed ware and elongated trenches to allow Austrians to advance under cover, saving hundreds of lives. The attack began at 5.00 am on October 27, after twenty-five minutes of artillery preparation. The Serbs were fooled and fled. Serbian positions were reached within five minutes, and many fleeing Serbs were taken captive. The offensive only stopped when men had become exhausted, and the tally of prisoners was too large for them to handle. The air filled with shrieking and moaning of the wounded, as well as the stench of corpses that had lain unburied in no-man's land for weeks. Trees were shot up, ground covered with shell holes and craters, and there were several hundred wounded on both sides. Kisch saw an Austrian captain with his entire head shot away, leaving only the neck and the left ear, his brand-new uniform soaked with blood. Two dead telephonists lay near him. The Serbs were ravenous and begged for food; they were fed generously. "Now that we are not shooting at each other anymore, we are brothers again." Some Serbs looked at the Austrians with enmity and submitted unwillingly to medical care. A great deal of booty was captured.[22]

On October 30, a report arrived of victories in Višegrad and Goražde in Eastern Bosnia, which had now been "cleansed" of Serbs. Patrols reported that Crna Bara (Serbia) had been cleared, opening the way to Serbia's grain-basket. On October 31, Kisch and his men were awakened early, ordered to march southeast in the direction of Crna Bara across abandoned Serbian shelters. At 9.45 am they entered the town. Apart from a few old people, this was a dead city, populated only with barking dogs, pigs, chickens, and cows. At least there was plenty to eat. The town reflected a higher living standard than others they had seen, with well-built houses, metal water pumps, and agricultural equipment. They found wine vats, preserved fruits, lard, and barrels of raki. In the evening, cows were driven to slaughter with whoops of joy.

The first day of November was relocation day. Patrols went back and forth, and at 10.00 am they marched off south, along the border into Serbia. They encountered obstacles in the form of barbed wire fences concealed in bushes and trees. Many trees had been chopped off, and Kisch could not understand why Serbs had not made use of these excellent defensive positions. At 1.00 pm they arrived in Badovinci, a prosperous—but abandoned—Serbian town. A wooden Serbian Orthodox church had fresh graves in its cemetery, a sign that some men buried there had been in action recently. About a hundred old people, mothers with babies and older children, along with the poor and the mentally disabled, had been left behind. They all looked apathetic and, when asked whether they wanted tea or coffee, they all said "raki." There was hardly a house without at least one barrel of homemade slivovitz.

On November 2—All Saints Day—the Austrians saw to it that the Serbian graves were neat and tidy, put crosses that wind has broken down up again, and cleared the roads to the cemeteries. At 11.00 am they marched off to Zminjak, and on November 4 arrived in Lipolist, where they took up positions in front of the main road. Lipolist was "just another Serbian village, with its barrels of apple and mulberry wine and raki." The village had a nice church with two towers, brick red tiles, and golden crosses. There were fresh graves in the church cemetery.

On November 6 another newspaper article carried a pompous note from Potiorek praising the army for its "glorious victories." Kisch found it scandalous. The winter campaign began on November 7 and, one day later, news arrived that Loznica had been occupied and 2,200 Serbs taken captive. It began to look as if Austrians were making progress: at 9.00 am, they attacked a nearby hill. Kisch was tasked with messenger duty. The grass through which he had to walk was head-high, and with each step he sank into the swamp. The ground was already covered with frost. The casualty figures from recent fighting were high; several of Kisch's friends had been killed.[23]

On Friday, November 13, it rained, on top of a severe frost the previous night. The mobile kitchen did not arrive, so, teeth chattering with cold, and almost insensate from hunger, they had to march off. But hunger, frost, rain, fog, nicotine addiction, rheumatism, heavy loads, and being soaked to the skin were not the worst thing about that day. The worst was the terrible mud that covered the entire region, making differentiation between roads and trenches impossible. It clung to clothes, boots, ammunition, rifles, everything. An entire regiment had to march single-file through the mud, in a line that was five or six kilometers long. Artillery pieces stuck fast, and had to be hauled out with oxen;

horses could hardly move. They met many suffering refugees, who were trying to return to their homes. In the afternoon, they finally arrived in Draginje-Bosnak, finding two pigs to butcher, cook, and devour. Lack of accompanying bread made them ill from ingestion of too much fat. Kisch was happy when midnight signaled the end of this unhappy day in Draginje (Serbia).

They marched off on November 14, meeting more and more returning villagers. Civilians become friendlier and offered the soldiers raki mixed with water, but Kisch was convinced that they would shoot them if they returned at night. At 3.30 pm, the Serbs opened artillery and rifle fire. The returning refugees, who still did not have a roof over their heads, were thrown into confusion.

More and more questions were being asked. Where were they going next? When would the next battle with Serbs take place? Backpacks felt heavier and heavier. On November 16 they arrived in Ub, a large, empty Serbian town. Kisch saw how, even as refugees, Serbs discriminated against Gypsies. Serbian artillery destroyed bridges over the Kolubara stream; they were quickly repaired by Austrian engineers. In pouring rain, Kisch's group reached Lajkovac (Serbia) on November 18. Mud was terrible and penetrated everything, but was at least partially covered when it started to snow. Kisch caught a bad cold and his back hurt. On November 20, the field hospital started to receive patients (including Serbs) with frozen limbs and rheumatism, as well as wounded (some of them seriously).

Kisch became convinced that what he could see of the army was being criminally mismanaged. Bribery ruled the roost, and treatment of ordinary soldiers was indescribable. In the officers' mess, they lived high on the hog, dining as if in a hotel. There were many shirkers, but some men were really ill: they had tuberculosis, weak hearts, inguinal hernias, and so on. But they already had this as civilians, and should not have been called up in the first place. "It's wrong that, when a man dies of tuberculosis in the field, his death is as 'heroic' as someone who dies from a bullet."

On November 27 the men marched out in the direction of Petka. The railway bridge over the river was blown up, but a temporary bridge had been erected. Three hundred prisoners were sent back to Lajkovac. Disorder continued: packages were received for soldiers who were already dead; money was sent back, but contents shared out (sometimes unequally, with stealing prevalent) among the men. The terrain was terrible, men had no reserves, and contemplated suicide.

The last month of this most awful of all years began. In the morning Kisch and his regiment marched to the north-west via Lazarevac, arriving in Vreoci—a suburb of Belgrade—that evening. The night of December 4 brought great excitement, and a flurry of orders. Men marched off, and took up position on the Sakulja Heights. However, man and beast were starving: they had received no provisions for four days. Men's shoes were in a terrible state: some men were barefoot, with frozen toes. Some developed frostbite, and had to have portions of their limbs amputated.

On December 5, Kisch received word that his regiment had been decimated. The Fourteenth and the Eleventh Companies were destroyed, others almost wiped out. Over 300 men had been lost, leaving the regiment with only 815 men. The afternoon of December 6, while Kisch was getting coffee, a shell exploded right next to him. The cook and one soldier were killed, five other soldiers seriously wounded. Men butchered an ox, which lay with its throat slit, amongst the corpses.[24]

On December 9, troops started their retreat, called by the officers a "position evacuation." The Fifteenth and Sixteenth Units had been pushed back with very heavy losses, in an attempt to stop a Serbian advance. Retreat continued in pitch darkness, baggage trains and artillery regiments blocking muddy roads. Kisch could not believe that Serbs were hard on their heels again, after apparent recent Austrian successes.

On December 10 they arrived in Stepojevac, where (they thought) they could finally sleep indoors again. However, rifle and artillery fire made it clear that the Serbs were still in pursuit. Shells started exploding in the town, and many wagons, horses still with feedbags on, streamed out, moving northwards. Chaos reigned; shells kept exploding amongst the houses, throwing clumps of mud into the air. Around 11.00 am, the Austrian artillery fired back. The wounded streamed in, shells exploded everywhere. This Serbian attack was unexpected: security had been lax. The main roads were packed with overturned field kitchens and wagons, and horse cadavers: everyone was travelling north.

On December 13, they arrived in Petrov Grob, where the troops finally established a fighting line. The first shells started to explode in the town around noon. The Hungarian troops disappeared, the right flank weakened, and a Serbian breakthrough threatened. Telephone communications were broken; nothing was done about maintaining defense of Belgrade. At 1.45 pm, a disorganized general retreat began: everyone wanted to go home. It started to rain, and darkness fell. At 7.00 pm they ascended a hill, from which the lights of Serb-occupied Belgrade could be seen in the distance.

On December 14, Kisch crossed a pontoon bridge over the Sava River. The bridge was jammed with carts and soldiers, and it took him over an hour to cross it. Belgrade disappeared into the distance. On December 15, six large detonations destroyed the three bridges from Austria into the Balkans. The day after, newspapers celebrated the Austrian Army's entry into Belgrade. The newspapers lied that Belgrade had been taken; in truth it had been vacated on November 29. Four out of fourteen days of the occupation had been wasted. Šabac (Serbia), with 10,000 Austrian sick and wounded, was again in Serbian hands. Kisch's skin itched; his clothes were full of vermin, skin covered with eczema.

On December 19, they continued their retreat to Ofutak.[25] In newspapers, Kisch read a ridiculously exaggerated and incorrect "huge Austrian victory over the Serbs in a battle from December 3 to December 7." In reality, King Peter, Princes Georg and Alexander had reentered Belgrade.

Christmas Eve was celebrated with extra rations of goulash, tea, and soup. The commander-in-chief proclaimed that the army had not been beaten, but that the offensive had to be halted because of "delayed arrival of equipment and ammunition." All sorts of lies were circulated by High Command, infuriating the troops who were there and knew what actually occurred. On December 30, Kisch reported the first fatal cases of cholera in Ofutak. The men were inspected for lice.[26]

New Year 1915 found Kisch's regiment still in Ofutak. The town swarmed with prostitutes, and a steady column of returning soldiers, stretcher bearers, and quartermasters passed through. The weather was bad; rain poured down. Men were inoculated with painful injections against cholera.[27] The cholera hospital at first refused to admit syphilis patients, but did so when ordered by rear echelon command. The streets were full of Serb civilians.

On January 12 the new Army Commandant Archduke Eugen was scheduled to visit troops. "Potemkin-like preparations" were made during the preceding two days, to create the impression of an enthusiastic army, ready to fight and die for the Kaiser. The Archduke inspected the troops, handing out medals. On January 13, the men received their second cholera inoculation. So far, thirty men had died of cholera.

On January 15, they were informed that the division was leaving for Josefdorf.[28] Did this mean that they were being transferred to the Russian Front, or simply fleeing from the cholera outbreak? Nobody knew. On January 18, men travelled over the Kaiser Franz Joseph Canal into Hungary. Winter descended on the area, with cold, ice and snow. In early February, Kisch and his comrades set off again, arriving in the Banat region.[29] They arrived in Debreczin (Hungary) on February 8. From there, they travelled on to Balnica (Poland).

Kisch commented on the high incidence of untreated frostbite amongst the wounded, which stopped their wounds from bleeding. There were several cases of self-mutilation.

For Kisch, Thursday, March 18, was the most fateful day in the war so far. He volunteered to deliver a seemingly unimportant order for the engineers, regarding the removal of some barbed wire. Kisch arrived at the headquarters in Wola Michowa (Poland), handed in the order, and had just sat down to lunch when a terrible explosion hit him on the head, knocking him to the ground. He did not lose consciousness, and realized that a shell had exploded right on top of him. Running out of the still smoking room to the physician-in-chief's office, he saw thick streams of blood pouring down from his head over his nose, ears, and shirt. He must have been hit elsewhere: his back, upper arm, and thigh were all bleeding. Medical orderlies and comrades carried him onto some straw.

Kisch acted as if he was dying, in hope of being transferred to Prague and not to a field hospital in the rear. The tragi-comedy continued when the physician arrived to examine him: he bandaged all the wounds, and asked whether anything else hurt. Kisch moaned "my back!" It turned out that his back wound had exposed the spinal column: it was also dressed. Kisch was more seriously wounded than he thought: he was transferred to a field hospital in Maniów (Poland), where further examination revealed a burst left and a damaged right eardrum. He was evacuated by train. On the way, he saw endless trains with Russian prisoners pass by. On March 21, he developed fever. He arrived in Vienna and, finally, in Prague where his mother was waiting for him at the railway station.[30]

The diary of Egon Erwin Kisch provides a blow-by-blow account of the failed Austro-Hungarian invasion of Serbia, the proximate Austro-Hungarian response to the assassination of Archduke Franz Ferdinand. The Austro-Hungarian Army, unprepared for large-scale fighting, failed to take the fighting spirit, readiness to fight, and patriotism of the Serbian Army into account, and were driven out with very heavy losses. A severe outbreak of typhus in the Serbian Army during the winter of 1914 halted hostilities, and Serbia was only occupied in late 1915 when combined armies of Austro-Hungary, Germany, and Bulgaria drove the Serbian army out across the mountains to the Albanian coast, whence they were evacuated to Corfu.

Uri Zvi Greenberg was born 1896 in Bialikamin,[31] to a line of Hasidic rabbis. By the time he was summarily conscripted, in August 1915, he was already a Yiddish poet of note. Greenberg fought during the crossing of the Sava River in the second Serbian campaign of October 1915, prior to the

Central Powers' attack on Belgrade. When the Austro-Hungarian forces forded the river, they launched an attack on enemy trenches encircled by barbed wire. Greenberg was one of the few survivors of the night attack. He saw his dead comrades hanging upside down on the wire, a sight that made a deep and lasting impression on him.

Greenberg wrote the second part of his first major work, written in Yiddish—*Ergits oif Felder*—to the sounds of cannons and machine guns, while in the trenches on the Sava River. His second work, *In Tzeitenes Roish* (written mainly in Yiddish), was written immediately after the war, in 1919. Both works, mostly in poetry and poetic prose, are suffused with his war experience.

> Wherever you step, there is a grave underfoot. Two feet under lies what is left of a man, with crushed skull, chest torn open . . . Forward! Bodies roll underfoot . . . I grind my teeth, and a twisted body lies there, a hole in his head. See what strange distortions bodies on the wire create! Are you sure that was someone? I remain alive, the moon will reveal to me a lake of human blood, with horses and hooves lying in it . . . By dawn's early light I'll see death moving away. I'll hear its mocking laughter at me.[32]

Greenberg's later poetry remains permeated with his war experiences. Abramson asserts that he suffered from severe post-traumatic stress disorder, perhaps even worse than Avigdor Hameiri did (see chapter 7). In his work *Emah Gedolah ve'Yareach* (Great Fear and the Moon), published in 1924, Greenberg writes:

> All young men fume in their graves; they rot and decay in the secret of the Carpathians.
> They will not fornicate with women because they decay.
> They will not feel hunger because they don't have stomachs.
> They will not thirst and drink because they have no lips
> Oh God, they don't have lips!

After the Serbian campaign, Greenberg was transferred to an office in Sarajevo (Bosnia). In 1917, when the war was clearly lost, he deserted and returned to Lemberg, where he remained in hiding until the war ended.[33]

Isidor Klaber, born in Vienna, was a medical student when war broke out, and served as physician's assistant. January 1915 found him on the Serbian

Front, after the Austro-Hungarian defeat by the Serbian Army. Along with his exhausted, wounded company, he found himself in a forest in the border between Serbia and Bosnia-Herzegovina, not far from Sarajevo. There was no dentist, and he learned how to pull teeth. He described Pesach celebrations in Sarajevo, in April 1915, held by the Ashkenazi and Sephardi congregations together. He had much to do as a medical orderly, treating cases of epidemic louse-borne typhus and meningitis. We will encounter him again on the Italian Front.[34]

Italian Front

The history of Jews in the Italian Army goes back almost as far as Jews in the Austrian military (chapter 2). In 1797, Napoleon and his army entered Ancona, abolishing the Jewish ghetto, and granted religious freedom to the Jews. Napoleon followed this with liberation of Jews in Venice, Verona, Padua and Rome, striking down the laws of the Inquisition. After papal reinstatement, Pope Pius VII took revenge on Jews living in the Papal States, forcing them into re-erected ghettos and making them wear the yellow badge. He was especially harsh to Sardinian Jews: aside from ghetto confinement, he forbade them from building synagogues.[35]

Jewish participation in movements for freedom and Italian unification began with the growing influence of republicanism and liberalism in cities of the peninsula. Piedmont, followed by Tuscany, were the first states to grant its Jewish citizens equal rights.[36] Tuscan Jews were allowed to enlist in the National Guard in 1847. After the collapse of the French monarchy in 1848, 235 Jews from Piedmont-Sardinia volunteered for military service, in the looming war with Austria. The Jewish volunteers formed the Seventh Company of Bersaglieri. Five Jews fought in the Lombard Legion of the short-lived "Roman Republic" (First Italian War of Independence); eight followed Garibaldi into exile. In 1854, Italian Jews from Sardinia-Piedmont, including Enrico Guastalla and Cesare Rovighi, volunteered to serve in the Crimean War. Jews fought against Austria in 1859. Both Guastalla and Rovighi served during the Second Italian War of Independence (1859–1860). There were already ninety Jewish career officers in the army of Piedmont-Sardinia at the start of the hostilities; 260 Jews served in the Piedmontese Army, and many were decorated for valor. Guastalla and Rovighi extended their service in further campaigns against Austria and Naples. The War of Independence yielded a new generation of Italian combatants. One of these,

Giuseppe Ottolenghi—a lowly cadet in the war against Austria—would eventually reach great heights. As the armies of Victor Emmanuel vanquished the Austrian Army and turned south, eleven Jews served with the *Garibaldini*, including Enrico Guastalla, who became one of Garibaldi's most trusted aides. Five Jewish officers obtained high decorations during the Neapolitan campaign. Jews were amongst the most fervent Italian nationalists and supporters of the Savoyard dynasty, and a disproportionate number of them served in the army. Eighty-seven Jewish soldiers saw action in the 1870 campaign to annex Rome. Giuseppe Ottolenghi served as attaché to the French Army during the Franco-Prussian War, was promoted lieutenant general in 1902, and served as minister of war from 1904 until his death in 1906. Other Jewish lieutenant generals included Emanuele Pugliese, Roberto Segre, and Angelo Arbib. Italy entered the war against Austro-Hungary in May 1915 with many Jewish officers.[37]

Italy, when it declared war on Austro-Hungary in May 1915, had, out of a total of about 35,000 Jews, 5,000–6,000 Jewish soldiers. The overall number of commissioned officers was 2,500–3,000—approximately 50% of all Jews serving in the war. Nearly forty Jews attained the rank of general during the war, and 700-1,000 Jewish soldiers earned decorations. Approximately 400–500 of these were killed during the war (399 confirmed fatalities, ranging from seventeen to sixty-one years old), and twice that number wounded. As in other armies, many Jewish soldiers were highly decorated (549 documented recipients). The high percentage of Jewish generals and other officers in World War I Italian army is noteworthy. Jews were active in army, navy (all branches), and air force, and several served in command positions. Colonel Angelo Modena began the war commanding an infantry regiment; by the war's end, he had been promoted major general. General Roberto Segre was cited for bravery at the Battle of Gorizia, and Colonel Emmanuel Pugliese distinguished himself during the battle of Vittorio Veneto, ending the war as a general. Jews also served in the navy, and three officers (Capon, Nunes, and Segre) went on to achieve the rank of full admiral.[38]

The Habsburg Jewish experience on the Italian Front is explored through summaries from diaries and memoirs of soldiers from Austria, Galicia, and Bukowina. The Italian Fronts in the Tyrol and Isonzo were perhaps the most savage of the war: Fighting was vertical, artillery had to be pulled up mountains, roads were narrow, weather extreme with deep snow alternating with mud, and shells and shrapnel ricocheted from mountains spraying men with metal and rock. Both sides tunneled into the mountain, trying to blow up one another's positions up. The diary of Adolf (Dolu) Rawitz compellingly describes the appalling conditions.

The disorder in Austro-Hungarian leadership expressed in diaries and memoirs from the Eastern Front and Serbia is mirrored in those from the Italian Front. The soldiers fought bravely and many of them had mountaineering experience, but the senior officers were disorganized, proper planning was often absent, and men complained vociferously about bad leadership. As described by Dolu Rawitz and Lilian Bader (whose husband served), a pernicious class distinction system ensured that educated soldiers became officers, and lived far better than ordinary soldiers. Antisemitism (mentioned in connection with Erwin Bader) was present, but not intrusive. Each memoir and diary emphasizes the ferocity of the fighting and the difficulty of terrain and weather. Dolu Rawitz was in the middle of the Battle of Caporetto, and comments on the difficult fighting terrain, as well as the chaos caused in the battle's wake, when soldiers entered Italian towns and looted supplies of food and drink, in such quantities and of such quality as they had not seen in years. Drunkenness became a severe problem, and digestive problems must also have occurred due to overeating, which lowered the soldiers' fighting ability. Rawitz also comments acidly on antisemitism of the Poles by whom he was imprisoned for a short while immediately after the end of the war.

The longer the campaign lasted, the worse shortages of all kinds caused by the blockade became, until by 1918 during the Battle of the Piave, the army was near starvation, poorly equipped, suffering from dysentery and malaria.

Isidor Klaber (chapter 4) was transferred to the Italian front as soon as Italy declared war, again working as a physician's assistant. A physician with whom he worked on the Isonzo was killed by a shot to the head, and Klaber was upset that he could not ease his last minutes with morphine. The bandaging station was filled with wounded, and cholera raged amongst the men, until it was brought under control by vaccination.[39] Klaber had to ride over the karst, to reach a group of men in the valley. He came under intense fire, and was lucky to return in one piece. After Yom Kippur, he was commandeered back to the Serbian Front, and a few hours later was lying in a trench with a graze shot to the head, watching Belgrade burn. He crawled to the nearest dressing station, and was evacuated, then spent three months in a Vienna hospital. After recovery, he was sent to Komorn,[40] where he worked in a reserve hospital, making sure that all cases of suspected cholera were isolated, until autumn 1916. He was then transferred, around Rosh Hashanah, to Lemberg,[41] where he spent winter in sub-zero temperatures. In summer 1917, Klaber was transferred back to the Isonzo in preparation for the Battle of Caporetto. Men got drunk on good Italian wine, and sick from unaccustomedly fatty Italian food. He was on the Piave during the influenza pandemic of 1918, which killed twenty to fifty million people worldwide. Malaria was very common in the swampy territory. He was infected with influenza himself, and transferred back to Vienna when the war ended.[42]

Paul Amman was born in 1884 in Vienna, and worked as teacher, author and translator. His war memoir chapter about his time on the Isonzo is aptly entitled "Into the meat-grinder."[43] His group was moved from Monte Lodin into the Gail Valley, to recover and regroup after the severe winter of 1915–1916.[44] An eighteen-year-old girl could be seen clearing the frozen snow on the roof with a pickaxe. They were moved to the Sessana military reservation: "a terribly stony place. One had to search for a crevice wide enough to accommodate a man between the sharp-teethed crags of limestone." Hardly twenty-five miles away, he saw a thundering, flaming *Dies Irae* of bursting shells and shrapnel. The Italian fliers spotted his column and bombed it. They were fired upon by small-caliber artillery. Piles of Italian corpses littered the ground near the front—"Count Cadorna's ultimate offensive energies."[45] His batman Kochlöffel helped clear a tunnel for Amman and his staff, to protect their field telephone. A bombardment began, and men crowded into the tunnel for protection. Kochlöffel produced a helmet for Amman from somewhere. Engineers arrived with pickaxes and shovels to build new trenches, but were pinned down by flanking fire from British-made machine guns. Death came from many directions. They marched to the foot of Mount Hermada, and Amman and his men cautiously climbed the stony slope.

Amman and his men ascended to an artillery observer's hide-out overlooking the Adriatic Sea. On 3.00 am on June 4, 1916, the offensive began with an hour-long artillery bombardment. Amman was unimpressed with the quality of Austrian leadership, nor was he satisfied with the quality of his equipment. His men came from all over the empire: a unit of Bosnian Muslims were particularly brave, and very anti-Italian. Their telephone was reinstalled on an abandoned ammunition dump on top of a fifteen-foot-high stack of live six-centimeter shells, and camouflaged by a tarpaulin. Wrestling with fear of being hit, Amman led his men out. Their immediate goal was to silence machine gun nests on a nearby hill. At 3.00–4.00 am, the throaty thunder of guns became an unforgettable howl, and white geysers of pulverized limestone rose all around. Men started to fire, slowly at first, then more rapidly. Amman and his men felt drunk, not with slivovitz, but perhaps from *Übermut* (overconfidence). Amman's strategy did not go according to plan: despite heroic attacks, enemy machine guns were not silenced. Many Italian strongpoints defended themselves with equal bravery. The two sides exchanged grenades. Suddenly there was a metallic crash to Amman's left: he had been hit, with two deep gashes behind his left ear.

Amman was bandaged, and continued on. His company was still firing artillery beyond the crest of the nearby hill. Had they silenced the machine gun nest? He did not know. Amman found a tunnel into which many wounded had crowded. Suddenly there was an ear-splitting bang, followed by a shower of steel and rocks. The British naval guns, from their rafts near Monfalcone, had opened up. A wounded man told Amman that his men had taken the machine gun nest. One of his men was hit from behind. Guns stopped firing, and Amman remained in the tunnel surrounded by badly wounded men. When evening fell, those who could tried to break out through the Italian infantry barrage. Amman met up with Kochlöffel again, and gave him hell for getting them both lost: they both groped into home territory again. Amman's wounds were treated, and he was evacuated. His main conclusion of all this fighting was: "the nonsense of it all."[46]

Philip Flesch, a Viennese of Hungarian origin, completed his schooling in 1914, volunteering for service in March 1916. He was sent straight to the Isonzo, and fought there until the end of the war. Losses were terrible: in one day his corps lost over 200 men and it took a long time to remove all coffins from their valley. In the final battle on the Piave River, he contrasted the exhausted, badly nourished, clothed, and equipped Austro-Hungarians with the endless supply of fresh, well-equipped, and well-nourished troops from the Entente. He commented on the complete breakdown of discipline when soldiers marched home.[47]

Lilian Stern, born 1893 in Vienna, married Erwin Bader, a Viennese physician in the Austro-Hungarian Army who served on the Italian Front, in 1918. Her comments on some aspects of the class-dominated structure of the Austro-Hungarian Army are instructive.

Peacetime military training was compulsory, but a strict distinction was made between men with and without higher education. The latter had to serve for three years, were paid badly, had to live in the barracks, could not be promoted higher than sergeant even for the bravest deed, and could not become officers. By contrast, men who had completed gymnasium had only to serve for one year in peacetime. After one year of service and successfully passing an examination, they automatically became reserve officers. They had many privileges, and were entitled to a batman. Professional soldiers formed a separate class, and often belonged to the nobility. This class system was reflected throughout the World War I Austro-Hungarian Army, with the broad, uneducated classes having to bear the heaviest burden. The same class distinction prevailed, to a greater or lesser degree, in armies of other warring parties.

Erwin Bader was, at first, head of an infectious disease hospital on the front line but was then transferred to the *Meraner Scharfschützen* (Meran sharpshooters), an elite unit, in the Tyrol. Because of their bravery, this regiment was awarded special privileges: they were able to draft their own men, form their own battalions, and choose and promote their own officers regardless of age, education, or social status. Bader reported for duty in the Tyrol early 1917, at the age of twenty-six, and was welcomed in friendly fashion. However, while in the mess hall, he heard a voice saying several times, as if during normal conversation: "damn the Jews!" Bader tapped his wine glass, stood up, and explained that he was not prepared to tolerate such an insult. Men convulsed with laughter: "the doctor is a Jew? Impossible! He doesn't look or dress like a Jew at all: no caftan, no side-locks, he even has blond hair!" Bader had a difficult time proving who he was, but after that he was held in the highest esteem for his service and excellent marksmanship. Appearances were deceptive.

When Bader joined the unit, it was stationed on the mountains of Valsugana. Their rugged peaks were covered with ice and snow for a large part of the year. The trench line was located in a hidden curve at 7,000 feet, with service buildings such as mess hall and medical station scattered in woods or higher up, behind the rocks. To get from one place to the other, men had to use improvised trails, or steps chopped into the rock. When snow and ice covered everything, ropes had to be used.

Bader returned to his regiment after a one-day leave with his wife, in time to storm the mountain fortress of Melette. His battalion was ordered to dig in; every day another regiment was ordered to storm the fortress, but turned back with terrible casualties. The plan was abandoned, after 30,000 Austrian casualties. The Italians opened up heavy artillery fire on the doctor's aid station, but he worked all day on the wounded, who were carried back by medical orderlies. When firing stopped at night, he went back to look for the dead: their faces and bodies haunted him. The doctor's battalion was withdrawn and Melette taken at a later time, when the war had shifted and the fortress was of no further importance, after further fruitless battles.

One night, Bader was summoned by his orderly: "The Italians are everywhere!" The commanding officer of the Austrians had fled, but a reserve officer gathered his men and, after bitter hand-to-hand fighting, the Italians were driven back. The lieutenant took up positions at the bridge with a machine gun and opened fire, killing the retreating enemy. It turned out that two Czech officers had previously crossed the lines to the enemy and arranged for the attack to take place. Bader reported that many Czech soldiers were escaping to the enemy.

During the Piave Offensive (June 1918), Bader was on Monte Majo overlooking the Po Valley, where he could see trainload after trainload of enemy soldiers brought up from the south. The Austrians were overwhelmed. Equipment was lacking, food very scarce. Men ate horsemeat, and suicide rates were high. Bader was in Vienna recovering from an appendectomy when the Armistice was signed.[48]

Joachim Schoenfeld from Sniatyn (now Ukraine), a small town in Galicia, was drafted and underwent harsh basic training. "A *Feldrabbiner* held a service for the Jewish soldiers who were being sent out to kill other Jews."[49] He was sent to the Isonzo after first being wounded in the leg on the Russian Front. He arrived at the Isonzo in time for the Trentino offensive in June 1916. His forces took the first Italian defense but suffered heavy losses and were halted at the second defense line. They fixed bayonets, prepared for hand-to-hand combat, and Bosnians placed daggers between their teeth. They stormed forward, but the Italians had fallen back. A few days later, the Italians attacked, and the Austro-Hungarians retreated to a strong, fortified position. This useless to-and-fro fighting was to be repeated countless times.

Schoenfeld's battalion was moved to the Carnic Alps: the Austrians and the Italians faced each other in trenches blasted from rock. The Austrians' side of the mountain was steep, and to reach the top a narrow road was blasted out in the form of a narrow rock serpentine. Accidents were common, and sometimes animals bearing heavy loads slipped and fell. Sudden avalanches were frequent. Supplies, ammunition, even guns had to brought up by hand and/or pack animals, at night, to avoid triggering an artillery barrage. An electrical cable was also available. For men not on duty in trenches, deep caverns were blasted from rock to provide shelter from bombardment: There were also bombings from airplanes and gas shelling, and exploding shells sent fragments of rock in all directions.

Deep below the mountain, the Italians began to blast a tunnel leading under the Austrian lines to a large chamber, which had to be filled with sufficient dynamite to blow them, together with part of the mountain, up. Schoenfeld observed a suspicious flow of gravel from a balloon high above the mountain, leading to suspicion that Italians were tunneling their way into the cavern where the Austrian command post was located. Counter-tunneling began immediately, about half a meter below the Italian tunnel. The Italians completed their tunnel, sealing the chamber with dynamite, but Austrian sappers broke in, cut the ignition cable, and removed a huge amount of dynamite down the cableway. The Austrians then proceeded to occupy positions that the Italians had evacuated in expectation of the explosion.

Schoenfeld's regiment was relieved, and he was awarded a second medal for bravery. He was active at the sixth Battle of the Isonzo, August 6 to 17, 1916. After battle, Schoenfeld was promoted second lieutenant. He missed August 7 and 8, but was on the front on August 9, and for the Ninth Battle of the Isonzo (October 31 to November 4, 1916). He was ordered into the trenches to replace a wounded lieutenant. Their barbed wire barriers had been destroyed, but Italians were beaten back by machine gun fire, and suffered heavy losses without gaining an inch of ground. Schoenfeld was appointed communications officer. Snow, ice, cold, and fog made military activity impossible and infantry could not move. Sporadic gunfire and bombardment from the air caused many casualties.

The troops, especially Jewish soldiers, mourned the death of Kaiser Franz Joseph on November 21. At the beginning of January 1917, Schoenfeld was promoted first lieutenant, and granted a three-month study furlough, to allow him to return to university and complete his interrupted studies. The Vienna Jewish community arranged communal seders for the garrison soldiers and those in hospital on Pesach.

After his study furlough ended, Schoenfeld returned to the front: the Italians again tried to overtake the Austrian positions, but were repulsed with heavy losses. During 1917, desertions began, especially by Czechs, Poles, and representatives of other Slav nationalities. One of the men was court-martialed and condemned to death. Six comrades from his platoon were ordered from the trenches to form the firing squad.

With German help, the Austro-Hungarians won the battle of Caporetto (October 24 to November 19, 1917), which began with a heavy poison gas bombardment. The Germans and the Austrians entered the captured regions, plundering military supplies, food, and drink. Schoenfeld's regiment reached the Piave, after which a stalemate of about a year ensued. French, British, and later American troops were dispatched to join the Italians, who had suffered terrible losses and large-scale desertions. Schoenfeld took part in the failed attack on the Piave in June 1918. He was in the Tyrolean Alps when the war ended.[50]

We encountered Adolf Mechner during the Brusilov Offensive in chapter 4.[51] Mechner was transferred to the Isonzo on October 14, 1917, in time for the Battle of Caporetto, which started ten days later. He was impressed at the enormous amounts of food and wine captured: they had been hungry for many months, and did the food and drink justice. They reached the walled city of Palmanova: retreating Italians had set fire to the houses, and Mechner's troops succeeded in putting the fire out, saving the town from burning down. They found large supplies of food, cookies, candies, bread, fruits, and cheese there as well. They progressed towards the Piave, but did not advance any further.

On January 1, 1918, Mechner was promoted ensign, entitling him to a batman. German reinforcements arrived, and a large joint offensive was planned. However, at least two days before the offensive was to begin, a Czech officer swam over to the Italian side, and gave the attack plan away. Mechner was named observation officer, given binoculars, and spent a great deal of time up a tree spying on the enemy. On May 31, Mechner was hit in the hand while in his observation post and, despite pleas to remain at the front, evacuated to Udine. He was lucky; the planned offensive was a fiasco due to Czech treachery. The Austrian boats in the middle of the Piave River were hit by artillery fire, and troops who had landed on the other side of the river were attacked by artillery. The Austrians lost 100,000 men. Mechner's wound healed well, and in July 1918, he was awarded the Large Silver Medal for bravery on the Italian front. He was at home in Vienna when the war ended.[52]

Fritz Lieben (chapter 4) was transferred from the Romanian to the Isonzo Front in September 1917.[53] They crossed the bridge at Slap (Slovenia), which had been shelled by the Italians, and arrived in a narrow mountain valley. They were visited regularly by Italian Caproni aeroplanes, apparently just for observation. On October 15 they were ordered to go to Tribusa, where they remained for ten days until the Battle of Caporetto began. By nocturnal forced marches, they travelled through destroyed towns: the only living creatures that they saw were hundreds of rats. They arrived in Caporetto and travelled through other Italian towns. One night, a fire broke out in the palazzo where they were quartered. A man played the piano on the burning town square, surrounded by flames—a Danteesque scene in the midst of chaos. Lieben remarked on the psychological effect of continuous combat on the men: excitability, excessive smoking, drunkenness—all signs of what we now recognize as post-traumatic stress disorder.[54]

Teofil Reiss's description of his brief time on the Isonzo differs significantly from that of his time on the Eastern Front (chapter 4). Nowhere, in

Reiss's description of his time on the Isonzo, does Reiss call the Italians "the enemy." There is no issue with Jewish oppression by Italians. His enthusiasm and willingness to help with medical and mess duties are not present, and it is apparent that he is sick of war. He walks around drunk, something he never would have done on the Eastern Front.

Reiss was transferred to the Isonzo, and travelled to Bozen on May 5, 1918 to receive medical supplies.[55] The day after, he made the acquaintance of young Stefani von Ferdigotti and took her out that evening: "Frln. Ferdigotti is a good and serious young girl, it's a pity that I can do nothing for her." His predilection for young ladies was obviously transferred from Eastern Europe to Italy. On Tuesday, May 7, after he received an "irritating" letter from his wife Pepi, Reiss and his company marched off on a stony road. He slept in a tent despite the cold and the mountain snow. They travelled on winding roads, it snowed continuously, and the tent in which Reiss had to sleep was cold and miserable. On June 15, the battle in Montello resulted in great losses in men and horses because their position, dug into a small cave, could be seen by the enemy. Fighting continued for several days, with dog fights in the air, yielding two dead and one wounded. The situation in the Austrian front lines was terrible; provisions were miserable. "If I was a simple artilleryman I could beg food from others, but I'm ashamed to do this." After the Second Battle of Piave, the Austro-Hungarian army was finished.

After attending a one-day course on gas attacks at command on June 3, Reiss returned to the line the next day. The Italians used long-range rifles. A direct hit on the canteen blew two men apart and severely wounded sixteen others. Shooting continued all night, and Reiss found shelter in a gully. The road was full of the dead and wounded. The dead were gathered together: hands, legs, everything mixed up in one grave with at least 100–120 dead. By June 8, it had become a little quieter and the dead could be buried. "Pepi writes that she is fixing an apartment up for us: God help that I too will live there."

It rained continuously. Reiss was soaked, and developed a cold. He drank a lot of rum and walked around drunk all day. "I have nowhere to lie down: it's pouring with rain, and I am sick of life. If I were not married I would shoot myself instead of suffering and living in fear of death every minute." On June 13, they marched off at 3.00 am in the rain, en route to Monte Longara. Provisions were barley soup and polenta, no bread. Their position in a valley on the road to Monte Longara was well built. At 7.45 am, the Italians began heavy-caliber bombardment on the valley road, firing every three minutes. "It's terrible to hear the shrapnel flying, and I pray God to stand by me. I am supposed to save lives, and am myself in danger." Coffee arrived at 11.30 am, but without bread. Reiss was hungry as a horse. Because the Italians were about to open fire, Reiss's unit opened blocking fire and the Italians responded; this continued until 4.00 am. Reiss eventually feel asleep in the cave from tiredness and hunger.

On June 14, Monte Longara was quiet before the storm, which broke the next day.[56] The offensive began between 1.00 and 2.00 am, with an artillery barrage on Reiss's battery; then the entire Austrian battery opened fire, sweat dripping from their faces. This continued until 9.00 am the next day, when firing ceased. After two more days of fighting, Reiss could not take it anymore and collapsed. He was diagnosed with "shrapnel concussion" and could not feel his feet. He was invalided home, apparently suffering from hysterical paralysis, which disappeared soon thereafter.[57]

Adolf (Dolu) Rawitz (plate 4) was born 1895 in Lemberg. In his handwritten diary, he described in detail his war experiences as an officer in the Austrian army on the Isonzo, and his critical attitude towards the war.[58]

His military career began on August 16, 1915, the day he enlisted. His first few weeks were spent in "miserable shacks," and he underwent basic training near Graz from November 10 through February 20, 1916. He developed pneumonia in March 1916, and was sent to Bruck an der Mur, to convalesce in a temporary field hospital erected in a gymnasium. After a leave in Prague and Vienna, he spent Yom Kippur in Graz.

On October 26, he arrived at the Izonzo Front in Hermagor. His workload was heavy, but he felt good about setting a good example to his men. Weather was lousy, but food was good. He took an officers' course in November: "we are divided into different classes. It is proven again that justice is a theoretical concept." He underwent shooting, fighting practice, and climbing instructions. Snow fell continuously, and lodgings in straw huts were miserable. Several men were wounded by a falling rock.

Kaiser Franz Joseph died on November 21, and was replaced by Emperor Charles. Rawitz and his comrades travelled into Villach, and looked at women "like ravening wolves." Rawitz underwent gas training, attending lectures. There was a festive Christmas Eve dinner in the presence of their captain. When he left, he wished them all a pleasant evening, but warned: "You youngsters—how easily holy Christmas can turn into a wild drinking party!" As a relatively abstemious Jew, Rawitz was ashamed when he saw how drunk some of the men became. On December 28, the men packed up in preparation for transportation to the front. By December 31, they were on Mount Planina (Slovenia): "our position there appears quite simple and primitive."[59]

On January 6 [1917], a man fell down the mountain, and could not be saved because of lack of torches and ropes. The first-aid patrol arrived too late: they brought him back dead. Snowfall was heavy and continuous, and men had to shovel a path to the unit's headquarters. By January 18, the snow stopped, but thunderstorms began instead:

> Thunder and lightning, just like mid-summer. To this is added the noise of thundering avalanches rolling down from high mountains around us. It's really frightening. When I go out at night to inspect our positions in the milky darkness, I can't see more than two paces in front of me: I hop like a blind man, and, in my mind's eye, see the ghostly appearance of the "white death." What will happen to us if it continues like this? We have little to eat, and when scanty provisions from the front are finished, we will be in a really bad way. Let's hope that things won't get this bad!

By January 19, all precipitation had stopped, the wind died down, and the landscape was beautiful: "The skies were bright and clear, and the surroundings so peaceful that my footsteps disturbed the silence." On February 14, Rawitz was promoted sergeant. On March 6, he and his men were warned that the Italians were preparing an offensive: spotlights soon appeared in nearby mountains, aimed at several Austrian positions. Rifle fire and hand grenades were unceasing. The Italians fired right into the Austrian positions in their caves with rifles and hand-grenades. "These cursed Italians don't even need to aim!" During subsequent withdrawal, many men were split up from their units, and wounded. By April 7, Rawitz was in a bad mood, caused by the failed Austrian offensive, increasing rain, snow, and wind, and spring that refused to come. He was given building work that was beyond his strength. On May 1, Rawitz was promoted officer cadet:

> I'm not sure who is more pleased, myself or those who chuckle when they see me. In two days' time, more enemy activity is predicted. The fact that success isn't assured scares me, and makes me tense. On one side, fear of the price of failure, on the other, ambition and my aspiration for a successful outcome. My ambition, under the existing circumstances, appears pathological, or at the very least sinful, to me.

From May 1 to 2, Rawitz undertook an intelligence tour of the surrounding area. He descended into a narrow depression, a kind of an avalanche delta, with huge accumulations of snow fallen from the mountains. From there, he continued with his men to the east slope of the adjacent mountain, where the enemy had not penetrated. A sudden flight of a night-owl hiding between the trees frightened them. After a short rest, they marched west, looking for a suitable lookout point. Rawitz arranged their uncomfortable observation post in a small crater created around a tree by snow that had melted and poured down. He was embedded in ice to his shoulders, so that he could not even turn around. At 9.00 am, after seeing everything there was to see; he and his men descended carefully, partly by creeping, partly by rolling,

After another observation trip on May 5, Rawitz was so exhausted that he did not want to work anymore. Their activity did not go as planned. They climbed up too late, reached the wrong place, and could not cut the enemy wire. Although they were seen and shot at, his group returned unharmed, and eight members of the trip were put up for medals. Rawitz's desire for a short rest after this inspection never came true:

> I'm not a lazy person, but when they constantly burden me with activities that are above and beyond, while others do almost nothing, it's too much for me and I feel exhausted. From yesterday my toes ache terribly: perhaps they got frostbitten on a recent trip.

On July 12, Rawitz reported from Mount Seluggio. Improvements and building on their position were necessary, because of continuous shelling. Between June 10 and July 6, 1917, Rawitz was on leave in Prague. He returned to the same frequent shelling of his position. On September 16, Rawitz and his men were transferred to another mountain position: from the heights, their outlooks could observe the enemy's trenches. On October 1 the weather changed, there came fog, snow, and heavy rain, which made the watchtower's job very difficult.

On October 24, the battle of Caporetto (Karfreit) began:

> The mountain, soaked in our blood, is now in our hands. Our forces have taken about 50,000 prisoners, among them over 700 officers. A large amount of weapons and war material has fallen into our hands, including 300 cannons. We announce our victory![60]

On October 28, Rawitz and his unit crossed the swollen streams with great difficulty, reaching the border road. There was deep fog: clothes were soaked through and began to freeze. They continued to pursue the enemy, battling an Italian rearguard. They found a pig, which was ceremoniously butchered. "The soldiers' faces shone with grease and enjoyment. Wine was poured." In the afternoon they continued, reaching Ovaro, and lodged in a hospital. Several of the men finished the hospital wine very rapidly, and staggered back to their unit.

By November 1, Rawitz reported that soldiers were becoming brutalized from too much food and, especially, too much wine. Several men were missing, having fallen asleep after they became drunk. They grabbed provisions from retreating Italians at the railway station. At the bridge crossing above Tagliamento, the Italian rearguard suffered losses. Rawitz's unit was ordered to drive the enemy north and south of Ampezzo hills. A unit of mountain cannons chased the Italian riflemen away. The unit changed direction to the northern heights of the road. To enter or leave their positions they had to pass through a curtain of Italian cannon fire. With luck, Rawitz led his unit away from the fire unharmed. On November 3, the unit attacked the southern Ampezzo hills, with another unit clearing out the surrounding heights. The Italians tried unsuccessfully to blow up the bridge. Rawitz's unit used wagons to ascend the mountain. The ascent was difficult, impeded by enemy attack. Because of unfavorable topography, Rawitz and his group were sent to the other side of the ravine, to attack the enemy from the rear. The battle ended in confusion. Afterwards, there were terrible difficulties associated with carrying the many dead and wounded down the mountain.

On November 4, Rawitz's unit had to cross the Tagliamento River and attack the nearby heights. He commanded the front, and men ascended the steep slope with difficulty. They forced the enemy to the edge of the forested heights by cannon fire. "Scandalous flight of Corporal Alber and his men." They clung to the slope until reinforcements arrived. Rawitz was surprised at the ferocity of enemy machine guns. They pursued the enemy until they took the valley. On November 5, Rawitz was awarded the Large Silver Medal for Bravery.

On November 6 at 2.00 pm, Rawitz's unit left Ampezzo. There was a traffic jam on the way, due to "stupid instructions given by high command." They advanced to the left bank of the Piave, taking large numbers of Italian prisoners, many completely drunk. Rawitz commented on the "Roman pride" of Italian officers. They advanced to the left bank of the Piave. The road was under fire from machine guns and shells. They could not advance further, because explosions of the giant ammunition stores continued until 2.00 am, and spent the night in mountain huts on the heights overlooking the Piave, eating cheese and smoking. Rawitz commented acidly on general plundering by Austro-Hungarian soldiers who had not seen such food and drink for years. His entire unit was completely drunk on Italian wine. "Corporal Firipass has to be dumped on a wagon like a slaughtered pig." The population joined in the looting: American flour and sacks of coffee lay in the streets.

Rawitz's unit was ordered to help block the Valley at Longarone, to stop the enemy from moving north. In Castellavazzo, they were informed that the Edelweiss Division and a Württemberg alpine division had broken through the Tramonti road to Longarone and taken prisoner an entire Italian division. On November 12 the unit marched off from Longarone. Traffic was blocked because command had not taken the blown up bridge into consideration, so it took five hours to march five kilometers. There was no order, and no proper division of duties by command. Mail finally arrived and a great deal of boozing followed; an officers meeting was called to discuss the drinking problem. The unit travelled on, arriving in Feltre on November 28.

On November 30 they departed for Terza, near the old front. Due to usual bad organization, ammunition did not arrive in time and artillery did not arrive at all, forcing the Austrians to attack gunfire with bayonets. Italian fliers bombed the army, and there were huge traffic jams on the roads, with columns five men wide blocking lines of cars bringing gas canisters, large-caliber shells, and mortar batteries. A new breakthrough, planned for December 1, proved unsuccessful. They arrived in Terza at 11.00 pm, and quartered in the destroyed town.[61]

On December 1, they continued on to Roncegno. Everything was bungled. They reached Roncegno at 4.00 pm, but had to wait for six hours until they were assigned a place to sleep. After a twenty-four-hour rest, and a "small adventure with our innkeeper's daughter," they travelled on, but there was another mix-up. After another rest, Rawitz's unit received instructions that they were being replaced.

From this point onwards, Rawitz's diary gradually becomes more disorganized; by 1918, entries are irregular, and interspersed with personal correspondence. On January 1, 1918, he reported an attack in the Adige Valley. "The innkeeper, Alma Sofia, and the girl from the kiosk . . ." On March 1, he was still on the mountain, reporting the danger of avalanches. After leave in Vienna and Lemberg, he was back with his unit by March 27, in time for Pesach. There was severe shelling by the superior Italian cannons. Rawitz complained bitterly that command did not allow the Austrians to prepare properly. "It's a disgrace: if they ever had to mount an offensive, it wouldn't succeed, and the men will be the whipping boys." Their division was strengthened by German storm troops.

The Second Battle of the Piave was mounted on June 15 and, to no one's surprise, failed. One of Rawitz unit's two thirty-pounders was useless even before the attack began, and the second did not fire properly in presence of the Italians' much better firepower. Losses were heavy, including many among the Kaiser's "elite troops." On July 27, Rawitz's unit was relieved. They travelled to Trieste, where he spent "some pleasant social hours in the cellar with Magdalena." He spent time through September 27 alternating between leave and scouting duty on the nearby mountain. Thick fog descended upon everything.

> We quickly grasped that we could make hay while the sun shone, and a happy grape harvest ensued. In pots, steel helmets, baskets, we brought the wonderful fruit over to where we were positioned. I was there as well, and although each time I passed through our columns I was soaked with water from the leaves, I didn't pass up picking grapes with my own hands and, as a natural result, tasting them. I might have gone on and on tasting them if evening hadn't fallen and we had to stop. Our mood was happy and joyful, as if we were drunk. There is magic in grape harvesting.

The Italians began their final attack on the Piave on 24 October. Rawitz was bitter that this was their reward for the breakthrough at Caporetto the previous year. The Austrian suggestion for an armistice looked to him like unconditional surrender.

> The Italians seem very sure of themselves, but despite this their methods are despicable and cowardly. They approach our positions with Austrian hats and steel helmets during the day, and try with hand gestures, and cries to entice the guards to surrender and cross over the lines. Casualties are heavy.
>
> This swinishness should already have ended. Men stand around indifferently; their mood is like that of prisoners. Each one feels abandoned by orders from the rear. If disorder in guard duty doesn't change in the near future, I cannot be responsible for the consequences. Evacuation begins. They are burning documents at command. Preparations for what is called an "ordered retreat."

On November 3, Rawitz received news of the impending Armistice, but apparently, the Italians didn't wish to abide by it. They dispatched messengers for negotiations. The Austrian forces must lay down their weapons and leave their positions, retaining only personal arms, and retreat north, regardless of the Italian forces approaching in the same direction. "Conduct of the Italians proves that Austria has surrendered unconditionally, Chaos. Sauve qui peut."

Rawitz gained the impression that the commanders were running away, leaving the front-line soldiers to remain self-sacrificingly at their posts, "obey orders exactly," and be taken prisoner. "The war has ended for us; we remain alive, but with bitter feelings. For what purpose, and in whose name, did we spill our blood? Perhaps we were destined to survive the present chaos to live better and freer lives." Roads were packed with retreating armies, and civilians were hostile. "Great joy amongst Czechs. Scandalous behavior of Czech officers. They befriend the soldiers. Feeling of honor—cowardice. Exploitation of incidental gains." By November 6, the number of prisoners was so large that Italians had no idea what to do with them: they turned into an undisciplined rabble. Without any discipline, the Bosnians attacked their fellow-prisoners' huts, destroyed them, and set fire to the wood. There was fury about the disgraceful implementation of the armistice. "They have betrayed us and sold us in an abominable fashion."

Rawitz commented on prisoner camp life:

> I run around like a caged bird. I hate the grey wall preventing me from looking out into the distance. Numbers of prisoners get larger and larger and tents sprout up like mushrooms after the rain. It's scary to see human waves moving to and fro. The Italian guard is becoming stricter, and they keep watch over us with machine guns. In everything they do, including their relation with us, they reveal their inborn cowardice, and fear of their former enemy whom they haven't succeeded in overcoming on the field of battle.

Rawitz joined up with a Polish division on November 11. They were transferred onto trains, with Czech officers and men, traveling through Italy to the Adriatic coast, which they reached on November 16. Rawitz continues:

> My first weeks of imprisonment are filled with unpleasant incidents caused by dirty politics. I am powerless, because of lack of experience. Conduct of the current commander of the Polish army, who

calls himself "democratic," in relation to the Jews is more than disgraceful. It's clear that he and his comrades will not want Jews in their future army, apparently for the good of their party.

By November 29, Rawitz's November 23 request to be received into the Polish army had not yet received a reply, while his comrades' applications were approved within twenty-four hours. In this way, he was informed that anti-Jewish antagonism did not allow him to be an equal member of the army. He asked that his request be nullified.

> Relinquishing hope to return home more rapidly didn't appear as bad as I had originally thought. My personal and national honor remains without any personal feelings of guilt. Physically I am a prisoner, but spiritually I am free.

On December 6 Rawitz became ill with fever and pharyngitis, and was transferred to an Italian field hospital in Caserta. "No one here is seriously ill, and yet almost every day someone dies in our unit." Rawitz remained in captivity, in reasonable conditions, through early 1919, and was finally repatriated on March 22, 1919.[62]

Dolu Rawitz's diary is unique in describing his experiences as an Italian prisoner after the Armistice. He reports antisemitism in the Polish Army, and several perceived cases of Czech perfidy. Sated on Italian provisions they had not seen for years, and suffering from severe privations after the Battle of Caporetto, the Austro-Hungarian army disintegrated after the unsuccessful Battle of the Piave. Although, with the aid of Germany, they had won the Battle of Caporetto, a combination of exhaustion, lack of supplies, and the greatly increased Entente forces brought in for the 1918 Battle of Piave was too much for them.

Paul Amman mentions the bravery of Bosnian soldiers: this is in direct contrast to reports of Bosnian cowardice by Bernhard Bardach (chapter 4). Descriptions of Czech betrayal by Edwin Bader, Adolf Mechner, and Dolu Rawitz correspond to those by many other soldiers. It is difficult to judge the veracity of statements about "Czech treachery." While this did occur, it was perhaps not as marked as some diaries and memoirs lead one to think. Individual opinions may have been colored by factors other than those of purely military nature (chapter 1). At any rate, sweeping statements about Slav or Czech treachery in the Habsburg army must be taken cum grano salis.

The war correspondent of *Egyenlőség*, Dr. Ludwig Magyar, gives a Hungarian's point of view, with the following reports from the Isonzo Front, published on February 27, 1916.

In his first story, Magyar recounts that Hungarian soldiers built a camp in the limestone karst plateau near Trieste, with barracks and stone and wooden houses in which to rest after battle. Everything necessary for the life of a soldier was available: a coffee house, an inn, a movie theater, a bath, a relaxation room, officers' quarters, a smokehouse, a bakery, a store, a hospital, and a sickbay. When Magyar was guided through this "fairy tale town," and shown its beautiful houses, with streets large and small, his guide, an artillery captain from Budapest, said that there was a Catholic church in every barrack, and even a Jewish prayer house—a makeshift synagogue in the middle of the karst rock, in a place where soldiers could rest, a few thousand paces behind the front. It was simple, bare house made of wood, with benches inside made of hardly shaved planks. Italian planes flew over, shells exploded behind and shrapnel in front of it. Every Friday night candles were lit, and each Saturday one could hear the solemn prayers of Jewish soldiers. Each week the rabbi from the nearest Honvéd division held services, and the temple was always filled.

Magyar asked, how this prayer house was built and who was responsible for this? The story was simple. Jewish soldiers had built it themselves in their leisure hours. Now they had a chaplain, they were happy that they could enter the prayer room and pray together. When war finally ended, liturgical objects would be brought home.

The central character of the second story was Dr. Isidor Rosenfeld, a Hungarian lawyer with a wife and children. The war had made him into an artilleryman: he had already been awarded a medal for bravery, and helped eject the Italians from San Michele.

The Italians had prepared their third offensive, which began on Yom Kippur. Rosenfeld, instead of praying and fasting, had to serve as artilleryman on this holy day. The bombardment destroyed telephone cables, which had to be repaired. On the firing line, every artilleryman had to be at his post. Rosenfeld put on his tallit, prayed, and repaired the telephone communications. He stood on the firing line and prayed, observed the enemy and prayed, did his duty and prayed, shells exploded near him and he prayed. He fought and fasted, repaired telephones and fasted, gave reports and fasted. His comrades all looked with respect at the artilleryman with the tallit who remained a Jew, through bombardment, mind-numbing shelling, and the roaring, howling concert of explosions.[63]

By May 1918, the condition of Austro-Hungarian troops on the Italian front had become impossible Chief of the General Staff Field Marshal Svetosar Boroević (1856–1920) noted shortages of everything, especially meat, fat, and flour. It was impossible to feed the troops properly, all were undernourished. He stated that, without increased rations and other supplies, no significant progress could be made. Hungary did not provide its necessary share, and expected supplies from Ukraine had not yet arrived. Increased bread rations were, therefore, under the current conditions, impossible. There was also a severe shortage of horse fodder. As noted above, after the Second Battle of the Piave, the Austro-Hungarian army was finished; within the ensuing months the empire disintegrated into its separate national constituents.[64]

Ottoman Front

Although the Ottoman Front was predominantly Turkish domain, Central Powers soldiers also served there. Mention has been made in my previous book of Dr. Natan Wolf of Germany, who served in the Battle of El Kafr in 1918.[65]

The impetus for sending the Austro-Hungarian troops to the Turkish Front came from Enver Pasha.[66] After preparation and outfitting in Slovenia, a contingent of artillery, motorized troops, and medical corps consisting of twenty-two officers and 813 men were sent to Beer Sheba.[67] These included a small number of Jewish soldiers who functioned as commandos. Austro-Hungarian citizens living in Palestine were also recruited.

Egyenlőség describes the arrival of two k.u.k. formations in Jerusalem in summer 1916:

> The city was decorated with Turkish, Austrian, Hungarian, and German flags, and soldiers entered the city to the strains of *Gott erhalte*.[68] A festive banquet was organized by the Lämelschule that evening, with representatives from the consular corps and all branches of the Central Powers present.[69] The Jerusalem Professor and k.u.k. Chaplain M. D. Gross arranged leave for all Jewish k.u.k. soldiers the day after to show them around holy sites of the city, and they were all presented with prayer books and tefillin.
>
> Soon after them, the second k.u.k. division arrived, containing three Jewish officers and many non-commissioned officers. A festive service was organized in the Lämelschule, and it was edifying to see

all the Jewish soldiers reciting the prayer for the Kaiser in Hebrew.

Several Austro-Hungarian Jewish soldiers were killed in Palestine. The first casualty among them was the Hungarian Nándor Kohn, who died of septicemia after a knee wound following the battle of El Arish in July 1916.

Twenty-two-year-old Hungarian artilleryman Lajos Gonda was killed by shrapnel during the First Battle of Gaza in March, 1917. A comrade wrote to Gonda's parents:

> We buried him under a palm tree and stood at his grave broken-hearted, reciting *kaddish*. Just before he died, he asked us to inform his dear parents of his end: he was fully conscious, and recited the *Sh'ma* just before he died.

Twenty-one-year-old artilleryman Nissim Behmoiras (Benshiras), a Sephardic Jew from Adrianople, who worked in the k.u.k artillery in Palestine as a translator, was wounded by machine-gun fire on July 20, 1917, and died of his wounds a few days later.[70] Delegations from the German, Austrian, and Turkish armies attended his funeral. Chaplain Horovicz (see chapter 6) gave the funeral oration, followed by a military salute. Thus ended the hopeful life of a twenty-year old. He was buried on the Mount of Olives.[71]

Celebrating holidays in Palestine and its environs must have been a special experience, as described in an October 1917 issue of *Egyenlőség*. Soldiers on the Sinai Front were given leave to celebrate High Holidays and Sukkot courtesy of chaplain Benjamin Horowicz. Initial services took place in the large officers' tent, equipped like a prayer locale and held in presence of the General Staff under the leadership of General Kress von Kressenstein.[72] In consideration of large numbers of Turkish soldiers and officers, a Turkish officer translated the prayers from Hebrew and German into Turkish. At the conclusion of the service, prayers were said for the Sultan and the Kaisers Wilhelm II and Charles. The next day, the chaplain accompanied by officers visited the Gaza Front, where the commanding k.u.k. Captain Arensdorf placed a beautiful garden at their disposal for other services. After explanation of the significance of the coming festivals, *mincha* (afternoon service) was recited under the heavens. Austrian, Hungarian, and German officers obtained leave to travel to Jerusalem. Soldiers on the front were given leave to celebrate the holidays in a nearby Jewish colony.

Many Jewish soldiers and officers were present for services in various Jerusalem synagogues. A large group gathered in the synagogue in German

Square. On the second day of Rosh Hashanah, *mincha* was recited at the Holy Wall. On evenings after Rosh Hashanah and Yom Kippur, the Austrian and Hungarian officers and soldiers were guests of Rabbi Horowicz. On the first night of Sukkot (Tabernacles), the officers gathered in the *sukkot* (booths) on German Square, to celebrate the festival.[73]

Conclusion

Although the Austro-Hungarian army entered the war disorganized and improperly equipped, and was driven out of Serbia and Western Galicia and Bukowina during the first months of the war, bravery was not lacking. The Tyrol and Isonzo campaigns represented perhaps the most brutal terrains of the war, and the Austro-Hungarian armies came very close to occupying Venice after the Battle of Caporetto. They were only prevented from doing so by the shortages caused by the blockade, and infusions of fresh troops from other Entente countries, which they could not hope to match. Except for the last few months of war when the empire came apart and individual diary reports of Czech treachery such as by Lilian Bader, there is no clear difference in the patriotism and bravery of Jewish soldiers of individual nationalities. Although cognizant of bad leadership on all levels, Egon Kisch, a Prague Jew, fought as bravely as any man in the midst of the slaughter that was the 1914 Serbian front.

Endnotes

1. Judeo-Spanish, or Ladino, is a Romance language derived from Old Spanish.
2. C. Clark, *The Sleepwalkers: How Europe Went to War in 1918* (New York: Harper Collins, 2013).
3. H. Strachan, *The First World War*, vol. 1, *To Arms* (Oxford: Oxford University Press, 2003), 335–347.
4. P. C. Appelbaum, "Infectious Diseases during the First World War," paper presented at Perspectives of the Great War International Conference "World War One," Queen Mary's College, August 10–14, 2014.
5. E. E. Kisch, *"Schreib das auf, Kisch!" Das Kriegstagebuch von Egon Erwin Kisch* (Berlin: Erich Reiss Verlag, 1930), 7–9.
6. M. Rauchensteiner, *The First World War and the End of the Habsburg Monarchy, 1914–1918* (Vienna, Cologne, and Weimar: Böhlau Verlag, 2014), 185–191.
7. Franz Werfel (1890–1945) was an Austrian Bohemian novelist; Robet Musil (1880–1942) was an Austrian philosophical writer.
8. Kisch, *"Schreib das auf,"* 11–27. Kol Nidrei (All Vows) is an introductory prayer on Yom Kippur eve.
9. A recipe for viral, bacterial, and parasitic fecal-oral infections.
10. Kisch, *"Schreib das auf,"* 27–52.

11 On October 6, 1908, Austria-Hungary announced annexation of Bosnia and Herzegovina, territories under Austro-Hungarian rule but formally within the sovereignty of the Ottoman Empire since 1878. This almost became a casus belli.
12 Most likely, bacterial dysentery, spread by contaminated water.
13 Kisch, *"Schreib das auf,"* 53–84.
14 Count István Tisza de Borosjenő et Szeged (1861–1918) was Prime Minister of Hungary between 1913 and 1917.
15 The Drina and Sava are tributaries of the Danube.
16 Kisch, *"Schreib das auf,"* 85–116.
17 Sremska Rača (Serbia).
18 Kisch, *"Schreib das auf,"* 116–132.
19 Signs of emotional lability probably due to post-traumatic stress disorder.
20 Probably *in Bosnia Herzegovina.*
21 Kisch, *"Schreib das auf,"* 132–145.
22 Ibid., 146–168.
23 Ibid., 169–195.
24 Ibid., 195–220.
25 Futog, suburb of Novi Sad (Serbia), near the Hungarian border.
26 Epidemic louse-borne typhus was so prevalent on both sides of the front during 1914 that the Central Powers did not return to press the attack that winter, for fear of being decimated (see note 4).
27 A killed cholera vaccine, administered repeatedly, offered only low-grade protection.
28 Žabalj (Serbia).
29 The Banat is a geographical and historical region in Central Europe currently divided among three countries: the eastern part lies in Western Romania; the western part in North-Eastern Serbia; and a small northern part lies within South-Eastern Hungary. Before 1918, it was part of the Austro-Hungarian Empire.
30 Kisch, *"Schreib das auf,"* 221–294.
31 Bilyi Kamin (Ukraine).
32 Translated into Hebrew and cited in D. Canaani, *Le'Nogah 'Ets Rakav* (Merhavia: Sifriyat Po'alim, 1950), 19.
33 G. Abramson, *Hebrew Writing of the First World War* (London and Portland, OR: Vallentine-Mitchell, 2008), 68–91.
34 I. Klaber, *Selbstbiographie* (New York: Archives of the Leo Baeck Institute, [1940]), ME 1451, 5–11. Pages are numbered by hand in the bottom right corner.
35 B. Weider, "Napoleon and the Jews," aish.com, accessed March 11, 2021, http://www.aish.com/jl/h/h/48945221.html; "Rome's Ghetto: The Ancient Jewish District," *Virtual Roma*, accessed March 11, 2021, http://roma.andreapollett.com/S1/roma-c9.htm.
36 N. Ausubel, *Pictorial History of the Jewish People from Bible Times to Our Own Day throughout the World* (New York: Crown Publishers, Inc., 1959), 198–199.
37 C. Roth, *The History of the Jews of Italy* (Philadelphia, PA: Jewish Publication Society of America, 1946), 457–484; idem (ed.), *Encyclopedia Judaica* (Jerusalem: Keter Publishing House, 1971), vol. 7, 955, vol. 11, 1559, and vol. 12, 1523–1524; R. M. Dainotto, "The Italian Risorgimento and the Questione Romana," in *The Italian Jewish Experience*, ed. T. P. Di Napoli (New York: Stony Brook University Press, 2000), 108–109; Ausubel, *Pictorial History of the Jewish People*, 200.
38 Roth, *Encyclopedia Judaica*, vol. 9, 1127, vol. 11, 1559 and 1575, vol. 13, 1379, and vol. 14, 1114; N. R. M. de Lange, *Atlas of the Jewish World* (New York: Facts on File, 1992),

64; P. Briganti, *Il Contributo Militare degli Ebrei italiani alla Grande Guerra 1915–1918* (Turin: Silvio Zamorani, 2009), 1–105 and 169–218; Idem (ed.), "It Contributo Militare degli Ebrei Italiani alla Grande Guerra," Proceedings of a conference held in the Center for Historical Studies, Bologna, December 6–9 (Bologna: Centro di Studi Storico-Militari "Generale Gino Bernadini", 2010), 1–14; V. Wilcox, "Between Faith and Nation: Italian Jewish Soldiers in the Great War," in *The Jewish Experience of the First World War*, ed. E. Madigan and G. Reuveni (London: Palgrave Macmillan, 2019), 188–192; Lia Toaff, personal communication. Battle of Gorizia (Sixth Battle of the Isonzo): August 6–17, 1916; Battle of Vittorio-Veneto: October 24–November 3, 1918.

39 A safe water supply and sewage disposal system would also have been necessary.
40 Komárom (Hungary).
41 Lviv (Ukraine).
42 Klaber, *Selbstbiographie*, 5–11.
43 P. Amman, *Memoirs and Reminiscences. Into the Meat Grinder. Isonzo: May 25 to June 4, 1917* (New York: Leo Baeck Institute [1918]), AR 7157, box 1, folder 3.
44 Unless otherwise mentioned, all locations are in modern-day Italy.
45 Count Luigi Cadorna (1850–1927), Chief of Staff of the Italian army during the first part of World War I, was known to be brutal and careless with men's lives. He was sacked after the Battle of Caporetto.
46 Amman, *Memoirs*, 1–117.
47 P. Flesch, *Mein Leben in Deutschland vor und nach dem 30 Januar 1933* (New York: Archives of the Leo Baeck institute, 1942), ME 132, 2–3. The Second Battle of the Piave River (June 15–23, 1918), was a decisive victory for the Italians (bolstered by other members of the Entente) against the Austro-Hungarian army, and a decisive blow to the empire.
48 L. Bader, *One Life is Not Enough: Autobiographic Vignettes* (New York: Leo Baeck Institute, 1956), ME 784, 91–99.
49 A unique feature of World War I. Jews served in all armies (chapter 1).
50 J. Schoenfeld, *Shtetl Memoirs: Jewish Life in Galicia under the Austro-Hungarian Empire and in the Reborn Poland 1898–1939* (Hoboken, NJ: Ktav Publishing House, 1985), 142–174.
51 A. Mechner, *My Family Biography, 1897–1984* (New York: Archives of the Leo Baeck Institute, 1981), ME 822.
52 Mechner, *My Family Biography*, 116–127.
53 F. Lieben, *Aus der Zeit meines Lebens. Erinnerungen* (New York: Leo Baeck Institute, 1960), ME 207a.
54 Ibid., 116-123.
55 Bolzano (Italy).
56 The Austrian Offensive, also called the battle of Solstice, began on June 15 and expanded onto the Plateau of Asagio, location of Monte Longara. It ended on June 23 with a decisive victory for the Italian army.
57 T. Reiss, *Tagebuch eines jüdischen Soldaten* (New York: Archives of the Leo Baeck Institute, [1919]), DS 135 A93 R45. Hebrew translation published in 1995 by Reiss's son and other relatives. T. T. Reiss, *In the Line of Fire: a Soldier's Diary 1914–1918* (n.p.: Createspace Independent Publishing Platform, 2016), 310–324. Page numbers in the German original.
58 A. Rawitz, *Diary of Adolf Dolu Rawitz* (New York: Archives of the Leo Baeck Institute, [1918]), ME 1340. A Hebrew version (Jerusalem: Leo Baeck Institute [2000-2003] has been used for pagination.
59 Ibid., 1–11.

60 The Battle of Caporetto (Twelfth Battle of the Isonzo, the Battle of Kobarid or Karfreit) was fought between Italy and the Central Powers between October 24 and November 19, 1917, near Kobarid (now in North-Western Slovenia, then part of the Austrian Littoral). The Austro-Hungarian forces, reinforced by the German units, were able to break into the Italian front line and rout the Italian forces opposing them. The battle demonstrated the effectiveness of storm troopers and infiltration tactics. Use of poison gas by the Germans played a key role in the collapse of the Italian Second Army.
61 Rawitz, *Diary*, 12–22.
62 Ibid., 23–61.
63 "Bilder vom Isonzo," *Dr. Bloch's Österreichische Wochenschrift*, March 24, 1916, 206–207.
64 Österreichisches Staatsarchiv/Kriegsarchiv/FA/NFA/HMK-AK/AGK do. 5. Armee AK-Isonzo 955, vol. 10, 67–68.
65 P. C. Appelbaum, *Loyal Sons. Jews in the German Army in the Great War* (London and Portland, OR: Vallentine-Mitchell), 196–197.
66 P. Jung, *Der k.u.k. Wüstenkrieg: Österreich-Ungarn im Vorderen Orient 1915–1918* (Graz, Vienna, and Cologne: Styrian Verlag, 1992). Ismail Enver Pasha (1881–1922) was the Turkish War Minister and one of the principal architects of the Armenian genocide.
67 G. Sajó and R.-T. Fischer, "Die jüdischen Soldaten des Kaisers im heiligen Land," in *Weltuntergang. Jüdisches Leben und Sterben im ersten Weltkrieg*, ed. M. G. Patka (Vienna, Graz, and Klagenfurt: Styria Premium, 2014), 120.
68 *Gott erhalte Franz den Kaiser*, the old Imperial anthem.
69 A synagogue founded with Austro-Hungarian support.
70 Previously in Bulgaria, now Edirne (Turkey).
71 A. Gaisbauer, "K.u.k. jüdische Gräber in der Wüste und am Ölberg," *David*, June/July 1991, 14; Jung, *Der k.u.k. Wüstenkrieg*, 171. Sajó and Fischer, "Die jüdischen Soldaten des Kaisers," 123–125; N. Schwake, "Nissim Bemoiras," in *Weltuntergang. Jüdisches Leben und Sterben im ersten Weltkrieg*, ed. M. G. Patka (Vienna, Graz, and Klagenfurt: Styria Premium, 2014), 218.
72 General Friedrich Freiherr Kress von Kressenstein (1870–1948) was a member of the group of German officers who assisted in the direction of World War I Ottoman army.
73 "Feiertage an der Sinaifront," *Dr. Blochs Österreichische Wochenschrift*, November 23, 1917, 743–744.

CHAPTER 6

Austro-Hungarian *Feldrabbiner*: Tallit, Torah, and Tobacco

With approximately 350,000 Jews fighting for the Habsburg Empire during the Great War (chapter 2), Austro-Hungary quickly realized the value of Jewish chaplains, and began to integrate them into the army, first on the Eastern, then the Italian Front. Their number would, during the course of the war, exceed 100 (see below). By contrast, approximately 100,000 Jews fought for Germany, but the German government was slower in supporting and giving rank to their approximately forty-five chaplains and chaplains assistants.[1] Tsarist Russia, with approximately 180,000 Jews serving in the army, didn't permit Jewish chaplains.[2] Italy, Austro-Hungary's other main protagonist, had about 5,000-6,000 Jewish soldiers serving, a large number relative to approximately 35,000 Jews living in Italy in 1915 (chapter 5). Despite low numbers, soldiers were provided with chaplains by the Italian government.[3] Austro-Hungary differed from other protagonists by presence of imams for Bosnian Moslem soldiers. Unique interactions between chaplains of different faiths will be explored in this chapter.

Austrian chaplains were exposed to many non-Jewish nationalities living in their theater of operations. This association has received scant attention in the literature. German chaplains wrote at length about presence (or absence) of antisemitism in the army, whereas—as will be seen—this was largely absent from the writings of Austro-Hungarian chaplains. Antisemitism was present in the Habsburg Army, but, despite lack of a formal *Burgfrieden* (chapter 3), was officially censored, increasing noticeably only during the last two years when it became clear that the war couldn't be won, and scapegoats were sought. There was also no *Judenzählung* (Jewish census): the Austro-Hungarian Army rejected a similar decree, due in part to efforts of Rabbi Adolf Altmann.[4] Jewish civilians in Eastern Europe saw the Central Powers' armies—German and

Austro-Hungarian—as liberators, compared to Russian oppressors. This was to be turned on its head two decades later, when these Jewish communities were destroyed during the Holocaust by the same armies they had seen as liberators a few decades earlier. The Central Powers' armies encountered Eastern European Jewry on the eve of its destruction. The tsarist oppression of Russian Jews provided the Habsburg Jews with a potent reason to go to war, to free their oppressed brethren in the Pale of Settlement.

There were striking differences in the way the Jewish Austro-Hungarian chaplains were treated by authorities compared to their German counterparts. The Austro-Hungarian chaplains were commissioned captains, with specially designed uniforms. On parade, they wore black clothing and a black half-top hat with two-centimeter-wide gold braid; in the field, field-grey with black velvet collar tabs. The rank of captain (ninth-grade officer status) was denoted by three narrow gold cuff borders.[5] Official salary, access (where possible) to officially authorized kosher kitchens, even for Russian prisoners of war (plate 5), and provision with ritual prayer objects to celebrate services were routine.[6] The fact that the army facilitated holiday services, and went to great lengths to provide kosher catering, encouraged Jewish soldiers in Monarchical loyalty. Where there were no Jewish communities, such as on the Italian front, the soldiers themselves set up kosher kitchen facilities and provisions. That so many Austro-Hungarian Jewish soldiers felt an obligation to keep kosher while serving in the field, reflects the presence of large numbers of Orthodox Jews from Galicia, Bukowina, and Northern Hungary.[7] In some cases, men attempted to exist on bread and water until they were able to obtain kosher food.[8] As reported by Rabbi Tauber, kosher food was not available for long periods and—to sustain life—Orthodox Jews were forced, against their will, to eat non-kosher food, giving rise to severe religious conflicts. In the German army, kosher food was provided from private communities, usually on chaplains' initiative; most soldiers came from Reform or assimilated backgrounds where keeping kosher was not a priority. Of all chaplains in the German Army, only Rabbi Alexander Winter reported refusing non-kosher food, existing on bread and tea until kosher food became available.[9]

Apart from this difference, the duties of Austro-Hungarian and German chaplains were similar: spiritual care, holding services, conducting burials, visiting the sick, providing care packages, and reading material. Both groups displayed "über-patriotism" of their respective fatherlands, which might today seem ridiculous, but must be taken with the spirit of time and place. Looked at with spectacles of the time, the Jews were perhaps the only Habsburg subjects who fully accepted the real nature of the Monarchy in a supranational Empire.[10] Nowhere have I placed words in their mouths which they themselves did not write. This "über-patriotism" can also be seen in the German Army, for example, in Rabbi Bruno Italiener's sermon during August 1914.[11]

Austro-Hungarian chaplains took it upon themselves to provide spiritual care for Jewish prisoners of war, mainly from Russia, but also from Serbia. Separate services were sometimes provided; at other times services were held with the rank and file (as with the 1916 Isonzo service arranged by Rabbi Link, with prisoners from Russia and Serbia present). Rabbi Kurrein described separate spiritual care of Russian prisoners. This special care reflected a noteworthy degree of religious tolerance in Habsburg armies. Rabbis, Christian (predominantly Catholic) chaplains, and imams provided care—including last rites—irrespective of faith, as was the case with Catholics, Protestants, and Jews in the German Army. German Jewish chaplains also looked after Jewish prisoners, but their military authorities did not go as far as the Austro-Hungarians in this regard.

There is lack of written information on chaplains' Eastern Front experiences during 1918. This might have been due to transfer to the Italian Front after the two Treaties of Brest Litovsk,[12] and deteriorating conditions, with shortages of everything, during the last year of the war, because of the blockade. Rabbi Aron Tänzer served in the German Bug Army through 1918, and described food shortages and chaos in Ukraine during the last year of the war. In 1918, he attempted to arrange Pesach and High Holiday celebrations, although by autumn of 1918 he was a sick man, worn out by duties.[13] Bernhard Bardach describes in detail increasing shortages during the last two war years.[14]

This chapter presents writings of Austro-Hungarian Jewish chaplains in their own voices. It is hoped that, thereby, a gap in existing knowledge will be filled, proving my above assertions. The chapter begins with the pre-1914 situation, but concentrates on the war itself. To try and preserve continuity, writings are presented sequentially, compared with those of German counterparts serving on the Eastern Front at the same time. Chaplains sometimes alternated between Russian and Italian fronts. After the 1917 Russian Revolution, the Eastern Front disintegrated, and chaplains were transferred to Italy.

Throughout the war, German chaplains published numerous articles and booklets containing holiday sermons outside of regular newspapers. The reader is referred to my previous book for English translations of many of these.[15] By contrast, Austro-Hungarian chaplains published much less. I could find no separate publications analogous to those from German chaplains. German chaplains' writings are often more self-directed and congratulatory than those of their Austro-Hungarian counterparts. Rabbi Leo Baeck, disciple of the neo-Kantian Hermann Cohen, often lapsed into metaphysical musings which had little value for the troops, and no counterpart in his Austro-Hungarian colleagues.[16]

The greater the number of Jewish soldiers in Habsburg armies, starting in the nineteenth century (chapter 2), the more pressing became the need for military chaplains. However, despite the fact that Christian chaplains had long been a feature of the Austro-Hungarian army, the Monarchy initially refused to formally appoint Jewish chaplains.

According to von Weisl, two Hungarian rabbis of the Pest Reform community were appointed as chaplains during the Kossuth rebellion (1848 to 1849); Rabbis Brueck and Einhorn were court-martialed with two other rabbis after the rebellion failed, but then freed.[17] Rabbi Ignác Einhorn was appointed chaplain by General György Klapka, commander of the Fortress of Komárom, on September 11, 1849, during the Hungarian uprising.[18] Rabbi Leopold Löw from Szeged is generally considered to be the first field rabbi, but he never received an official appointment.[19]

The first Jewish chaplain to serve (unofficially) in the Habsburg armies was Rabbi Jozef Szántó (1816–1874), appointed in 1859 during the war between Italian Savoy and France. Lack of festivals and small numbers of Jewish soldiers in this war precluded holding of services, hospital visits and burials, and little is known of his activity. According to Wolf, at the start of hostilities between Austria and Prussia, Rabbi Szántó was reappointed. He was sworn in on July 23, 1866, but due to short duration of the war, he could not take up his position, and was dismissed from the army. According to Rabbi Alexander Kisch (see below), Rabbi Adolf Ehrentheil of Bohemia volunteered his services as chaplain in 1866. He received no military appointment, but worked voluntarily with wounded, helping with correspondence and burials. After the war, when Jewish chaplaincy received official government recognition, Rabbi Ehrentheil was named Chaplain of Reserves. Both he and Rabbi Kisch worked together to plan military prayer books, suitable uniforms, and harmonize Jewish law and ritual with military necessity.[20]

When in 1906 parliamentary representative Dr. Benno Straucher from Bukowina brought up the issue of peacetime military rabbis in the *Reichsrat*, War Minister Heinrich von Pitreich countered that "rabbis are found everywhere where soldiers are located. I don't believe that additional chaplains duties will be too much for them."[21] Until 1914, rabbis were appointed in the

Landwehr, but all served as "reserve chaplains," and were only called into service during time of war.

During the late nineteenth and early twentieth century, the Habsburg rabbi most closely associated with chaplaincy was Alexander Kisch (1848–1917). In 1874, immediately after accepting his first pulpit in Brüx.[22] Rabbi Kisch reported to military authorities to be "registered as chaplain in case of mobilization." Military rules did not foresee appointment of Jewish chaplains during peacetime, so he was named "chaplain of reserves" and later "*Landwehr* army chaplain" or "chaplain second class" on September 5, 1874. Rabbi Kisch served as chaplain for the few Jewish soldiers in the Brüx garrison and, when the Bosnian campaign began in 1878, volunteered for duty. However, the war ministry had already selected another candidate, Rabbi Wilhelm (Vilmos) Bacher (1850–1913) from Szeged and later Budapest. Bacher served as chaplain in Bosanski Brod (Bosnia Herzegovina). After the war, he was dismissed and returned to civilian life.[23] Rabbi Kisch became rabbi of the Prague Meiselova Synagogue in 1886, and was appointed chaplain to the many Jewish soldiers in the Prague garrison on September 28, 1886. His request to be named "chief rabbi of the k.u.k. Prague garrison" was denied on November 15, 1896, on grounds that, despite full recognition of his services, the title did not exist, and granting of military rank to a civilian was not permitted. Nothing daunted, Rabbi Kisch continued his duties, and wrote of this period:

> I held regular services, undertaking spiritual care for all Jewish soldiers, not only in garrisons of Prague and its suburbs, but also in the whole of Bohemia. Although remuneration for costs incurred was offered several times, I rejected this: this freedom allowed me to thoroughly grasp all military customs and usages, so foreign to me beforehand. I was always greeted in the friendliest fashion, even in highest military echelons.[24]

The problem how to make Jewish religious ritual compatible with military service was compellingly described by Karl Emil Franzos (1848–1904) in his novella *Moschko von Parma*.[25] The Galician Jewish community of Barnow is gripped with a terrible sense of sadness, when one of its young members decides to become a soldier. The community as a whole admonishes him:

> . . . to remain true to the dietary laws, all prayers and rituals. He who does not, commits as great a sin as he who raises his hand to his

parents, because he raises his hand against God. Not even the slightest compromise is possible. One who wants to become a soldier is not a Jew anymore: he loses his contention for joy in the Hereafter.[26]

Rabbi Kisch adopted a more conciliatory tone to this problem, building upon initial exhortations of Rabbis Yechezkel Landau of Prague in 1789 (chapter 2) and Aron Karfunkel of Silesia, to fulfil as many of the commandments as exigencies of war allowed.[27]

Rabbi Kisch was "prevented from carrying out my long-practiced activity as eldest and first Jewish chaplain" by a stroke. He was forced to retire as "subsidiary chaplain" on December 31, 1914. This did not prevent him, against physicians' advice, from visiting and taking care of sick and wounded, holding a memorial service for fallen Jewish soldiers killed at the Prague Jewish cemetery in 1916. One of his sons, Bruno Kisch, served as senior physician in the *Landwehr*. Alexander Kisch died on December 8, 1917.[28]

The nineteenth century saw first appointment of chaplains in the Prussian Army, during the Franco-Prussian War. Four chaplains were appointed on an ad hoc basis from civilian communities (notably Dr. Isak Blumenstein), provided with free transportation and lodging, but not rank or remuneration. The practice was discontinued after the war.[29]

When World War I broke out, there were already nine chaplains in the k.u.k. army, twelve in the k.k. *Landwehr,* and eleven in the k.u. Honvėd army.[30] By the time the war ended, 133 chaplains from all parts of the empire (76 k.u.k., 29 k.k., and 28 k.u.) had served on all fronts.[31] Each chaplain held the rank of chaplain of the reserve, and had at his disposal a "field chapel" consisting of a Torah scroll, tallit, ten sets of tefillin, ten Hebrew prayer books, and a silk skullcap.[32] Such liturgical objects were not routinely provided in the German army. The duties of the chaplains in the Austro-Hungarian army were similar in many ways to those described in my book on German Jewish chaplains, but differed in some aspects due to the heterogeneity of Habsburg Jewish soldiers following their difference in region of origin, socio-economic status, education, and (importantly) the notable presence of Orthodox Jews.[33] The large numbers of Orthodox soldiers from Galicia, Bukowina, and Northern Hungary contrasted sharply with largely assimilated German Jewish soldiers. Jewish army chaplains played an important role reintroducing assimilated Jews to traditional religious practice, and introducing traditional Jews to more "modern" forms of worship. Even if they came from Orthodox backgrounds, rabbis also had a secular education and were trained in fine universities and modern religious seminaries. The multilingualism of many Austrian chaplains (chapter 1) allowed them to converse in several languages, facilitating communication. In Hungary, paragraph 29 of the "Law of the Armed Forces" stated that every rabbi graduating from the rabbinical seminaries in Budapest or Pozsony[34] was allowed to apply for chaplaincy, if he 1) possessed at least a cum laude level degree; 2) was younger than forty; 3) led a morally upright life; 4) had Hungarian citizenship and good command of the language; 5) was physically fit; 6) had served at least three years as a civilian rabbi.[35] This high educational level was also seen in German-Jewish chaplains, who were generally less Orthodox than Austro-Hungarian counterparts.[36]

By comparison, German Jewish chaplains had to create (and initially pay for) their own uniforms, were not commissioned but held initially unpaid honorary rank, with no officially sanctioned kosher kitchens or access to liturgical objects. Apart from a red cross band on the right arm and a Magen David around their necks, uniforms were irregular, and often included a Boer-War type slouch hat. Italian chaplains wore distinctive uniforms, including a beret affixed with the Crown of Italy on top of a five-pointed star.[37]

As soon as Italy declared war on Austro-Hungary in May 1915, Angelo Sereni, President of the Italian-Jewish Community Committee, and Angelo Sacerdoti, Chief Rabbi of Rome, worked together to create the Italian military rabbinate, comprising nine chaplains (eight lieutenants with Rabbi Sacerdoti as captain), and three vice rabbis. Rabbi Rodolfo Levi of Pitigliano (Tuscany) was one of the first to sign up. Unlike their Catholic counterparts, Italian chaplains were not authorized to conduct services in the front lines, but worked in the rear. The Italian Magen David Adom (Jewish Red Cross) petitioned authorities for prayer books and other necessities for Austro-Hungarian Jewish prisoners of war in Rome and other areas during the 1916, 1917, and especially 1918 High Holiday periods.[38] Chief Rabbi Marguelis of Florence requested that soldiers be allowed to celebrate Pesach and High Holidays at the front. The prisoner of war department in Santamaria requested matzot for prisoners of war during Pesach 1917, and a request came in September for High Holiday prayer books, also for prisoners. Italian chaplains had the same problems with organization, weather, and bad roads as did their Austro-Hungarian counterparts. Their duties included providing spiritual care for the soldiers, supplies of liturgical objects (to prisoners of war as well), assistance with promotions, communicating with families at home, helping trace missing soldiers, organizing services on High Holidays such as those in Verona in 1917 for the First, Sixth, and Seventh armies. Extra rations and matzot for Pesach were a particular problem, solved by private fundraising.[39]

It is not my aim to list the names, demographics, and military details of each Austro-Hungarian *Feldrabbiner*. Peter Steiner has listed seventy-seven chaplains in the consolidated k.u.k. army (forty-seven of Hungarian origin), nineteen in the k.k. *Landwehr*, and eighteen in the k.u. Honvéds.[40] Ákos Biró lists seventy-eight chaplains in the k.u.k. army, and confirms eighteen in the k.u.[41] To this list can be added Rabbis Moses David Gross and Benjamin Halevi Horowicz, both of who served on the Palestine Front.[42] It is rather my intention to present and analyze thoughts and writings of those who wrote about their experiences.

Habsburg Jews were much more heterogeneous than their German counterparts. As described by Rabbis Tauber and Bertisch (see below), Orthodox soldiers required spiritual care by a chaplain conversant in Torah and Talmud. This was not the case for assimilated Jewish soldiers from large cities such as Vienna, Budapest, and Prague.

The cited sections do not reflect the author's opinion. The goal of this chapter is rather to give these long-dead men a voice to tell their story of war, as they saw and experienced it. With luxury of a century of reflection and intervention of the Holocaust, it is easy for us to mock their patriotism and positive opinions, but at the time these emotions were real and immediate. It is noteworthy that, as soon as war was declared, an abbreviated prayer book was published for Jewish soldiers in the field.[43]

Austro-Hungarian chaplains were based not only in the field, but also in garrison cities. Relations between garrison chaplains and their corresponding Jewish communities were not always smooth. Rabbi Salomon Funk (born in 1867 in Szőgyén),[44] based in Budapest, refused to countenance appointment by the Pressburg[45] Jewish community of their own purportedly "Orthodox" chaplains, who he felt did not have sufficient broad Orthodox education.[46]

Rabbi Arnold Frankfurter, born in 1881 in Sobotište (Slovakia), came from a distinguished family of rabbis, and studied at the Universities of Vienna and Berlin. From 1908 he worked as rabbi of the *Israelitischer Tempelverein* in Vienna, and on February 1, 1909 he became military chaplain in the Austrian army within the reserve unit. From 1914 through 1918, he served as chief chaplain of the Jewish military garrison in Vienna, An article written by Rabbi Frankfurter to the Vienna *Israelitische Kultusgemeinde* (IKG) in 1915 defined his view of the chaplaincy; this is significant, because nothing had previously been formalized.[47] By comparison, German Jewish chaplains' responsibilities were not formalized: they worked on an ad hoc basis, with aid of frequent conferences to coordinate their activities.[48]

On December 25, 1914, Rabbi Frankfurter wrote a letter to the Vienna Jewish community informing them of his appointment as head of the Jewish military chaplaincy, which had taken place in Vienna on December 16, 1914. He defined the previously informal role of Jewish chaplains in the Habsburg army:

> This activity is new. No instructions, analogous to those prescribed for chaplains of other faiths, has been obtained. Still more, the service area of the Second Army is large, including Lower Austria and areas of Bohemia and Moravia. Regular services must be held in all these places. Our duties must include religious instruction in some cadet schools, blessing troops before they depart into the field, visiting the wounded, bestowal of last rites to fallen comrades, stewardship of military registers, and solemnization of wedding ceremonies in the chaplain's jurisdiction. Spiritual care of captured prisoners is also the chaplain's domain.

At least once a month, services were to be held, with sermons in German and Hungarian, for the Vienna garrison. Three types of services for High Holidays were envisaged: 1) "German" for German-speakers reflecting the more disciplined "Vienna Rite": a traditional liturgy with a vernacular sermon; 2) one in Hungarian; and 3) a third with Orthodox Galician rite. Monthly services were also arranged in the garrison prison. By comparison, it may be assumed that most German services were of a more liberal, Reform nature.

Rabbi Frankfurter considered visiting the sick and wounded, and providing gifts, money, and reading material, to be an integral part of chaplains' duties, especially for patients strange to the area, for whom communication with families back home was so important. Services for the dying and funeral rites were an essential part of his responsibilities. The mostly Russian prisoners of war in the military command area also fell within the chaplain's duties. They were to be visited monthly, and services for them arranged, where possible (plate 6) All religious laws possible were to be observed, including kosher food restrictions, the supply of matzot for Pesach, and the relief of prisoners' work detail on festival days. If possible, camps were to be equipped with a permanent prayer room with a Torah. The Rabbis also were to visit the camp hospital, and supervise the burial if a prisoner of war died. Rabbi Frankfurter tried his best to fulfil these recommendations, and in 1915 he published a sixty-page trilingual pocket prayer book. He was assisted in his enterprises by two deputies, Rabbis Ernst (Ernő) Deutsch (1866–1950) and Rudolf Ferda (1889–1944) (plate 7).[49]

Rabbi Frankfurter wrote with the conviction and belief of his time. Jews were amongst the most loyal members of Kaiser Franz Joseph's polyglot Empire, and, despite widespread antisemitism, had been granted rights which did not exist in countries like Germany and Russia. Rabbi Frankfurter was convinced of the self-evident rightness of his cause. Both he and other chaplains regarded care of Russian prisoners of war as an integral part of their duties.

In the September 4, 1914 issue of *Die Wahrheit*, Rabbi Abraham Frankl from Ungarisch Brod published an article summarizing the history of Jewish chaplains in Germany and Austro-Hungary.[50] He referred to Biblical priests who served as the first chaplains as the "anointed for war" (Talmud Sotah 42a) Rabbi Leo Bertisch (see below) expounded on this Biblical theme, drawing parallels between the role of priests in ancient Israel and that of modern-day chaplains. After the military decree of 1869 allowed Jewish theologians as chaplains into the army, Frankl was the first to volunteer, but was not called into active service. His functions were limited to patriotic speeches on ceremonial occasions, leading services, visiting the sick and wounded, taking care of their correspondence, and giving funeral orations at the graves of soldiers who had been killed.[51]

Rabbi Gabriel Schwarz from Zagreb (1872–1942) studied in the *Landesrabbinerschule* in Budapest and the Jewish Theological Seminary in Vienna in 1886–1896, and served in Croatian communities until the outbreak of the war. With the initial mobilization against Serbia, he was appointed chaplain in a *Landsturm* brigade, where he remained through the end of 1914.[52] For three of these five months he served either in, or up to five kilometers behind, the trenches, where "my ears got used to the rifles clatter and my nerves to whistling of shrapnel and shells." He learned to develop gallows humor, awaiting death each day. Firing took place mainly in the afternoon and evening, lasting all night. When tethered balloons appeared on the horizon, he and the men learned to hide, as Isaiah (26:20) wrote, "enter your rooms and shut the doors behind you; hide yourselves for a little while until his wrath has passed by."

On one occasion, a piece of shrapnel hit twenty paces from his shelter and he was lucky to escape unscathed. "Piles of corpses and wounded men lay around me, and, remembering my dear ones at home, I raised a tearful eye, uttering a silent thanks to our Lord in Heaven." Amidst all the dead and dying—which made an indelible impression on him—he became the spiritual head of a soldiers' community. During the course of his five months' service he got to know every one of the approximately fifty soldiers personally, and regularly visited the sick and wounded. His little "community" grew, as additional Jewish soldiers voluntarily made their way to him. His knowledge of German, Croatian, and Hungarian facilitated communication with Jewish and non-Jewish soldiers. Because of continuous operations there were no formal services, but every Friday evening and festival he managed to gather a *minyan* together, and hold an improvised service.[53] No Jewish soldier exhibited the desire to withdraw or hide from his religion; his congregation included ordinary soldiers, non-commissioned and commissioned officers, and physicians. Non-Jews also participated, and Rabbi Schwarz was happy to see that they listened attentively to what he had to say. On Hanukkah, Jewish and a large number of non-Jewish soldiers gathered together, and in no time the wooden shack was filled. After evening service ended, lights were lit, and Hanukkah songs sung, Rabbi Schwarz explained the significance of the festival to the men in Hungarian: the festival lights signified the light of the Lord, illuminating the path to victory. The reaction of the non-Jewish soldiers to his words filled him with joy, and made the toil and effort of the past five months worthwhile.

On Rosh Hashanah eve, Rabbi Schwarz found himself in the neighboring town, separated from his Jewish flock, depressed at being alone. He was joined at table by two Catholic ministers, two judges, and a few Christian officers. One of the ministers raised his glass and wished Rabbi Schwarz Happy New Year in so friendly and sincere a way that he forgot his loneliness and cheered up. On Christmas tables were turned, and Rabbi Schwarz returned the favor for the Catholic chaplains, cheering them up and making them feel better. Rabbi Schwarz also officiated over burials, regardless of the soldier's religion. He felt as if he was hearing the words of Malachi 2:7 that "the priest is the messenger of the Lord of Hosts."[54]

Rabbi Max Béla Fischer (born in Pressburg in 1883) was appointed chaplain in 1914, and served as the contact point for all chaplains in different crown territories for delivery of prayer books and gifts from home including matzot and cigarettes.[55] A similar position did not exist for German chaplains, who mostly depended on local communities for their needs. In the same year, Rabbi Fischer was appointed chaplain with the Patriotic Benevolent Society of the Red Cross in Lower Austria, and chaplain for Red Cross sanatoria, including the Rothschild Hospital. For this, he was provided a monthly stipend of 100 crowns. He was decorated for his activities, which included serving the Vienna IKG as military and civilian rabbi. His war experiences are set out in a photograph and correspondence album, with postcards of thanks from many sources.[56]

Rabbi Sámuel Schlesinger, in peacetime a rabbi in Monor, Hungary, volunteered as soon as war began, and was initially attached to a Honvéd division on the southern part of the Eastern Front (no. 1 Honvéd Military District). He served throughout the war.

In a feuilleton "Spiritual Care in the Trenches," published November 1914, he remarked on the high regard in which he was held by the officer's corps. He attended the wounded and dying at dressing stations, where he offered comfort and encouragement, and had the task of burying several Jewish officers, bringing two back to Bosnia, so that they could be buried within the empire. The High Holiday services went solemnly, with Rabbi Schlesinger acting as rabbi and prayer leader. *Selichot* (penitential prayers) were recited at 3.00 am, with assistance of Christian guards. He prayed in Hungarian, so that they too could understand. The same Christians assisted him in putting on tefillin, which they had observed before, at home.

For Rosh Hashanah 1914, those who were not active on the front line gathered in a small room at the dressing station. They already had a Torah scroll from the authorities, and Rabbi Schlesinger obtained candles from the nearest town. The front line was only a few kilometers away. The congregation consisted of officers and men; doctors hurried back and forth from services to dressing stations and back. During the afternoon, Rabbi Schlesinger visited the front lines, to pray with those soldiers who could not leave their posts. The enemy was only 100 meters away. He recorded his exchange with the soldiers.[57]

The 1914 autumn holidays found Rabbi Arthur Levy from Germany on the Eastern Front. He arranged leave for men to attend Rosh Hashanah services but could not personally attend, because of his visit to High Command. He commented especially on good treatment of Russian Jewish prisoners of war by the German Army, and their inclusion in services. No mention is made of special catering for festive meals, nor (specifically) of Yom Kippur. Soldiers celebrated Sukkot (Tabernacles festival) eve in a local synagogue with shot-up windows and ceiling, and were welcomed into homes of the local Jewish population.[58]

The youngest Jewish chaplain in the armies of the Central Powers was, according to the *Allgemeine Zeitung des Judentums*, the twenty-three-year-old Hirsch Lebovics. He was born in 1893 in a small Hungarian town where his father was rabbi. After obtaining his rabbinical diploma, he became rabbi of Mitrovica (Vojvodina/Serbia) in 1915. He volunteered as chaplain that same year.[59]

The historian and philosopher Adolf Altmann (plate 8) was born 1879 in Hunfalu, and ordained rabbi in 1907.[60] He had been chief rabbi of Salzburg for eight years and, when war began, was head of the congregation in Meran.[61] He volunteered for the chaplaincy as soon as war was declared. When Italy declared war on Austro-Hungary, in May 1915, he served voluntarily in the Tenth Army, without pay, as subsidiary rabbi on the Isonzo front, visiting field hospitals, officiating at burials, solving personal and other problems, and holding field services. He travelled to the front regularly despite harsh terrain and weather, and was proud that he served the men irrespective of religion. His sermon on the death of Kaiser Franz Joseph was widely circulated.[62]

Reports from Austro-Hungarian chaplains become more numerous in 1915. Rabbi Meir Tauber (1880–1942) was born in Stanisławów. He studied at the Vienna Rabbinical Seminary and, after obtaining his doctorate in philosophy, served as professor of religion in state gymnasia in Waage Neustadt and Lemberg.[63] He saw service as chaplain in the k.k. *Landwehr* between 1915 and 1918 on Galician and Isonzo Fronts. His war experiences were reported in three consecutive articles in *Dr. Bloch's Österreichische Wochenschrift*.

The first article reported Rabbi Tauber's initial impressions. Proper performance of a chaplain's duty depended upon regular close contact with soldiers. For this, an appointment to an active division was optimal, compared to service in the rear, where service was limited to local field hospitals and issuance of death certificates. His community consisted of about 550 soldiers; many Orthodox, bearded *Landwehr* men from East Galicia and North Hungary, with special need for religious edification. Many had attempted, under great difficulties, to adhere to Jewish dietary laws until, lacking strength from proper nourishment, they had been forced to eat in the communal mess. Moved by their devotion, Rabbi Tauber tried to lighten their conscience by drawing attention to the unusual conditions, reminding them that, in a godly cause such as a war with antisemitic Russia, any ritual loses its binding power. Tauber likened the Russians to Amalek, Israel's age-old, eternal enemy.[64] The soldiers were thankful for communal Sabbath and festival services, which provided a *minyan* now and then. Rabbi Tauber tried to encourage bravery, and always impress upon soldiers the significance of this war for the fatherland in general, and Jews in particular. He used examples of poor Jewish families abused and expelled from their homes by the Cossacks, to drive the point home and motivate the men,

Preparations for Pesach 1915 posed special difficulties, but military authorities were "very helpful indeed." Government money was used to purchase 1,300 kilograms matzot, and every opportunity was used to provide

Jewish soldiers with kosher food. Cattle were ritually slaughtered, and food prepared in specially cleaned mobile kitchens with separate containers. Rabbi Tauber led one seder evening, giving the other to a Jewish physician. Soldiers who were not on duty gathered in a specially prepared room, each man with a glass of wine, matzot, and a war *hagadah* (seder prayer book). After *kiddush* (blessing over wine), a young military physician asked the four questions, and the assembled men read out in chorus the story of the Exodus from Egypt. Both mornings, prayers were recited Hasidic style, with a great deal of active participation and singing. By comparison, seders were held throughout the German Army, but kosher meat had to be obtained from home.

Rabbi Tauber brought matzot, newspapers, books, chocolates, cigars, and the like for the sick and wounded, which pleased them greatly. He described a wounded man who requested a visit when he felt that the end was near. It was late at night and Rabbi Tauber travelled five kilometers to the hospital. The man welcomed him with tears of joy, they both recited the Confession of Faith, and the wounded man fell asleep, exhausted from excitement. He lingered for another three days.

Prayers for the dead on the last day of Pesach 1915 were moving and uplifting, with tears in everyone's eyes. *Mincha* (afternoon service) was held in the open and very solemn. "A beautiful spring day, the sun is setting; sturdy young men stand in rank and file, one of them reciting the prayers loudly." Rabbi Tauber used Deuteronomy 22:1–4 to expound on harm caused by the Russians to Jews in the Pale of Settlement, and what must be done about it.

Rabbi Tauber also saw, with the commandant's assistance, to establishment of a Jewish military cemetery. All Jewish soldiers who died, in battle or field hospital, were brought here and buried according to Jewish rite, with a formal *chevra kadisha* (burial society). Jewish soldiers acted as pall-bearers.[65]

There were no similar problems with Orthodox practice for Jewish soldiers in the German army who were largely assimilated, with needs focused primarily on material matters.[66] Orthodox chaplains such as the Carlebachs left almost no war writings on the subject, and only Rabbi Alexander Winter mentions problems with obtaining kosher food.[67]

Rabbi Arthur Levy, a German chaplain working in the same area, reported murders and pogroms in more than 215 places from Łódź in December 1914. He reported that some Jews were hanged in their synagogue, in prayer robe and tallit on Yom Kippur, others from balconies of their homes on return from synagogue, after their wives were sent to get the rope, and left dangling for a day. Young girls drowned themselves rather than submit to the Cossacks, and one rabbi was saved only by the entry of German troops, after his house and property were destroyed by fire. As so often happened, Jews were accused of hiding telephones in their tallitot, acting as German spies, and expelled from their homes. 15,000 small traders were robbed of their property and turned into beggars. Rabbi Levy published all this as an open letter to American Jews, after his initial report in the *Berliner Tageblatt*, but was not believed.[68]

Rabbi Tauber's second report dealt with the large scale offensive against the Russian Front in West Galicia.[69] The attack began on Lag Ba'Omer (May 2, 1915), the Jewish "weapons-festival."[70] He declared a field service for this day in the Jewish military cemetery which he had laid out in Zakliczyn (Poland). Rabbi Tauber recited *mincha* and, in his talk, connected heroic battles from the time of the Romans with heroes fighting and dying now for Kaiser and Fatherland.

Rabbi Tauber movingly described his experiences in the medical unit. Wounded arrived from all sides—on foot, by any available conveyance and (where possible) Red Cross vehicles—after having received first aid at the front. Seriously wounded came with head or abdominal wounds, or bullet wounds to the leg and foot with fractures.[71] Physicians did their difficult job, concerned with immediate, and best possible, treatment of the injuries. Chaplains assisted with gifts from home, food or drink, a cigarette, but most of all by personal participation:

> These heroes bear their physical pain with equanimity: their suffering is more psychological, in that they are now condemned to inactivity. Russian breakthroughs have been stopped, and pursuit of the enemy has begun all along the line.

Often, during his travels, Rabbi Tauber encountered hundreds of wounded who, wounds already dressed, were on their way to the next field hospital. He provided them with small gifts such as chocolates, newspapers, and cigarettes from his own supply, refreshing the exhausted men with cold tea.

His descriptions of the suffering of Jewish civilians caught in between the Russian army and the armies of the Central Powers are very moving:

> While icons hung out of windows almost always protected Christian houses from damage, Jewish homes were destroyed, or completely plundered. In one village, Jewish houses on the square and in adjacent streets were used as stables.

Refugees lost everything. Rabbi Tauber visited several abandoned homes from which all furniture had disappeared. Floors were torn up, window frames torn out; the Russians used wood for fuel. Horses were quartered in upper floors, manure decomposing in stinking heaps. The synagogue, erected only a few years ago at great expense, had been turned into a stable, after all furnishings had been dragged away. Rabbi Tauber was told that in presence of the Jews—who were not allowed in—their synagogue had been plundered and desecrated. The Russians harassed the Jews, because they saw in each Jew an Austrian spy. Many were led away and disappeared without a trace, others threatened daily with deportation. Notices on street corners, which Rabbi Tauber could still see, stated:

> Experiences have clearly shown hostile behavior of Jews from Poland, Galicia, and Bukowina. Each time they leave this or any other district, which is then occupied by our opponents, violent measures are taken against the population sympathetic towards us: Jews incite Austrians, and those of German nationality, against us. To prevent atrocities against our loyal population, and protect our soldiers from Jewish espionage along the front, Jews are forbidden to remain in our military district, or enter the district west of Jarosław [Poland]. To prevent defamation of the peaceful, sympathetic population and countermand Jewish espionage, hostages may be taken: One hostage for every peaceful civilian punished by Austrians or Germans, and for each captured Jewish spy, two hostages to be taken and threatened with death. This measure is taken solely to punish Jewish disloyalty and atrocities against the peaceful, sympathetic local population.

An eminent Jew from Jodłowa (Poland) described his suffering to Rabbi Tauber for a whole hour. He had, under threats, to indemnify invoices against large amounts of money for wood that he had delivered, but for which little had been paid. He was beaten and forced to leave his house with his wife and nine children. When he returned a few days later, he found it completely looted, and was fortunate to escape being taken away as a hostage. Russians went on the rampage in Ropczyce and Sędziszów, where houses were destroyed and plundered, and in Rzeszów, where homes and stores of refugees were plundered.[72] Rabbi Tauber's descriptions of Russian depredations against Jewish civilians only differ from those of Rabbis Arthur Levy and Gustav Sicher (see below) in degree.

Rabbi Tauber's third article began by describing a meeting with German officers at the start of the 1915 Dunajec Offensive.[73] One asked him when he thought that he would return to his hometown of Lemberg. His reply caused him some embarrassment. The town was so far away, there were so many pessimists who did not wish to believe that it would soon be reconquered, that, following desire rather than logic, he said he would like to be there by the end of July. "So late?" the German staff officer said laughing. "We'll be there earlier. In two weeks we'll reach the river San, where we will try to stop the Russians. We'll be in Lemberg around the middle of June." Facts proved the soldier's confidence correct, and Rabbi Tauber felt lucky to have participated in the victorious progress of the armies of the Central Powers.

Rabbi Tauber was present during the reconquest of Lemberg in June 1915. Austrian troops reached the Russian positions on the San in the middle of May:

> A difficult battle for the river crossing, that unfortunately claimed many victims, began. A beautiful, communal military cemetery was laid out by the medical corps at the forest edge, tastefully decorated by the town's civilian population and the [Christian] division chaplain. Mass was read daily, and it was a beautiful sight to see how, on holidays, the colorfully dressed population knelt with soldiers at the graves, praying silently for salvation of the dead. In Leżajsk [Poland], very near the front, where soldiers fallen in battle were brought, rows of soldiers' graves were laid out in the Jewish cemetery, lovingly tended by the local Jewish population. Many soldiers lay in unmarked graves, because it wasn't always possible to bring their mortal remains back from the front for burial.

Rabbi Tauber went on to describe four weeks of uninterrupted fighting on the San River. Russians had to withdraw, soldiers crossed the river, and saw before them a picture of devastation. The entire town at the river's edge was burned down; only chimneys remained, as if to designate the once so peaceful individual homesteads, and their dispossessed inhabitants. His unit crossed into Russia; he was overwhelmed with curiosity about what was happening in this country and its people, including Poles living under Russian domination, but mainly about the Jews, who had undergone such repression and persecution. After a long march, they reached Tarnogród (Poland), where they were quartered in the Russian archbishop's house. It was a small Polish town, with a largely Jewish population (the Jewish community of Tarnogród numbered about 600 families). There were two synagogues, many small prayer houses, and an old Jewish cemetery. The population were mostly poor: agricultural merchants and moneylenders. Rabbi Tauber visited the synagogue, in the midst of the Sabbath, and beheld a sad picture: "bags, clothes, bed sheets, household utensils lay around, and amongst them pale, anxiety-filled faces murmuring prayers." Jews from Sieniawa (Poland) and surroundings had found refuge here, when they were driven into Russia by Cossacks. Many local Jews had hidden in the synagogue to prevent being dragged away, but also because Russians had filled them with terror of the Germans' "murdering, thieving passion." Ironically, the owner of an estate told Rabbi Tauber that two Cossack officers had declared to him that they must, on higher authority, burn the building down. The owner invited the officers in for a splendid dinner, and during the meal servants mentioned that Germans were coming. The officers fled with the other Cossacks, and the estate was saved. Each Jew in town was suspected of being a spy. All were driven out, after which abandoned dwellings were robbed and plundered by fleeing Cossacks and the local population.[74]

The view by Rabbi Tauber of the situation in Lemberg is instructive. Lemberg lay right in the path of the invading army. When Russians conquered most of Galicia and Bukowina in summer 1914, thousands of Jews fled, fearing for their lives. Although some reports of Russian atrocities may have been exaggerated by war propaganda, there is no doubt that Jews who remained suffered greatly under Russians, who (rightly) regarded the Jews of Galicia and Bukowina as loyal Habsburg subjects. When Lemberg was liberated during the Gorlice-Tarnów Offensive, Galician Jews rejoiced, but the situation in cities such as Lemberg remained difficult.[75] An-sky describes the burning of Brody, and Russian persecution, murder and expulsion during early months of the war.[76] The initial situation once the Russians had left was chaotic, and time was required to restore order.[77]

Service in field hospitals was an essential part of chaplains' duties. Rabbi Edmund (Ödön) Kálmán was born 1896 in Kunszentmárton (Hungary), and studied between 1906 and 1911 at the Jewish Theological Seminaries in Budapest and Breslau, respectively.[78] After obtaining his doctorate, he became chief rabbi in Jászberényi (Hungary). He served with the k.u. Honvéd Army throughout the war.

An August 1915 feuilleton described a dressing station on the Eastern Front, on the Russian border. Wounded were brought there from Posadów (Poland) during twelve days and nights, at the violent climax of the battle.

Enemy wounded, left behind when the troops fled, were also cared for. Rabbi Kálmán described the scene:

> You, little river striving towards the far-off Bug, how engorged you have become with Russian blood! It's neither fairy-tale nor exaggeration, but the bloody truth. The river of blood flowed to the Bug, bringing the last greeting of thousands and thousands of soldiers home to Russia. Sighs, moans, wails of soldiers—Hungarian, Austrian, Russian, Croatian, Romanian, Polish—flowed into each other: national differences disappeared, they were nothing but suffering people. We walked amongst them: chaplains of four religions, whose differences disappeared until only one religion remained, the holy religion of help to the suffering.

In the beginning, when numbers of wounded at the dressing station were still relatively small, each chaplain tried to provide words of comfort to wounded and dying. Ritual objects were brought from wagons. Chaplains sought liturgical objects, symbols of religious usage at home. All recognized that the wounded looked upon them as physicians owing to red crosses on their arms; it was decided that all should wear chaplains' coats decorated with gold lanyards. Rabbi Kálmán felt as if the chaplains stood in Temple vestments, holding services while visiting the wounded. Each man had his own request. One wanted a cooling compress on his hot forehead, another a few drops of lukewarm milk on his parched lips. Another wanted his comrade's knapsack behind his head. A fourth asked for help writing a card to his family, telling them that he was alive. A fifth needed reassurance that his broken, shot-up arm could still be saved. A sixth needed to be quietened down so that he did not bleed to death, a seventh, a brother's hand before embarking on the long road to the other side.

The wounded became ever more numerous. Prayer shawls, which Rabbi Kálmán had brought with him to shroud bodies, were exhausted, as were small mezuzot that he handed out; and the wounded arrived in even greater numbers. Some came themselves, others were brought in on stretchers or wagons. There was no time to find out to which religion a man belonged, and after a while, chaplains of all four faiths stopped looking. On Rabbi Kálmán's suggestion, they decided to give up separate religions: there was only one flock, one shepherd: "We provide a religious word to he who thirsts, in God's name. We are priests of the one God, all called to this bloody place for one and the same purpose, so we should divide the work up as brothers."

From then on, they made no distinction in religious activity in care of wounded souls. Only when a soldier had reached the end and was about to die, was his own chaplain called to him:

> I will never forget the time when a Tyrolean private convulsively pressed my hand to his lips with his last strength, and, ever more softly, whispered tremulously to me with lips gradually growing stiff: "Our Father ... Dear Father ... Dear Father ... Credo." So the poor man stammered, while to my right a young father from Siebenbürgen sputtered the first line of *kaddish* [prayer for the dead]: "*Yisgadal veyiskadash* ... my children ... *sh'mei rabo* ... my dear children."[79] My Catholic colleague wiped the sweat from his forehead.

Jewish chaplains in armies of all countries (except the Russian army, which had no Jewish chaplains) endeavored to provide spiritual assistance regardless of religion. This was especially the case in the Habsburg army, with its mixture of Catholics (including Eastern Orthodox), Protestants, Jews, and Moslems. This care also extended to prisoners of war, but was not always reciprocated.

A Russian prisoner lay wounded in another part of Rabbi Kálmán's dressing station. At first, the chaplains approached them with the same love, but two scenes occurred which alienated them from this "evil-hearted nation." One idealistic physician was walking along rows of wounded, asking the Russians about their wounds and their pain. He bent over closer to one of them because he did not hear his words, wanting to examine him more closely. The Russian, with a sudden movement, swung his hitherto concealed pocket knife. "Even here, hate had not stopped working in the Russian and Cossack heart." Shuddering, they walked away from this "depraved man who raised his weapon of murder against his benefactor." From then on, the Russian wounded were housed in separate barracks.

The second incident contrasted the patriotic feelings of local Jews, opposed to the Russophile feelings of Ruthenians The Jewish population of the small town came en masse to visit the wounded. Each brought a little pot or basket filled with refreshments, food, wine, mineral water, or other useful things. Early in the morning people were out and about; rich and poor brought gifts to defenders of their fatherland. At first, the chaplains were pleased to see the population's ministrations. The town had a Jewish community of about 6,000, and ten charitable institutions. Rabbi Kálmán called the leaders of these institutions; encouraged by their rabbis, it was resolved that men would bring milk and bread, and women would bring stewed fruit. Jewish men arrived with milk, and Jewish women gave water to the thirsty.

Then, Ruthenian women came with their gifts, at first only a few, but then more and more. A surgeon started to look with increasing irritation at the Ruthenian women bringing gifts. In the end, he approached Rabbi Kálmán, shaking with rage: "Look around and see: the Ruthenians bring their gifts only to the Russian wounded, and only the Jews look after our own men. Just look!" They saw a genteel, older Ruthenian lady with five or six servants approaching the dressing station. The servants were carrying baskets packed with good things: wine, roasted meat, bottled fruit, white cake, even small head cushions. People made way for her, and the Ruthenian women kissed her hand. The Jews bowed to her, frightened: she must have been a noblewoman. When she entered the fenced off room, she gave a few bites to Austro-Hungarian wounded, then walked decisively to Russian wounded and gave them most of the ample food. "Did you see that?" the physician said angrily. "I won't tolerate it anymore. These insolent people care only for the Russian prisoners, while the Jews are the ones who take care of our own wounded. I will not allow any more of this!"

The area was closed off, and the chaplains, together with medical corps, handed the gifts out properly, to all wounded alike:

> The physician pressed my hand. "You can be proud of members of your faith!" he said. "Let us get to work." He went back to mend broken bodies, and I to raise broken souls.[80]

Rabbi Artur/Arnold Grünfeld, whose pulpits before the war were in Jihlava (Czech Republic) and Eger (Hungary), volunteered as soon as war began. In summer 1915, he was appointed chaplain of the Thirteenth *Landwehr* Infantry Division. Excerpts from two of his letters during the summer of 1915 emphasize many difficulties of fighting on the Eastern Front.

In a first brief communication on June 9, 1915, Rabbi Grünfeld wrote that provisions were plentiful, especially because Russians left enormous quantities of white flour behind. Drinks at meals consisted of wine and mineral water, and once they even "liberated" a barrel of good Hungarian beer. There was lack of safe drinking water, with outbreaks of typhoid and cholera all over the front. Similarly, German chaplain Aron Tänzer described an outbreak of cholera near Krasnystav (Poland).[81] Rabbi Grünfeld served together with officers, physicians, and veterinarians (essential because of large numbers of horses). Roads were terrible: "Unending sand on roads and mud and filth on rainy days are peculiarities of this country, in which I have wandered around for more than two months." This sentiment is echoed by everyone who served on the Eastern Front.[82]

Rabbi Grünfeld remarked on the region's fertility, which—he felt—would help defeat Russian plans to starve them out. He saw miserable dwellings, from which the tower of a Russian Orthodox church stood out, alternating with neglected Jewish villages, on whose population the departing Russians took out their anger. Travelling further, Rabbi Grünfeld held services for soldiers wherever he could, even in half-destroyed prayer houses.[83]

Ludwig Golinski served as chaplain in the k.u.k. army throughout the war. His correspondence provides an example of mutual compassion shown by chaplains of all faiths, in the Austro-Hungarian army. In 1915, he received a letter from an Eastern Orthodox chaplain via one of his Jewish colleagues. It is not clear exactly to whom this letter was addressed:

> I am enclosing a letter which I recently received from an Eastern Orthodox chaplain, a former comrade. As a Pole, his German is not good. But the friendly human sentiments are more significant than language. Unfortunately, we Jewish chaplains cannot be everywhere, so the more gratifying it is when chaplains of other faiths care for sick and wounded Jewish soldiers. The card reads (literally):
>
> "Laskow, June 14, 1915[84]
>
> Dear friend, I am contacting you again after a five-month interval. Remembered love for a good comrade does not die, and I hope to see you again. I have been on ten days' leave with my family, and found them all in the best of health, despite the Russian occupation.... I have a request: there are sick Jews in my hospital. It pains me that I have reading material, especially prayer books, for everyone except these poor men.... Be so good as to send me five Jewish soldier's prayer books, which you might have. I am convinced that you will not fail to fulfil my request, and send you and everyone else my best greetings, Peter Ezaus."[85]

Rabbi Gustav Sicher was born in 1880 in Klatovy (Czech Republic). After initial medical studies in Vienna, he changed to the rabbinate and obtained his doctorate at Charles University in Prague. After beginning his rabbinical career

1906 in Nachod, he subsequently served as chaplain in the k.k. *Landwehr* in Cracow throughout the war, and was highly decorated.[86] Rabbi Sicher described the entire High Holidays and Sukkot season on the Polish Front 1915 in three newspaper articles, communicated by Rabbis Halberstamm and Rosenmann from Mährisch-Schönberg.[87]

The first article refers to Rabbi Sicher's sojourn in Wilkołaz, between Kraśnik and Lublin (all in Poland). There, he handed in his first report of High Holidays celebrations to Command. In a meadow in front of an estate, he wrote the New Year's wishes to his home community. Alongside him lay a handsome Russian officer, who had just died from a shot through the intestines. Farms were burning in the distance. A Russian plane flew over and was fired upon; it seemed to waver for a moment, but then suddenly raised itself up and flew away. Then came the order for strategic redeployment, so they marched through Galicia, penetrating into Russia again from another side across the Weichsel.[88]

Rabbi Sicher enjoyed his visit to Kraśnik, where he escaped from the suffering of the dressing station, and was pampered by the local Jewish innkeeper. He was promised *machzorim* (High Holidays prayer books) and shofars, and celebrated Rosh Hashanah in Galicia. On Sunday afternoon of September 20, the day before the start of the holiday, they arrived at a swampy, mean meadow in Podlesie, a miserable village near Radomyśl.[89]

A soldier from the baggage train found the only Jews in the town: this pleased Jewish soldiers, because they knew they would get a warm place to sleep, eat kosher food, and be able to hold services. The room was in a gin mill that resembled all village taverns, with bare walls and empty shelves. The innkeeper, his pregnant wife, and children stood in an adjacent room. The wife knew nothing about her eldest son, who was in the army: communication with the outside had been broken. She had a feverish rash brought on by fear of Cossacks. Rabbi Sicher advised the family not to run away, as they would not get far and only get stuck in the muddy, filthy streets, where the enemy could overtake them after having destroyed their home, and shoot them. It was better to hide in the cellar. The man agreed, but the woman fled to Radomyśl with her children. In the evening Rabbi Sicher arranged a *minyan* in the house. The room was scrubbed, and the table between the two beds served as the pulpit, on which he placed two candles. The host obtained freshly slaughtered poultry from Radomyśl. The prayer leader had a rough and ready wagoner's voice, with which he prayed relatively well.

The *minyan* consisted mostly of men from the medical corps and a few Ulans. Rabbi Sicher expounded on the Biblical text that God alone sees what is hidden from Man. No one at the beginning of the war anticipated that a year later they would be celebrating the next Rosh Hashanah in the field. At the end, he blessed the soldiers, and they sat down to dinner: a piece of fish, chicken, and chicken soup. The sparse meal tasted wonderful, because they found out that they could rest here for two days: "A Happy New Year in the field indeed!"

During the night many remained awake: not only because solemn thoughts at the beginning of the New Year hung heavy over them, but because of the battalions of flies and other insects. In the morning men prayed attentively, without prayer books and shofar (which had not arrived despite having been promised). The kindly commandant, a surgeon-major, was present at services. The men eked out an after-services lunch as best they could. A flea or two in the food bothered nobody. A few men were upset that the delicious slivovitz that someone had requisitioned in Radomyśl had already been finished, and nasty glares were cast at the Polish servant, who was suspected of the dirty deed.

Rabbi Sicher spent the holiday evenings with the men, learning about their opinions, cares, and wishes. The second festival morning, he prevailed upon their imperturbable prayer leader to shorten the service: they had to march off soon, and he wanted to preserve the commandant's goodwill for the coming festival days. After services, their valiant prayer leader was back at work with his horses. They marched off that afternoon, over appalling terrain. Luckily, the march was short, and they secured wonderful accommodations in an estate with large, clean rooms.[90]

The second article describes how, after several night journeys on bad roads, Rabbi Sicher and his men arrived in Żabno (Poland) on the eve of the penitential Sabbath between Rosh Hashanah and Yom Kippur. The impoverished Jews of Żabno—the rich had already fled—were terrified of the Russians. They had not been able to celebrate Rosh Hashanah according to ritual, because war emergency demanded that they had to work on the roads.

Rabbi Sicher started preparing for the approaching Yom Kippur. Luckily, almost the entire division had been quartered in and around Żabno, so he was not far from command. A member of the general staff told Rabbi Sicher that his written request had made a good impression on the general, so an addendum was made to orders from division command: "If soldiers of the Jewish faith are in their quarters, they should attend services according to the directive of Chaplain Rabbi Sicher." At 4.00 am, they marched off on terrain that was so bad that one of the heavy pack-wagons flew into the air, bursting apart in the middle of the road. Rabbi Sicher spent the Sabbath praying, sleeping in the hut of an old pig farmer on a baronial estate. During the evening, he sat with other officers and physicians in the cool, spacious hall of the baron and his son, drinking tea. They were not far from Cracow, and could only guess at their real destination.

At 3.00 am, they were awakened and ordered to march northwards, in the direction of Russian Poland. Baggage trains, artillery pieces, and ammunition wagons clattered on the pontoon bridge over the Weichsel to Russia. Their first day back on the Russian soil was foggy, with a cool wind blowing under a pale grey sky. They arrived in the small town of Koszyce (Poland). Local Jews were overjoyed at their arrival, and Rabbi Sicher was offered good lodging, reading material, tea, and food, but they could stop there for only fifteen minutes. He found the Jews in this area better off and cleaner than those in Krasnik and Zaklików (Poland). As was the case elsewhere, Jewish civilians anxiously awaited the protection of the Austro-Hungarian army.

Rabbi Sicher's first lieutenant brought a few hundred field prayer booklets, which the war ministry had sent earlier that year. The booklets had been mislaid by the Vienna IKG. Order was not a hallmark of the Austro-Hungarian Army. They spent the night in the meadow in front of the Dobiesławice (Poland) town hall where they ceremoniously requisitioned a rare drink—beer. On the second day, they arrived in Kazimierza Wielka (Poland), and were quartered in a sugar factory. The town's Jews were pleased to see them, and opined that, although their economic situation under the Russians was good, they would be happier under Austrian rule. Like so many Jews in the empire, they spoke of Kaiser Franz Joseph with love and reverence.

Front line fighting on Yom Kippur complicated orderly services. The day before Yom Kippur, they departed, arriving that afternoon in a wretched rural area. The medical corps unit was quartered in the local estate. Rabbi Sicher asked the young Polish caretaker if he had a free room for a service for Yom Kippur eve which was about to begin; he responded "no." Unfazed, Rabbi Sicher went directly to the home (if it could be called that) of the only Jew in the area, to establish a service. The room was miserable—a stable in Western Austria looked better.

The poor man gave Rabbi Sicher what he had to eat: potatoes, a little soup in a glass, barley, tea. Rabbi Sicher nibbled reluctantly, chewing on a goose bone which he had left over from Kazimierza Wielka. They only just managed a *minyan*: the polite *Landwehr* brigade commandant gave his two Jewish orderlies two days' leave over Yom Kippur, so that they could participate in services.

After piously murmured introductory prayers, Rabbi Sicher ordered the room swept and the chickens removed. Then their prayer leader began the *Kol Nidrei* prayer with the usual melodious wailing chant.[91] On hearing this, the man's wife collapsed with a tremendous howl, followed by the children's wailing when they heard their mother's cries. Most of the soldiers wept, thinking of their loved ones back home. Rabbi Sicher gave a short talk before the blessing, but was interrupted by the woman several times. They were visited by dogs, cats, and chickens, who lived in the room as well. Despite everything, the mood was solemn. The soldiers slept with the Jewish family, also in the stables. Rabbi Sicher slept inside the ambulance.

At 7.00 am on Yom Kippur morning they marched off. In consideration of Jewish soldiers, Rabbi Sicher descended from the ambulance, and marched along with them, fourteen kilometers on terrible roads up and down hills. After five hours of exhausting marching they arrived at another estate, with a forester's house adjacent to the manor house. Here, too, they discovered a Jewish tenant, a better one than the previous unpleasant individual. During early afternoon Rabbi Sicher tried to reconstitute a *minyan* again, but the sergeant commanded their prayer leader to clean the horses. Another hour passed before Rabbi Sicher could go up to the forester's lodge, where the surgeon-major called the sergeant and relieved his man from duty. By the time Rabbi Sicher fetched him from the stable, and brought him to the prayer leader's platform, it was already 1.00 pm, and the service began with the Torah reading. The prayer room was better than the previous day, but stank badly because of an adjacent alcove with a small child in it. A little cat walked over the leader's prayer book, and dogs and chickens paid temporary visits. They prayed in the sticky air of the low-ceilinged room, uninterruptedly and not very gracefully, until the end of the holy day. Rabbi Sicher led the *ne'ila* (concluding) service. Their breakfast meal was not princely: a few potatoes, apples, sour milk, tea, and black coffee.[92]

The third article focuses on the Jews of Staszów (Poland), which Rabbi Sicher's unit entered after Yom Kippur. Two days earlier, the Russians had shot members of a *minyan* dead just before the concluding service. The prayer leader, a widower and father of nine young children, was hanged from a corner lamppost in the market square. He was still dangling in his white prayer robe, before Rabbi Sicher's company cut him down. A young, educated man from a good family who thought that, by knowledge of Russian and persuasiveness, he could prove the Jews' innocence, was also shot dead. The day after his execution, the Russian military chancery announced—too late—that Jews, who had been falsely accused of starting a fire in revenge, were innocent, and that the arsonist had been found. At the end of such a Yom Kippur, the Jews of Staszów did not break their fast with appetite.

Soldiers were quartered there the Sabbath after Yom Kippur. Horror could still be seen and felt in every face. Sabbath hymns were sung, but in subdued tones, without the usual festivity. The grandmother, a virtuous woman, spoke with Rabbi Sicher until deep into the night about evils of which people are capable. A Jewish deputation arrived, asking for permission to bury the innocent victims of the Russian caprice—who at present lay under a thin layer of earth in a meadow—in the Jewish cemetery. Approval by command was given, through Rabbi Sicher, whose report continued:

> I only saw a tabernacle hut once during the entire festival, on the first evening in Klimontów (Poland), where we arrived late, and established a dressing station. Sights requiring strong nerves and a stout heart were seen. Shrapnel flew over Klimontów daily. A dead Jewish woman lay in a room, killed by a wall that had fallen in when a missile hit her house. Other Jews sought shelter in their cellars. In one house which I entered at midnight, they had crept up out of their shelters. They were happy to see me: we went up to the hut in the attic and I recited the blessing over the wine. During the first two days of Sukkot, the terrain was so bad that it trumped all that had gone before. One physician's assistant was wounded, after flying out of his little vehicle. Dark of night made proper orientation difficult, and it poured with rain. When one has to flee onto the coachman's seat and the wagon is stuck and cannot move, wind-driven rain blows painfully through sodden limbs. So it was that I arrived at a farmer's cottage in Garbów (Poland) on the second day of Sukkot, frozen into a block of ice.

Rabbi Sicher cut wood, while the regimental physician heated the room. Because blankets arrived only the next day, a bundle of straw served as a blanket on dripping clothes. They spent the rest of Sukkot in Garbów. Crossing the "streets" of this "charming" backwater was a bold undertaking, which one had to consider twice before taking the risk of sloshing deep into mud and filth. Muddy water poured from above and below, every small rise a slide, every level catwalk a lake. The clay hut belonging to the only Jew in town was their prayer room. A few Jews who had travelled to Sandomierz (Poland) to fetch the traditional "four species" had been murdered in the forest by Cossacks, so men had to be satisfied with thinking about their symbolic significance.

During the intermediate Sabbath, they assembled in the same place for services, to the sound of cannons crashing and machine guns clattering. *Hoshanot* were performed on Hoshanah Raba, but there was no *minyan* for Shmini Atzeret. It poured with rain, and Rabbi Sicher shared an attack of influenza with the Protestant chaplain. Because it wasn't possible to have a *minyan* in the flood outside for men divided in different camps, he decided to spend Simchat Torah on a bundle of straw in the cottage, but his arrangements were interrupted by a command to depart immediately. They arrived at their destination the afternoon of the second day, delayed by bad roads. The sound of enemy artillery on the other side of the Weichsel was their accompanying music. Suddenly, a large shell exploded about 500 meters from Rabbi Sicher's wagon, and danger from exploding shells was very real. They hurried, accompanied by cracking and whistling fire, to escape from the firing line, arriving at their destination the next afternoon. Rabbi Sicher had only an hour to rest there, and fell into an exhausted sleep in the wagon with the wounded. From there, they travelled in the direction of Dęblin. On the way the following Friday afternoon, the Jewish and Eastern Orthodox chaplains, travelling together in cheerful mood on the coachman's seat of the wagon carrying the wounded, had the "great honor of being regarded as essential military personnel by the enemy." Two well-aimed shots landing at feet of the officer's valet marching alongside were meant for them, but missed.[93]

This long description in three parts by Rabbi Sicher is unique amongst Austro-Hungarian chaplains, in that it covers the entire fall festival period (the High Holidays and the seven days of Sukkot). It is interesting on several levels. The articles demonstrate that their author adapts to sometimes appalling conditions and tries his best to arrange services even in the midst of battle and in the humblest locations. His descriptions of the bad roads are typical, as are the descriptions of ruined towns and suffering Jews. Murders and depredations by the Russian soldiers are similar to those described by Rabbi Arthur Levy, just fewer in number. The Russians routinely murdered the Jews without first bothering to ascertain their guilt. Rabbi Sicher is a modest man, and thinks nothing of bedding down and cutting wood along with his men. His only care is to provide services and spiritual comfort, as best he can. On Yom Kippur morning when services cannot be held, he marches along with the troops and forgoes the comfort of travel by wagon. He is a typical kind and compassionate Austro-Hungarian chaplain, whose actions speak louder than words.

Rabbi Albert Schweiger was born in 1878 in Topolcany. His father was the well-known Talmudist Rabbi Yizhak Schweiger.[94] Like Rabbi Grünfeld, Rabbi Schweiger served in Jihlava before the war. Dr. Richard Löwi describes a 1915 seder evening in the Carpathians, with Rabbi Schweiger officiating. His report confirms good relations between all the soldiers, and between chaplains of different faiths:

> The seder evening of the Forty-Third k.u.k. Infantry medical unit will long remain a pleasant memory of a beautiful, moving event, for those who participated. In a wretched location high in the Carpathians, about fifty officers and officer candidates and 100 soldiers gathered; many had to stand in the street because there was no space in the two adjacent rooms. Despite the cold, everyone stayed until the end. Chaplain Dr. Albert Schweiger, in peacetime rabbi of Kremsier, deserves special praise.[95] He ensured that, with agreement of command, invitations were sent to all Jewish soldiers in advance, to give them the opportunity, where possible, to observe the laws of Pesach. The commander of the medical unit extended his support in every way, not only making possible the difficult supply of food, but also availability of other supplies.
>
> After *ma'ariv* (evening service), seder celebration began. Many eyes filled with tears in memory of past seder evenings celebrated with their family. After blessing the wine, Rabbi Schweiger gave a spirited talk, which made a deep impression on those present. He explained the significance of the holiday, and expressed the wish that, just as the Almighty delivered our ancestors from the Egyptian yoke, he would deliver our fatherland from the enemy in whose land their fellow Jews were oppressed. He ended his talk with a threefold hurrah to the Kaiser, in which those present enthusiastically participated. Then a young, recently promoted lieutenant read the four questions to the rabbi, who read the entire Pesach prayer book, accompanied by many explanations. The somber initial mood became ever more joyful and confident, and at the end everyone sang Pesach songs together. The men parted in a happy mood after the celebration with the pleasant consciousness of having been able to express their religious feelings here, in the secure expectation of being to celebrate the holiday next year at home. The commandant and Catholic division

chaplain attended the seder.[96]

Rabbi Schweiger described the 1915 High Holidays in the k.k. *Landwehr*: The army advanced, through pouring rain and roads turned into muddy quagmires. Soldiers were exhausted from fighting both enemy and elements. Although Rabbi Schweiger made arrangements well in advance, the day of preparation for Rosh Hashanah was difficult. Troops started advancing in the early morning through pouring rain: roads were swamped and almost impassable. Knee-deep mud and constant rain made evening services impossible.

Next morning, fields were awash with rain and mud. The only acceptable place for the services was the building in which the wounded were being cared for. Officers and men gathered together for prayer. Rabbi Schweiger gave a sermon before the blowing the shofar. He explained that Rosh Hashanah was also called the Day of Judgment, because God made judgment on all peoples, and the Almighty would punish the Russian state because of its acts of horror against Jews. Prayers were shortened, because the sick and wounded were waiting outside for urgent medical treatment in the same room. Improvisation and shortening of services were necessary under such conditions.

Conditions improved prior to Yom Kippur: the rain stopped, and the sun shone. With foresight, a meal was arranged for the Jewish soldiers in preparation for Yom Kippur. A beautiful hall in a lovely castle with all modern conveniences was put at their disposal to hold the services. Rabbi Schweiger introduced the holy day with a talk, explaining the significance of Yom Kippur in the field. After that, *Kol Nidrei* was intoned and the service continued. On Yom Kippur day they recited all prescribed prayers, led by an excellent prayer leader. During the morning, special devotion and emotion reigned when Rabbi Schweiger recited the memorial prayer for the dead. In the afternoon they rested, but the day's devotion was interrupted with orders to advance. The commandant agreed that Jewish soldiers could continue services and catch up next morning at dawn. After conclusion of the service, all entreated The Almighty that they be granted a new year in which they would witness a happy peace, to be able to celebrate next year's festivals safe in the circle of their loved ones.[97]

Rabbi Aron Tänzer celebrated the 1915 High Holidays with the German Bug Army in Brest Litovsk. Despite havoc wrought by the departing Russians, he held Rosh Hashanah and Yom Kippur services in the plundered Great Synagogue. Some Russian prisoners also participated.[98] It is difficult to envision such a fastidious, rigorously disciplined man being comfortable in ad hoc circumstances with stinking huts, and mud up to his knees. His iron sense of duty prevailed whatever the conditions, but complaints were regularly voiced in his diary, and a note of self-congratulation sometimes crept in. This stands in contrast to the Austro-Hungarian chaplain who adapted to the most adverse conditions without complaint.

As has been noted, the Austro-Hungarian army was more forthcoming in fulfilling the religious and dietary needs of the Orthodox Jews than was the case in any other country. Official army rules for Pesach celebration in the field were published in February 1916.[99] They are cited in full, as an example of this unique cooperation:

> According to an announcement from the Jewish chaplaincy in *Wiener Zeitung* no. 84 of January 19, 1916, Passover (*Osterfest*) begins on April 17, 1916 in the evening, and ends on April 25, 1916, at dusk. During that period, Jewish soldiers are to be provided with kosher food.[100]
>
> 1. In all positions where Jewish communities can be found, this can be done through them in cooperation with station command, against payment of a sum equal to the daily food ration.
> 2. Where there is a Jewish community but for whatever reason p. 1. cannot be carried out, kosher food must be provided by local (military) management. In such cases, provision of matzot and ritually slaughtered meat must be taken over by relevant authorities, in cooperation with the nearest Jewish community. In such a case, preparation of kosher food in a separate kitchen must be supervised by men themselves. When this occurs, it is recommended to gather all Jewish soldiers in the garrison together, so they may use the same kitchen.
> 3. In places where there is no Jewish community, see p. 2.
> 4. Where the total number of Jewish soldiers is less than twenty, preparation of kosher food under their own direction cannot occur, unless done without additional payment by military authorities. Offers by individual community members are permitted.
> 5. Directions for the erection of a kosher kitchen:
>   a. Instead of bread, matzot must be provided;
>   b. Either new cutlery, plates, bowls, and all cooking utensils are to be used, or else they must be heated in water with a hot brick placed into it;
>   c. No bread or anything related to fermentation may be brought

into the kitchen;

d. Slaughtered meat must be prepared ritually (soaked and salted);

e. Potatoes are preferred as vegetables but, due to current difficulties, legumes are allowed;

f. All other ritual dietary laws, such as separation of milk and meat, must be rigorously observed during these eight days.

All other questions related to this subject must be referred to the Jewish chaplaincy in Vienna.

6. The following refers specifically to the Vienna garrison: field command must count the number of soldiers, including sick and prisoners of war, requiring kosher provisions and provide these to the local chaplaincy, along with accommodation requirements. The Jewish chaplaincy must be in contact with the public soup kitchen "Einheit," 2 Malzgasse, which is set up for mass catering, to arrange catering, and to advise the field command of different troop units and authorities that are involved.

Any troop unit or authority that can undertake these provisions at their own cost must do so and notify field command and the Jewish chaplaincy.

As compensation, all troop units and authorities must send relevant food ration money to the Jewish chaplaincy in Vienna, to pay the soup kitchen authorities.

7. In prisoner-of-war camps (for prisoners and their guards), see pp. 2. and 3.

8. It is expressly noted that additional expenditure for provision of kosher provisions should not occur. If, for any unforeseen reason, the above is impossible, additional costs may be incurred and command should be informed in time.[101]

In 1916, German chaplains Aron Tänzer, Leopold Rosenak Sali Levi, Arthur Levy, Jakob Sonderling, and Leo Baeck held Pesach services and seders for hundreds of officers and men in areas across the entire Eastern Front. Matzot and other provisions were obtained from home communities and lodges. As was the case with the German chaplains throughout the war, order and punctuality reigned where possible. Ad hoc arrangements were avoided, and borrowed liturgical objects did not arrive at the last minute. Like their Austrian counterparts, German chaplains tried to alleviate civilian suffering and include the civilian population into their holiday celebrations.[102]

In June 1916, Rabbi Adolf Altmann was officially named k.u.k. *Feldrabbiner*, and appointed chaplain in the reserve for the war's duration in Army Group Archduke Eugen. In this capacity, he was awarded the Golden Service Cross with Crown and Ribbon by Emperor Charles, in recognition of his service. In March 1917, Rabbi Altmann met officially with Conrad von Hötzendorf, and discussed increasing antisemitism in the Austro-Hungarian Army. By that time, the *Judenzählung* of 1916 had been performed in the German Army,[103] and Rabbi Altmann worked to help exclude this from consideration in Austro-Hungary.[104] Conrad von Hötzendorf was no friend to the Jews: his antisemitism seems to have been opportunistic, however, and did not prevent promotion of Jews to high rank. He harbored no racial animosity towards Jews, distinguished clearly between "international" and "national" (that is, Austro-Hungarian) Jewry, and valued the bravery of his Jewish soldiers. His feelings about Catholicism were also mixed, so he may have felt doubtful of organized religion in general.[105]

Rabbi Altmann's intention was to set down his war experiences in diary form after the conflict was over. He handwrote a table of contents and obtained letters of recommendation from Conrad von Hötzendorf, as well as many other high-ranking officers. It is our loss that this diary was never written, and that whatever sermons he gave to the troops during the war were not documented.[106]

Altmann published a unique feuilleton for Hanukkah 1916, taking the festival theme to encourage making virtue of necessity, because of blockade shortages. Read today, this article might sound absurd, but sentiments were real at the time and the article must be interpreted in that light. By the end of 1916, the blockade had had a devastating effect on food supply, especially on the home front. Soldiers could forage and buy provisions in large cities like Warsaw and Vilna, but at exorbitant prices; rationing at home by that time had become severe, and only got worse. Rabbi Altmann wrote:

> And so we light the dear candles, which illuminate our sad and dark present state from our glorious past, for the third time during the war. None of our other festivals owe their existence so directly to occurrences during war like Hanukkah. None speaks to our hearts as strongly with reference to tremendous happenings which we are witnessing, like the festival of lights. Tiny flames of these historic lights should be an admonition to a higher order, to understand the signs of the times.

Rabbi Altmann pointed out how memories of old Hanukkah celebrations connected with those in their own times both militarily and economically. They constituted a call to bravery and dedication, telling of the Maccabean victory and encouraging its imitation. The story of the miraculous Hanukkah light represented an incompletely appreciated heavenly signal of victory:

> When man himself becomes a blessing, everything around him is strengthened. We hear about Joseph: "thus the Lord's blessing was upon all that he owned, in the house and in the field." (Genesis 39:5). This blessing from God, confirmed by man, is seen in our own day through satisfaction and frugality: they are postulates and foundations of true love of fatherland.

Rabbi Altmann posited that if they emulated the Maccabees in their perseverance against scarcity and believing in God's power, miracles would happen for them, such as swift conquest of much of Romania and access to the Romanian wheat fields and other agriculture. He ended by calling for consecration, and understanding of blessings that can be found in scarcity.[107] Rabbi Altmann must have known how serious the effects of the blockade were, especially later in the war, but the above feuilleton must be viewed as patriotic encouragement to the troops in time of scarcity.

The first report of chaplains arranging services on the Italian Front occurred in 1916.[108] During fierce fighting in 1916, Rabbi Tauber organized and conducted troop and civilian Yom Kippur services in Laibach.[109] An anonymous attendee described this service, held by Rabbi Tauber together with Rabbi A. Deutsch.

Just before *Kol Nidrei*, the narrator described a brightly lit festival hall full of Jewish soldiers, and civilian families from Laibach. Excitement could be seen on every face, as if to say: "Something is about to happen which only a Jew can understand." Rabbi Deutsch rose onto a small platform. The rabbi's voice was heard as a salvation, and heaviness in the air disappeared like fog. Everyone awoke after the sermon, as from a trance, when the cantor's strong, sad voice resonated. The service ended at 9.00 pm.

On Yom Kippur morning, after *shacharit* (morning service), Rabbi Tauber gave the sermon, depicting a great house in which peace would reign and concluded: "and the children shall return within their borders" (Jeremiah 31:17). After *mussaf* (additional service), Rabbi Tauber entered the military prayer room, where Rabbi Deutsch was leading another service, took the latter over, and left Rabbi Deutsch to proceed with the general service.

After the concluding service, the men partook of the ritual break-fast meal, after having first received a kosher meal on the eve of the fast. Rabbi Tauber visited the Russian-Jewish prisoners of war, who also participated in services, and for whom free meals were provided. He reported:

> When I entered the room where prisoners of war were receiving free kosher meals, I observed a wonderful scene. Fifty men sat around tables. Each had—apart from a plate of food—grapes, other fruit, and a quart of wine. I will not forget the joy of these men, their thankful spirits, their cheerful, if slightly forced, mood. Their facial expressions said: "You have looked after us, prisoners of war, so well on Yom Kippur."[110]

Many letters attested to how men appreciated their Jewish chaplains. An anonymous soldier reported on Rabbi Tauber's assistance setting up services during 1916 High Holidays on the Isonzo. Units were located on an exposed part of the front and, to gather at the appointed place, men had to pass through the firing line. This did not prevent soldiers from streaming together from their positions in large numbers the day before the festival. According to division commands, each man was equipped with rucksack, tent sheet, and cover, with provisions for three days (including the Sabbath after Rosh Hashanah), and the day before and evening of Yom Kippur. They made sure to arrive in time to have meals cooked, be fed and bivouacked, and not to have to march back to their positions during festival days. Because of insufficient initial allocation of chaplains to the Isonzo Army, no chaplain was initially available, but this deficiency was reversed soon after (plate 9). Rabbi Tauber took up the initial call, with assistance of Ensign Dr. Siegfried Steiner.

Rabbi Tauber proved an excellent choice: he had only one day before the High Holidays, during which he hastily collected the necessary ritual objects, including Torah, shofar and kosher wine, from the rear, and had these brought to the men, who were gathered far out in the front line. At the last minute, just before the festival began, an automobile with these objects rattled in, joyfully greeted by the men. Because of heavy traffic at the front, they did not have much hope that the ritual objects would come in time. Local brigade medical officers put a large empty hospital barracks at the men's disposal. Blankets, tent sheets, white cloths and candles, rapidly turned the barracks into a worthy prayer room.

It gave ordinary soldiers great joy to see how Jewish officers at services provided an example to the men, with open-handedness and devoutness. In the coastal mountainous terrain, an area where in peacetime no Jews would have gathered for prayer, a glorious Jewish congregation, filled with faith in God and brotherhood, developed. Such a spirit, reports the anonymous soldier, was only possible in the field, under the war's spiritual impact together with the destiny-laden solemnity that constituted the mood of the holy days.

Volunteer prayer leaders were excellent. Honvėd Lieutenant Samuel Bein was especially fine in leading the additional service and *Kol Nidrei*: the pathos of his prayer and beautiful voice were moving. It was uplifting to see how officers searched out older *Landwehr* men, who were fathers, for *aliyot* so that they could gain spiritual strength and recite blessings for their families.[111] This contrasted with the usual practice, according to which *aliyot* were mostly given to those who donated to Jewish national or war charities. "The shofar sound was imprinted in our memories, framed by thundering artillery fire rolling over us from the nearby front."[112]

Bėla Diamant (born in 1885 in Spácza) served as k.u.k. chaplain during the last three years of the war.[113] Like Rabbis Bertisch and Tauber, he emphasized the Orthodox make-up of many soldiers entrusted to his care. He described a 1916 Sunday afternoon service held in one of his regiments, with large numbers of Galician Jewish recruits. After services, he informed the men that they had to bury a Jewish Honvėd, who had died in the local field hospital from a shot to the head. He formed them up and in closed cortege they marched to the cemetery. The picture of this Jewish company, these bearded *Peyes-Juden* (sidelock Jews), appealed to him in a special way. Having arrived at the cemetery, he had to wait for the hearse. He conversed with the men in the meanwhile, noticing that one after another left his group. After a short time, they all returned, one with a handful of money, saying: "Herr Rabbiner, we request that you send half of these 100 crowns, which we have collected amongst ourselves, to each of the two widows of our fallen comrades. Tell them that we'll send this amount to them every month."

Rabbi Diamant wanted to call out with all his strength: "Hear and take note, you antisemites! This is the true spirit of the Polish Jew!"[114]

Rabbi Samuel Link was 1871 born in Neutra.[115] He studied at the University of Vienna and Berlin Theological Seminary, obtaining his rabbinical diploma in 1895 followed by his PhD at the University of Bern in 1905.[116]

When war broke out, he was a rabbi in Pilsen (Czech Republic). He served as chaplain in the k.u.k. Italian army from 1916 to 1918. When he took up his office in South Tyrol, he found that services were led by a Polish cantor in the Orthodox, "undisciplined" manner. Rabbi Link attempted to "educate" his more traditional congregants in modern service rites, without traditional noisy, disorganized participation. Initially mistrusted, he became beloved for his sincerity, and was awarded the Golden Service Cross with Crown and Swords. The following are two reports of his activities.

The first report is written by an unnamed soldier from the South Tyrol. The writer arrived at the Palazzo Venditti, and followed a few soldiers to the first floor. At the top of the stairs he found a *Landwehr* man with fixed bayonet at the door. "A religious service under armed guard?" But the chaplain, whom he met in the antechamber of the hall where the service was to be held, explained: guards were there because of prisoners of war whom he had brought along, and had to take back to camp after the service. "Have you attended a religious service in the field before?" the chaplain asked. The writer said no, this was the first time he had even heard of this.

Rabbi Link told him that weekly services had been held in town before his arrival by a Polish cantor who had officiated in an East Galician village, now serving in the *Landwehr*. The writer's first impression was an untidy room, in which fifty men stood around, yelling confusedly, or moving around frantically, as if one wanted to "surpass" the other in piety. Most were Jews from Orthodox Galician communities who knew no other kind of service. Others, used to a quieter service, felt uncomfortable with the customs of this majority. The Orthodox soldiers at first approached the writer with distrust, but were soon convinced that he was at least as good a Jew as the loudest amongst them.

When Rabbi Link—a modest man in wrinkled cassock—and the writer entered the room, soldiers rose. The chaplain saluted them, and sat in front of a little table decorated with a white embroidered cloth. The writer took his place on a back bench: about twenty rows of benches had been obtained from a local school, so that about 200 soldiers could be seated, but more came, so they had to stand in side corridors. A strange scene emerged: a classroom-like room with low school children's benches on which soldiers now sat, many with grey beards and tattered uniforms. The high windows overlooking the Via Lunga, one of the noisiest streets in the town, were shut. One soldier lit the candles in the two silver candlesticks on the little table next to the rabbi, another handed out small Hebrew prayer books.

Austro-Hungarian soldiers sat in front rows, caps on heads. Some of them were old and some very young; there were university men, farmers, city types, merchants, Galician village Jews with long, black, beards. Some had typical Semitic features but others, such as three Tyrolean *Landwehr*—whom nobody would have thought were Jews—did not. Infantry, dragoons, artillery, sappers, railway, *Landwehr*—all were represented. Officers sat in side rows. Many shirts exhibited decorations: bravery and service crosses, and a few Iron Crosses. A black-bearded Galician infantry corporal, looking exactly like a Talmud student, wore the Large Silver Medal for Bravery and Small Silver and Bronze Bravery Medals. One Tyrolean was decorated with the Golden Medal for Bravery.

Prisoners of war sat in back benches: Russians, and three Serbs. The Russians were mainly tall and slender with blond—sometimes very blond—hair, looking nothing like the Galicians so often identified as Jewish racial types. The private first class serving as cantor donned his tallit, approached the platform, and started to sing the introductory Sabbath hymn, *Lecha Dodi*:[117]

> He is no singer, by God's grace, this cantor: his voice is flawed and coarse. But, somehow, I don't know how, its effect, with the sad melancholy of the old hymns which have remained the same for hundreds of years in their sobbing, wailing, humble-contrite pleading, is harrowing. Others pray with him in an undertone; here and there someone tries, from old habit, to raise his voice above the others: but he looks at the chaplain self-consciously and immediately lowers his voice. Many sit, heads deeply bowed between intertwined hands; others stare into a distance which we cannot fathom, murmuring prayers untiringly. Russians pray from memory, bowing deeply from time to time and raising their voices moderately. A young Serb in the back row prays standing, tears running over his deeply sunken cheeks . . . Everyone joins in the hymn, and the beautiful melody soars aloft rejoicing, filling the room, pulsating through closed window into the street outside, causing passersby to stop and listen.

Rabbi Link's sermon expounded on the weekly Torah portion, and then he spoke of everybody's cares and worries:

> . . . always more warmly, always more brotherly, always more thrillingly . . . A master of discourse hides in this delicate, humble man. Sometimes his voice swells through the room. "It's not enough just to

do your duty," he declares, "think that you are Jews, and must therefore do more than your duty, to silence our enemies. Let no-one dare call you cowards, forgetting that Judah the Maccabee, the Hammer, was your ancestor."

The service ended with the Austrian National Hymn *Gott erhalte*. Everyone approached the chaplain and thanked him in his own way; the city dweller with a warm word, the farmer standing stiffly at attention, saluting. Under the beautiful old palazzo portico men slowly disappeared, some gesticulating, already in dispute over exposition of the weekly Torah portion. Under watch, prisoners of war came down, but they too seemed to walk straighter.[118]

This article powerfully portrays the mélange of nationalities in the Austro-Hungarian Army. Contrary to preconceived prejudices, Jews did not necessarily have Semitic features. Some of the bravest and most decorated soldiers were the most Orthodox, whose greatest joy was to noisily expound Torah and Talmud, whenever possible. One can imagine the shock of assimilated Austrian Jews on their first encounter with a raucous, disorganized, Eastern European Orthodox service: they must have thought they were in another world, another religion. Prisoners of war were incorporated into services as much as possible. In synagogue, all were equal.

In another 1916 letter, Samuel Goldfand (presumably one of Rabbi Link's congregants) reported on Rabbi Link's participation in a memorable Shavuot (Pentecost) celebration in the field:

In this solemn-dark time, during which so many thousands look at life through veils of tears, it does one good to report a festival with real Jewish communal spirit. Our recent Shavuot festival was just such an uplifting festival celebration.

Deep emotion welled through the approximately 350 assembled soldiers when Dr. Bloch (no relation to the newspaper editor), using Jewish citations, praised Rabbi Link as a religious, selfless man who, despite great deprivations, regarded it as his highest duty to ease pain and misery wherever he could. Rabbi Link modestly thanked the officer for his kind thoughts, and concluded with a prayer of thanks to God and Fatherland.[119] This modest acceptances of thanks and congratulations by Rabbi Link contrasts sharply with the diary of Rabbi Tänzer, replete with self-congratulatory entries (no doubt well-deserved) about his talks and sermons.[120]

Rabbi Bernard Hausner was born in 1874 in Chortkow,[121] Ordained by the rabbinical seminary in Vienna, he received a doctorate in philosophy from the German University in Prague. He spent time from September 3, 1914 to June 22, 1915 (Russian occupation of Lemberg) working with Jewish and Russian authorities to alleviate the situation of Jewish civilians, who were subjected to pogroms, mass arrests, forced labor, beatings, murder, rape, and robbery by the Russians.[122] When the Russians evacuated Lemberg, he volunteered, serving as chaplain in the k.u.k. army first on the Galician and then the Italian Front during the last three war years.[123] He wrote about his experiences as *Feldrabbiner* in 1916 and 1917, sending the following letter from the Isonzo in 1916 through an unnamed writer:

> From the Isonzo Front: In one hour I must go to my troops for the Yom Kippur service. During Rosh Hashanah, I arranged eight services in my section. I was able to participate, alternating, in only four of these. This represented a lot of work, but I was happy to participate. All our prayers for victory will hopefully be heard, because we are fighting in a righteous cause.

The services followed prescribed ritual. Commanders of five regiments and younger officers alike were accommodating, helping Rabbi Hausner with arrangements. "Even the smallest hint of antisemitism in the field was held thoroughly in check." Rabbi Hausner had, during recent days, received a legion of *Liebesgaben* (gifts from home) as a result of a request in Dr. Bloch's newspaper. Money was used to purchase large amounts of cigarettes, soap, and chocolate, and distributed amongst the men, including those in his own regiment.[124]

Rabbi Hausner reported on the ferocity and tragedy of battle in 1917:

> An unforgettable scene unfolded before me: Amongst troops marching into the fire and shrapnel of battle on the next hill are many of my acquaintances. One Christian soldier approaches me asking for a prayer book . . . Towards evening the men return, on foot and in ambulances, many severely wounded. Who could do justice to the scene, with its endless suffering and misery? Nobody who hasn't seen and experienced war can truly understand its horror.[125]

Dieter Hecht has recently published an excellent monograph describing the duties of Rabbi Hausner during the war, including his work on the

Hilfskomittee in Lemberg after the Russian invasion, and his subsequent service on the Isonzo,[126]

Rabbi Viktor Kurrein was born in 1881 in Linz and studied at the Vienna Jewish Theological Seminary, graduating with a doctorate in philosophy in 1904.[127] He served as rabbi and chaplain both for k.u.k. armies and prisoner of war camps. Appointment of a Jewish chaplain whose sole duties were to Jewish prisoners of war appears unique. The following is an extract from his 1916 feuilleton on the chaplain's duties towards prisoners of war. It shows a remarkable amount of consideration given to the Russian Jewish prisoners of war by the Austro-Hungarian authorities:

> One evening, two men passed by me in a Salzburg street;[128] I paused to hear what they were saying to each other: "A disarmed enemy isn't an enemy anymore. Only men with weapons are our enemies, against whom we must fight. Therefore, a prisoner isn't an enemy anymore: he is a man like you or I." These words, from modest people, in the language of ordinary folk, demonstrate a noteworthy unprejudiced way of thinking. Since then, the more I visit the prisoner-of-war camp, the more I think of those words: "prisoner-of-war camp!" What had one understood of this concept before? Today, we visualize a town with 30,000 or more inhabitants, clean, cared for, with picturesque streets and gardens, electric lights, mail, a fire brigade, a coffee house, church and cemetery, administrative center and offices. Certainly, this town (albeit smaller) has something curious about it: a town without women and children! Perhaps such a prisoner-of-war camp was Paradise for Adam, before creation of Eve.

Rabbi Kurrein was in charge of two camps, each with its small community of Jews. Many prisoners worked in industry or agriculture. Whenever he asked Jewish prisoners how they were treated, they replied that they were doing well, lacking nothing. Rabbi Kurrein facilitated correspondence: Yiddish was written with German instead of Hebrew letters, so that it could pass censors.

For Pesach, new barracks were constructed, with two new kitchen facilities, cutlery, cooking material, and provisions according to the Jewish law. Matzot, kosher meat, and wine were made available at state expense. Prisoners were allowed to cook for themselves, eat their meals, hold services and seders in another large barracks. Rabbi Kurrein gave his first sermon and brought gifts from home, *hagadot,* and cigarettes. A library was founded, and Rabbi

Kurrein contributed all superfluous Hebrew literature that he had to it. Prayer and psalm books, tallitot and tefillin were provided partially at personal cost, partially with the cooperation of his home community of Teplitz-Schönau, from whom he also received a Torah scroll, an altar cloth, and a *parochet* (cover for the Holy Ark).[129] The Torah ark, prayer leader lectern, table, and candles were prepared by the prisoners, and the room papered over. Thus, they had a permanent prayer room for their *minyanim* (see plate 6). They even studied Torah every day, and when he gave his monthly sermon, his "community" crowded so tightly together that the room was almost too small.

Professionals amongst the prisoners were occupied in their own jobs, and their diligence and expertise earned high praise. No faith-related hindrances were put in their way: farmers and even Catholic chaplains sent to Rabbi Kurrein for prayer books for the Russian Jews—another example of interfaith cooperation. The government and military cooperation—at all levels—in the care for spiritual needs of the Jewish prisoners, and the lengths to which authorities went to look after these men, is remarkable.[130]

Rabbi Samu(el) Lemberger, a civilian rabbi from Pozsonyszentgyörgy, applied for a field rabbi reserve position when war began.[131] Lemberger was sent to the Eastern Front with the Thirty-Ninth Honvéds on August 1, 1914, and took part in several bloody battles in Galicia from 1914 through 1916, after which he was sent to Transylvania. He became the most highly decorated Jewish chaplain in the k.u. army: awards included the Knight's Cross of the Order of Franz Joseph on the ribbon of the Merit Cross with Swords, Golden Merit Cross with Crown on the ribbon of the Military Medal Cross, Military Jubilee Cross of 1908, Officer's Badge of Honor of the Red Cross with War Decoration, and Emperor Charles Troops' Cross.[132]

One of Rabbi Lemberger's articles from the Romanian Front was published in *Egyenlőség* in 1916 and translated into German. It reports that Rabbi Lemberger was on the point of travelling to an adjacent battalion, to hold a service, when an older sergeant introduced himself, asking whether he had buried Ensign Leopold Löwi, in a cemetery near the Romanian border. It turned out that Rabbi Lemberger's young friend Leopold Löwi—who had died heroically two weeks before, during storming of a Romanian border elevation, and been buried this side of the border, to rest in the earth of his homeland—was this man's brother. He had arrived with the last company, and when he left the trenches he had come upon the grave of his younger brother.

Another tragic case: a few days previously Rabbi Lemberger had been called to another burial. Before the funeral he looked at the dog tags of the young comrade who was to be laid to rest, and confirmed with heavy heart that the dead man's father was also serving with them. Luckily, the father was several kilometers away, otherwise Rabbi Lemberger would have had to witness the dreadful image of a soldier-father grieving at the grave of his soldier-son.

The wounded were not kept long at the front where Rabbi Lemberger served. Only in exceptional cases, where a serious wound and immediate transport could endanger healing, did they keep the wounded there for up to a few weeks. So it was with poor Ensign Friedrich Fischer. At the head of his Honvéds, he attacked a Romanian elevation occupied by the enemy, was wounded in the abdomen, and developed peritonitis.[133] He was treated at the front and his condition improved for ten days. There was hope for his recovery, but he suddenly became weaker, and died three days later. The young man was loved like a blood relative by all who knew him. He had already been awarded two Silver Medals for Bravery. For his last heroic deed, which saved the situation, he was awarded the Golden Medal for Bravery, but did not live to enjoy it: he had already died. Rabbi Lemberger concluded:

> We also have moments that uplift the heart. To spend Rosh Hashanah and Yom Kippur here amongst hundreds of front soldiers, see reverence with which services are filled, and the devotion, loyalty and love of the faith of our fathers: these experiences compensate us for all difficulties. The religious thoughts of some of our comrades are wonderful to behold.[134]

Chaplains were not averse to front-line duty. On February 2, 1917, during an infantry attack on an Italian trench position, before the storm troops jumped out of the trenches and charged, Rabbi Béla Diamant, ministering to the troops, encouraged everyone to fight. He remained with the attack groups throughout the battle and contributed by his personal presence to its successful outcome. His actions were mentioned in dispatches. In an article published in a March 1917 issue of *Dr. Bloch's Österreichische Wochenschrift*, an anonymous writer emphasized Rabbi Diamant's courage and scorn of death, as well as the fact that, although located at the corps command, he preferred to stay in the front line.[135]

Like their German counterparts, the Austro-Hungarian chaplains held conferences to share information and exchange ideas.[136] A rabbinical conference was held in Trieste between May 6 and 7, 1917, for all chaplains in the Fifth Army under chairmanship of Rabbi Tauber, to discuss current issues. Decisions were made, including proposal for convocation of a general chaplains' conference, to expand the development of the Jewish chaplaincy. The Chairman of the Trieste Congregation as well as Dr. Chajes (chief rabbi, IKG Vienna) made themselves available to assist. Dr. Chajes attended the conference as observer. All attendees gathered for a communal photograph (plate 10).[137]

It is interesting to note that Dr. Majer (Meier) Samuel Balaban (1877–1942), noted historian of Polish and Galician Jews, was also an ordained rabbi, who often mediated between military authorities and Jewish communities.[138] At the end of December 1916, after a six-week informational trip in June through the Austro-Hungarian occupation area in Poland, Balaban was appointed *Oberfeldrabbiner* of the entire k.u.k. occupation army, responsible for organization of spiritual care and representation of the local chaplains before the high command and the Christian chaplains.[139]

Late in May 1917, *Dr. Bloch's Österreichische Wochenschrift* carried a series of articles unique in the World War I Jewish chaplaincy, all by Rabbi Leo Bertisch from Przemyśl. Rabbi Bertisch was born in 1877 in Stanislau.[140] He obtained his doctorate in 1915 from Charles University in Prague, and served as chaplain of the reserves during 1917, first at command in Vienna, and later in Przemyśl. The articles originate from Deutschbrod and Leitmeritz.[141]

His introductory article on the need for Jewish chaplains was followed by three lengthier articles, expounding on the relationships between the first chaplains of the Jewish people—the priests and the High Priest—and present-day chaplaincy. Rabbi Bertisch is an excellent example of the need for Orthodox chaplaincy training. These articles would have meant little to assimilated Jews from Liberal/Reform backgrounds, but have been very welcome amongst Orthodox soldiers well acquainted with his Torah and Talmud citations.

In his introductory article, Rabbi Bertisch pointed to Deuteronomy 20:2: "When you are about to go into battle, the priest shall come forward and address the army. . . ." From this text, Rabbi Bertisch deduced that, in ancient times, priests had the same duties as modern-day chaplains. They reminded soldiers of God with their words, and they also had religious and patriotic duties. "What other function could they have had, according to the Biblical text, in the upcoming war? In which other capacity could they have served, other than that of modern chaplains?"

Rabbi Bertisch cited Talmud and commentaries, referring to Jewish chaplain as the "anointed for war," whose purpose is to work with troops on religious and moral issues. Talmud Sota 42a remarks that not every priest, but only those specifically chosen, that is, the "anointed ones," must go before the soldiers prior to the battle, and speak to them. Only these priests have the right to be entrusted with such a mission.¹⁴²

In his first article, Rabbi Bertisch compared the swearing-in of Jewish soldiers en route to service in the field, then and now. During the current war, all departing men were assembled in uniform, divided into groups according to language or religion. All their officers, commanders, and chaplains assembled before the men, and the National Anthem played while the regimental flag was raised. Then, the commandant usually gave a short talk to the assembled men, reminding them of their duties. They were divided into groups by a chaplain, who gave a short talk, reminding men of their duties to fatherland and law, but also to religion and God. General swearing-in then took place in each soldier's mother tongue, troops were dismissed by their commanders, and marched off.

Rabbi Bertisch compared the modern swearing-in ceremony with the one described in Deuteronomy 20:2–4:

> It shall be, when you are come nigh into battle, that the priest shall approach and speak to the people, and say to them: "Hear, O Israel, you approach this day into battle against your enemies: let not your hearts faint, fear not, and do not tremble, neither be terrified because of them; For the Lord your God is He Who goes with you, to fight for you against your enemies, to save you."

Rabbi Bertisch cited this speech by priests to soldiers going into the field as an example for modern Jewish chaplains who had the task of addressing their own troops going into the field.¹⁴³

In the second article, Rabbi Bertisch expounded further on chaplaincy duties devolving on priests and high priests. He pointed out that one Talmud tractate devotes an entire section to chaplains, named originally the "anointed for war." He used Biblical passages (Deuteronomy 20:2), Talmud (Sotah 42a), and commentaries to show how the original name *cohen* ("priest") was changed to "anointed for war."

Bertisch continued by expounding that, in the same way as every Jewish and non-Jewish chaplain today carried ritual objects necessary for holding a service, so did the "anointed for war." Numbers 31:6 continues: "and the holy articles from the sanctuary in his hand." In ancient times, the "anointed for war" went to battle with the "holy articles." Rabbi Bertisch deduced the different purely religious functions of present-day chaplains from the above texts. These included holding services, visiting the sick, and presiding over the swearing-in of troops.

Later in this article, Rabbi Bertisch described a second, purely military, function of the chaplain in the ancient army of Israel, according to Numbers 31:6 "and trumpets for signaling in his hand." There are no commentaries on these trumpets. But, as Rabbi Bertisch noted, they signify the priest's military duties: he is obliged to sound the trumpet as a signal to summon the community and break up camp. In Numbers 10:1–8 we read how the Lord commanded the making of two silver trumpets, used for calling the congregation and directing their movement. When both were blown, the congregation was to gather at the door of the tabernacle of meeting. If only one was blown, only leaders, heads of divisions of Israel, were to come. When the trumpets sounded advance, the camps on the east side began their journey. When advance was sounded a second time, the camps on the south side began their journey. When the assembly was to be gathered together, trumpets were to be blown, but not to sound the advance. Latter-day chaplains' duties had more emphasis on the spiritual and the supportive, and not just the purely military issues.

Rabbi Bertisch pointed out that nomination and selection of chaplains is also described in the Bible. Not every priest was entrusted with this mission—only those selected and destined for this purpose. In other words, only those who were the "anointed for war" could stand before the people and the soldiers before they went out to war, only they had the right to assume this function (see Talmud Sota 42a).

He expanded on differences in ritual clothing (uniforms) of ordinary priests (chaplains) and the High Priest (chief chaplain), and the Talmudic differences of opinion concerning the rank of the "anointed for war." When the "anointed for war" went out to battle, he wore the prescribed four priestly articles of clothing (robe, girdle, miter, and drawers), but could borrow the *Urim* and *Tummim* from the High Priest, even if he was an ordinary priest.[144]

The High Priest enjoyed highest prestige, and was the most influential personage in ancient Israel. He was head of the priesthood, and the entire sect. He represented the entire Jewish nation in that, as part of his assignation, he carried the names of the twelve tribes in the stones on his breastplate. There was also an inscription on his forehead plate next to the scapular garment "Holy to the Lord." This high dignity obligated special holiness. The High Priest's service consisted of first-line religious supervision. In the entire Jewish state, only the "anointed for war" could occupy the high position, authority, and dignity of High Priest, and wear at least some of the High Priest's ostentatiously decorated garments.

If these ancient priests were everything for their people, Israel, the more so were they for their fellow Jews during times of war, out in the field. Thus, Bertisch expounded, they could best be recognized during the present war, where thousands of Jewish soldiers were far from their homes, parents, wives, and children. They could find comfort, advice, strength, and edification only with their chaplain, just as in ancient times Jewish soldiers found all this in the "anointed for war." Therefore, it is not surprising that the Jewish sages understood, so long ago, to equip priests with power and respect, dignity and authority, to allow them to function at the front as the High Priest functioned at home. Rabbi Bertisch noted that the Jewish chaplains were well respected in all warring countries. In the Austro-Hungarian army, in contrast to other professionals such as physicians and jurists, chaplains were deployed as captains immediately upon entering active service, instead of having first to serve in a subordinate rank.[145]

His final article continued with an exposition on whether or not a chaplain must possess theological knowledge:

> When we speak about the Jewish people, we refer to the great masses of Jews in the East: in Russia, Galicia, Bukowina, Hungary, and Moravia, or else specific cities such as Vienna, Berlin, New York. The few Jewish soldiers from Bohemia, Lower Austria (apart from Vienna), Upper Austria, Salzburg, the Tyrol, etc. do not come into consideration because, with few exceptions, they are indifferent to religion. But when, for example, we speak of a Galician or Hungarian regiment, where they are 100 to 200 or even 300 to 400 Jewish soldiers present, we must not forget that most of them can study Pentateuch with commentaries. Many can also chant the Torah or study Gemara, because most have been to traditional Hebrew school in their youth, and many have also gone to Talmud schools.

Rabbi Bertisch asked: how should a chaplain behave when he comes in contact with soldiers who immediately start to recite Torah to the chaplain when they meet? When such a man wished to hear Torah from a chaplain, he wanted to involve the chaplain in a mutual "Torah discussion."[146] A soldier who had theological knowledge became so excited that he forgot, or did not even think, that he stood before his superior in the form of a chaplain. If a chaplain did not answer his questions, or participate in theological debate, he immediately forfeited position and authority.

Rabbi Bertisch concluded that a chaplain must possess and master Talmudic and even theological knowledge, so that he could speak to the troops, but also expound Torah and Talmud to them. The only other comparable country where such rabbinical knowledge would have been necessary was Russia, which took no spiritual care of their approximately 180,000 Jewish soldiers, a large part of whom were Orthodox.[147]

By 1917, the Allied blockade had given rise to increasingly severe food shortages. Indeed, most war correspondence of Central Powers soldiers between 1917 and 1918 is concerned with food. In this light, provision of festive holiday meals took on a new meaning. A letter from a grateful congregant to Rabbi Tauber after 1917 Pesach services reads:

Esteemed Herr Rabbiner!

Powerfully moved by our being able to celebrate Pesach in the field, it is the desire of all us in staff and command to express our heartfelt thanks to you for your generous, beautifully arranged Jewish initiative, providing ritually prepared food for us—especially for our brave Jewish comrades fighting in the furthest trenches, during this holy Passover festival.

We are all aware of the great deed that you have done! What great efforts you have had to make, to achieve your goal, so beautifully achieved! Matzot in the trenches! Ritually prepared meat at such a time! Who would have thought this possible during Pesach even in 1915 or 1916? What at that time counted as Utopia, you, Herr Rabbiner, have brought this year to ennobling reality.[148]

A letter in a 1917 issue of *Jüdische Korrespondenz* shows influence of the blockade even on inflexible Jewish dietary laws:

The rabbinate of the Vienna IKG feels the need—because of exceptional shortage of provisions caused by the war—to allow, for this Pesach only, consumption of beans, peas, and lentils, as long as, before the beginning of Pesach, it is in its original state, carefully examined, together with all *chametz* [leaven], and sent packaged accordingly.[149]

Chaplains on the Eastern Front often took it upon themselves to try to better the conditions of the suffering local Jewish civilian populations, caught in-between two powerful armies.

Rabbi Reuben Färber was born in 1869 in Oświęcim (Poland). He was ordained 1896 in Galicia, and studied Semitic languages in Berlin and Strassburg, where he obtained his PhD in 1901. When war began, he was rabbi in Mährisch-Ostrau.[150] Beginning in August 1917, he served for ten months as chaplain in the k.u.k. Fourth Army in Vladimir-Volynsky, and then transferred to Cholm.[151] His services to the Jewish community during this time, plus a letter of thanks from the chairman and members of the board of the Vladimir-Volynsky Jewish community, published in *Dr. Bloch's Österreichische Wochenschrift* of June 1918, are summarized below.

His activities led to the Vienna *Israelitische Allianz* reinstating their previously cancelled monthly subvention, and even raising it. The division of benefits was entrusted to suitable administrators, with Rabbi Färber at their head. For many months, he labored to compile a directory of the poor, defining how much support they needed. He founded a twelve-member community board to help him in these activities. Out of the chaotic conditions in which 12,000 souls (mainly the poor and wretched) of the congregation found themselves, a well-ordered community was created. The neighboring town of Ustilug requested, and obtained, command approval for Rabbi Färber to similarly organize their own community.[152]

A section for Jewish schools was attached to the community board, to give teaching a modern, secular—in addition to the religious—direction. A campaign to clothe poor children during winter was held, which included charity evenings under the chaplain's protectorate. This led to establishment of a permanent clothing association, headed by a member of the committee, which at the time of writing had collected about 10,000 rubles for purchase of shoes and other articles of clothing, to be distributed amongst poorest children. 5,000 rubles were earmarked for providing wood to the very poor. For Pesach, the committee was able to provide an additional 15,000 rubles to support the poor during the festival. Rabbi Färber supervised the Jewish soup kitchen, school, and rabbinical college. He paid attention to the *mikveh* (ritual immersion bath) and, despite significant difficulties, a diligent bath supervisor was appointed. Under his leadership, there was a significant improvement in order, hygiene, and administration of the main synagogue.

Rabbi Färber's principle throughout was to centralize all branches of community life, so that the single threads all came together in the hands of the community board. The article concluded:

> Dr. Färber has inspired deepest thanks of our town for his selfless service, beneficence, organizational ability, and love of his Jewish people extending to all aspects of our community. The board regrets his departure, and, with all parties involved, wishes him luck from their heart in all his activities on behalf of Austrian Jewry. We thank him also for many hours of uplifting services and his learned and enjoyable sermons.
>
> What chaplain Färber has achieved as mediator between the Jewish population and military administration can only be alluded to here in brief. God will reward him for his efforts and service. After peace returns, this will be a golden page in the history of our community. As a sign of our thanks, the community has elected Dr. Färber a permanent honorary member of this community. Vladimir-Volynsky. May 27, 1918.[153]

Little more than two decades later, the Jewish community of Vladimir-Volynsky, together with the entire Jewish culture of Eastern Europe, was destroyed by the annihilating antisemitism of the Holocaust.

In an article written towards the end of the war, Rabbi Färber set out the three different Jewish religious rites in the Austro-Hungarian army (Liberal, Conservative, and Orthodox).[154] How would an Orthodox chaplain be received by assimilated troops, and a Liberal chaplain by Orthodox soldiers? Levels of acceptance differed: Orthodox Jews from Galicia and Bukowina did not look kindly on a Liberal rabbi who ate in the mess, not adhering to all religious practices, without deep knowledge of Torah and Talmud. This point is also alluded to by Rabbi Bertisch. Rabbi Färber proposed that a *Kollegium* with one representative of each of the three rites be elected, to advise the War Ministry where chaplains should be placed, depending on the religious adherence of the soldiers involved.[155] There is no evidence that this suggestion was followed.

It is interesting to compare Rabbi Färber's activities with those of Rabbi Tänzer, an indefatigable soup kitchen organizer in the German army. Given the appalling conditions and his wide service area, Rabbi Tänzer achieved fully as much as Rabbi Färber. This, despite strict German army protocol, compared to the more relaxed Austro-Hungarian military administration under which Rabbi Färber worked. Rabbi Jacob Sänger, a German chaplain in the Balkans, also assisted Jewish civilians: however, he did not go through prescribed channels and received a stern reprimand.[156] One can imagine that the Austro-Hungarian army allowed more independence, and less reliance on official paperwork, than its German counterpart.

By the end of 1917, with peace between the Central Powers and Russia and Ukraine in sight, military activity shifted to the Isonzo. Rabbi Grünfeld, originally stationed on the Eastern Front (see above), described Yom Kippur services on the Italian Front, a month before the start of the Battle of Caporetto on October 24:

> Slowly, the heavily laden truck winds its way up the dusty mountain road. It's Yom Kippur eve and in a few hours I hope to be with my brave soldiers. On Rosh Hashanah, I assured them that, if possible, I would spend the holy day with them. On my request, division command gave the order by telephone for as protected a place as possible near the reserve division, to hold two services. Jewish soldiers in our regiments have acquitted themselves with great bravery.

They were located near the front, which was about to erupt. Destroyed houses, with large craters everywhere, showed how easily the road through which they were passing could be reached by Italian shells. Rabbi Grünfeld passed safely through the dangerous valley with wretched villages, arrived at his provisional goal, and awaited advance guard of the medical division for arrival of orders.

According to command direction, about 200 soldiers and a number of officers assembled at a forested mountain slope, to celebrate Yom Kippur. The melody of *Kol Nidrei* sounded eerily beautiful, about three kilometers from the front lines. Gradually, impenetrable darkness fell. After the service, Rabbi Grünfeld spent time with his men, and then departed, in the middle of the night, so that he could lead a service the next morning for soldiers in another regiment.[157]

Yom Kippur day services were held on a forested mountain slope from which one looked deep into the valley. But this time there was no peace like the night before. Within a few hours, seven enemy planes appeared above: from all corners, anti-aircraft artillery thundered against them. Rabbi Grünfeld reminded the soldiers about Jonah's words during a wild storm: "I am a Hebrew and I worship [only] the Lord, the God of Heaven" (Jonah 1: 9). Like Jonah, they pledged, in this difficult hour, unbreakable loyalty to God and Israel. The service continued despite external disturbances. Sounds of the holy *Unetaneh Tokef* ("Let us proclaim the power of this day's holiness") prayer sounded reverently from the lips of the prayer leader, a cantor in private life. Near where they prayed, an enemy plane was shot down and plummeted to earth.[158]

Rabbi Schulim Ochser served in the k.u.k. army during 1917 and 1918. Before the war he was a high school teacher in Tarnopol.[159] He was not yet officially ordained when war broke out, and advised not to hold services for the troops.[160] He was attached to a division before and during the Battle of Caporetto.

The week before Rosh Hashanah, the column was shot out of its position and conducted to a new and dangerous valley. Rabbi Ochser (who had by now been ordained) was requested to hold an early morning service on September 9. The directive was issued quickly, and the neighboring units rapidly notified. Everybody went to bed on time, because the next day's march would be arduous. At 9.00 pm, they heard a shell whooshing. The Christian chaplain, who shared the room with Rabbi Ochser, believed that they could go to sleep, because the shell seemed to be an errant one. However, in less than ten minutes, shelling scattered their unit to the four winds.

On Sunday morning, Rabbi Ochser gathered the men together, and the morning service proceeded. A few Orthodox Jews gathered around their rabbi, and prayers rose from anguished throats. Everyone rejoiced at the arrival of the New Year. Thanks to the men's efforts, a splendid prayer room was arranged, with the ark, a prayer platform, a pulpit, a table, and seats for non-commissioned officers, rabbi, and officers to the right. The two Rosh Hashanah days passed solemnly. Although none of the Jewish soldiers in the front lines were given leave, the group still contained more than 200 members. Yom Kippur passed in an even more reverent atmosphere: most soldiers did not leave the prayer house after the *Kol Nidrei* service; one of the guards read and expounded on the Talmud tractate dealing with Yom Kippur (Yoma) with deep understanding.

When Yom Kippur was drawing to an end, airplane bombs pelted down on the area, but the resounding tone of "The Lord He is God" (signaling the end of the fast day) overwhelmed the roar of the bombs, and everyone left the house of prayer unharmed. The Orthodox soldiers had a harder time on Sukkot. During one of the holiday services, the entire group of houses where their prayer room was located was shelled. On October 8, services had to be interrupted twice. During the afternoon service, the barometric pressure of a shell tore the windows, frame and all, from the wall, and they flew onto those praying. Rabbi Ochser cancelled the morning service, and on the afternoon of October 9 they were scheduled to take leave of the festival period. However, things turned out differently. Shells exploded around them at twenty-five-second intervals. The rabbi, an assistant physician, and a medical corps lieutenant took shelter in the priest's house, so they could go back to services as soon as it became quiet again. At the last minute, they were joined by the captain and the pharmacist. Suddenly it became dark, there was a crash, and chaos ensued. The poor physician was mangled, and laid to rest at 11.00 am in the adjoining cemetery. The severely wounded lieutenant and the wounded rabbi were transported to the nearest field hospital.

The stress proved too much for Rabbi Ochser: he had to be hospitalized for severe nervous exhaustion, but recovered, at least to some degree, and returned to service. Chaplains (and all other front soldiers) must have returned from the war with varying degrees of post-traumatic stress disorder. This is the only report I could find of a Central Power Jewish chaplain suffering from this condition and it should be noted that it is reported by someone else, not the rabbi himself.[161]

The longer the Italian war lasted, the more chaplains care was provided on that front, despite weather and transportation problems. Plate 11 depicts celebration of Simchat Torah on the Isonzo in 1917 (Jewish year 5678).

Rabbi Arthur Rosenzweig was born in 1883 in Teplitz. After study in Berlin and Heidelberg he obtained his doctoral diploma in 1907; he became a rabbi in Aussig in 1909 and professor at Charles University in Prague.[162] Rabbi Rosenzweig served as chaplain in the k.k. *Landwehr* from November 1916 through the end of the war. The following is an extract written by Elsa Köhler (probably a nurse) describing a Hanukkah 1917 celebration organized by Rabbi Rosenzweig, location unspecified.

Soldiers crowded onto narrow, roughly timbered wooden benches. Near them sat a small group of Russian prisoners of war, and on the other side the officers. The writer gazed over the narrow, whitewashed room, whose only wall decoration was garish posters advertising recent movies. Her eyes wandered from these fake impressions of joy, distress, and death, and rested upon the solemn assembly of grey men, who had perhaps been acquainted before the war with life's joys, but now had looked distress and gruesome death in the face.

Rabbi Rosenzweig stood in black, wrinkled cassock next to the white-clothed table upon which the festive Hanukkah menorah decorated by candles sat enthroned. First sounds of afternoon service were heard from the prayer reader; he swayed back and forth with the sing-song melody. Soldiers prayed with him, and the room filled with familiar sounds:

> After the evening service, six candles lit up the bare, prosaic cinema room, turning it into a House of God full of holiness—a house of peace and rest, in which tired soldiers found a piece of home for a short time: "'Not by might nor by power, but by my Spirit,' says the Lord Almighty" (Zechariah 4:6) echoed through the room. Chaplain Rosenzweig explained, modestly and kindly, the meaning of this festival. He told of the heroic deeds of the Maccabees, and transitioned to the heroic deeds of young Jewish soldiers and men of our time, twentieth-century Maccabees.
>
> A prayer for the dead was recited by the Russian prisoners of war with solemn, high-pitched, strange-sounding voices. Their faces, into which suffering and longing for their family had etched harsh suffering lines, were pale and careworn. Many had tears in their eyes. They too had their dead and their graves: the bones of their ancestors lay in the ground of a faraway region. But behind the lowered lids, the soul's antechamber, images of the past arose as well: Images of happy, sunny family life, so marked in the Jewish faith.

After services, the chaplain distributed gifts. It was moving to see how these war-hardened, battle-tested men became children again:

> They looked with large, expectant eyes at each plain, brown box that contained all the wonderful things that would be handed out to them. Like small schoolboys with their teacher, they held their arms out to the chaplain: "Please, Herr Rabbiner, I have received nothing yet. Please for me. Please for me." The barrier between the soldiers and the rabbi cracked, gave in from the crowding, and almost collapsed. One by one, gifts appeared from the plain, brown, marvelous boxes that seemed to be almost bottomless, handed by the rabbi to happy recipients.[163]

As late as the last Pesach of the war, Rabbi Grünfeld was still serving in the field. A report from Captain B. describes a Pesach service on the river Piave. By spring 1918, the blockade made provision of one kilogram of matzot per man something of a miracle.

> Only about fifteen men came, although many Jews were registered in that division. This indifference to religion of our mostly West Austrian Jewish brothers was felt painfully by those present. The service was very dignified. A Russian, who had come over to our side during the Russo-Japanese War and is now serving as an Austrian soldier, led the service well. After that chaplain Rabbi Grünfeld from Eger gave an uplifting sermon. It was the first day of the month (*Rosh Chodesh*), and he spoke about the coming Pesach holiday. At the end of the service he handed out prayer books. Because of distance, a kosher kitchen couldn't be erected, but each man received one kilogram of matzot. Perhaps it will be possible to give Jewish soldiers leave during the two festival days, so that they can participate in the communal kosher kitchen in D., where the chaplain is located. This chaplain is very active and holds services nearly every day.[164]

Isidor/Israel Kohn served as chaplain on the Italian front during the last year of the war. He left a description of an abandoned synagogue in occupied Italy towards the end of the war:

> The synagogue is located at the corner of two busy streets in the town center. Entering through a private home with the sign "Entrance to the Shul" in Italian on the wall, one comes upon a small, clean courtyard, whose three sides consist of the fire wall of the adjacent houses: the fourth side is the front of the synagogue. In peacetime Vittorio was a favorite Venetian summer resort. In contrast to many beautiful villas in the town, the synagogue appears simple and unadorned. The small entrance room contains an artistically built copper washbasin. Through a narrow staircase of about twelve steps one enters a passage which leads, through large double doors, to the sanctuary. Bright light, which can be screened off by side shutters, shines into the sanctuary from high windows. The floor is covered in marble. Rows of benches appear on both side walls. The ark, richly decorated in wood with white and gold overlay, is situated in front. Because the ark is in the front, benches are on the side and the middle is empty. For the women, narrow galleries are built into both sides and the

back wall. On one side wall there are two tables of honor, one listing, in Hebrew, names of families who have provided large donations. On the other, in large Italian letters, names of those remembered during *yizkor* [prayer for the dead] appear. There are several Torah scrolls, without silver and other decorations, in the ark, as well as numerous prayer books, Bibles, prayer books printed in Venice in 1710 "for German and Italian rites." According to an inscription, the synagogue is ninety years old. Apparently there had been about forty-five well-off Jewish families in the town before the war, but they had fled, with only a few left.[165]

Rabbi Adolf Kelémen was born 1861 in Dutovlje.[166] After studying at Berlin and Budapest Theological Seminaries, he officiated at various Hungarian pulpits—the last of which was Fogaras—for twenty-five years until, at age fifty-three, he volunteered for service as soon as war began.[167] He served on the front from October 18, 1914 through May 22, 1915. During his time in the trenches, he held services with sermons for the Thirty-Second Honvéd and the Eighty-Second k.u.k. Regiment. He also served in the *Nyíregyháza* Garrison Hospital (Hungary).

At age fifty-six, his sense of duty led him to request reactivation from the Royal Hungarian Honvéd Minister. Rabbi Kelémen could easily have stayed in the rear, but his feeling of duty pressed him to front line duty. He was seriously wounded by a shell splinter on the Romanian front in March 1917 and brought to a field hospital, where he died as a result of his wounds.

I could find only one report written by Rabbi Kelémen, from the Carpathian front on May 4, 1915. The words reflect patriotism that made a fifty-three-year-old volunteer for war duty, and apply for reactivation three years later:

> I felt a great longing to visit the field of battle, to see it with my own eyes and give aid and comfort to those brave souls who are sacrificing everything and doing their duty to King and Fatherland.[168] It was a lovely, sunny Sunday, and the beauty of the Carpathians filled me with a sacred spirit, as if the area had been turned into a gigantic House of God. When I arrived at our Honvéd regiment, I asked permission to address the men, emphasizing that my short talk would be non-denominational.

The captain was pleased to accept, and in five minutes I was surrounded by hundreds of brave Hungarian brothers. When I looked into their faithful eyes, the strength of my youthful principles was renewed: the medieval barriers of prejudice must be torn down! All of us—children of the same soil, the same Fatherland—must regard each other as equals, devoted to one another! I spoke to the dear Honvéds from an overflowing heart, and it felt like a religious service for all my fellow men. The captain was visibly moved, and invited me to say a few words to his men in the front line trenches. We walked through rocky roads and ravines and small, almost impassable mountain paths, and eventually arrived at our goal, a Carpathian summit. Artillery pieces roared, rifles cracked, and bullets hissed—the Russians were only 200 yards away. Men came out of their trenches, to hear the word of the Lord on such a beautiful Sunday morning. All of us thought little of our own short lives, but rather of the holy war for the benefit of our great and good Hungary, united in the service of God.

After shaking everyone's hand, I returned to the captain's dugout. As a remembrance, he gave me a Russian rifle, cartridge case, and cartridges, and we returned to our original position. I parted from him under clear, starry skies. I will donate my gift to the Hungarian-Jewish war museum, and carry the memory of that day in my heart forever![169]

Rabbi Kelémen's age alone makes him unique. He is the only serving chaplain I could find in the armies of the Central Powers who died on the front. His sense of duty and love of fatherland require no elaboration. Schweitzer asserts that Rabbi Kelémen died of pneumonia, and not directly of his wounds.[170]

In summary, the perusal of writings and actions of Austro-Hungarian Jewish chaplains have led me to the following conclusions: These were modest men, imbued with supranational loyalty to the empire, which made them count amongst the most loyal of the Kaiser's subjects. They wrote little, but acted greatly. They asked no credit for themselves, and were only concerned with the welfare of the men entrusted to them, including prisoners.

With help from military authorities, greater than could be ascertained for most other countries, these chaplains tended the religious needs of their heterogeneous flock. This included Orthodox Jews with needs different from those of assimilated coreligionists. In no other army could Orthodox Jewish soldiers both request and obtain a chaplain who made time to sit and democratically expound Torah and Talmud. Tradition requires that respect is accorded to the most learned scholar irrespective of rank, and some chaplains may have had under them soldiers whose Torah and Talmud knowledge exceeded their own. This required a kind of humility that made these chaplains special.

Military authorities saw to it that there were garrison chaplains in the large cities, and also provided (where possible) required liturgical objects, that remained in the units. Kosher kitchens were erected on holidays such as Pesach, and religious needs of Jewish prisoners—mainly Russian—were looked after, even to the extent of providing a special chaplain, Rabbi Kurrein, whose sole job it was to tend to the religious needs of the prisoners of war. Even during 1918, when food supplies had almost been exhausted at home and on the front, Jewish chaplains managed to provide matzot for Pesach on the Italian Front, where the Austro-Hungarians were still fighting.

The Torah and Talmud expositions of Rabbi Bertisch stand out: I could not find their equivalent in the writings of chaplains from any other army. Russian rabbis had this knowledge in plenty, but were not permitted to serve as chaplains. Death as a result of wounds received in action by Rabbi Adolf Kelémen at the age of fifty-six is unique. The only other example I could find was Rabbi Abraham Bloch, Chief Rabbi of Lyon, killed in battle in 1914 at the age of fifty-five.[171]

After the war, the chaplains returned to their respective communities. Tragically, many of these brave, patriotic rabbis were to be murdered in the Holocaust, and their communities destroyed, making information about their ultimate fate difficult. Rabbi Frankfurter was beaten to death in Buchenwald; Rabbis Tauber and Balaban died in the Warsaw ghetto; Rabbis Altmann, Schweiger, Grünfeld, and Ferda were murdered in Auschwitz.

Endnotes

1 S. Hank, H. Simon, and U. Hank, *Feldrabbiner in den deutschen Streitkräften des ersten Weltkrieges* (Berlin: Hentrich & Hentrich, 2013); P. C. Appelbaum, *Loyalty Betrayed. Jewish Chaplains in the German Army during the First World War* (London and Portland, OR: Vallentine-Mitchell, 2014).

2 Y. Petrovsky Shtern, *Jews in the Russian Army, 1827–1917. Drafted into Modernity* (New York: Cambridge University Press, 2009), 248–268; idem, personal communication.

3 C. Roth, *The History of the Jews of Italy* (Philadelphia, PA: Jewish Publication Society of America, 1946), 508; N. R. M. de Lange, *Atlas of the Jewish World* (New York: Facts on File, 1992), 64; Lia Toaff, personal communication.

4   P. C. Appelbaum, *Loyal Sons. Jews in the German Army in the Great War* (London and Portland, OR: Vallentine-Mitchell, 2014), 239–283; E. Schmidl, *Habsburgs jüdische Soldaten, 1788–1918* (Vienna, Cologne, and Weimar: Böhlau Verlag, 2014), 119.
5   *Adjustierungsvorschrift für das k.u.k. Heer*, part 7, "Normal Verordnungsblatt für das k.u.k. Heer," no. 23 (Vienna: Druck der k.k. Hof- und Staatsdruckerei, 1918), 5.
6   Schmidl, *Habsburgs jüdische Soldaten*, 133–134.
7   Bukov(w)ina is a historical region located on the northern slopes of the Central Eastern Carpathians and the adjoining plains. Formerly part of the Austro-Hungary Empire, it is now shared between Romania and Ukraine.
8   M. L. Rozenblit, *Reconstructing a National Identity. The Jews of Habsburg Austria during World War I* (Oxford and New York: Oxford University Press, 2004), 96–97. First published in 2001.
9   Appelbaum, *Loyalty Betrayed*, 294–295.
10 Rozenblit, *Reconstructing a National Identity*, 8.
11 Appelbaum, *Loyalty Betrayed*, 121–123.
12 Brest (Belarus). The treaty with Ukraine was signed on February 9, 1918, and that with Russia on March 3, 1918.
13 Appelbaum, *Loyalty Betrayed*, 216–234.
14 B. Bardach, *Carnage and Care on the Eastern Front. The War Diaries of Dr. Bernhard Bardach*, trans. and ed. P. C. Appelbaum (New York and Oxford: Berghahn Books, 2018), 191 et seq.
15 Appelbaum, *Loyalty Betrayed*.
16 Ibid., 145–173. Hermann Cohen (1842–1918) was a German Jewish philosopher and one of the founders of the Marburg School of Neo-Kantianism.
17 W. von Weisl, *Die Juden in der Armee Österreich-Ungarns. Illegale Transporte* (Tel Aviv: Olamenu, 1971), 22f, note 3. Lajos (Louis) Kossuth de Udvard et Kossuthfalvan (1802–1894) was a Hungarian lawyer, politician, and Governor-President of the Kingdom of Hungary during the 1848–1849 revolution against the Habsburg Dynasty. A joint army of Russian and Austrian forces defeated the Hungarian forces and, after restoration of Habsburg power, Hungary was placed under martial law; it took until 1867 for it to regain equal status.
18 Anonymous, *Magyar Front* 13, no. 2 (2011): 12; Á. Biró, "Jewish Military Chaplains in the Austro-Hungarian Armed Forces During World War I," *Acta Ethnographica Hungarica* 59, no. 2 (2014): 1–10, here 1. Komárom (Hungary), Komárno (Slovak Republic): a town on both sides of the Danube.
19 D. J. Hecht, "Der König rief, und alle, alle kamen. Jewish Military Chaplains on Duty in the Austro-Hungarian Army during World War I," *Jewish Culture and History* 17, no 3 (2016): 205.
20 G. Wolf, *Josef Wertheimer. Ein Lebens- und Zeitbild. Beitrag zur Geschichte der Juden Österreichs in neuerster Zeit* (Vienna: Herzfeld & Bauer, 1868), 151–152; idem, *Die Geschichte der Juden in Wien 1156–1876* (Vienna: Alfred Hoelder, 1876), 167; A. Kisch, "Zur Geschichte der israelitische Militärseelsorge in Deutschland und Österreich. Zugleich Erinnerungen aus meiner 42-jährigen Tätigkeit als Militärseelsorger," *Allgemeine Zeitung des Judentums*, December 8, 1916, 582–584.
21 "Juden im Österreichischen Heere," *Dr. Bloch's Österreichische Wochenschrift*, July 6, 1906, 451.
22 Most (Czech Republic).
23 A. Kisch, "Zur Geschichte der Israelitische Militärseelsorge in Deutschland und Österreich. Zugleich Erinnerungen aus meiner 42-jährigen Tätigkeit als Militärseelsorger,"

Allgemeine Zeitung des Judentums, December 15, 1916, 595–597; W. Güde, "Fallbeispiel: Rabbiner Dr. Alexander Kisch als k.k. Landwehrrabbiner. Zugleich ein kleiner Beitrag über die Anfänge der jüdischen Militärseesorge in Österreich-Ungarn," in *Jüdische Soldaten— Jüdischer Widerstand in Deutschland und Frankreich*, ed. M. Berger and G. Römer-Hillebrecht (Paderborn: Ferdinand Schöningh, 2012), 185. According to Schmidl, Kaiser Franz Joseph had one military chaplain each appointed for Italy and Bohemia on June 26, 1866, but the war ended before they could take up their positions. See E. A. Schmidl, *Juden in der k.u.k. Armee 1788–1918. Jews in the Habsburg Armed Forces*, vol. 11 of Studia Judaica Austriaca (Eisenstadt: Österreichisches Jüdisches Museum, 1989), 140; K. Frojimovics, G. Komoróczy, V. Pusztai, and A. Strbik (eds.), *Jewish Budapest. Monuments, Rites, History* (Budapest: Central European University Press, 1999), 201–211.

24   A. Kisch, "Zur Geschichte der Israelitische Militärseelsorge in Deutschland und Österreich. Zugleich Erinnerungen aus meiner 42-jährigen Tätigkeit als Militärseelsorger," *Allgemeine Zeitung des Judentums*, February 23, 1917, 94–95; idem, "Zur Geschichte der Israelitische Militärseelsorge in Deutschland und Österreich. Zugleich Erinnerungen aus meiner 42-jährigen Tätigkeit als Militärseelsorger," *Allgemeine Zeitung des Judentums*, March 2, 1917, 103–105; Güde, "Fallbeispiel: Rabbiner Dr. Alexander Kisch," 180–196.

25   K. E. Franzos, *Moschko von Parma* (Stuttgart & Berlin: G. Cotta'sche Buchhandlung Nachfolger, 1921). First published: Leipzig: Duncker & Humblot, 1880. Karl Emil Franzos (1848–1904) was a popular Austrian novelist of the late nineteenth century. His works, reportage and fiction, concentrate on the multiethnic corner of Galicia, Podolia, and Bukowina, now largely in Ukraine.

26   Ibid., 14.

27   T. Zlocisti, "Die Einsegnung der jüdischen Soldaten in Breslau, 1813," *Im Deutschen Reich*, September 1900, 443–445. Cited in: E. Lindner, *Patriotismus deutscher Juden von der napoleonischen Ära bis zum Kaiserreich* (Frankfurt am Main: Peter Lang, 1997), 61. This injunction is based upon a text published in 1842, based on reminiscences of a witness to the occasion. See E. Kerstenberg-Gladstein, *Neuere Geschichte der Juden in den böhmischen Ländern*, vol. 1, *Das Zeitalter der Aufklärung 1780–1830* (Tübingen: J. C. B. Mohr, Paul Siebeck, 1969), 70–72; A. Kisch, "Zur Geschichte der Israelitische Militärseelsorge in Deutschland und Österreich. Zugleich Erinnerungen aus meiner 42-jährigen Tätigkeit als Militärseelsorger," *Allgemeine Zeitung des Judentums*, December 8, 1916, 582–584; Appelbaum, *Loyal Sons*, 9.

28   Güde, "Fallbeispiel: Rabbiner Dr. Alexander Kisch," 195–196.

29   Appelbaum, *Loyalty Betrayed*, 15–24.

30   D. J. Hecht, "Feldrabbiner in der k.u.k. Armee während des ersten Weltkriegs," in *Weltuntergang. Jüdisches Leben und Sterben im ersten Weltkrieg*, ed. M. G. Patka (Vienna, Graz, and Klagenfurt: Styria Premium, 2014), 69.

31   Hecht, "Der König rief," 206. In his recent book chapter, Hecht lists a total of 113 chaplains, but several who served between January and November 1918, through the end of the war, are not included. See D. J. Hecht, "Austro-Hungarian Jewish Chaplains between East and West. Rabbi Bernard Dov Hausner (1874–1938) during World War I," in *Jewish Soldiers in the Collective Memory of Central Europe. The Remembrance of World War I from a Jewish Perspective*, ed. G. Lamprecht, E. Lappin-Eppel, and U. Wyrwa (Vienna, Cologne, and Weimar: Böhlau Verlag, 2019), 92.

32   Schmidl, *Habsburgs jüdische Soldaten*, 132–135; Hecht, "Feldrabbiner," 69; idem, "Der König rief," 203–216.

33   Appelbaum, *Loyalty Betrayed*.

34 Pozsony county was an administrative county (comitatus) of the Kingdom of Hungary. Its territory lies in present-day Western Slovakia.
35 Á. Biró, "Rabbis in the Austro-Hungarian Armed Forces," *Magyar Front* 13, no. 2 (2011): 13; Biró, "Jewish Military Chaplains," 3.
36 *Ranglisten des kaiserlichen und königlichen Heeres* (Vienna: K.k. Hof- und Staatsdruckerei, 1916), 1004; ibid. (Vienna: K.k. Hof- und Staatsdruckerei, 1917), 1343; ibid. (Vienna: K.k. Hof- und Staatsdruckerei, 1918), 1674–1675; Appelbaum, *Loyalty Betrayed*, 311.
37 P. Abbina, "La Participazione Ebraica alla Grand Guerra: il Rabbinato Militare," *Shalom*, January 3, 2009, 1–3; Lia Toaff, personal communication.
38 Archivio Storico della Comunità Ebraica di Roma, Archivio Contemporaneo, Fondo Comunità Israelitica di Roma, b. 146, fasc. 1, letter of May 23, 1915; ibid., b. 147, fasc. 1, letter of July 11, 1915; ibid., b. 147, fasc. 1, letter of September 11, 1916; P. Briganti, personal communication; Lia Toaff, personal communication.
39 Abbina, "La Participazione Ebraica," 1–3; V. Wilcox, "Between Faith and Nation: Italian Jewish Soldiers in the Great War," in *The Jewish Experience of the First World War*, ed. E. Madigan, G. Reuveni (London: Palgrave Macmillan, 2019), 194–200.
40 P. Steiner, "Namensliste der Feldrabbiner in der Österreich-ungarischen Armee des ersten Weltkrieges," in *Weltuntergang. Jüdisches Leben und Sterben im ersten Weltkrieg*, ed. M. G. Patka (Vienna, Graz, and Klagenfurt: Styria Premium, 2014), 77–79. At the start of the war, the k.u.k. chaplains branch was named the *k.u.k. israelitische Seelsorge*, and the k.k. branch was named *Militärseelsorge*. See A. Feller, "The Jewish Military Chaplaincy," *The Galitzianer* 25, no. 3 (September 2018): 7–13.
41 Biró, "Jewish Military Chaplains," 6–8.
42 G. Sajó and R.-T. Fischer, "Die jüdischen Soldaten des Kaisers im heiligen Land," in *Weltuntergang. Jüdisches Leben und Sterben im ersten Weltkrieg*, ed. M. G. Patka (Vienna, Graz, and Klagenfurt: Styria Premium, 2014), 119–125.
43 *Gebetbuch für israelitische Soldaten in Kriege* (Vienna: Verlag des israelitischen Kultusgemeinde Wien, 1914).
44 Svodin (south-west Slovakia).
45 Bratislava (Slovak Republic).
46 Hecht, "Feldrabbiner," 71.
47 Central Archives for the History of the Jewish People, AW 357/2, letter to Israelitische Kultusgemeinde, August 5, 1915.
48 Hank, Simon, and Hank, *Feldrabbiner*, 488–591.
49 A. Frankfurter, "Die k.u.k. Militärseelsorge in Wien," *Jüdische Korrespondenz*, October 10, 1916, 1–2; Hecht, "Der König Rief," 209–213.
50 Uherský Brod (Czech Republic).
51 "Der Feldrabbiner," *Die Wahrheit*, September 4, 1914, 7–8;
52 Reserve unit consisting of men from thirty-four to fifty-five years of age.
53 Quorum of ten men necessary for a communal service.
54 "Ein Österreichischer Feldprediger," *Allgemeine Zeitung des Judentums*, February 12, 1915, 76–78.
55 Bratislava (Slovak Republic).
56 Hecht, "Feldrabbiner," 71–72; Central Archives for the History of the Jewish People, AW/3111.
57 Feuilleton, "Seelsorge im Schützengraben," *Dr. Bloch's Österreichische Wochenschrift*, November 6, 1914, 771.
58 Hank, Simon, and Hank, *Feldrabbiner*, 325–327.

59 "Der jüngste jüdische Feldrabbiner," *Allgemeine Zeitung des Judentums*, June 9, 1916, 269.
60 Huncovce (Slovak Republic).
61 Merano (South Tyrolean Italy).
62 A[dolf] Altmann, *A Filial Memoir*, Yearbook of the Leo Baeck Institute 26 (1981); M. Altmann, "K.u.k. Feldrabbiner Dr. Adolf Altmann an der Kriegsfront (1915–1918) in Begegnung mit Feldmarschall Conrad von Hötzendorf und anderen Armeekommandanten," special addition, in *Ein ewiges Dennoch. 12 Jahre Juden in Salzburg*, ed. M. Feingold (Vienna, Cologne, and Weimar: Böhlau Verlag, 1993), 492–509.
63 Ivano-Frankivsk (Ukraine); Nové Mesto nad Váhom (Slovak Republic); Lviv (Ukraine).
64 Exodus 17:8–16.
65 M. Tauber, "Feldpostbrief eines jüdischen Militärseelsorgers," *Dr. Bloch's Österreichische Wochenschrift*, April 16, 1915, 289–290.
66 Appelbaum, *Loyalty Betrayed*.
67 Hank, Simon, and Hank, *Feldrabbiner*, 248–249; Appelbaum, *Loyalty Betrayed*, 294-295.
68 "Tells of Russians' Murder of Jews," *New York Times*, February 4, 1915, 3:2.
69 The Gorlice–Tarnow Offensive, the Central Powers' main offensive effort of 1915, caused complete collapse of Russian lines and retreat far into Russia. The continued series of actions lasted most of the campaigning season for 1915, beginning in early May and only ending due to bad weather in October.
70 A holiday celebrated on the thirty-third day between the second night of Pesach and Shavuot, which occurs on the eighteenth day of the Hebrew month of Iyar. It is interpreted by some as anniversary of death of Rabbi Shimon bar Yochai, a leading sage and mystic. Children across Israel go out and play on this day with bows and arrows.
71 In the pre-antibiotic era, penetrating abdominal wounds were uniformly fatal, due to peritonitis.
72 All three cities in Poland. M. Tauber, "II. Brief des Feldrabbiners Dr. Tauber," *Dr. Bloch's Österreichische Wochenschrift*, June 18, 1915, 453–455.
73 The Battle of Dunajec (a river in Southern Poland), which began in early May, 1915, was the first major battle of the Gorlice-Tarnow Offensive.
74 M. Tauber, "Dritter Feldpostbrief des Feldrabbiners Dr. M. Tauber," *Dr. Bloch's Österreichische Wochenschrift*, September 28, 1915, 713–715.
75 Rozenblit, *Reconstructing a National Identity*, 50–51.
76 S. An-sky, *The Enemy at his Pleasure. A Journey through the Jewish Pale of Settlement During World War I*, transl. and ed. J. Neugroschel (New York: Metropolitan Books, Henry Holt & Co., 2002), 3–110.
77 Ibid., 125–159.
78 Wrocław (Poland).
79 Siebenbürgen: Transylvania. The Hebrew words are the opening line of the mourner's *kaddish*, old Ashkenazi pronunciation.
80 "Der Verbandplatz (aus dem Tagebuch eines Feldrabbiners)," *Dr. Bloch's Österreichische Wochenschrift*, August 13, 1915, 618–619. Ruthenia is a cross-border area of Eastern Europe mainly comprising Ukraine, but also the contiguous areas of Belarus, Slovakia, and Hungary, with a distinct language and culture. Ruthenians are members of the Rus' people with an Eastern Orthodox or Ruthenian Uniate Church religious background. In the Austro-Hungarian context, Ruthenians are Ukrainians.
81 Appelbaum, *Loyalty Betrayed*, 182–183. Cholera is a human-specific infection, so horses could safely drink the contaminated water.

82   "Aus Briefen des k.k. Feldrabbiners Dr. Arnold Grünfeld," *Dr. Bloch's Österreichische Wochenschrift*, July 23, 1915, 555. Rabbi Grünfeld was taking part in the Gorlice-Tarnów offensive, which liberated Lemberg, Przemyśl, Warsaw, and Kovno, forcing Russians to evacuate most of Galicia and Poland. The drinking water on the Eastern Front was contaminated with dysentery, typhoid fever, and cholera, and outbreaks occurred amongst civilians. Bernhard Bardach (Bardach, *Carnage and Care*) spends a great deal of time describing the bad, sometimes impassable roads.

83   "Aus Briefen des k.k. Feldrabbiners Dr. Arnold Grünfeld," *Dr. Bloch's Österreichische Wochenschrift*, August 13, 1915, 610. At this stage, Lemberg had already been liberated.

84   Lasków (Poland).

85   "Feldpostbrief des Feldrabbiners Dr. Ludwig Golinski," *Dr. Bloch's Österreichische Wochenschrift*, June 25, 1915, 474.

86   Kateřina Čapková, "Sicher, Gustav," *YIVO Encyclopedia*, accessed March 13, 2021, www.yivoencyclopedia.org/article.aspx/Sicher_Gustav. Náchod (Czech Republic).

87   Šumperk (Czech Republic).

88   Vistula.

89   All towns in Poland.

90   "Feldpostbrief des Feldrabbiners Dr. Sicher mitgeteilt von Rabbiner Dr. Halberstamm, Mähr.-Schönburg," *Dr. Bloch's Österreichische Wochenschrift*, September 17, 1915, 705–706.

91   "All vows." Prayer that introduces Yom Kippur eve.

92   "Feiertage im Felde. Aus Briefen des Feldrabbiners Dr. Sicher mitgeteilt von Rabbiner Dr. Rosenmann in Mähr.-Schönburg," *Dr. Bloch's Österreichische Wochenschrift*, September 28, 1915, 732–733.

93   "Feiertage im Felde. Aus Briefen des Feldrabbiners Dr. Sicher mitgeteilt von Rabbiner Dr. Rosenmann, Mähr.-Schönburg," *Dr. Bloch's Österreichische* Wochenschrift, October 29, 1915, 811–812. Hoshana Rabah, Shmini Atzeret, and Simchat Torah are all part of the seven-day Sukkot festival. The "four species" (*arba'at haminim*) (Leviticus 23:40) consist of *etrog* (citron), *lulav* (closed date palm tree frond), *hadass* (myrtle tree bough with leaves), and *aravah* (willow tree branch with leaves).

94   Topoľčany (Slovak Republic).

95   Kroměříž (Czech Republic).

96   "Ein Sederabend im Felde," *Dr. Bloch's Österreichische Wochenschrift*, April 16, 1915, 293–294.

97   A. Schweiger, "Die hohen Festtage im Felde," *Dr. Bloch's Österreichische Wochenschrift*, October 8, 1915, 737–738.

98   Appelbaum, *Loyal Sons*, 192–194.

99   Austrian Military Command Order no. 38, February 17, 1916, 1—no. 4348, 1—no. 3213.

100 In general, this is covered by Decree no. 1, 2188/1639, January 28, 1916, in Military Command Order 23/16.

101 "Peßach in der Armee," *Jüdische Volksstimme*, March 30, 1916, 3.

102 Hank, Simon, and Hank, *Feldrabbiner*, 557–558; Appelbaum, *Loyalty Betrayed*.

103 Appelbaum, *Loyal Sons*, 239–283.

104 Schmidl, *Habsburg jüdische Soldaten*, 119.

105 F. Conrad von Hötzendorf, *Private Aufzeichnungen. Erste Veröffentlichungen aus den Papieren des k.u.k. Generalstabs-Chef*, ed. K. Peball (Vienna and Munich: Amalthea-Verlag, 1977), 19, 288, 313–314; L. Sondhaus, *Franz Conrad von Hötzendorf: Architect of the Apocalypse* (Boston, Leiden, and Cologne: Brill Academic Publishers, 2000), 223.

106 Altmann, "K.u.k Feldrabbiner Dr. Adolf Altmann," 502–570. Photocopies of handwritten dedications are given on 538–570.
107 A. Altmann, "Der Segen in Wenigen," *Dr. Bloch's Österreichische Wochenschrift*, December 22, 1916, 839–840. On August 28, 1916, Romania declared war on Austro-Hungary, and Germany responded with a declaration of war the following day. Generals Erich von Falkenhayn and August von Mackensen took control of this new front and, by December 1916, led their troops to a decisive victory, overrunning much of Romania and occupying Bucharest by December 9, 1916. The verse often referred to regarding Hanukkah is: "'Not by might nor by power, but by my Spirit,' says the Lord Almighty" (Zechariah 4:6).
108 Italy declared war on Austro-Hungary on May 23, 1915, and against Germany on August 28, 1916.
109 Ljubljana (Slovenia).
110 Anonymous, "Yom-Kippur in Laibach," *Dr. Bloch's Österreichische Wochenschrift*, October 17, 1916, 693–694; It is not clear whether this refers to Aron or Adolf Deutsch (Steiner, "Namensliste," 77).
111 Singular *aliya*: the process of being called up to recite blessings over a Torah portion.
112 "Von der Isonzofront. Ein Feldpostbrief," *Dr. Bloch's Österreichische Wochenschrift*, December 8, 1916, 798.
113 Špačince (Slovak Republic).
114 "Ein Feldpostbrief," *Dr. Bloch's Österreichische Wochenschrift*, February 11, 1916, 105.
115 Nitra (Slovak Republic).
116 M. Brocke, J. Carlebach (eds.), *Biographisches Handbuch der Rabbiner. Teil 2 Die Rabbiner im Deutschen Reich 1871–1945* (Munich: De Gruyter Saur, 2009), 404.
117 "Come, my beloved" is a hymn welcoming the Sabbath as a bridegroom welcomes a bride.
118 "Jüdische Feldgottesdienst in Süd-Tirol," *Jüdische Volksstimme*, October 11, 1916, 3. The melody of the Habsburg National Anthem, Gott erhalte Franz den Kaiser, with melody by Josef Haydn (1732–1809) from the second movement of his Kaiserquartett (Hob. III, 77), was subsequently used in the Deutschlandlied, which became Deutschland über Alles.
119 S. Goldfand, "Ein denkwürdiges Schewuothfest im Felde," *Dr. Bloch's Österreichische Wochenschrift*, June 15, 1917, 380–381.
120 Appelbaum, *Loyalty Betrayed*, 175–238.
121 Chortkiv (Ukraine).
122 Hecht, "Austro-Hungarian Jewish Chaplains," 99–104.
123 Asaf Kaniel, "Hausner, Bernard Dov," *YIVO Encyclopedia*, accessed April 9, 2021, yivoencyclopedia.org/article.aspx/Hausner_Bernard_Dov; Feller, "The Jewish Military Chaplaincy," 11.
124 "Ein interessanter Feldpostbrief," *Dr. Bloch's Österreichische Wochenschrift*, 3 November 1916, 718.
125 "Unsere Helden am Isonzo." *Dr. Blochs Österreichische Wochenschrift*, 13 July 1917, 442-443.
126 Hecht, "Austro-Hungarian Jewish Chaplains" 99-109.
127 *Biographisches Handbuch der Rabbiner*, 359. Not included in the lists published by Steiner, "Namensliste," 77–79.
128 Two large prisoner-of-war camps were located in Anif und Grödig, near Salzburg. See M. Rauchensteiner, *The First World War and the End of the Habsburg Monarchy* (Vienna, Cologne, and Weimar: Böhlau Verlag, 2014), 832.
129 Teplice (Czech Republic).
130 "Im k.u.k. Kriegsgefangenenlager bei Salzburg," *Dr. Bloch's Österreichische Wochenschrift*, February 11, 1916, 114–115.

131 Szentgyörgy (Slovak Republic).
132 E Biró, "Rabbis in the Austro-Hungarian Armed Forces," 14.
133 See note 71.
134 "Episoden vom rumänischen Kriegsschauplatz," *Dr. Bloch's Österreichische Wochenschrift*, December 29, 1916, 847.
135 "Feldrabbiner Béla Diamant," *Dr. Bloch's Österreichische Wochenschrift*, March 30, 1917, 202.
136 Appelbaum, *Loyalty Betrayed*, 299–306.
137 "Kongreß der Feldrabbiner," *Dr. Bloch's Österreichische Wochenschrift*, June 1, 1917, 349–350. The photograph in Hecht, "Feldrabbiner," 69 has the date as February, not May.
138 Hecht, "Feldrabbiner," 71.
139 "Oberfeldrabbiner für das jüdische k.u.k. Okkupationsgebiet," *Jüdische Korrespondenz*, March 13, 1917, 3; F. M. Schuster, *Zwischen allen Fronten. Osteuropäische Juden während des ersten Weltkrieges 1914–1919* (Cologne, Weimar, and Vienna: Böhlau Verlag, 2004), 279–281.
140 Ivano-Frankivsk (Ukraine).
141 Havlíčkův Brod, Litoměřice (Czech Republic).
142 L. Bertisch, "Pastorierung israelitischer Mannschaft anläßlich der Eidesleistung von Marschformationen und die heilige Schrift," *Dr. Bloch's Österreichische Wochenschrift*, May 25, 1917, 323–324.
143 L. Bertisch, "Der Feldrabbiner und die heilige Schrift," *Dr. Bloch's Österreichische Wochenschrift*, June 14, 1918, 360–362.
144 The *Urim* and *Tummim* were attached to the High Priest's breastplate with small chains and bands. They consisted of two sheets, held together by a richly colored girdle to form one whole. There were two onyx stones in each shoulder, with six of the twelve tribes of Israel engraved on each. The two stones were firmly connected with buckles, and the girdle under the chest held both parts of the breastplate together. The front of the breastplate carried twelve different stones in four rows of three, with names of the twelve tribes of Israel. The *Urim* and *Tummim*, which indicated responses to questions posed to the High Priest, were in the upper open side. A miraculous illumination of the twelve stones indicated an affirmative answer.
145 L. Bertisch, "Der Feldrabbiner und die heilige Schrift," *Dr. Bloch's Österreichische Wochenschrift*, June 21, 1918, 380–381. In addition to the four priestly garments worn by every priest, the High Priest wore four more garments, including the *Urim* and *Tummim*.
146 Study of Torah or Talmud is traditionally done in a group, so that expositions may be compared and argued over.
147 Y. Petrovsky Shtern, personal communication; L. Bertisch, "Der Feldrabbiner und die heilige Schrift,'" *Dr. Bloch's Österreichische Wochenschrift*, June 28, 1918, 394–396.
148 "Letter to the Editor," *Dr. Bloch's Österreichische Wochenschrift*, April 20, 1917, 242.
149 "Hülsenfrüchte für Pessach," *Jüdische Korrespondenz*, March 15, 1917, 3. "Konferenz Österreich-ungarischer Feldrabbiner," ibid.
150 Ostrava (Czech Republic).
151 Volodymyr-Volynskyi (Ukraine); Chełm (Poland);
152 Ustyluh (Ukraine).
153 "Dank des Kultusvorstandes in Wladimir Wolynski an Herrn Feldrabbiner Dr. Färber," *Dr. Bloch's Österreichische Wochenschrift*, June 14, 1918, 369; Also published in *Die Wahrheit*, 14 June 1918, 7.
154 Different from the modern American Conservative movement.

155 R. Färber, "Unsere israelitische Militärseelsorge," *Hickls Wiener judischer Volkskalender*, 1917–1918, 46–47.
156 Appelbaum, *Loyalty Betrayed*, 175–238. The section about Rabbi Sänger appears on 206.
157 Travel by vehicle on Yom Kippur would have been permitted by the exigencies of war.
158 A. Grünfeld, "Yom-Kippur im Felde," *Dr. Bloch's Österreichische Wochenschrift*, October 19, 1917, 661.
159 Ternopil (Ukraine).
160 Courtesy of E. A. Schmidl: "Bericht über die Tätigkeit der k.u.k. Feldrabbiner in der k.u.k. 24. J. D. bis Ende Dezember 1917," Österreichische Kriegsarchive.
161 "Feldrabbiner Dr. Schulim Ochser," *Dr. Bloch's Österreichische Wochenschrift*, November 9, 1917, 712–713; S. Ochser, "Feiertagsende," *Dr. Bloch's Österreichische Wochenschrift*, December 28, 1917, 821–822. "The Lord He is God" (1 Kings, 1: 39) is proclaimed at the conclusion of the Yom Kippur services.
162 Ústí nad Labem (Czech Republic).
163 "Chanukkahfeier im Kriegspital." *Dr. Bloch's Österreichische Wochenschrift*, January 18, 1918, 40–41.
164 "Jüdischer Feldgottesdienst an der Piave," *Dr. Bloch's Österreichische Wochenschrift*, April 12, 1918, 215.
165 "Eine Synagoge in dem besetzten Gebiete Italiens," *Dr. Bloch's Österreichische Wochenschrift*, May 3, 1918, 267. The town referred to is known as Vittorio Veneto.
166 Dutovlje (Slovenia).
167 Făgăraș (Romania).
168 Franz Joseph was the King of Hungary.
169 "Feldpostbrief eines Honved-Feldrabbiners." *Die Wahrheit*, May 14, 1915, 4–5.
170 "Heldentod eines Feldrabbiners," *Dr. Bloch's Österreichische Wochenschrift*, March 2, 1917, 132–133; "Zum Andenken des unvergeßlichen Feldrabbiners Dr. Kelemen," *Dr. Bloch's Österreichische Wochenschrift*, July 27, 1917, 477; G. Schweitzer, "Hungarian Neolog (Progressive) Rabbis during the Great War (1914–1918)," in *Jewish Soldiers in the Collective Memory of Central Europe. The Remembrance of World War I from a Jewish Perspective*, ed. G. Lamprecht, E. Lappin-Eppel, and U. Wyrwa (Vienna, Cologne, and Weimar: Böhlau Verlag, 2019), 119.
171 P.-E. Landau, *Les Juifs de France et la Grand Guerre. Un Patriotisme Républicain 1914–1941* (Paris: Editions CNRS, 1999), 195–210. The legend that Rabbi Bloch was killed by an enemy shell while bringing a crucifix to a dying soldier has not been authenticated.

CHAPTER 7

Captives of the Tsar in European Russia, Siberia, and Central Asia

Introduction

It has been calculated that at the beginning of June 1915, 6,470 officers and 457,800 men had been taken captive by the Russians. By war's end, these figures had increased to between 1.5 million and over 2 million. According to several estimates, there were 57,178 officers and 2,330,000 other rank prisoners in Russian prisoner-of-war camps. Of these, 411,000 died in captivity (17.8% of the total). The vast majority of these captives comprised Austro-Hungarians – 54,146 officers, and 2,057,000 other rank prisoners. Of these, 31% were Hungarians, 30% German Austrians, 7% Romanians, 5% Poles, 3% Czechoslovaks, 3% South Slavs, 2.5% Jews, and 0.5% Italians.[1]

There are many statistical data available on this subject, none properly verifiable. It must be kept in mind that these figures have been used to support claims and arguments to quantify suffering and express specific points of view on inhumane conduct, victories, defeats, bravery, and cowardice. With reported numbers between 1.5 and as high as 2.8 million, between 17% and 31% of a total number of approximately 9 million men serving in the Austro-Hungarian army were taken prisoner.[2] No book on the Austro-Hungarian army in World War I is therefore complete without a detailed analysis of their prisoner-of-war experiences. The great majority of the Austrian soldiers were taken prisoner by the Russian army. Of the others, some were taken captive by the Italian army during the final Battle of the Piave in November 1918. Some soldiers were captured by the Serbs during the 1914 offensive. Of these, a portion were released when Central Powers occupied Serbia in late 1915, but others were taken back to Corfu by the Serbian army after their retreat to the coast.

Many Austro-Hungarian soldiers were taken prisoner in very large "batches." For example, 119,000 (93 staff officers, 2,500 officers) were captured when the fortress of Przemyśl surrendered on March 22, 1915, and 100,000 during the "Black and Yellow" offensive of August 26–October 13. During the brutal Carpathian Winter War (January to April 1915), 180,000 Austro-Hungarians were captured. An estimated 200,000 soldiers were taken during a single three-day period within the Brusilov Offensive in spring 1916. Rachamimow and Pastor estimate that 300,000–380,000 soldiers were captured during the entire Brusilov Offensive, which exhausted both the Austro-Hungarian and the Russian armies. Because of extreme weather in the Carpathians during the winter offensive of January 23–April 30, 1915, the exact numbers of prisoners taken amongst the 793,000 men lost was never defined.[3] Russian prisoner-of-war camps were unique in that they also contained approximately 100,000 stranded enemy civilians, travelers, hostages, and people removed from a war zone such as Przemyśl.[4] The Breithaupt novel describes this in detail (see below).

Neutral countries like Sweden, Denmark, Spain (which rarely participated), and (until they declared war on the Central Powers) the United States took it upon themselves to assist in the care of Russian prisoners of war via the Red Cross. Private individuals played important roles. In particular, the Swede Elsa Brändström ("the Angel of Siberia") achieved iconic status for charitable activities amongst German-speaking prisoners, and was briefly considered in the early 1920s for the Nobel Peace Prize.[5] Highborn Austro-Hungarian noblewomen volunteered and provided greater or lesser amounts of assistance. Countess Nora Kinsky (1888–1923) did yeoman service in founding field hospitals and visiting thousands of prisoners of war in camps throughout Russia and Turkestan. She returned home in 1918 after the Russian Revolution, but died soon after in childbirth.[6]

J. C. Engle has argued that weather, climate, and terrain, together with unsatisfactory leadership, played a large part in depressed morale, high captivity and desertion rates.[7] Habsburg troops were deployed in three different areas during the first war year, spreading their ranks thin. In Serbia, unlike other theaters of operations, significant resistance from guerilla (*komitatschi*) formations was encountered, indistinguishable from civilian population. This, combined with natural barriers such as woods and cornfields (often mined), and problems crossing the flooded Drina and Sava Rivers, sapped morale. On the much longer Galician Front, long, exhausting marches, hasty retreats and frivolous assaults sapped fighting spirit, and brutal winter fighting in the

Carpathians was without discernable military purpose. By the end of 1915, the Habsburg Army had suffered 2.1 million casualties, partly due to reckless frontal assaults early in the war. This resulted in desperate attempts to avoid the front. There were the added hazards of extreme weather, lack of protection, insufficient food and supplies, and the development of what we now know to be post-traumatic stress disorder.[8]

No longer able to cope, the Austro-Hungarian soldiers used a variety of methods to escape the firing line: self-inflicted gunshot wounds, feigning illness, temporary poisoning by ingestion of oleander leaf or mixtures such as chewing tobacco, rum, and dynamite, or, most desperate of all, self-infection with gonococcal pus.[9]

Both Engle and the Hungarian poet Géza Gyóni (who died in Russian captivity in 1917) reported that soldiers taken at the fall of Przemyśl were suffering from scurvy and "shell shock," which made them susceptible to capture and sapped fighting spirit.[10] The Jewish-born future Stalinist dictator of Hungary, Mátyás Rákosi, reported on freezing conditions during the Carpathian campaign that sapped the soldiers' will to fight. "Becoming captured under these conditions did not appear frightening."[11] This phenomenon became widespread, with the result that entire battalions used the opportunity to "fall into captivity."[12] This apathy was carried to the camps, especially during long Russian winters: the longer the war lasted, the more prisoners suffered from increasing depression and lack of interest. A similar response was found in Russian soldiers—often badly fed, clothed, trained, and equipped *muzhiks* who had no idea why they were fighting and had nothing invested in the war.

Once prisoners were brought—often over long distances, during which they were frequently robbed of all their possessions—to clearing camps in Darnitsa near Kiev, and Ugreshskaya and Kozhukhovo in Moscow, where they were sorted for onward transportation.[13] Nationality played a role in the prisoners' final destination: Slavs, Romanians, Italians, and soldiers from Alsace-Lorraine went to European Russia, while Germans, Austrians, and Hungarians were sent to Siberia and Turkestan. That is not to say that the best run camps were always in European Russia: some of the best-run camps were in Siberia. But Slavs generally did receive better treatment. The Polish officer Roman Dybowski described how, in the second half of 1916, German and Slav prisoners were separated, and the Germans were often given better quarters.[14]

For rank-and-file soldiers, the conditions in Russian camps were harsh; but officers, with their monthly allowance of 50–75 rubles, depending on their rank, lived well until the February Revolution ate away at currency value.[15] Imre

Nagy, future Communist Prime Minister of the 1956 revolutionary Hungarian provisional government, was wounded and captured during the 1916 Brusilov Offensive.[16] Although he had not finished high school, Nagy was assigned to the intelligentsia barrack for volunteer high school graduate ensigns, reserve officers, and those with some university education. They were exempted from daily work, and camped—like officers—away from ordinary soldiers. They passed the time with athletic activities, newspaper publishing, reading, amateur theatrics, music, and other cultural pursuits.[17] The novel by Breithaupt (see below) describes differing camp conditions and interactions between the rank-and-file soldiers, officers, and civilians in a Transbaikalian camp.

Mortality rates for Russian prisoners of war were high: around eighteen percent.[18] Rachamimow has published a well-researched book on this subject, drawing from works by Davis, Rauchensteiner, and others; and Wurzer has added significant information to the store of literature. Since Russian War Archives were only opened for research in the 1990s, only Rachamimow and Wurzer have included them in their studies. Wurzer in particular includes entire sections in the original Russian.[19] Although German prisoners also spent time in Russian captivity, their numbers (approximately 167,000) were far below those of Austro-Hungary, making their overall prisoner of war status, mainly in Britain and France, very different from their Austro-Hungarian counterparts.[20]

With approximately 350,000 Jewish soldiers in the Austro-Hungarian army, and prisoner capture rate between the minimum of 17% and maximum of 31%, the total number of Jewish soldiers taken captive by Russians would be anywhere between 59,500 and 108,500. This chapter focuses on diverse experiences of Jewish prisoners in Russia and Central Asia. It posits that the treatment of Jewish prisoners was similar to that of their Christian counterparts. However, Russian antisemitism did play a role in some circumstances, in particular in the brutal behavior of Cossack troops. Relations between prisoners and civilians were generally positive irrespective of religion. Large number of Jewish and non-Jewish civilians from cities such as Przemyśl and Lemberg were expelled from their homes and imprisoned along with soldiers because of suspected espionage and collaboration with the Central Powers.[21] These civilians had no formal rights as prisoners of war.[22] During captivity, many assimilated Jewish soldiers came into contact for the first time with Jews from all over the wide Russian Empire—not only from the Pale of Settlement, but also from large cities such as Moscow, and Eastern areas, including parts of Turkestan such as Tashkent, Kokand, Astrakhan, and Bukhara.[23] Jewish civilians living in Siberia usually came there as a result of their flight from the Pale of Settlement.

The interaction between Austro-Hungarian Jewish soldiers and Russian and Central Asian Jewish civilians has not been adequately documented, and little is known about the life of Jewish civilians in Central Asia during World War I. Not only did Austro-Hungarian Jewish soldiers come from diverse ethnic and geographic backgrounds within the empire, they also differed widely in religious adherence. This complicated relations with each other, with Christian soldiers, and with civilians. By contrast, German Jewish soldiers were more homogenous.

Attempts to recruit prisoners of war in the Bolshevik cause began immediately after the October Revolution. Magyar, German, and Jewish prisoners were the first groups approached, and a congress of "International Social-Democratic POWs" was summoned to Samara in the end of January 1918. Delegates formally requested (and were given) permission to join the Red Guards These included the future leader of the Hungarian Soviet Republic, Béla Kun. The total number of prisoners of war who served with the Red Army at some time or another ranged from 50,000 to 190,000.[24]

Russian captivity was a unique experience because prisoners witnessed firsthand the results of the Russian Revolution and its effects on all parts of the country. This added to existing lack of organization, and played a role in delayed prisoner repatriation. As Rachamimow states, an estimated 430,000 prisoners—mainly from Austro-Hungary but also from Germany and Turkey—found themselves in Siberia and Turkestan during the Russian Civil War, and were only repatriated during 1921–1922. The last batch of Austro-Hungarian prisoners were sent home from the port of Vladivostok in 1922.[25] Prisoners returning home encountered a population not interested in hearing about the travails of Russian captivity. For Jews, this lack of interest was magnified many times over by their concern over the rise of National Socialism, and interest disappeared completely in the light of the horrors of the Holocaust. Time is overdue to revisit this issue, and see what we can learn from the prisoners' experiences.

This chapter—the first of its kind on this subject of which I am aware—utilizes diaries, books, and memoirs of Austro-Hungarian soldiers in Serbian, Russian, and Central Asian captivity. I assert that the entire Austro-Hungarian war experience cannot be properly understood without taking into consideration their massive numbers of prisoners, mainly taken by Russia.

Memoirs of Adolph Epstein and Hans Kohn describe odysseys through Central Asia and encounters—including a Pesach seder—with Bukharan Jews. Kaspar Blond's travel odyssey takes him through Persia and Mesopotamia, arriving in Aleppo in time to bear witness to the Armenian genocide before traveling home. This chapter also contains a summary of the first English translation of Avigdor Hameiri's book *Bagehinom shel Mata* (Hell on Earth), published more than eight decades ago. The book contains an extraordinary cast of characters and sheds light on conditions in different camps, interpersonal relations between prisoners and Russian military and non-military personnel, and meetings between Jewish prisoners and Russian Jews living mostly in the Pale of Settlement. Hameiri's direct experiences of the Russian Revolution, including a meeting with Symon Petlyura, are unique.

Georg Breithaupt's semi-fictional description of life in a prisoner of war camp in Transbaikalia provides unique glimpses into camp life, and prisoner-prisoner and prisoner-soldier interactions. It emphasizes the little-known fact that many thousands of Jewish civilians were exiled together with captured soldiers.

Reports of the brief imprisonment of Austro-Hungarian prisoners by Serbia in the brief 1914–1915 campaign are sparse, and this chapter adds to literature on the subject.

At least early in the war, officer prisoners lived well, and on friendly terms with the local civilian population, exemplified by Arnold Hindls's life in Novosibirsk.[26] The overall mortality rate of approximately 18% in Russian prisoner of war camps compared to prisoners in Britain, Germany, Austro-Hungary, and Italy (2–7%) appears due more to laziness, disorder, and indolence than organized cruelty.[27] Events such as the typhus outbreak in Totskoe on the Samara River in winter 1915–1916 which killed as many as 17,000 out of 25,000 prisoners, and widespread prisoner abuse while building of the Murmansk railway—where 25,000 forced prisoner laborers died, and 32,000 suffered from scurvy, typhus, tuberculosis, typhoid, and cholera between July 1915 and October 1916—undoubtedly occurred, but these were ultimately stopped, and deliberate cruelty was not the norm.[28] The only group singled out for their barbaric acts were Cossacks. Overall, the conditions for Jewish prisoners in the Russian camps reflect those reported by Wurzer and Rachamimow for all Central Powers prisoners, set down at the beginning of this chapter.

The contents of these memoirs support the premise that there was little significant difference in treatment between Jewish and non-Jewish Austro-Hungarian prisoners in Russia and Central Asia. Hameiri confirms oppression of Jews living in the Russian Pale of Settlement, but he himself experienced no discrimination from Russian authorities on religious grounds. Kaspar Blond does not specifically report that he is Jewish. Epstein and his comrades were allowed to attend synagogue and seders in private homes in Central Asia, despite the fact that there were no Jewish chaplains in the Russian army. Jews in the local prisoner-of-war camp were able to have their dead buried by the Kokand Jewish community.[29] Far more, prisoners discriminated against one another based upon nationality: Czech against Magyar and vice versa, non-Slav against Slav; and religion: Christian against Jew. Antisemitism was present amongst prisoners, both officers and men. In the Breithaupt book, the Jewish doctor Rubens accepts Gersdorff's traditionally "genteel" Prussian antisemitism but feels that cultured men can bridge such gaps.

Mention is made below of the usefulness of "auto-fiction" to better describe war experiences at a distance. Works by Hameiri and Breithaupt cannot be easily classified, and lie between memoirs—covering both simple chronicles and more detailed analysis—and fiction, allowing the writer to describe life more vividly, even if partially fictionalized. Holtzman argues that reality generally confirms Hameiri's texts, whether in relation to the nature of war, the Russians, or his portrait of Russian Jews.[30] The number of confirmable facts in Breithaupt's book also argue in favor of its authenticity (see below).

Infectious diseases described by Breithaupt, Hameiri, and Blond in their books are similar to those reported by Wurzer, and wreaked havoc amongst soldiers and prisoners on the Eastern Front.[31] Venereal disease was rife; apart from salvarsan, introduced in 1911 for treatment of syphilis, no antibacterial agents existed, and treatment could only be supportive. Smallpox was very rarely encountered on the Western Front, because of uniform vaccination; in Central Asia it could and did exist, and spread amongst largely unvaccinated civilian and military population. It may be assumed that inoculation against typhoid fever and cholera, the rule for most combatants on both sides, was not as widespread in the Russian army. Breithaupt's physician protagonist Rubens is well versed in epidemiology of infectious diseases; he does all he can to prevent their spread by improving the water supply and sewage disposal systems, separating the camp kitchens, ventilating the rooms and cleaning out the barracks as much as possible, and making clean clothes available, to decrease loads of lice and other insects.

Experiences of Epstein and Popper in the Bukharan Jewish communities of Tashkent and Osh (which have ceased to exist, having transplanted mainly to the United States and Israel) are unique, as are their descriptions of a Bukharan synagogue, a Bukharan seder service, and polygamy amongst Bukharan Jewish men. As described by Breithaupt, the propensity of Galician Jews to view everything as a business opportunity, even building a synagogue alcove in the midst of a filthy, dark barracks, is typical. Large-scale exile of Jewish civilians left them no option but trade, if they were to survive.

Kaspar Blond provides details of a little-known theater of war operations—the failed efforts of the Central Powers to mobilize Central Asian and Persian Muslims in a holy war against the Entente. He ends with a chilling picture of the Armenian genocide by the Turks. Christian onlookers witnessed the atrocities silently, without attempting to help. This was a harbinger of things to come during the rest of the twentieth and the twenty-first century. When writing about his *Lebensraum* policy in the east, Hitler commented: "Who, after all, speaks today of the annihilation of the Armenians?"[32]

Diaries, Books and Memoirs

a. Serbia

Approximately 70,000 Austro-Hungarian prisoners were taken by Serbia during the 1914 campaign.[33] A letter from Alfred Kriegler published in a January 1916 issue of *Dr. Blochs Österreichische Wochenschrift* documents his nine-month Serbian captivity. After he was wounded four times on December 4, 1914, Kriegler was brought to a dressing station and taken captive three days later with 150 other wounded men. They were transported to Serb hinterland and divided amongst several field hospitals. In Üsküb, he was treated by Serbian, foreign, and prisoner-of-war physicians.[34] Three interned civilian women served as voluntary nurses. "Their dedication and sacrifice saved many lives." In the beginning, Jewish prisoners could live and make purchases in the town. Later, they were taken back to camp, to work on roads, railways, and in stores. Early August 1915, most Jewish prisoners were transferred to Novibazar as punishment, where they were "destined for hard labor, robbed of all freedom." At the end of October, men were brought, under escort, to Debar, for evacuation. This letter was sent from Salonika, from where Kriegler was presumably repatriated.[35]

A January 1916 feuilleton in *Dr. Blochs Österreichische Wochenschrift* reported a war diary of a soldier returning home from Serbian captivity. Its author was the travelling merchant Moritz Schwarcz who was taken captive by Serbs in December 1914, after the hard-fought battle for Belgrade (chapter 5). During the Bulgarian offensive he was taken from Nisch in the direction of Durazzo, then again from Novibazar to Struga, where he escaped, and found shelter with a Turkish farmer. Here he waited for the Bulgarian armies to liberate him. His diary deals with the time he spent in captivity between Belgrade and Struga.[36]

On December 16, his transport of 130–140 men was assembled and inspected. Wedding rings were taken from two men on both flanks. Schwarcz's sturdy lace-up boots were taken away, exchanged for sandals.

> Luckily I didn't have a fur coat, otherwise they would have exchanged that as well. Only prisoners in a position to pay 3 dinars for one army loaf or ½ kg of rusks captured from us received anything. We didn't starve, because each man who had some money bought food for those who didn't.

On December 23, they marched through snow, ice, and swamp to Mladenowac.[37] Schwarcz complained to the Serbian officer about how they were being treated; and the officer answered in rough German: "Yes, my children. War is no wedding!" Ill with fever, Schwarcz travelled from Mladenowac to Nisch in a wagon meant for pigs. The prisoner of war camp in Nisch consisted of five long wooden huts, into which men were packed. At midday they received bread and boiled beans, without fat or salt. For dinner there was only corn bread. Typhus raged amongst them: every day they buried 250–300 prisoners, mostly Czechs, whose resistance was apparently low.[38]

Many local civilians cared for the prisoners, some even lovingly.

> Today God sent us Frau Taler, wife of a rich Jewish agricultural merchant. She asked which of us wanted kosher food: naturally, all Jewish soldiers said that they did, and she provided 140 of us with lunch. The weak amongst us received chicken. She refused to take money, so we gave our dinars to comrades of other faiths.

> With what selfless dedication Herr Steiner cared for us, irrespective of religion! He kept watch on our severely ill, and I know of several whose dying eyes he closed.

On January 15, 1915, the president of the Nisch Jewish community appeared in camp, to inform men that command had approved their living outside of the barracks, as long as the community supplied, or guaranteed, one dinar per man. He asked whether they were prepared to work outside the camp as water carriers, woodcutters, or building workers. They happily agreed, and were allowed to leave the camp. On the outside, they could find out news from home, and receive money rapidly.

The men survived a freezing winter. Around the end of April, they read in newspapers, which were smuggled in, about disquiet amongst the Serbs. The unsuccessful Russian Carpathian campaign affected them greatly. The population of Nisch stated: "The fate of Russia is the fate of Serbia as well." Two prominent members of the Nisch Jewish community faced court martial because the military leadership had equated their help with facilitating the prisoners' correspondence and espionage.

On May 10, four of Schwarcz's comrades, who sent their correspondence through two local bankers, were interrogated by a military tribunal. They did not confess, and were thrown into prison. At midnight, they were brought to the Jewish cemetery, each given a shovel, and commanded to dig their own graves. The squadron escort showed the prisoners their rifles and cartridges and threatened them with execution if they did not confess. At that moment, a hussar dashed into the cemetery, bringing the command to return the prisoners to the court, because they had in the meanwhile established the innocence of the two Nisch Jews. "If the hussar had loosened his horse's reins, the four men would have died a martyr's death."

On July 8, Schwarcz read that the Central Powers had broken through the Russian Front at Gorlice. Even Serbian newspapers could not lie anymore about the fact that things were bad on the Northern Front. Schwarz and his comrades were sent to Novibazar, to work on water lines. They lived in town and the Turkish population treated them well.

On July 20, they were taken to work on the local railway line. Many of Schwarcz's comrades were killed by explosions. "I told the engineer, that our blood sticks to this building, but that our side will also use it." As soon as the Bulgarians invaded Serbia, they were the first to use the new railway.[39]

b. Avigdor Hameiri. Hell on Earth. Russian Imprisonment, Lice, and Suffering

Avigdor Hameiri's novel of Russian captivity is a unique work. We encountered him in chapter 4, during his period of active service (1914–1916). He was taken prisoner in June 1916 during the Brusilov Offensive, and saw the end of the war in Odessa, whence he immigrated to Palestine in 1921. His classic book describing his Russian imprisonment, *Bagehinom shel Mata* (Hell on Earth) was published in Hebrew in 1932 and apart from an annotated Hebrew version published in 1989, has lain dormant, unknown except by a small group of Hebraists, for over eighty years.[40] I have published the first English translation of this work.[41] Because it is freely available, I include a summary of salient sections. Interested readers are referred to the complete volume for more details.

Hameiri was taken prisoner in Chortkov, with his entire unit, in June 1916.[42] Accompanied by his two friends, who also appear in his previous book *The Great Madness*[43]—Pály, his steadfast Magyar batman, and Margolis, the adaptable *yeshiva* student with ready Bible and Talmud quips (see chapter 4)—he travelled, by foot and in louse-ridden *teplushka*, to the Darnitsa assembly area outside Kiev—a Babel of many languages and nationalities from all corners of the empire. He was briefly quartered with a civilian Russian family, bathed, and fed well. Hardly had he begun to enjoy the comforts of home, when he and his companions were rousted out. Their journey continued on a Dnieper steamer to a river estate with a packing house for hay managed by an antisemite reactionary. Hameiri got to know a local Russian Jewish family and was impressed by their tolerant orthodoxy and long-suffering acceptance of oppression. He found out that the estate manager was disposing of prisoners by inciting violent arguments between Czechs and Magyars, and throwing bodies in the river as fish food.[44]

They were transferred away in pouring rain by a guard whose instructions were to kill them and bring back their ears as proof that they were dead. The plan was foiled, and the prisoners continued by train to louse-ridden barracks in Homel, where the three friends were joined by a thin unwashed Gypsy named Latzi, who had never had any possessions and took everything that came simply and philosophically.[45] Hameiri again encountered the everyday oppression of kindly local Jews. He was struck by the curious combination in the Russian nature of cruelty and generosity of spirit. The prisoners were transferred again by *teplushka* to the "lair of the bear," Moscow. The Moscow prisoner-of-war camp was huge. Ostensibly just an assembly point, it was populated by a large community of corrupt men who profited by thievery, making a comfortable life for themselves despite cruelty of Czech guards. Hameiri was struck by the men's sexual liaisons with the city women: even Jewish women were not immune. Although men had wives back home, marriage often occurred, and many local women became pregnant. When their men abandoned them, suicide was common. Hameiri was unimpressed by the local member of the Swedish Red Cross, who profited from clothes and shoes sent by Kaiser Franz Joseph for the men by selling them on the black market, and did not care about the violence meted out to the prisoners by the Czech guards. He and his friends fell afoul of the authorities, and escaped from the city.[46]

They ascended a train, not knowing its destination. It became clear that this was a death train, transporting dying typhus prisoners to be buried alive in lime pits on the side of the road. Revolted, the three friends had no alternative but to continue. It turned out that the train's destination was a punishment camp in Shatsk with merciless Circassian guards.[47] Prisoners were treated with barbarous cruelty, whipped unmercifully (sometimes to death), and had to sit in freezing, unheated, rat-infested barracks for days at a time. Margolis was whipped so viciously around the face that he lost use of an eye. Prisoners died like flies of typhus, and rats gnawed their bodies open and fed on them. Nourishment consisted of stinking cabbage soup and inedible, gluey bread. Hameiri had the idea of passing himself off as a Circassian, asking for a Muslim prayer rug, on which the two Jewish men recited Jewish prayers, bowed down and facing Mecca. This pacified the guards somewhat and made their lives easier.

The friends managed to escape into the town and find transportation by wagon to the nearest station, but the driver dumped them in the middle of the freezing forest and rode off.

> We stand in a huge expanse of snow; the silence is deafening. In the middle of this silent expanse, under dark and gloomy skies, four wretched prisoners of war are walking, in a strange country, on an unknown road, at night. Sick, weak, suffering, we all pray together to the God of Jacob. Not even an echo can be heard—not from the leaden sky, nor from the fading borders of the infinite expanse of snow.[48]

The friends trudged onward through the cold dark night. Villagers slammed doors and windows in their faces. As retaliation for lack of hospitality, Margolis burned one of the barns down, and they fled, arriving at the camp in Nizhny Novgorod. This chapter, "The Menagerie of Souls," reads like an antechamber to the Holocaust. Although the Russians had ample food, prisoners were starved for no reason, and walked around like starving, emaciated shadow-men, whose description exactly fits the *Musulmänner* in camps like Auschwitz. An array of camp characters comes to life: a prisoner hurrying around, briefcase in hand, searching for his peacetime work; one constantly apologizing for starting the war; one who is constantly busy, running around doing who knows what; one who eats everything in sight including straw, sawdust, bandages, and blood from his suppurating abscesses. Most compelling of all is the resident scientist, suffering from scurvy and beriberi, who gives learned lectures to the starving prisoners on the food groups, fine, rich meals with wine that everyone should eat and drink, describing each mouthwatering delicacy in excruciating detail to his starving audience.

The prisoners were transferred again, this time to Kazan. In Kazan food was plentiful, but prisoners were forbidden to scratch their louse-ridden bodies. Those who dared were beaten to a pulp. A prisoner who dared to scratch was ordered to ingest a mug of soup with several of his body lice inside it, and promptly vomited the contents out. The prisoners were transferred again, this time to Vyatka. Hameiri was quartered as a servant in the house of the local doctor. One of the doctor's daughters had befriended a dark-haired (obviously Jewish) schoolmate, who visited often to practice piano together. The father came home, and when the Jewish girl saw him she fell down in a faint. She was one of the young Jewish girls whose only recourse to escape from the Pale of Jewish Settlement and go to secular school was to acquire a yellow prostitutes' card; the doctor was her examining physician ensuring that she was free of venereal disease. On seeing this, Hameiri was immediately discharged from the household.[49]

The travel saga continued: the four friends were transferred to a camp in Perm. Another character appears: Private First Class Gong, with an enormous head, which he required "to bring peace to the world—peace cigarettes, peace food, peace lice, even a peace war." From Perm, the journey continued through the Urals to Ekaterinburg. This chapter, "The Human Slaughterhouse," frighteningly resembles the cruel experiments of Nazi doctors like Josef Mengele. Prisoners were operated on by two doctors—one Czech, one Russian—in experiments on limb amputation, eye removal, open massage of a living heart, tongue extirpation, intestinal examination, and so forth. Most (but not all) of these were done under anesthesia. However, for the second group of (physiological) experiments on the body's response to painful stimuli, prisoners remained awake. After the patients' wounds were healed (if they survived), they were taken away to be murdered and buried in a far-away pit. The prisoners hatched a plot, murdered the doctors, and a nurse ran screaming into the town to alert the police. Previous nurses had tried to do this, but were shot before they arrived. Authorities arrived, strict measures were taken, culprits punished, and mutilated prisoners compensated financially. This is the salient difference between Russian and Nazi camps in the two respective wars. Russian cruelty was mostly due to isolated individuals in isolated places without adequate supervision, and stopped when complaints were made and effective measures taken.[50]

The travel odyssey continued, and the prisoners' train descended from the mountains into the immense wastes of freezing Siberia. The prisoners passed through a well-run camp in Omsk, but Hameiri was too listless, weak, and disinterested to get off the train, let alone escape. They travelled through Tomsk, arriving at a camp in Nizhneudinsk, run by cruel Czechs who tortured prisoners mercilessly. The same stinking soup was served. Hameiri vomited into his mug but was forced to drink the mixture down by a ruddy-faced Czech guard: he vomited convulsively and collapsed. Pály was so incensed that he spat in the guard's face. As punishment, his trousers were removed; tapeworms with which he had been previously infected, now expelled from his rectum, were forced down his mouth at bayonet point, and he was choked to death. Hameiri, Latzi the Gypsy, and Margolis were prostrate with grief. Despite Pály being a Calvinist Magyar, *kaddish* was recited over his grave.[51] A Magen David was carved on his wooden cross, with the words: "Here lies Infantryman Gergo Pály, who died an honorable death in the twenty-second upright year of his upright life. May his soul be bound up in the bond of life."[52]

The train journey continued through Eastern Siberia. During the trip via Irkutsk to Yakutsk, Hameiri got to know a Yakut sentry: a decent sort, who explained the Yakut religion of shamanism to them. The men travelled on foot from Yakutsk to Verkhoyansk, one of the coldest towns (-50°C) on earth. In order not to freeze to death overnight in a drafty barn, the men slept on horse dung and huddled together for warmth. Next morning, they were tasked to dig out a village which had been covered by a recent avalanche and in which everyone was dead. Vodka inside the houses revived them.

Travelling now in the opposite direction, the prisoners arrived at a camp in Irkutsk, full of virulent Catholic antisemites who murdered Jewish prisoners at every chance they got. To the suffering described in previous camps, a terrible outbreak of syphilis was added here. Prisoners were fixated on sex: they ruminated, sang, told lurid stories, molded erotic statues out of horse dung and masturbated on them. The camp scientist gave a learned lecture "on different forms of copulation of various creatures." A powerful German Christian was lured by promises of a beautiful Jewish maiden on their return home, to systematically kill all the antisemites, and murder of Jews ceased.[53]

The three remaining friends escaped from the camp in Irkutsk in emptied latrine barrels that were carried away by local Samoyeds.[54] Safely out of the camp, they climbed out of the stinking barrels with great relief, washed the excrement off with snow, and continued on foot. They walked on and on across vast snow-covered Siberian tundra until they had no strength left. Suddenly lights flickered in the distance. Inside one of the village houses, they saw a daughter and her mother, baking bread. The father had been exiled for helping an Austrian prisoner of war, so the two women were alone. The daughter let the three men in and extended hospitality. Because the two women conversed in Russo-Yiddish, their Jewishness was apparent. The daughter Raechka fed them and gave them milk. The mother protested vigorously: "look what happened when we tried to this before?" But Raechka barred the door with her arms and refused to give the men up. She gave all three men hot water to bathe and clean themselves, and boiled and scrubbed their clothes to clean them and get rid of lice. Clean and sated, they went to sleep over the baking stove with clean blankets. In the morning they found their clothes spotlessly clean and folded. She fed them again generously, and let them sleep their fill. When the two women heard that Hameiri and Margolis were Jewish, their eyes filled with tears. Raechka was a picture of Jewish beauty: long black hair cascading down shapely shoulders, dark eyes, and sensuous mouth. Hameiri wondered how she would find a Jewish husband in this wilderness. The three parted reluctantly from the two women with tears in their eyes and journeyed onwards. This chapter, "A Daughter of Israel," is one of the most beautiful of the book.[55]

Onwards, via Sayansk and Semipalatinsk,[56] to a well-run camp in Orenburg, where even the food was good. Hameiri and his friends were confronted by a "mad costume party" of prisoners masquerading as actors, writers, and playwrights. The camp was "run" by a prisoner called "Royal Highness," who lorded it over other prisoners. Margolis let the secret out that none of these men were who they said they were, and the culprits were punished. Prisoners forced the three friends away from the camp. This thoughtless act by Margolis prevented them from staying in the Orenburg camp, and would ultimately cause his death.

They journeyed through an area settled and farmed by Ural Cossacks. To their surprise and contrary to the often barbarous Don Cossacks, they were treated with kindness and hospitality. One old man took them with his cart to the nearest camp, in Uralsk.[57] A terrible place: the camp was heated, and glabrous drops of water fell from ceiling to wooden beds and floor, causing putrid fungi to grow. The camp was full of scurvy. In one of the rare descriptions in World War I prison literature, homosexuality is described in detail. The sight of two prisoners with horrible scurvy rictuses having sex with one another was too much for Hameiri, making him feel ritually impure, a state worse than mere uncleanliness. In one of the most gruesome scenes in the book, Margolis sat on the plank of an outdoor pit latrine, but slipped and fell into the pit of excrement.

After flailing around, he sank underneath and was drowned. No one helped him. Hameiri screamed convulsively and collapsed. Admitted into the camp hospital, he slowly recovered. Latzi was alive, having survived a bout of typhus. A kindly Russian official offered to allow Hameiri and Latzi to travel to Kiev. A Jew from the local community told Hameiri that they had retrieved Margolis's body, washed it and given him a ritual Jewish burial.

> A Jewish burial.
> As if this changes anything.
> Nevertheless, I feel a kind of relief. They took him from the stinking pool of shit and buried him in a Jewish grave.
> Strange how much better that makes me feel.[58]

On the way to Kiev, Hameiri—now only with Latzi to accompany him—stopped off at a camp in Sarov. A "holy sister" dressed as a Russian orthodox nun, accompanied by a "priest" appeared, to "bless and comfort" the prisoner officers (not the men). When the rank-and-file soldiers saw that they were being excluded, they became so angry that the two "comforters" had to flee. But the "holy sister" left a message behind, informing the men that she had syphilis. A few weeks later, to the officers' fury, symptoms began to appear. Latzi became infected with typhus, and died. Hameiri was now alone and inconsolable.

Hameiri's travels began again. On the train, he saw clear signs of the Russian Revolution: red flags on every street corner and cheers for Kerensky.[59] The *teplushka* was clean and louse-free, sprayed with carbolic acid, and the guard friendlier. The train stopped in Saratov, where camp food was good. Hameiri was set to work cleaning a town street. How good it felt to work again![60]

Hameiri's heart sank when he was told his next destination: Shatsk! On the way, he contemplated suicide—he could not go through that cruelty again. When he arrived, he noticed that the old inhabitants were still there—apparently, the stinking cabbage soup had some nutritional value. The Circassian guards were also there, but all signs of cruelty had disappeared, and a red flag hung over the camp roof. Hameiri and his two new camp friends escaped easily, arriving at an assembly point in Ryazan. They were surprised, looking out of a first-floor window, to see, in a nearby house, a Jewish family, with mother and young daughters giving the carpets, the furniture, and the other things in the house a thorough cleaning. It was Pesach eve. The men, much moved, looked on while the master of the house and the family performed the first seder. In a moving description, they participated in the second seder ceremony from afar, imitating each ritual dipping, with cups for each of the ritual four cups of wine. Everyone said the *Shecheyanu* prayer together, eyes full of tears.[61] The next morning, the youngest daughter arrived with large helpings of Pesach food and matzot for the men. Hameiri told a friendly Russian official that he had friends in Kiev, and he allowed him to be transferred there. In Kiev, spring had arrived.[62]

The trip had come full circle: Hameiri was back in Darnitsa, at another camp with cruel Czech guards who punished the prisoners psychologically. By bribing a Russian guard, he became part of a work detail in Kiev. Work, spring, and fresh air made him feel a great deal better. Amongst workers in the Kiev factory, he met his wife-to-be, Ginda Abramovna. With the help of old Zionist friends in Kiev and a non-Jewish lawyer, his release was secured. The book ends with a few chapters about quarrelsome Zionists in Kiev, and a meeting with Symon Petlyura. Hameiri lived through the Russian Civil War in Odessa, describing the pogroms and desolation brought by the Reds and Whites on the Jewish population. The book ends on a powerfully compassionate note: on his way to visit a friend in the Cheka, Hameiri meets that same ruddy-faced Czech who was instrumental in Pály's murder, being led to his execution. For reasons which were not clear to him, Hameiri intervened on the Czech's behalf and secured his release. "I return home and hear that my permit to enter the Land of Israel has been secured. Sanctified, I am ready for the Land of the Prophets."[63]

Hameiri's two war books are difficult to classify. Apart from one scene of Grand-Guignol gruesomeness in *The Great Madness*, in which Cossacks drink blood mixed with wine, with a head on the table, a torso under it, and another prisoner nailed to the wall (chapter 4), the book offers exact historical facts. *Hell on Earth* is another matter. Holtzman has characterized this book as "auto-fiction," placing the author at a distance from himself and from the gruesome circumstances (see above). The gist of Hameiri's narration is true: his personal sketches of his three friends reflects their authenticity, as do his other sketches of people and places. The reasons for his constant transferal from camp to camp are unclear. Many times it seems that he and his friends jump from the frying pan into the fire. Hameiri's descriptions begin to blur and sometimes become hallucinatory in the second part of the book, but their nucleus of authenticity is undoubted. The cruelty of some guards, the description of the freezing Siberia, lice, Siberian wastelands, and his finely brushed descriptions of people are crafted with attention to authenticity.

The noted Red Cross assistant, art critic, and novelist Julius Meier-Graefe (1867–1935) describes his time as a prisoner of war in Nizhneudinsk (which he calls Nadinsk) in a positive light.[64] Differences between his experience and that of Hameiri may be due to the different attitudes of camp commandants, guards, and staff. Hameiri is one of the few World War I writers who describes prisoner homosexuality. I believe that he returned from the war with what we now call post-traumatic stress disorder, which made him difficult to live with for the rest of his life. One of the great writers and poets of pre-independence Israel, and the only writer to describe his World War I experiences in Hebrew, Hameiri has unfortunately been largely forgotten.

c. Arnold Hindls: Novosibirsk and Berezovka

Arnold Hindls was born in Leipnik in 1885, qualified as an engineer, and was in the midst of his one-year volunteer service when war began. His war memoirs, mainly of his time in Russian captivity, are excerpted below.[65]

Hindls was captured, with approximately 100,000 other Austro-Hungarian soldiers, during the 1914 Carpathian campaign, in an attempt to cross the frozen Nida River in Poland the night of December 23, 1914. Under armed Cossack guard, prisoners marched for eight days to the nearest railway station. They were given food, clothes, winter boots, and travelled further, past Moscow, across the Urals, finally reaching Novosibirsk, on the Ob River. They were quartered in bunker-like buildings built deep into the earth, with wooden ceilings and lice-ridden bedding planks. The weather was freezing, and the first impression of their new home devastating. They convinced Cossacks to allow them to have a Russian steam bath and delouse themselves. They tried to find quarters in the town, where conditions were better and food cheap, but their potential hostess had been threatened with the death penalty for housing escaped prisoners, so they had no alternative but to return to camp.

Hindls informed authorities that he was a "building engineer," and was told that the chief architect was looking for an engineer who specialized in reinforced concrete. Hindlis met with the architect, and was given employment, quartered in the architect's house, and treated like a family member. He was tasked with planning a reinforced concrete bridge over the Kamenka River.

A serious typhus outbreak in bunkers where men were housed led to them being closed down: all men were taken to other camps, or housed with town families. Each officer received fifty rubles a month, which was more than sufficient: twenty rubles were enough to pay for board and good food. Stores were full of provisions, with plenty of meat and chicken. They used the remaining money to buy warm clothes for the Siberian winter, and had their laundry done.

Hindls was given a general project for planning of a citywide electricity station, and an abattoir for the developing town, so he had plenty to do.

The short Siberian spring gave way to summer, and men were allowed to bathe in the river Ob. They keep their underpants on, whereas, to their amazement, Russians of all ages and both sexes bathed naked. The beautiful idyll in Novosibirsk did not last, and in autumn 1915 Hindls and his comrades were transferred. They passed through Krasnoyarsk and Irkutsk, arriving in Berezovka, a town with a large prisoner-of-war camp in Transbaikalia near the Lena River.[66]

Conditions in Berezovka were strict, and became stricter with time; it sometimes took months before strictly censored letters and packages arrived. Hindls's men joined the several hundred officers captured at the fall of Przemyśl on March 22, 1915, and a few captured Turkish officers. Four men shared a room, which was freezing in winter. They were allowed into town, under escort. War news was difficult to come by, available only via Russian command.

Amongst approximately 4,000 officers in the camp were men from every profession. To keep the men occupied, each of them gave lectures on his profession, Hindls on his previous activities in Novosibirsk. Compared to plentiful provisions in Novosibirsk, food became scarcer in Berezovka, and shortages began to occur. There was no fruit or vegetables, and even for a time, no bread. Scurvy, tuberculosis, and furunculosis appeared, and Hindls contracted tuberculosis. After examination and hospitalization, he was classified a war invalid, valid for prisoner exchange. Shortages of baking flour worsened, and they made do with a kind of buckwheat gruel. Milk was scarce in winter, but was sometimes available for purchase as frozen cubes, and was either consumed or made into butter. In place of meat, the prisoners bought a frozen, stinking, rock-hard 300-kilogram bear carcass, which took Hindls's appetite away.[67] Grapes were available from a nearby town, and prisoners made their own "wine."

Along with food shortages, went shortages of everything else: shoes, paper, leather, fabric, and so forth. The camp regime became ever stricter. During an inspection visit by a general from military command, a Russian soldier attacked him with an axe, shattering his skull. As punishment, the rebellious soldier had to dig his own grave in front of the cemetery wall. He was shot in the presence of the entire Russian garrison, and the grave filled up. The general was given a hero's funeral. After the Bolshevik revolution, the graves of Russian soldiers who revolted were opened, and bodies buried next to the general.

After the Bolshevik Revolution began, communications with home were broken, and Hindls's hopes for a prisoner exchange dashed. Many soldiers used the resulting chaos to try and escape: one of Hindls's comrades succeeded in escaping through Manchuria via China to Tibet, where he was received by the Dalai Lama.

After the revolution, Hindls lived through the beginning of the civil war between the Reds and the Whites, including the Czech Legion. In late autumn 1918, Hindls and his fellow prisoners were transported further east in cattle trucks. They travelled through Harbin, capital of Manchuria. After endless travelling, they arrived at Ussuriysk, about eighty kilometers from Vladivostok. The train was attacked by yelling Cossacks, but Hindls and his men were unharmed and able to send a telegram to the Red Cross in Vladivostok announcing their arrival. After witnessing the chaos caused by the continued Russian Civil War, he was finally repatriated home by ship in 1920.[68]

d. Georg Breithaupt. Life in a Transbaikalian Camp. Lice, Heat, Neglect, and Infectious Diseases

In 1919 Georg Breithaupt published a novel entitled *The Fight for Survival*, set in a Russian prisoner-of-war camp near the fictional Transbaikalian town of Andarinsk near the Mongolian border. Details are too accurate (see below) for this to be anything else but an autobiography by a prisoner physician.[69] The first extended English excerpts from this vivid and compelling book (difficult to obtain even in the original) are presented here.

The novel begins in June 1915 during the great typhus epidemic in the prisoner-of-war camp at Andarinsk, which was probably Berezovka, in Russian Transbaikalia.[70] Hindls (see above) describes this camp, with many of the problems delineated by Breithaupt.

It was time for daily morning prisoner officer's roll call. But before it took place, an order from prisoner barracks commandant, Lieutenant Colonel Sommer, was read out. At 10.30 am, surgeon Major Dr. Julius Rubens appeared: "a small, daintily built Semitic-looking man with large nose, sensuous lips, melancholy eyes, and intelligent brow." The door opened, and a Russian non-commissioned officer appeared, looking for Dr. Rubens: he must pack his things and report immediately to the commandant. There was a severe and increasing outbreak of typhus in the camp for ordinary prisoners, on the other side of the river. Before he left for the sick barracks, Rubens reported to ranking German camp officer Major von Horn.[71] Horn also wanted to know about "Sister Frieda," who plied her trade in the officers' camp, giving out that she was a Red Cross sister. The major secretly wondered whether this dandified Austrian Jew would be tough enough to withstand the task set him, and gave him the large sum of 563 rubles for expenses. Rubens promised to report back, if he did not die of typhus in the meanwhile, and departed.[72]

Dr. Julius Rubens came from a well-off Austrian Jewish merchant family. Thirty-five when the war began, he was working as a specialist in internal medicine in Vienna, and became physician in chief of a Galician *Landwehr* battalion in the Carpathians. He was captured, with his entire battalion, in November 1914.

Rubens stepped out into the blinding summer light, and was nearly knocked over by a brutal stinking Cossack horseman with a pockmarked face. He arrived at the office of the Russian commandant of the enlisted soldiers' camp. An elderly Jew—*Landwehr* Infantryman Samuel Rosenduft—with a shrewd face, beard, and side locks, sidled up to him, offering his services as a translator and general factotum. On the way to prisoners' camp and his new quarters, Rosenduft told him of rampant disease in the prisoners' barracks: there was no proper medical assistance, and men were dying like flies.

On one side of the stream, the main camp appeared, with watchtowers and Cossack posts. The endless Central Asian steppes extended in every direction, and Rubens sank to his ankles in sand and dust. Lines of low wooden barracks with tin roofs appeared. Here and there Rubens saw wooden latrines, surrounded by thousands of flies. Groups of barefoot men with bare chests and tattered trousers picked lice out of their filthy shirts. Rubens and Rosenduft crossed the bridge over the stream. On the other side of the river were more barracks, stores, officers' quarters, and barracks for a Siberian Cossack regiment. This second group of barracks had been used as a quarantine area, but it became obvious that this was impractical, given lack of order. About 3,000 prisoners, most taken captive during the fall of Przemyśl, were housed in both barracks.

They entered the typhus camp, about two dozen windowless wooden barracks, in between them one wooden latrine.[73] On one side of the hill, caves had been dug in the earth. Nearby, stood a little whitewashed house with green windowpanes and a veranda. This side of the camp was full of half-naked emaciated figures, clothed in tatters. Despite the vermin, the sick prisoners fled inside barracks and caves to escape boiling midday heat. The heat, the stink of unwashed bodies and latrines, and the dusty air took Rubens's breath away. Rosenduft led Rubens into a large wooden barracks with rooms and offices emitting a terrible smell. One of these rooms was where Rubens was to stay; an adjacent one would be his "sick room," a smelly little room with two rows of wooden pallets: here and there a motionless figure lay wrapped in a blanket.

Rubens told Rosenduft to tell his Russian escort that he refused to live in such a pigsty, and was returning to officers' camp. After a whispered conversation, Rosenduft informed Rubens that, on payment of five rubles, he would be allowed to stay in the little white house vacated by a Russian artilleryman. The little house was filthy, most doors were shut, carpets were dirty, and bugs were crawling over the walls. Apart from the veranda, the house had three rooms, including a functioning kitchen. Rubens chose a corner room, a little less dirty than the others. Rosenduft told him that the Russian Dr. Pushkin would acquaint him with rules and regulations, but had no idea when he would visit again. Rubens must begin at once, with Rosenduft serving as batman. Rubens wanted to visit the patients, and gave Rosenduft ten rubles to do some shopping.

Rubens entered one of the rooms. Coffee, milk, sugar, bread, butter and sausage lay on the table, around which three prisoner medical orderlies in tattered clothes sat, eating and smoking. They were Müller, a snobbish Berliner who had recently been in the field, a fat short Hungarian named Farkas, and Huber, a large, typical Viennese rapscallion. Rubens called them to attention: discipline was badly lacking.

He performed his first inspection, asking why so few patients were present. Farkas explained that others were scared of becoming infected; also, severely ill men could not be brought here because of lack of stretchers, so they simply died in the barracks. Rubens was furious: no sick book, no diagnoses, no details, nothing! Pushkin was supposed to visit every eight days. If possible, he sent typhus patients to the nearby garrison hospital, which seldom had space for them. Rubens started to examine patients. Clothed in rags, they were living skeletons with waxy faces, crawling with lice. Already the first patient appeared to be in the last stages of typhoid fever, and none of the patients had received treatment. Rubens found a man dead from louse-borne typhus lying on an upper pallet. Out of the original ten patients three had died (two of typhus, one of typhoid).[74] Rubens disinfected his hands thoroughly, and left the hellish room.

The doctor's examination room was dirty, sparsely furnished with a table, a chairs, an examination bed, and a cabinet with a few disinfectants and medications. Rubens made a long list of his needs, and gave Farkas fifty rubles for purchases. The Russian non-commissioned officer in "charge" of medical matters walked in. He had Mongoloid features with cunning slits for eyes, flattened nose, and rubbery lips. He wiped the sweat off his brow, spat, cleaned his nose thoroughly with his finger, and sat down, threatening Rubens with imprisonment: he had received no orders about him. After long and complicated-sounding financial negotiations with the Russian—who was illiterate—Rosenduft calmed the waters. On his way back, Rubens inspected the dreadful conditions in the latrine. Back in the house, he found that his rooms had been cleaned, and a fresh mattress had been brought. Rosenduft cooked dinner and finally, after a long day, Rubens went to sleep.[75]

The next day, Rubens arrived at the sick barracks to find about 1,000 ragged, confused, evil-smelling men milling around the door, waiting to see him. One man showed Rubens the suppurating abscess under his nose; another, wounds on his bare feet; another pointed to his back. Rubens could hardly get through the door. He prohibited the patients from entering the examination room through the sick room, in which typhus and typhoid patients lay, so the men entered through the window.

Genuinely sick prisoners were mixed with the healthy who came out of curiosity. The heat and the stench made the air inside the examination room unbearable, and opening the window made it worse. All patients had the same complaints about inedible food and lack of decent clothing and shoes. Rubens interviewed the men for hours, but the number of men in front of the window only increased.

After lunch, Rubens started to examine the remaining men. There were twenty-eight cases of typhoid, nineteen cases of typhus, one scarlet fever, one severe rheumatic joint fever, and the rest had serious tuberculosis. Rubens ordered them to remain. Rosenduft promised to speak to the Russian in charge, named Seliwanow, to discuss needed improvements, including necessity of beds in a hospital separate from the sick room, which was full to bursting.[76]

Rubens visited barracks no. 70, where a patient seriously ill with rheumatic fever had been reported. It was a long windowless barn, with one door at each end. Rubens was greeted by a mixture of penned up men and makhorka.[77] A "barracks doctor"—someone who had "studied medicine,"—was present. Rubens gave instructions to make the man as comfortable as possible, and send him to the sick room the next day.[78]

They entered the camp office, a bare room with a table and writing material, some chairs, and a few pallets on which men lay snoring. Rubens roughly woke the clerks up. One of them—a Jew, Itzig Holzmann—told Rubens that nothing useful could be gained from Seliwanow today, because last night he beat up his wife, whom he caught in bed with a prisoner. Holzmann found Seliwanow in bed with a hangover. After he was given five rubles, Seliwanow verbally approved the delivery of the beds.

This time, with better order, the sick room visit was easier and quicker: only a few severely ill men had been transferred from the barracks, and no one died during the night. The rheumatic fever patient arrived, was made comfortable, and given salicylic acid.[79] For most of the sick, Rubens had little to offer except better nursing care, nutrition, and hygiene. He took his first look into the kitchen where food for the sick was prepared, and was greeted by a swarm of flies that contaminated everything before it was eaten.[80] He determined that this plague must be diminished by, for example, better storage of corpses before burial.

In this particular camp—which looked like a colony of disturbed ants—700–800 men were housed in two sections. Few were hale and hearty, most looked emaciated and dirty, with dull, expressionless eyes. Rubens emphasized the necessity of removing men with infectious diseases from barracks, and cautioned them not to drink unboiled water or kvass prepared with contaminated water.[81] Typhoid patients did not all need to die, if they were treated properly.[82]

Rubens visited earthen burrows, where some men lived. There was no straw bedding, and sand blew through cracks in the ceiling, coating everything. The Russians had stolen the ceiling wood. Each burrow held twenty men. The latrine hole serving the burrows was in the same awful state, covered with flies, as the others. Twelve men sat together on one wooden plank. When the latrine was full, it was pumped out by a Mongolian sewage removal unit; the stench was so awful that nobody could breathe. No disinfection was performed.

Rubens and Farkas moved slowly through the crowd of unwashed men clutching their eating utensils, waiting for food. Rubens thought that they looked like carnivores in the zoo, before feeding time. There were two kitchens, each containing a huge oven and three embedded cauldrons. On a long table, pieces of cooked meat, peeled and unpeeled potatoes, cabbage, onions, and "something green" were laid out. Two cauldrons were filled to overflowing with fatty soup, the other one with boiling water for tea. Men got only tea for breakfast; lunch was soup containing meat and a piece of bread, and dinner was kasha. Provisions had become scantier with time, and meat was now available only once a day. Rubens tasted the soup: a thin meat broth with a few small pieces of meat and potato. Bread was made of bran mixed with black flour, it was soggy and not properly baked. Six men each received one loaf of this bread, thirty centimeters in diameter. This particular kitchen prepared meals for 1,325 men. No one controlled whether men received proper provisions and no one had any idea of exactly what these provisions were. Stealing and black marketeering were rife. All three cooks were Czechs. One of them, apparently, came from a Prague hotel.

Men waited impatiently outside the kitchen, grumbling vociferously. The soup was thin, the barrack commanders and the Czech kitchen staff kept all meat for themselves. Jews had better food, for which they paid extra. Separate nationalities stood in groups. Hungarians cursed loudest, and Jews negotiated amongst themselves, waving their hands in the air. The cook opened the door, and the men crowded in like vultures. Food distribution took a long time; Rubens noticed that the barrack commandants each took an extra portion of soup. In the second kitchen, where food had already been doled out, cooks were also Czechs.

The barn-like sheds all looked similar: filth an inch deep, wooden pallets, about two hundred men packed into each barrack. Flies swarmed everywhere. Barracks in which a German was in charge looked better and men cleaner. The barracks in which Jews were the majority was commanded by a Polish Jewish sergeant. The door was closed, and in the semi-darkness Rubens heard a cacophony worse than a zoo aviary. Many Jews had side-locks and (despite the oppressive heat) were dressed in heavy caftans. Cigarettes, makhorka, tobacco, lamps, chocolate, clothes, shoes, every kind of food—everything was for sale, and each Jew offered his wares to Rubens at a cheaper price. There were facilities for moneylending and currency exchange, at competitive rates. Most civilians had been captured during the occupation of Przemyśl, exiled under suspicion of spying. Some men were praying in tallit and tefillin, and a Jewish prayer room, with candles and books, had been erected in one of the corners. Rubens was astonished: "What a people these *Ostjuden* were! Devotion and profiteering, religious needs and a well-developed business sense—mixed up in the same people!" The Jewish barracks were filthier than all others so far.

Rubens was surrounded by a crowd of undisciplined, gesticulating Galician Jews, talking and complaining at the same time; news that there was a Jewish physician in camp had spread like wildfire! Rubens told them that both their makeshift synagogue, and merchandise stands had to go: they were filthy, and barracks must be thoroughly cleaned and aired out. There were empty barracks available for praying and trading.

In contrast to undisciplined Jewish barracks, the next barracks, with only Hungarian prisoners, was too disciplined. One of the prisoners, a sergeant, walked around with a dog whip; the prisoners looked like beaten dogs.

During the afternoon, Rubens found the sick room cleaner and more ordered; even the rheumatic fever patient was feeling better. Holzmann had plundered the camp store: eleven iron bedsteads with wooden pallets and small wooden cupboards for each bed now stood in the sick room kitchen, with two tables and some chairs. There was a severe lack of water for men to wash in. Rubens ordered that water had to be brought in from the stream and properly boiled before drinking, to avoid typhoid. He also stated that all men had to be treated equally, to lessen the likelihood of bad blood between different nationalities. One of the barrack commanders mentioned the stinking fish soup that they received twice a week for lunch; the Russians liked it, but the prisoners loathed it.[83]

Amongst the prisoners, Rubens's gaze fixed upon *Unteroffizier* (noncommissioned officer) Werner von Gersdorff, because of his dignified appearance. This Prussian nobleman was suspicious of the "little Jewish doctor," His frame was emaciated, but traces of elegant bearing remained. He had started to study medicine but lost interest, and became a lawyer. Gersdorff's attitude softened when Rubens addressed him politely, and invited him to tea on his veranda. He told Rubens that he had been severely wounded in the Carpathians by a saber cut to the head and chest, which left him unconscious. Plundered, frozen, almost bled out, he arrived at a field hospital, where three bone splinters were removed from his skull. After an eventful journey during which his wounds became infected and two-and-a-half months in Lemberg, he was sent by cattle car via Moscow to the camp in Andarinsk. Gersdorff resented being treated like an ordinary soldier despite his noble origins, whereas Rubens, "the small insignificant Jew, whose Galician grandfather probably sold shoelaces, had enough money here to live well, be treated with respect, and put in charge of 3,000 men."

Gersdorff reflected that this was the first time in months that he had eaten at a set table, and did not to have slurp soup from a communal pot with a wooden spoon. They discussed the war and camp conditions. Gersdorff explained that the men in the barracks did not really live: they vegetated, demoralized by cold, hunger, and boredom. Jews, who stole everything to make a profit, constituted the greatest camp danger. Gersdorff suddenly stopped, realizing that Rubens was a Jew. A soldiers' canteen, where they could buy their own things, was a necessity. Most "barracks commandants" were too lazy to maintain discipline, making sure that only their own lives counted. There were also many open homosexual encounters between prisoners.

Rubens observed Gersdorff carefully: despite his tattered appearance and previous suffering, he was still a nobleman with a principled, strong will. He recommended that the first thing to be done was to forbid the men's immediate superiors from reporting them to the Russians. The men must be given something to do, because an idle mind was the devil's workshop. They must be allowed to do their own laundry, provisions must be improved, and a pharmacy and canteen provided. Russians provided nothing out of their own volition, and everything would cost money. Rubens asked whether Gersdorff could assist him in his endeavors. Gersdorff was astonished, and asked for time to think about it. Rubens invited Gersdorff to lodge with him, and join him for dinner.

Gersdorff had a lot to think about: a meal at a table set with cutlery and crockery, someone who treated him with respect, an opportunity to help bring order into chaos, a chance to get back at the Russians for their maliciousness. His innate sense of Teutonic thoroughness made him think through all aspects of this matter. No matter how good an impression Rubens made, he would still be working under a Jew, and an Austrian Jew at that. Would men take orders from a non-commissioned officer? What about money? He had not a kopek to his name here, and any money he requested from home would take months to arrive. To take up this job, he must be properly dressed, with a batman. Nobody takes orders from a badly dressed man. But the most important consideration was that he would be out of his filthy barracks. What should he do?

Gersdorff eventually told an astonished Rubens that he must reject the offer, and shared his concerns about three essential issues: health, sense of responsibility, and money. Rubens addressed his health issues: all would disappear with time and proper nutrition. His low rank should not be a problem with the Austrians, and Rubens would speak to the handful of Germans. Gersdorff would be addressed as *Herr Doktor* because of his law degree. Money was the biggest problem, but Rubens had an idea: how about obtaining a loan, which Gersdorff would pay back when his money arrived from home. Although he had no camp credit, Rubens would stand guarantor for him.

Gersdorff made sure that he would be working independently, not under Rubens. He admitted that he was (and had always been) an antisemite; Rubens countered that he had already seen that, but two educated men could agree to have differences of opinions.

The next day, the loan was secured. Rubens signed for 450 crowns (due by war's end), at a usurious interest rate of 50%. At this exchange and interest rate, everyone involved stood to make a lot of money. Rubens was ashamed of the entire business, but beggars could not be choosers and the money was badly needed.[84]

Gersdorff thought back to that awful day when he embarked on the trip to Siberia, packed into a cattle car with thirty-nine other men, some suffering from typhoid fever. The Russians had promised to let them off the train for a while in Chelyabinsk, the next train stop. Gersdorff heard that, recently, five coaches of Turkish prisoners, sealed because of louse-borne typhus cases, had been left unattended on the tracks for eight days. When they were finally opened, signs of cannibalism were evident.

He thought of the interminable train journey: Moscow, Samara, Chelyabinsk, Omsk, Krasnoyarsk, Irkutsk; his trip across the Urals; Lake Baikal with its enormous ice-covered water surface and tunnels in the steep mountain slopes at the water's edge through which the train passed. Finally, they reached the prisoner of war camp near Andarinsk: a shabby one-storied wooden barracks on the river bank. In his new position, Gersdorff's professional sense of organization got the upper hand, and he made suggestions to improve conditions. Although unpopular, he quickly became an important person in camp. Ironically, the only prisoners who liked him were the ones he most despised—the Galicians in the *Judenbaracke*. The next day, Rosenduft ceremoniously gave Gersdorff a hundred-ruble bill. Gersdorff had not seen so large a ruble denomination before, and asked for change. He ordered the barber for noon, and wrote home requesting the money.[85]

Returning from the sick room, Rubens found a new man: Gersdorff was resplendent in a new suit of clothes and shoes: he had shaved and had a haircut, and a livid scar could be seen on his scalp. Rubens told him that Dr. Pushkin had paid him a visit—an Odessa Jew who had some training in Germany. By German standards he was not qualified, but by Russian ones he was. A dandified fop reeking of perfume, who spent as little time in the camp as possible, he agreed to all of Rubens's requests except the fish soup—every Tuesday and Thursday this is eaten for lunch all over Russia! He approved medicines, disinfectants, more barracks and latrines, and a separate kitchen for patients in the sick room and the hospital—all on condition that it did not cost extra, and Russians did not have to make an effort to get anything done.

Suddenly, someone knocked on the door. Rubens was surprised to see a woman; she was medium height and plump; her short blue dress exposed a pair of strong legs. The tight blouse accentuated her figure, she had sensuous lips and greedy grey eyes, and wore a soldier's hat on her untidy blond hair. She was the same "Sister" Frieda Schimpfke who lived earlier in the officers' camp. Rubens was attracted to her: he had been without female company for too long, and she was not wearing a corset because of the heat. He told her that Major von Horn had forbidden her to call herself a Red Cross sister: she angrily denied the charge. Gersdorff was not pleased to see her. His noble bearing, clean clothes and excellent appearance attracted Frieda. She greeted Gersdorff, and left, promising she would return. Rubens warned Gersdorff of the dangers of venereal disease: according to Major von Horn, before the war—far from being a Red Cross sister—she was a Berlin prostitute.

In order to bring about improvements, Seliwanow had to be bribed with a monthly supplement of ten or fifteen rubles. More money, in the form of a "war loan," needed to be squeezed out of the Galician Jews, with possible additional assistance from the governments of Austro-Hungary and Germany, as well as the Red Cross. The neutral Americans also needed to be approached.

Rubens and Rosenduft crossed the bridge from the communicable diseases camp to the Russian barracks. They saw the Russian soldiers with Russo-Mongolian women and elegantly dressed ladies; ten prisoners hitched to a truck were laboriously hauling water from the river. On the way to the Russian commandant's headquarters, they saw a group of prisoners being mercilessly beaten, for some infraction or other.

Only Rubens was allowed into the officers' quarters, because he had an official permit. He greeted his former roommates. They had barracks fever, and wanted to break out to neutral Mongolia. Rubens warned against it, but promised to keep their plans secret. He reported to von Horn's private quarters, informing him of the progress made. Horn suggested a telegraphic request to the American consulate and the Swedish Red Cross representative in Moscow, and promised to collect money amongst other German officers. Von Horn treated Rubens with respect, a Prussian nobleman speaking to a Jewish parvenu. Second in command, First Lieutenant Sommer, told Rubens that he had heard of an American consul visiting a prisoner-of-war camp in Siberia, and promised to try and arrange a visit.

Rubens and Rosenduft returned to the other side of the camp, where Gersdorff awaited, resplendent in new clothes, Gersdorff crossed the bridge to the other side of camp for the first time since his internment, looking for Frieda Schimpfke, whom both Rubens and von Horn regarded as a danger to the physical and moral well-being of prisoners. Her room was in disarray, and air smelled of cigarette smoke, cheap perfume, and dirty washing. An open-shirted Russian soldier sat at the table drinking tea. Frieda stood at the mirror in her stockings, combing her beautiful blond hair. After a short conversation in Russian with Frieda, the Russian left, giving her a ruble note; Gersdorff and Frieda were left alone in her room.

She said that von Horn, a fellow-German, was responsible for her living so miserably. When Gersdorff told her how Horn was going to assist Rubens improve camp conditions, she reacted like a bull to a red rag, but promised not to interfere. Frieda threw her arms at him, ample breasts falling out of her open blouse. Gersdorff pushed her away brutally, calmed her down, and quickly left. Thus rebuffed, how could she take revenge on both Germans for their insults? Perhaps by getting the Russians to lock Horn up? She was just a simple woman, trying to survive.[86]

The next morning, working together in the sick room, Rubens warned Gersdorff about the great danger of typhus-carrying lice. Farkas reported ninety-seven sick, with seven mortalities. Rubens introduced "Herr Dr. von Gersdorff" to the orderlies, who were not pleased: another superior to give them orders! Gersdorff remembered what he had learned during his time at medical school, and slipped back into the routine of symptoms, diagnosis, and treatment. They were in the middle of rounds, when he heard the news: the American consul had arrived, and was actually in the barracks! They met in front of one of the caves: the consul was taking photographs of the latrine pumped out by Mongolian workers dressed in sheepskin coats and boots, despite the heat. "Good," thought Rubens, "let the American consul get a good look at the mess here!" The American was elegantly clad, his face non-committal. He introduced himself to Rubens as Smith, the American consul in Moscow. Their Russian escort, Titoff, was a corpulent, puffed up dandy resplendent in new uniform: he was the son of a rich Andarinsk tea merchant, and had profited mightily from owning both camp canteens. Rubens gave the consul a long list of complaints, mainly imprisonment of officers who refused to follow petty orders, use of men to pull water wagons like animals, night plundering by Cossacks. The consul laughed thinly: "I know the story by heart: I have heard it many times from other camps." He promised to try and help. But, after all, his mission was only to observe and report: everything else was the duty of other officials. Why waste good American money? The Russians would only steal it. He entered the sick room with Rubens, but Titoff, scared of becoming infected, remained outside. Smith and Titoff departed for Andarinsk, to forget about the camp and enjoy some schnapps.[87]

Rubens and Gersdorff reflected on the American: he did his duty and nothing more: but then what more could be expected from an egotistical nation of shopkeepers? Rubens and Gersdorff visited the Russian field hospital, which was under supervision of a questionably qualified Czech prisoner doctor and Czech prisoner staff. After a disrespectful delay, the Czech physician—who has been having his afternoon nap—appeared, and showed them around his hospital, which had about two hundred beds. A separate infectious diseases section contained overcrowded areas for patients with louse-borne typhus, typhoid, diphtheria, scarlet fever, measles, and erysipelas. Smallpox patients lay in a separate room: the disease was apparently brought in by the Cossacks from Mongolia. These patients lay, apathetic and emaciated, faces covered with disfiguring, hemorrhagic pocks. There was also a separate tuberculosis room. Other patients in the field hospital, not suffering from infectious diseases, were mainly cases of rash and boils (lack of hygiene), and venereal diseases. The entire area, into Mongolia, was rife with venereal diseases, too many to be treated in any hospital, so most walked free in the community. Rubens and Gersdorff decided to examine each prisoner in their barracks for venereal diseases: this had not yet been done. Both men left with a poor opinion of Czechs in general, and Czech physicians in particular.

By next morning, three more men had died in hospital. Pushkin had not yet fulfilled his promise, and Rubens was worried that they only had enough disinfectants and medication for one more day, with typhoid cases rising. Rubens hurried to the Russian commandant, whom he found with Frieda, and extracted a promise from him to sort everything out with Pushkin. After lunch they passed through the Russian camp on the way to town for a day's visit. It became apparent that Russian soldiers were treated no better than prisoners of war by their own officers.

Andarinsk was a mixture of Russian soldiers, young schoolgirls with short skirts, Cossacks, Transbaikalians of every type including Mongols, well-dressed Japanese, and Chinese smoking opium pipes. Some houses were well built, with some well-appointed stores and electric street lighting. But Andarinsk was really a Potemkin village with an outside veneer of civilization. Russian soldiers, young Jewish girls with downcast eyes accompanied by their less-than-beautiful mothers, Cossack horsemen with supposed criminals in tow, Mongolian ponies, and camel caravans all vied for place in the streets; and a cacophony of Russian, Chinese, Mongolian, Central Asian languages, and Yiddish was heard.

Rubens and Gersdorff entered the pharmacy, the real reason for their visit. Rubens handed the pharmacist his list of bandages and medicines costing almost a hundred rubles. In case Pushkin's promises did not come through, Rubens bought the supplies with his own money. While he was weighing everything out, the pharmacist complained "about Jewish black marketeering." The nearest garrison was so far away, in Irkutsk, that no control could be exercised. Civilians frequented opium dens in the Mongolian quarter, and alcohol flowed in rivers, despite the formal Russian ban on alcohol. There were so many brothels and bathhouses, with such lack of morals amongst civilian and military, that the entire town resembled one big brothel. Only Jews had an ordered family life, but pogroms sometimes occurred and street crime was rife. The town was full of venereal diseases; smallpox and bubonic plague were carried in from Mongolia. Smallpox had a high mortality rate because the locals were not vaccinated.

Although Mongolia was nominally under Chinese suzerainty, in reality it—and the area to the north—was ruled and controlled by Russia. The pharmacist warned against trying to escape through Mongolia to China, because the Russian government had a standing reward of fifty gold rubles for each captured prisoner. The prisoners who tried to escape were executed horribly by roving bands of Cossacks, who loved nothing better than hunting down humans.

Before Rubens and Gersdorff returned to their camp, they visited the officers' camp and talked to officers who were about to try to escape. Documents were exchanged, new identifications checked and rehearsed. Men were not encouraged by the picture of Cossack human hunters in Mongolia. Rubens and Gersdorff took leave of the escapees, and returned to the soldiers' camp, tired and worried about the officers' escape plans. Should they both try to escape as well?[88]

They were fortunate that they bought the pharmacy supplies: without them they would have run out of medicine on Sunday. The two men went on a surprise barracks inspection: none of their instructions had been followed, even in the Jewish barracks. Rubens yelled himself hoarse, and the men returned to the sick room to meet replacements for the fired orderlies who had been very pleased to escape from unwanted duty.

That evening, they suddenly heard wild yelling in the camp: Cossack horsemen were riding down anyone unlucky enough to escape. Nobody knew why this sudden attack had occurred. One prisoner lay dead, his skull split in two: he could not flee because of a bullet wound in the leg. Another man lay, face slashed open by a whip. While Gersdorff was examining him, Cossacks attacked again like wild beasts, yelling and whipping or sabering anyone in their path. Finding no more victims outside, they rode into the barracks that contained men with infectious diseases. Luckily, the prisoners had climbed to the upper pallets. The Cossacks' hate-filled, pockmarked faces and stink of sweat, filth, makhorka, leather, and rotgut filled the barracks. Gersdorff called out to the prisoners: "Beat these animals to death!" As if electrified, the prisoners rose up and threw everything in sight at one of the attacking Cossacks. In a few moments, the Cossack was reduced to bloody pulp. He lay on the floor motionless, but the prisoners still hurled objects at him, filled with blood lust, a desire for revenge for past humiliations and privations. On Gersdorff's advice, the prisoners cleaned the blood away, wrapped the body in a blanket, and tossed it into the half-full latrine. The authorities would surely not notice one missing Cossack. One prisoner was dead after the second attack, and six wounded.

Early next morning, the camp was suddenly surrounded by Russian guards. Authorities had heard that von Horn had planned an uprising for today in the typhus camp. He was arrested, and Cossacks attacked last evening to intimidate prisoners and prevent their escape. After a suitable bribe, Seliwanow agreed to let Gersdorff report to the commandant about this affair. The two men came up with a plausible story: they knew nothing of any rebellion, and guaranteed that everything would remain calm, allowing them to continue their work. Two prisoners had been killed by Cossacks, and many wounded and beaten up.

With a smirk, Seliwanow told Rubens that four escaped officers had been captured again: Frieda had betrayed everyone for money. Gersdorff complained to Titoff—substituting for the commandant, who was in town—that Russians had contravened international law by what the Cossacks had done. Titoff denied any knowledge of this: the Cossacks had merely been ordered to restore order and prevent escapes. He confirmed that Frieda had lied, to take revenge on von Horn. Gersdorff asked Titoff what kind of threat unarmed, half-starved prisoners constituted, and what excuse there was for the murder of two unarmed prisoners in contravention of the Geneva Convention. Titoff agreed to remove the guards from the camp and apologized in flowery English for what had happened, saying that he personally intervened to ensure that Rubens and Gersdorff were not arrested.

Suddenly Gersdorff heard a commotion outside. Three beaten, bloodied, chained men were being brutally led into the camp by a band of Cossacks. One had a bloody stump instead of a right hand. They were part of the group of four who tried to escape the previous night. Gersdorff went to help them. In the so-called "lock-up," he found, together with the three escapees and Major von Horn (whom he was not allowed to see), fifteen men all crowded in the filthy prison, and all in miserable condition. Some of the men had been there since last winter; no one had been to see them before. Through the keyhole, he saw von Horn sitting with his head in his hands. One of the three escaped officers had committed suicide from despair. Gersdorff promised the other two men to do what he could, bribed the guard to call Pushkin and make sure that both men were treated as officers and released, and departed.

Gersdorff returned, and told Rubens of the horrors he had seen, but he started to feel ill with cold shivers: he had become infected with louse-borne typhus. The end of the novel does not reveal whether Gersdorff survived, and readers are left to draw their own conclusions. At any rate, "Rubens had done his best."[89]

There are several references in the Breithaupt novel to events that are corroborated by other sources. These reference lend credence to the authenticity of Breihaupt's narrative. Mention has already been made of Seliwanow. There is also a reference to "Sister Klara" in an incident in Berezovka, when a German Captain Hagen tried to organize a mass escape of the entire camp to the Chinese border, which was ninety kilometers away. A German-Polish nurse, "the lovely Klara," betrayed the plan to the camp commandant.[90] The incident with the Turkish prisoners forgotten in a closed train is described by the Swedish envoy Rütger Essèn in connection with a trainload of Turkish prisoners from Omsk: approximately forty prisoners froze to death.[91] Brändström reported that in December 1914, 200 Turkish prisoners suffering from cholera were sent north in closed wagons, which were only opened after three weeks, leaving only sixty men alive.[92] Yanikdag described how, in winter 1915, of 800 Turkish prisoners shipped to the Priamur district of Siberia, only 200 survived the trip.[93]

Other details in this book also ring true, such as the relationship between Jews and non-Jews (including refined Prussian antisemitism); animosities between different Habsburg nationalities; Russian sloth and predilection for bribes. Russian camp authorities are not innately cruel; they are merely lazy and content to leave things as they are. Rubens—an educated Austrian Jewish physician—looks on *Ostjuden* with curiosity, as though they are a type of animal in a zoo, and Rosenduft is every ready to make a fast buck. This kind of gentle disparagement for members of one's own faith could only have been penned by a fellow Jew. Gersdorff's harrowing journey from the place of his captivity to his final destination is mirrored by other authors, especially Hameiri (see above). The book depicts interactions between prisoner soldiers and officers, and Russians and prisoner officers. Dissatisfaction with the assistance given by American neutrals has also been reported by other sources.[94] The description of a multiethnic Russian town on the Mongolian border, replete with bathhouses and brothels, Chinese opium dens, and Jewish prisoners trying to make a living by trade, is authentic, as is the description of the myriad infectious diseases (including smallpox), which plagued prisoners and civilians alike. As stated, the town alluded to in the novel was probably Berezovka. Finally, this novel gives one of the very few descriptions of World War I prisoner homosexuality.[95]

e. Hans Kohn. Turkestan and Siberia

Hans Kohn was born in Prague in 1891, joined the army, and was taken prisoner during the Carpathian campaign March 1915. From then until January 1920, he remained in Russia. In his autobiography, he describes captivity in Central Asia and Far Eastern Russia (including Siberia).[96]

Kohn was initially held captive in Samarkand, a city he describes as having colorful bazaars and narrow winding streets flanked by walled-in houses with charming courtyards, "an oasis of luxuriant green in the desert."[97] They were held in a Cossack summer training camp where, apart from primitive medical conditions with high incidences of malaria, typhoid fever, and louse-borne typhus, life was not oppressive. They had their own organization, food was plentiful and cheap, guards friendly, and they were even allowed to visit the town. Kohn found, amongst the population, a number of Bukharan Jews.[98]

In February 1916, Kohn escaped from camp, trying unsuccessfully to cross the desert into Afghanistan. After three days of wandering and exhaustion, he was recaptured. Because he was deemed an escape risk, he was transported to a remote outpost in the Pamir Mountains, near the border of Chinese Turkestan.[99] During the five day journey by train, ox-drawn cart, and horse, he developed a severe case of malaria, apparently cured by the 12,000-foot altitude of the prison camp. Possibly because of the high altitude, malarial mosquitos were absent. During March, Kohn witnessed three springs: the first in Samarkand before they left, the second in Osh where they waited for a few days or their escort, and the third, "a very timid and tender spring in the high and rarified air of Gulcha."[100]

Because Russians expected resistance from the inhabitants of Turkestan after mobilization for front labor service in 1916, Kohn was sent away in June 1916: he travelled by train via Samara to Khabarovsk, capital of Far Eastern Russia (in reality a camp in Krasnaya Rechka).[101] Despite guards, a few of Kohn's fellow prisoners succeeded in escaping through train windows, so the last part of their journey was made by barred *teplushkas*. They were placed in well-built houses normally used by staff officers, with four or five men locked in each room. Except for prison inmates and guards, they were allowed to see no one.

Winter 1916/1917 was hard, with food shortages not only for prisoners but also for the local population, because of the breakdown of Russian transportation due to war. The March revolution ended the prisoners' solitary confinement;[102] Red Cross books and periodicals were made available, and Kohn organized a series of lectures on philosophy and Russian civilization.[103] Kohn spent 1917 through 1920 in Siberia. He was sent to Novosibirsk in April 1918, where he remained for seven months, after which he and his comrades were transferred to Krasnoyarsk at the end of 1918, in the midst of the freezing Siberian winter. In Krasnoyarsk, a large camp with more than 10,000 prisoners, prison life was comfortable (the best of his entire captivity), with rich intellectual life and greater liberty in contacts with the local population. In early 1919 he paid a visit to Irkutsk and made contact with the local Jewish community. No longer a prisoner, he moved from the camp in Krasnoyarsk to Irkutsk, took Czech citizenship and joined the cultural section of the Czechoslovak Legion as civilian assistant librarian. By mid-November 1919, the White Army had been driven back and he saw that the Bolsheviks would win the Russian Civil War. In 1920, after an eventful trip through Manchuria to Vladivostok, he was repatriated.[104]

f. Adolf Epstein and Georg Popper. Bukharan Synagogues and Seders; Escape through the Russian Hinterland[105]

Adolf Epstein, a twenty-nine-year-old post office official from Prague, begins his memoirs as a lieutenant in an infantry division on the Carpathian Front February 1915. He and almost his entire regiment were captured, and driven by Cossack troops through half of Galicia on foot. While they were on the march, Przemyśl fell, and crowds of new prisoners—among them Lieutenant Georg Popper, former vice-director of a Prague bank—joined Epstein's group (plate 12). They were led in triumph by the Russians from one end of Lemberg to the other, and transported to Kiev, whence they were transferred to the south-east, to "Turkestan, land of the thousand and one nights," travelling for days and nights through ice and snow until they reached the warmer regions of Central Asia. They saw their first camels, and travelled along the Aral Sea through the endless steppes. At the end of April, they arrived in Tashkent, capital of Turkestan.[106]

In Tashkent, men were divided up into several barracks. Epstein and Popper were placed, with about 100 officers, in a large stone barracks on the banks of the Salar River, with guardrooms and a large room for officers. With help from a Serb prisoner, they made themselves understood, and were allowed by Russian guards to arrange purchases of straw, other sleeping necessities, and furniture, and to run their own kitchen. When they were taken into the city (strictly under watch) for a steam bath, they were fascinated by the multitude of nationalities: Kyrgyz, Turkmen, Uzbeks, Tajiks, Afghans, Persians, Indians,

Chinese, and small-statured Bukharan Jews dressed like Muslims. The men wore long coats of heavy silk, usually yellow with green or blue stripes and a black silk cap instead of a turban. The women were dressed in brightly colored Muslim robes, without veils (plate 13). Young girls had their coal-black hair braided and decorated with coins. Wife and child rode behind the husband, on the same horse.

Officers obtained a monthly allowance of fifty rubles, of which about half was spent on provisions, and men passed the time with all sorts of games. They heard almost nothing from outside until they ordered their own newspapers: Popper translated the articles into German, and every evening the newspaper was read aloud after dinner. They obtained maps, trying to follow the course of the campaign. During the summer heat, men were allowed to bathe in the nearby stream. Sleep was difficult in summer, with temperatures as high as 40–50°C, and the men built clay huts on the river. However, due to the danger of malaria mosquitoes, Epstein preferred to sleep in the now almost empty large room.

Heat took its toll with the intensified spreading of infectious diseases such as typhoid and typhus fever, cholera, smallpox, but especially malaria because of the stagnant water. Of 200,000 prisoners of war held in Turkestan, about 22,000 had died by the end of 1915. The officers camp was reasonably free of infectious diseases and, because men walked around naked, lice-free. Prisoner physicians treated patients as best they could, but were often infected themselves. Russians paid no attention to hygienic precautions, and men were left to fend for themselves.[107]

Strict rules of confinement were relaxed during Easter 1915 for Catholic, Protestant, and Jewish festivals, allowing officers and men to have contact with the civilian population.[108] On the first two seder evenings, practically all Jews in the barracks attended synagogue. The second evening was spent in the Bukharan synagogue. Because they were amongst the richest inhabitants of Tashkent, the Bukharan Jews spared no expense in its building. Protected from the street, it was situated in a courtyard surrounded with linden trees. Inside the synagogue was decorated in Moorish style, walls and pillars coated with sunlight-reflecting gold. Walls were covered with multicolored carpets and covers, and the floor had thick Persian carpets. Along walls on all sides ran one long bench, on which, like Muslims, men sat on cushions in crossed stocking feet. Those who could not find a place squatted around the altar in the middle of the sanctuary. Torah scrolls, rolled in multicolored silk covers and richly decorated with gold and silver plate, stood in the open ark. In the gallery at the back, covered by a silk curtain, women sat on cushions. Services were noisy: everyone prayed loudly, and children, who were allowed to come up to the altar, could be heard crying. The Bukharans in their tallit-covered, colorful coats, swaying as they prayed, were a magnificent sight. Unfortunately, Epstein and his comrades did not get the opportunity to get to know the Bukharan Jews better during their time in Tashkent.[109]

By contrast, they did get a chance to get to know the other local Russian Jews, almost all of whom spoke either German or Yiddish. They were not kindly disposed toward Russians; but admired and feared Germans, and were friendly towards Austrians, who appreciated the pretty local young women. The prisoners' freedom of movement did not last long, and was soon cancelled, apparently in retaliation for bad treatment of Russian prisoners in Austro-Hungary.[110] The prisoners' situation was also affected by unsuccessful escape attempts, which were punished by imprisonment in a strict regime camp on the Caspian Sea. Epstein described culinary problems with the Hungarians, who wanted their food more highly spiced than the other prisoners, and regarded vegetables such as yellow turnips as "bird food."

In fall 1915 they were visited by their first Red Cross Commission, and held a festive meal with splendid food on Christmas Eve. By that time, even civilians started feeling food shortages, and prisoner abuse began to occur. The monotony of prison life gave rise to arguments and quarrels amongst the bored men. In July 1916, an anti-Russian rebellion occurred in Turkestan.[111] The Russians begin transferring the German and Austro-Hungarian officers to Osh and other locations in Turkestan, or Siberia. Epstein and Popper were both transferred to Osh.[112]

They travelled part of the way to Osh by goods wagon, passing the Kokand area with its cotton and rice fields.[113] The huge Tien Shan mountain range between Central Asia and China could be seen throughout the journey. Because of proximity to China and Afghanistan, another great mix of nationalities could be seen. The final leg of the journey was on foot, through the Central Asian steppes. Osh was 1,000 meters above sea level, about 100 kilometers from the Chinese border, unreachable because of the intervening mountains, 3,000–4,000 meters of height, with strictly guarded passes. The climate was dry, excellent for prevention of infectious diseases. The town's population consisted of several hundred Russians and about 40,000 Kyrgyz and other nationalities. The men were housed in barracks in the Russian part of the town. After they were joined by prisoners from other parts of Turkestan, there were about 200 Austro-Hungarian officers, half German- and half Hungarian-speaking, with a few Croatian and Czech physicians. Men were allowed to bring their belongings with them from Tashkent, and soon organized themselves quite comfortably, although they were bored and depressed when the Kaiser's peace offer was turned down by the Entente at Christmas time.[114]

Early 1917, they followed newspaper reports of the Russian Revolution with great interest. The treatment by their Russian guards improved, and the overthrow of the tsar was met with rejoicing by civilian and military Russian population. They celebrated Pesach 1917 in a Bukharan synagogue, and were surprised to be invited to the subsequent seder. The men were divided amongst several families. The Russian guards soon agreed when they were told that good wine would be offered to them as well. Epstein and Popper were invited to the home of a rich cotton merchant, with bedrooms on the ground floor and the women's rooms one floor up. Although their host was a modern man, the seder was celebrated according to ancient rite. A low platform, richly covered with silken cloths and carpets, filled the room. Seating cushions were placed on the platform. Finely wrought vessels and cups stood on the low table. Men wore long, heavy silken coats, with silken caps on their heads. The host's two wives with their children sat on one side of the table, hair glistening with adornments, with beautiful shawls over their shoulders.[115] They had beautiful, delicate faces with almond-shaped eyes. The two charming twelve-year-old girls had their hair plaited in two small braids, with unusual head decorations. Each guest had a bowl in front of him. Because it was impossible to walk around the table, dishes had to be served on it. The daughters of the house managed this by walking nimbly over the table with black-stockinged feet, pouring the heavy, red Turkestan wine out for each guest. The pilaf, which reminded the men of Serbian meat and rice, was carried in a large bowl.[116] Dessert was a baked dish.

Table talk revolved around the war. Their host explained that Bukharan men had the right to marry more than one wife, if the first one remained barren. After he did so, however, his first wife bore him a child, so now he had one child from each wife. When Epstein asked how the two wives managed together, his host laughed. Each wife had her own bedroom, and they shared domestic chores. The Jewish women in Osh did not wear a veil, in contrast to the local Muslims, but still, their role was to work, not speak. Both wives sat quietly at dinner, whispered to each other, and stood respectfully when their husband honored them with a word. When Epstein and his comrades told their host that they were allowed only one wife, he refused to believe them. They returned to barracks full of wine and new impressions.

The men used the long summer to bathe every day. Their Russian escorts did not mind, because the men could not escape naked. On Yom Kippur, the prisoners visited the local temple, which, in contrast to the one they visited in Tashkent, was simply adorned. During the Torah reading, two Bukharans attacked each other; one drew a revolver, the other a knife. Women rushed from their sections, and separated the men. The prisoners' Russian escort anxiously ordered them back to the barracks.

Meanwhile, economic conditions deteriorated: everything became more expensive, and severe inflation developed. Food shortages began, and acquisition of provisions became the prisoners' primary concern. Horses and even dogs were eaten. From 1917 onwards, Turkestan was closed off from the rest of Russia by the White guards. Winter brought more privations: there was a severe shortage of food and heating material, and the prisoners' freedom of movement was restricted. News came of peace negotiations in Brest-Litovsk, and escape now seemed possible.[117] Flight through the high mountain passes to China, or via Persia, Afghanistan or the Caspian Sea, seemed out of the question, and they were left with possibility of escape through the Russian hinterland.

In mid-March 1918, after the Treaty of Brest-Litovsk, a mixed German-Danish deputation visited Epstein's camp: they advised against escaping because of a prisoner exchange was supposed to begin shortly. The prisoners were not sure what to do, but Epstein and his comrades determined to escape. They collected their belongings and obtained permission to visit Tashkent, under excuse of visiting the local dentist. False passes were obtained.[118]

They commenced their flight on March 26, 1918. Kokand, the center of the cotton industry, had been destroyed, and ruined bales of cotton, which could not be transported because of lack of wagons, lay on both sides of the street.[119] They travelled part of the way by rail, arriving in Tashkent at 10.00 pm. Because the city was under siege, they had to spend the night at the station. They rented a car and found a tiny room. Pesach food was obtained from the local Jewish community for the ten-day period. Further flight seemed difficult because railway communications into the Russian hinterland had been interrupted. Life in Tashkent had become very expensive. Galician Jewish civilians, taken captive during the conquests of 1914 and 1915, had been released, but were not allowed home in case they joined the army, so they were now engaged in trade. Epstein and his comrades borrowed 3,000 rubles, which enabled them to travel to Vyazma, in the Smolensk district of European Russia.

As soon as railway communications were restored, they prepared to depart. They chose May 1, a Communist holiday, which coincided that year with the

Russian Easter, because they reckoned that military discipline would be relaxed on that day. They sold their uniforms to local Polish Jews and, before they left, visited the local military cemetery to pay respects to comrades who had died in captivity. They boarded the train and passed through the Urals; all went well until, two hours from Orenburg, the train stopped. There were rumors that the train must go back because there was fighting around Orenburg, but finally the train proceeded and arrived in the city, where, for the first time in months, they were able to obtain white bread.

On March 4, they travelled on to Samara. The station was full of Red guards, and they tried to sit in the waiting room as inconspicuously as possible. Because Red guards were inspecting travel documents, Epstein and his comrades went into the city early the next morning. They decided to take a freight train to Tula, so as to avoid the Red guards, and hide in a *teplushka* behind the stove. They arrived safely in Tula, and then proceeded via Orel to Kursk, where they arrived on May 9, 1918. The men reported at the local Danish consulate as soon as they could. The consulate put the men up in a villa for eight days, during which ample provisions for the road were purchased in the town prior to leaving for Lgow in Poland on May 15.[120] They passed the demarcation zone in the dead of night, and were again in Austro-Hungarian territory.[121]

Upon their return, they heard the terrible news: fifteen of their comrades who had tried to escape after them, had been murdered. Simmering dissatisfaction with Russian rule culminated in a full-scale uprising of the Central Asian peoples in late 1918 and early 1919, and nearly 200 prisoners—both officers and men—were murdered in the chaos by bandits and militia. Nineteen men, who had married Russian women, remained behind in safety.[122] Epstein thought of his murdered comrades with great sadness, and vowed to remember them.[123]

g. The Odyssey of Kaspar Blond: Persia, Mesopotamia, the Ottoman Middle East, and the Central Powers Campaign in Persia

Kaspar Blond was born in 1889 in Czernowitz.[124] He studied medicine in Vienna, and in 1913 he served as one-year volunteer. The war interrupted his medical studies. From August 4, 1914, Blond was active as assistant physician in the Czernowitz garrison hospital. Because Czernowitz was the first town occupied by the Russians, Blond was taken captive very early, on September 24, 1914. He was transported to Turkestan, and imprisoned in Ashkhabad and Tashkent where he served as camp physician.[125] He escaped from Ashkhabad on November 6, 1915, and began a travel odyssey that would take him through Persia, Mesopotamia, and Turkish Syria, where he witnessed the Armenian genocide at first hand. On return to Vienna, he was transferred to Palestine in early 1917, due to his knowledge of infectious diseases. He remained there until the end of the war.[126] His travels through Persia, Iraq, and Ottoman Syria are diarized[127] and provide a unique perspective on a little-known theater of operations.

Blond escaped from Ashkhabad, with three comrades, in civilian clothing with bulging pockets and double-soled shoes. They marched across the steppe with a Turkmen guide; the terrain became mountainous, and an icy wind blew. The mountains they were crossing formed the border between Turkestan and the Persian province of Khorasan. They struggled up the bare rocky mountain in the middle of the night and crossed the border into Persia.[128]

They travelled through the ice-cold night, arriving exhausted and half-frozen in a small Persian town in Khorasan around midnight. Next day, they marched off along a fast-flowing mountain stream in a south-westerly direction. On the way, they stopped in a village where Blond and his comrades were introduced as "great physicians," and soon surrounded by people with all sorts of conditions. They spent the night in a mud hut "together with an old Persian with red-dyed finger nails and beard, two young Persian women, two children, and a host of vermin," and then continued east, washing properly in a mountain stream for the first time since their departure. They were welcomed by the local Khan's son in a nearby village.[129]

Accompanied by the Khan's son, they continued to the next village, where they enquired whether any Cossacks had been seen in the area. The Khan's son led them to the local governor's palace. The governor's brother welcomed them and took them around the local bazaar. They met a twenty-one-year-old German Balt who, on the way to volunteer at the German mission in Tehran, was captured by Russians on suspicion of espionage, and escaped. He told Blond and his comrades that they all (including himself) were under house arrest. The Cossacks had previously warned the Persians to give neither aid nor comfort to the soldiers of the Central Powers, and the Tehran regime was Russia-friendly. After several days, they were brought before the governor. They persuaded him that they were not spies, and he agreed to let them go. Blond was impressed by the anti-Russian feeling of the inhabitants in Khorasan.[130]

Blond and his comrades left the town riding on mules. They arrived in Tabor, where they were suspected of being Russians in disguise, and fled a few hours later. They crossed the mountains, reaching the Great Salt Desert, where lack of water soon made itself felt. After an exhausting journey of thirty hours, they reached a small settlement, where the local leader, informed of their impending arrival by the governor, revived them with yoghurt, cheese, bread, and tea. On November 20 they set off on foot and, after a few days, approached the main Mashhad-Tehran road. They found out that there was a large Cossack encampment halfway between the two cities, and assumed that the Cossacks were awaiting their arrival. They made a wide berth around the Cossack camp and, after eighteen hours of exhausting travel, with wounded, bleeding feet, reached the main road again.

While they were resting, eating, and drinking tea in the next village, two riders approached, and told Blond and his comrades to follow them, to save them from the Cossacks who had already heard of their approach by telegram. They continued by the main road via Damghan. The two men left, but no sooner had Blond and his comrades settled down to dinner, thinking that they were at last safe from the Russians, when news came that they must depart at once because fifty Cossacks were pursuing them. They arrived in Dowlatabad, where they spent the night. They were all given tickets and travelled, dressed as Turkmen, in the Persian post-chaise to Tehran. On the way, they heard that the Central Powers mission in Tehran had had to relocate in the southern city of Qum because of threat of Russian attack; later they heard that the Austro-Hungarian representative had returned to Tehran. They arrived in the capital of Persia on November 30, and reported to their military attaché.[131]

In Tehran they encountered properly equipped Austrian soldiers moving freely through the city (plate 14): a great contrast to emaciated prisoners to whom they had become accustomed in the prisoner camps. About 300 Austrian and Hungarian soldiers had reported to their Tehran mission since the war began, all with travel odysseys. Few had the luck, like Blond and his comrades, of finding an anti-Russian Persian governor, and many others died on the way, leaving their bones to bleach in the desert. The prisoners who reached Tehran were, on command of the Austrian attaché, formed up in two detachments, in service of the German army. In Tehran, Muslims were encouraged to join a holy war against the Entente after their defeat in the Dardanelles.

Blond and his comrades were seconded to an Austrian detachment and remained in Tehran for eleven days, before they fled Tehran following rumors about a possible Russian invasion.[132] They arrived in Hassanabad, where they met up with a Persian gendarmerie regiment who spoke pessimistically about a local tribal revolt against the Cossacks. On December 15 they reported to the German consul in Qum, becoming part of a German detachment. Blond described fighting in Persia:

> In Persia, war cannot be compared to a European war waged even fifty years ago. In a country with neither trains nor factories, where cities still have walls, towers, embrasures, and battlements, war takes on a medieval character. The bearded, sinewy Persian irregular cavalry, with flintlock and breech loading rifles, look like images from the Crusades or the Thirty-Years War.[133]

Merchants in Qum were "swimming in gold." Most Persian politicians were parasites, who did not have their country's welfare at heart. The Germans had money: why not take it from them? Bazaar prices in Qum had doubled since the Germans arrived.[134]

Schünemann, the head of the German detachment, was supposed to prevent the Russians from invading Qum, and loosen their grip on Iraqi Kurdistan.[135] News from the "fighting front" was chaotic; the fighters left Qum for Kashan in the south, in an attempt to make the local gendarmerie stand fast and prevent a Russian breakthrough. The town stood like a fortress in the wild steppes, surrounded by walls and ramparts, home to bandits preying on caravans. From Kashan, they travelled through rain and snow to Isfahan. Schünemann was apparently planning a takeover of Tehran with help of the scattered troops from the Central Powers and supporters in the Persian gendarmerie. He enlisted help from those calling themselves *mudjahids* (plate 15): warlike Afghan tribes, layabouts, thieves, the "scum of the earth" of some Persian tribes only motivated by hopes of booty.[136] It was January 1916. Schünemann and his men were pursued by the Russians and, in order not to be encircled and cut off, left Isfahan for the safety of the nearby Zagros Mountains, in the direction of Sultanabad. The Austrian contingent contained men from almost all parts of the empire: Germans, Romanians, Poles, Czechs, Ukrainians and Jews, Croats and Slovaks, Magyars, and Bosnian Muslims. Snow began to fall, turning the highlands into a wilderness of snow and ice. Finally, they reached the Persian province of East Luristan, near the border with Mesopotamia.[137]

The group was joined by the Austrian vice-consul of Sultanabad—who had surrendered the city to the Russians—with his small contingent of men. The journey over the Zagros Mountains was hazardous. Starving and half-dead from malaria (previously contracted in Turkestan) and other diseases, they staggered into Borujerd. The overall military situation remained unclear, with rumors swirling, and credible information was difficult to get. Finally, it became clear that the German cause in Persia was lost. The Central Powers had overestimated the degree to which the Persians would support their cause.

They struggled on through Eastern Luristan, reaching Nahavand, from which they had to flee because the Russians were at their heels. In the vicinity of the town they saw, for the first time in Persia, properly built trenches and fortifications. After more than eight hours in the saddle, they reached Sahneh, where Blond finally found a field hospital. There, he could help treat the men with severe frostbites, malaria, and other diseases. They travelled on to Kermanshah, where the Austrian detachment was relieved of duty and dissolved. On the way eastwards, they saw the panicked Persian gendarmerie fleeing in the opposite direction, and Blond was again astounded at the naïveté of the Central Powers when dealing with the Persians. In Mahidascht, there were so many Turkish wounded that Blond swam in "blood, pus, and piss." Uniforms were drenched with blood, wounds already septic upon arrival, and many wounded had lost a great deal of blood. Doctors were so exhausted that they could not stand straight anymore. Blond received orders to transport the wounded over the border from Persia via Kurdistan to the nearest town with a field hospital in Turkish Mesopotamia.[138]

Blond arrived in a little Mesopotamian border village on March 1, 1916. A severe outbreak of epidemic louse-borne fever erupted: it was not clear whether this originated locally, or had spread from Baghdad. Not only were clothes and coats infested with lice, but lice crept into the wounds of the Turkish soldiers in the local field hospital. Blond became infected himself and was transported by caravan, in a semi-conscious state, to Baghdad.[139]

In Baghdad, Blond slowly recovered and, as soon as he could, took over medical responsibilities for the sick and wounded. In Baghdad, he became interested in an infection called "Aleppo boil," which he had seen previously in Turkestan and Persia. It caused boil-like swellings on hands, feet, and face, and only affected the Austrian prisoners in Turkestan during their second year of captivity. Because the infection was seasonal, Blond postulated an insect vector. He took skin and soft tissue biopsies, and sent them to Vienna for investigation.[140]

From Baghdad, Blond travelled through Mesopotamia. On the way to, and in Aleppo, he encountered at first hand victims of the Armenian genocide during spring 1916. I cite his compelling report in full, in my translation, providing a fitting end to the chapter.

The brutality and horror, suffering and misery that I saw in these Armenian desert camps beggars description. Weeks after my return home, these fearful images still haunted me. Old-young children, starving young girls and women died a gruesome death in their multitudes. Corpses of unburied children lay around in the open, prey of wild dogs and jackals. I saw Armenian girls and women picking undigested corn from horse manure, washing the seeds in the Euphrates, and eating them. Nowhere did the misery of this unholy war strike me as strongly as in these Armenian desert camps. Even I, hardened by thirteen months of Russian captivity and accustomed to the sick and dying, was struck dumb at the sight of these concentration camps.

In Abu Kamal, I handed out all the bread that I could to the starving Armenians. They fell upon us like starving wolves and tore the bread from our hands: the stronger tore the bread from the weaker, and fled like beasts of prey, out of fear that the bread might be robbed from them. Our caravan was besieged all day by people acting like ravening wolves. Naked women and children lay in the dust moaning for bread in the most heart-rending fashion. I could not take a position on the Armenians and knew the treachery of which the Turks accused them, but who can forget the tortures of women and children? Can one learn to love a people whose government lets its own people slowly die of starvation in the desert? Thousands of young Armenian women were raped and sold as slaves.

Upon arrival in Aleppo—on my way to Constantinople, Bulgaria, and home—I made a flaming protest to our consul about what was happening. He showed me a book published by Turks that listed the Armenian transgressions. When I told him that the contents of this book did not interest me, he gave me friendly advice to say nothing further, if I wanted to return home safely. Since the days of Khmelnitsky, religious intolerance and bestial cruelty did not celebrate such inhuman orgies as I saw on the banks of the Euphrates. And there were Christians amongst the onlookers who could have prevented or at least moderated the brutality. They were Christians, and they did nothing. I curse this war.[141]

Endnotes

1. A. Rachamimow, *POWs and the Great War. Captivity on the Eastern Front* (Oxford and New York: Berg, 2002), 31-44; A. Józsa, *Háború Hadifogság, Forradalom. Magyar Internacionalista Hadifoglyok az 1917-es Oroszországi Forradalmakban* (Budapest: Akádemia Kiadó, 1970), 22, note 12. An earlier Hungarian source puts the number of Austro-Hungarian prisoners of war at 1,672,000. See B. Baja, I. Lukinich, J. Pilch, and L. Zulahy (eds.), *Hadifogoly Magyarok Története* (Budapest: Athanaeum, 1930), vol. 1, 75; P. Pastor, "Hungarian Prisoners of War in Siberia," in *Essays on World War I*, ed. P. Pastor and G. A. Tunstall (New York: Columbia University Press, 2012), 112. According to Rauchensteiner (personal communication), the total number of prisoners was around 1.5 million, with 200,000–300,000 Hungarians.
2. Rachamimow, *POWs and the Great War*, 31; Rauchensteiner, personal communication.
3. Rachamimow, *POWs and the Great War*, 31–34; 38; G. Wurzer, *Die Kriegsgefangene der Mittelmächte in Russland im ersten Weltkrieg* (Göttingen: V&R Unipress, 2005), 49–55, 106, 265; Pastor, "Hungarian Prisoners," 113.
4. G. H. Davis, "National Red Cross Societies and Prisoners of War in Russia 1914–1918," *Journal of Contemporary History* 28 (1993): 33.
5. E. Brändström, *Unter Kriegsgefangenen in Rußland und Sibirien* (Berlin: Deutsche Verlagsgesellschaft für Politik und Geschichte, 1922).
6. N. Kinsky, *Russisches Tagebuch 1916–1918* (Herford: Busse Seewald, 1987), 35–208; Rachamimow, *POWs and the Great War*, 180–185.
7. J. C. Engle, "'This Monstrous War will Devour Us All.' The Austro-Hungarian Soldier Experience, 1914–1915," in *1914. Austro-Hungary, the Origins, and the First Year of World War I*, ed. G. Bischof, F. Kasthofer, and R. Williamson (New Orleans: University of New Orleans Press, 2014), 146–147.
8. Pastor, "Hungarian Prisoners," 113–116.
9. Engle, "'This Monstrous War,'" 161.
10. G. Gyóni, "Just For One Night," in *The Lost Voices of World War I. An international Anthology of Writers, Poets and Playwrights*, ed. T. Cross (Iowa City: University of Iowa Press, 1989), 349–350; Engle, "'This Monstrous War,'" 146–147, 163–164.
11. M. Rákosi, *Visszaemlékezések, 1892–1925* (Budapest: Napvilá Kiádo, 2002), 195–208.
12. G. Milei, K. Petrák (eds.), *Tanúságtevők Visszaemlékezések Magyarországi Munkásmozgalom Történéből Magyarok a Nagy Oktober Győzelméért 1917–1921* (Budapest: Kossuth, 1977), 272.
13. Kyiv (Ukraine).
14. R. Dubowski, *Seven Years in Russia and Siberia, 1914–1921* (Cheshire, CT: Cherry Hill Books, 1922), 3–37; Rachamimow, *POWs and the Great War*, 54–60.
15. Rachamimow, *POWs and the Great War*, 97–99. Generals received 125 rubles per month.
16. Imre Nagy (1896–1958), Hungarian communist politician, was appointed Chairman of the Council of Ministers of the Hungarian People's Republic on two occasions. Nagy's second term ended when his government was brought down by the Soviet invasion during the failed Hungarian Revolution of 1956. He was executed on charges of treason two years later.
17. Pastor, "Hungarian Prisoners," 119.
18. Rachamimow, *POWs and the Great War*, 106–109; Wurzer, *Kriegsgefangene*, 49–55, 106, 265.
19. Rachamimow, *POWs and the Great War*; Wurzer, *Kriegsgefangene*.
20. Rachamimow, *POWs and the Great War*, 31.
21. Lviv (Ukraine).

22 Wurzer, *Kriegsgefangene*, 160.
23 Modern-day Central Asian Republics.
24 Rachamimow, *POWs and the Great War*, 121.
25 Ibid., 4–5.
26 Known at the time as Novonikolaevsk (the name was changed in 1925).
27 Rachamimow, *POWs and the Great War*, 107.
28 R. Nachtigal, "Seuchen unter militärischer Aufsicht in Russland. Das Lager Tockoe als Beispiel für die Behandlung der Kriegsgefangenen 1915-1916," *Jahrbücher für die Geschichte Osteuropas* 48 (2000): 363–387; Rachamimow, *POWs and the Great War*, 95, 111–114; Józsa, *Háború*, 129.
29 G. Cartellieri, *Hilfplatz D7 vermißt. Erlebnisse eines kriegsgefangenen Arztes* (Karlsbad-Drahowitz and Leipzig: Adam Kraft vermißt. 1936), 188. Reference to Jews only appears in the first few hundred copies, and was expunged by the National Socialists in subsequent printings.
30 G. Abramson, *Hebrew Writing of the First World War* (London and Portland, OR: Vallentine-Mitchell, 2008), 29–30, 51.
31 Wurzer, *Kriegsgefangene*, 105–116.
32 L. P. Lochner, *What about Germany?* (New York: Dodd, Mead & Co., 1942), 1–4.
33 M. Rauchensteiner, *The First World War and the End of the Habsburg Monarchy, 1914–1918* (Vienna, Cologne, and Weimar: Böhlau Verlag, 2014), 279, 833.
34 Skopje (Macedonia).
35 "Ein Feldpostbrief eines Gefangenen in Serbien," *Dr. Blochs Österreichische Wochenschrift*, January 28, 1916, 74. The Sanjak of Novibazar was an Ottoman administrative district until the First Balkan War (1912). It included the territories of present-day northeastern Montenegro and southwestern Serbia, as well as some northern parts of Kosovo. This region is also known as Raška, or Sandžak. Debar: Macedonia; Salonika: Thessaloniki (Greece).
36 Nisch: Niš (Serbia); Durazzo: Durrës (Albania); Struga (Macedonia).
37 Mladenovac (Serbia).
38 An epidemic of typhus and relapsing fever, which started in Serbia at the end of 1914, killed upwards of 150,000 people in a population of around four and a half million. Both diseases shared similar symptoms—high temperature, rashes, constant itching—and were spread by lice. They were highly infectious and often occurred together. While the exact start date of the epidemic was disputed, sources agreed that it ended in June 1915. Even in this short time the epidemic was devastating in a small country, where diseases spread rapidly.
39 "Das Kriegstagebuch des Moritz Schwarcz," *Dr. Blochs Österreichische Wochenschrift*, January 14, 1916, 48. Bulgaria joined the Central Powers on October 11, 1915 and, together with Austro-Hungary and Germany, invaded and occupied Serbia the following month.
40 A. Hameiri, *Bagehinom shel Mata. Reshimot Katzin Ivri be'Shevi Rusya* (Tel Aviv: Mitzpeh Publishers, 1931). An annotated version of this book was published in 1989 by Devir Publishing House (Tel Aviv).
41 A. Hameiri, *Hell on Earth*, trans. P. C. Appelbaum (Detroit: Wayne State University Press, 2017).
42 Chortkiv (Ukraine).
43 A. Hameiri, *The Great Madness*, trans. Y. Lotan (Haifa: Or Ron Publishing House, Ltd., 1984). Originally published as *Hashiga'on Hagadol* (Tel Aviv: Mitzpeh Publishers, 1929).
44 Hameiri, *Hell on Earth*, 1–120.
45 Gomel (Belarus).
46 Hameiri, *Hell on Earth*, 121–164.

47 Shatsk (Ukraine). Circassians are a mostly Muslim nation originating from the Northwestern Caucasus.
48 Hameiri, *Hell on Earth*, 165–217.
49 Ibid., 221–242. The "yellow ticket" (*zhyolty bilet*), жёлтый билет, the official prostitution license, permitted young Jewish women to live outside the Pale of Settlement.
50 Ibid., 243–260.
51 Jewish prayer for the dead.
52 Hameiri, *Hell on Earth*, 261–282.
53 Ibid., 283–309.
54 A nomadic Siberian ethnic group.
55 Hameiri, *Hell on Earth*, 310–328.
56 Semey (Kazakhstan).
57 Oral (Kazakhstan).
58 Hameiri, *Hell on Earth*, 329–347.
59 Alexander Fyodorovich Kerensky (1861–1970) was the leader of the Russian Provisional Government after the first Russian Revolution.
60 Hameiri, *Hell on Earth*, 363–378.
61 "Blessed are You our God, King of the Universe, who has granted us life (*shehecheyanu*), sustained us, and enabled us to reach thus occasion."
62 Hameiri, *Hell on Earth*, 379–393.
63 Ibid., 394–436. Hameiri's experiences in Odessa are described in his book of short stories, *Ben Shinei Ha'adam* (Tel Aviv: Hashachar, 1929). English edition: *Of Human Carnage—Odessa 1918–1920*, trans. P. C. Appelbaum (Middletown, RI: Stone Tower Publishers, and Boston, MA: Black Widow Press, 2020). Symon Vasylyovych Petlyura (1879–1926) was the Supreme Commander of the Ukrainian Army and the President of the Ukrainian National Republic during Ukraine's short-lived sovereignty in 1918–1921. He is usually blamed for the anti-Jewish pogroms. Petlyura was ultimately murdered in Paris. Cheka (*Chrezvychainaya Komissiya*) was Lenin's first secret police service.
64 J. Meier-Graefe, *Der Tscheinik* (Berlin: S. Fischer Verlag, 1918), 270–359.
65 A. Hindls, *Aus meinem Leben*, (New York: Archives of the Leo Baeck Institute, New York, 1966), ME 296, 61–97. Leipnik: Lipník nad Bečvou (Moravian part of the Czech Republic).
66 Ibid., 67–75. (Nizhnyaya) Berezovka was not situated in the Turkestan military area but rather in East Siberia, in the region called at the time the Irkutsk military area, south of Lake Baikal and north of Mongolia.
67 Bears may carry trichinosis, a potentially fatal roundworm infection.
68 Hindls, *Aus meinem Leben*, 76–97.
69 G. Breithaupt, *Der Kampf ums Dasein. Ein Ausschnitt aus der sibirischen Gefangenschaft* (Berlin: Verlag Carl Curtius, 1919).
70 Wurzer, personal communication. The German original states *Typhus*, making it impossible to distinguish between typhus and typhoid. Both were present.
71 It is clear that prisoner officers did not wish to visit the enlisted men's camp, which was physically separated from their own and much more dangerous because of rampant infectious diseases.
72 Breithaupt, *Der Kampf ums Dasein*, 11–32.
73 *Typhus* in German can either mean louse-borne typhus, or typhoid fever (an orally acquired infections caused by fecal contamination of the water supply). In this case the disease is called *typhus abdominalis* (typhoid). Both infections were rampant.
74 In some cases, the differences are given in the text.

75 Breithaupt, *Der Kampf ums Dasein*, 35–77.
76 A document in the *Rossiisky gosudarstvenny voenno-istorichesky arkhiv* (RGVIA, Russian State Military History Archives), f. 1468, op. 3, d. 440 describes the relationship between the commandant of the Berezovka garrison and the commander of a Cossack unit, *Unteresaul* Selivanov, and lists complaint's about Selivanov's treatment of prisoners (*O vzaimootnosheniyakh komendanta Berezovskogo garnizona i komandira kazachei sotni esaula Selivanova*).
77 A type of cheap Russian smoking tobacco.
78 Breithaupt, *Der Kampf ums Dasein*, 79–113.
79 Still the current standard treatment of rheumatic fever, which is an inflammation rather than an infection.
80 Flies can mechanically transfer fecal-oral infections.
81 A Russian national drink made from fermented bread.
82 Approximately eighty percent of typhoid patients recovered with proper nursing and nutrition, in the preantibiotic era.
83 Breithaupt, *Der Kampf ums Dasein*, 117–164. As I myself experienced on a Baltic cruise many years ago, Russians still love their fish soup.
84 Ibid., 167–204.
85 Ibid., 207–248.
86 Ibid., 251–304.
87 Davis ("National Red Cross Societies," 37) also mentions that both captors and captives mistrusted American consular officials.
88 Breithaupt, *Der Kampf ums Dasein*, 306–376.
89 Ibid., 379–415; An unrelated catastrophic typhoid fever epidemic occurred in Totskoe on the Samara River in European Russia during the winter of 1915/1916.
90 G. Brodde, *Russische Gefangenschaft und die Flucht durch die Bolschewiki* (Siegen: Montanus-Verlag, 1918), 35–36; B. Späth, *Als Kosak und Matrose unter Koltschaks Fahne in Sibirien* (Konstanz am Bodensee: Scheffel Verlag, 1925), 14–15.
91 R. Essèn, *Zwischen der Ostsee und dem stillen Ozean. Asiatische Probleme und Erinnerungen* (Frankfurt am Main: Frankfurter Societäts-Drückerei, 1925), 32.
92 Brändström, *Unter Kriegsgefangenen*, 22.
93 Y. Yanikdag, "Ottoman Prisoner of War in Russia, 1914–1922," *Journal of Contemporary History* 34, no. 1 (1999): 71–72.
94 G.H. Davis, "The Life of Prisoners of War in Russia, 1914-1918," in *Essays on World War I: Origins and Prisoners of War (War and Society in East Central Europe)* vol. 5, ed. S. Williamson, P. Pastor (New York: Columbia University Press, 1983), 170; idem, "National Red Cross Societies," 37.
95 Rachamimow, *POWs*, 11; Hameiri, *Hell on Earth*, 340.
96 H. Kohn, *Living in a World Revolution. My Encounters with History* (New York: Pocket Books, 1964). Originally published in 1964 in New York by Simon and Schuster.
97 Uzbekistan.
98 Kohn, *Living in a World Revolution*, 93–94. Bukharan Jews came from Central Asia, and historically spoke Bukhori, a dialect of the Tajik-Persian language. Their name comes from the former Emirate of Bukhara, which once had a sizable Jewish community. Bukharan Jews are one of the oldest ethno-religious groups in Central Asia and over the years developed their own distinct culture. Most lived in modern-day Uzbekistan and Tajikistan, but have since moved to Israel and the United States.

99 A high mountain range in Central Asia formed by the junction of the Himalayas with Tian Shan, Karakoram, Kunlun, and Hindu Kush ranges. The area is shared between Kyrgyzstan and Xinjiang (China).
100 Kohn, *Living in a World Revolution*, 95–96. Osh, Gulcha (Kyrgyzstan).
101 Rachamimow, *POWs and the Great War*, 92.
102 Between March 8–12, 1917 (new style), the tsar was forced to abdicate, and the monarchy was replaced by a Provisional Government.
103 Kohn, *Living in a World Revolution*, 97–98.
104 Ibid., 111–122. The Czechoslovak Legion were volunteer armed forces who fought together with the Entente to win the Allies' support for the establishment of an independent Czechoslovak state. The Legion was heavily involved in the Russian Civil War, where it fought against the Bolsheviks, at times controlling the entire Trans-Siberian railway and several major cities in Siberia. At the war's end, it was driven out of Russia by the victorious Bolsheviks.
105 A. Epstein, *Kriegsgefangen in Turkestan. Erinnerungen von Georg Popper und Adolf Epstein* (Vienna: Selbstverlag, 1935).
106 Ibid., 7–10. Modern-day Uzbekistan.
107 Ibid., 11–17.
108 There were no Jewish chaplains in the Russian Army (Y. Petrovsky-Shtern, personal communication).
109 Epstein, *Kriegsgefangen*, 18–19.
110 This is unlikely. Prisoners of war were generally treated well by Germany and Austro-Hungary. Propaganda played a role on both sides.
111 Major violence in Russian Turkestan broke out in 1916, when the tsarist government ended its exemption of Muslims from military service. The region erupted in a general revolt, centered in modern-day Kazakhstan and Uzbekistan, which was only put down by martial law. Thousands died or were massacred, and hundreds of thousands more fled, often into the neighboring Republic of China.
112 Epstein, *Kriegsgefangen*, 19–24.
113 The Khanate of Kokand was a Turkic state in Central Asia that existed from 1709–1876 within the territory of modern Kyrgyzstan. After that, it became a city in modern-day Eastern Uzbekistan. Jewish prisoners of war who died in the Kokand area were eventually allowed, after great difficulties with Russian authorities, to be buried according to Jewish rite in the local Jewish cemetery by the local population (Cartellieri, *Hilfplatz vermißt*, 188).
114 On December 12, 1916, Germany issued a note to the Entente suggesting a compromise peace. On December 20, President Woodrow Wilson called upon the Central Powers to make their proposal more specific—to no avail. On December 30, the Allies rejected the proposal, which they deemed unworthy of serious consideration.
115 The Torah does not outlaw polygamy. However, approximately one thousand years ago, Rabbi Gershom ben Judah (Rabbeinu Gershom) (c. 960–1028 or 1040) banned its practice. This ban was accepted as law by all Ashkenazi Jews, but was not recognized by Sephardic and Yemenite communities. Polygamy is almost nonexistent today even amongst Sephardic Jews, due to the fact that the overwhelming majority of them live in societies where polygamy is not legally and/or socially acceptable.
116 Rice is avoided on Passover by Ashkenazi, but not Sephardi, Jews.
117 Immediately after the November Bolshevik Revolution, Lenin initiated peace negotiations with Germany. The Treaty of Brest-Litovsk (March 3, 1918) took Russia out of the war.
118 Epstein, *Kriegsgefangen*, 25–37.

119 Cotton needs a lot of water to grow, and cotton fields filled with stagnant water became ideal breeding grounds for endemic malaria in this region.
120 Not to be confused with Lwow (Lviv), which was called Lemberg at the time.
121 Epstein, *Kriegsgefangen*, 38–56.
122 See Rachamimow, *POWs and the Great War*, 152, figure 4.4.
123 Epstein, *Kriegsgefangen*, 57–58. The Basmachi Revolt—an uprising against Russian Imperial and Soviet rule by the Muslim peoples of Central Asia—had its roots in 1916, when the tsarist government ended its exemption of Muslims from military service (see Kohn, *Living in a World Revolution*, 97). It was bloodily repulsed, and the countries of Central Asia became the Turkestani Autonomous Soviet Socialist Republic of the Soviet Union in 1924.
124 Capital of Habsburg Bukowina. Modern-day Chernivtsi (Ukraine).
125 Ashgabat (Turkmenistan).
126 P. Jung, "Der Militärische Weg Kaspar Blonds bis zu seiner Flucht 1915," *Österreichische Militärgeschichte*, vol. 5, *Ein unbekannter Krieg 1914–1916. Das k.u.k. Gesandtschaftsdetachement Teheran von Persien bis nach Wien* (Vienna: Verlagsbuchhandlung Stöhr, 1997), 28–32; M. G. Patka (ed.), *Weltuntergang. Jüdisches Leben und Sterben im ersten Weltkrieg* (Vienna, Graz, and Klagenfurt: Styria Premium, 2014), 219.
127 K. Blond, "Ein unbekannter Krieg. Persönliche Aufzeichnungen als k.u.k. Sanitätsfähnrich in Persien während der Jahre 1915/16," in *Österreichische Militärgeschichte*, vol. 5, *Ein unbekannter Krieg 1914–1916. Das k.u.k. Gesandtschaftsdetachement Teheran von Persien bis nach Wien* (Vienna: Verlagsbuchhandlung Stöhr, 1997), 33–93. First published in 1931 in Leipzig by Anzengruber-Verlag. No attempt has been made to trace every one of the villages and towns through which Blond and his comrades passed.
128 Ibid., 33–36.
129 Ibid., 36–39.
130 Ibid., 39–43.
131 Ibid., 43–47.
132 Ibid., 47–52.
133 Ibid., 54.
134 Ibid., 53–56.
135 Max Otto Schünemann (1891–1944).
136 One who struggles, or rides, for the sake of Allah and Islam. The word is still important, in today's context.
137 K. Blond, "Ein unbekannter Krieg." The photograph on 65 is a compelling image of the *mudjahids*.
138 Ibid., 67–78.
139 Ibid., 78–81.
140 Ibid., 81–84. "Aleppo sore" or "Delhi boil" (oriental sore) is a disease that affects skin and soft tissue, caused by a protozoan of the genus *Leishmania* (*L. tropica*) and spread by the bite of the *Phlebotomus* sandfly. Marked by persistent granulomatous and ulcerating lesions, it occurs widely in Asia and in tropical regions, where it is still prevalent.
141 Blond, "Ein unbekannter Krieg," 84–91. The 1915 Armenian genocide was the systematic extermination by the Ottoman government of its minority Armenian subjects. The Armenians were exiled from their historic homeland within the territory constituting the present-day Republic of Turkey, mainly Eastern Anatolia. The total number of people killed as a result has been estimated at between 1 and 1.5 million; Cossack hetman Bohdan-Zynovy Mykhailovych Khmelnytsky (c .1595–1657) led a revolt in 1648–1654 against the Polish Commonwealth. He is still remembered for his brutality, especially against the Jewish population of the republic.

CHAPTER 8. EPILOGUE

The Fate of Habsburg Jewish Veterans and Their Influence on Postwar Europe

It is not the aim of this book to report in detail on political and social developments of the truncated postwar Austrian Republic, and new countries created from the Habsburg Empire after the Treaty of Saint Germain in September 1919. Suffice it to say that the former Empire's Jews lost their cherished supranational identity, and were cast into whichever newly independent country they happened to be born or lived. Jews were amongst the old Empire's most loyal citizens, and in most regions—with exception of German Austria—their lives and loyalties were turned upside down. Bernhard Bardach's refusal to join the army of the new Polish Republic is a case in point:

> Despite the fact that I was born and bred in Lemberg, I refuse to choose the Polish Army, and will not belong to such a dissolute, corrupt, indolent nation. The Germans are not kindly disposed to the Jews, but at least they are cultivated, assiduous, and more honest, so I will join them.[1]

The influence of Jewish veterans in founding of the short-lived 1919 Hungarian Soviet Republic, and its influence after the latter fell, are of great importance. The reader is referred to standard texts on this subject, such as Rudolf Tőkés, *Bela Kun and the Hungarian Soviet Republic*.[2] In brief, although a Social Democratic Party had existed in Hungary for several decades before the beginning of the war,[3] true communism only began to gain traction in 1917, with formation of the Engineer and Revolutionary Socialists: the latter was formed by a Marxist study group of the Galileo Circle.[4] Workers Councils were developed, and strikes organized.[5]

By end of 1917, as many as 734,000 Hungarians were reported as captured, and imprisoned—mainly in Siberia and Turkestan.[6] On factory and workshop levels, contacts between prisoners of war and Russian Socialists were probably established as early as 1915.[7] Even before the February Revolution, the Russian government had allowed Czech, Slovak, and Southern Slav prisoners of war to leave camps and receive wages similar to those of Russian workers. These privileges were increased after the revolution. However, the conditions of non-Slav Hungarians, Austrians, and Germans did not improve, and many detainees were constrained to seek out radical Russian Socialist elements. This did not mature until the October Revolution.

By the time the war began, Béla Kun (Kohn) (1886–1938) had already become a Marxist.[8] After joining the army, he left for the Eastern Front in 1915; he was taken prisoner early in 1916, and shipped off to a prisoner-of-war camp in the Tomsk district. There, Kun met, and formed a Marxist study circle with, twelve to fifteen junior officers and enlisted men. After a stint in hospital, he obtained permission from the Bolshevik- and Menshevik-controlled Tomsk Soviet to live outside the camp. He joined the Tomsk regional branch of government, rapidly gaining a position of authority in the *guberniia* executive committee.[9] Similar events were occurring in European Russia and Siberia. In the Omsk district, for example, where 197,000 prisoners were Hungarian, Károly Ligeti, József Rabinovits and other former Galileists formed a revolutionary organization and joined the local Bolshevik faction. Similar groups were formed in Krasnoyarsk and Turkestan. Many future Hungarian revolutionary leaders (most of them Jewish) were recruited from the Tomsk group, and Béla Kun's Marxist writings proliferated. In early December 1917, Kun left Tomsk for Petrograd, where he met with Lenin.[10]

Due partly to Kun's efforts, a Hungarian Marxism study circle formed in Moscow in early 1918. Several of Kun's new prisoner-of-war comrades were to form the nucleus of his 1918–1919 government: Tibor Szamuely, Endre Rudnyánszky, Károly Vántus, Ernő Pór, Ferenc Jancsik, Frigyes Karikás, Ferenc Münnich, Imre Szilágyi, and József Rabinovits. Kun contributed to *Pravda*, and was tutored by Bukharin.[11]

The Hungarians prisoners of war in Russia played a disproportional role in Bolshevik activities during spring and summer 1918, making other nationalities apprehensive. As a result, many well-trained men (led by Jews) were available to join the Red Army to defend Russia and carry the revolution forward. Because Germany's defeat after the Treaty of Brest Litovsk was less predictable than that of Austro-Hungary, Hungary was regarded as the first country to turn Bolshevik after the war. To this end, the Moscow school (led by Kun and Szamuely) recruited activists from agitator schools in Moscow, Omsk, and other locations and trained them in Marxist theory, dialectics, and practice. Szamuely led the way, indoctrinating rank-and-file Hungarian prisoners, and Kun prepared a blueprint for a Communist takeover. As a result, by early November the Hungarian Communist Party was ready to seize power and establish the Hungarian Soviet Republic soon thereafter.[12]

The Hungarian war cabinet fell in late October, and was replaced by a cabinet of the former opposition under the premiership of Count Mihály Károlyi. However, the Monarchy's defeat left the new government vulnerable to a combined Romanian, Serbian, Czechoslovak, and French invasion. Winter was approaching, and the economic situation deteriorated, with food riots breaking out. Added to this, rifts appeared in the governing party. The Hungarian Social Democratic Party, which initially declined to exert actual power, changed its views, so that a dual-power situation developed. Unable to operate within the party, the revolutionary Socialists appointed themselves "keepers of the revolution's conscience," and Socialist opposition began large-scale reactivation, condemning the Social Democrats for their cooperation with the bourgeoisie. Kun returned to Hungary in November 1918 and provided a comprehensive plan for social revolution, splitting the Socialists and creating a Bolshevik-style Hungarian Communist Party.[13]

Kun and his group had the advantage of witnessing and participating in the Bolshevik Revolution from its inception. This experience helped them to adapt the system to Hungary. They established a party organization, drew up strategic goals, recruited new members—including the returning prisoners of war—and influenced veterans' associations. Their journal *Internationale* catered to radical writers, artists, and the technical intelligentsia. New members of Kun's group such as Gyulá Alpári, József Pogány, Jenő Landler, and Jenő Varga were recruited, and indoctrination and propaganda proceeded apace, especially in the December 1918 to February 1919 issues of *Vörös Ujság* (Red Newspaper) Kun was a tireless speaker in his cause, and his Communist Party gained inroads in more moderate Socialists and Social Democrats. The government was powerless to stop their venomous critique, and, on February 21, 1919, seized the Communist Party's printing presses and propaganda leaflets and briefly imprisoned the Communist leaders, including Kun.[14]

On March 21, 1919, one month after they were jailed and apparently neutralized politically, Kun and his comrades emerged from jail to form a coalition government with majority Socialists, and form the Hungarian Soviet

Republic. A combination of revolutionary experience in Russia by Kun and his comrades, bargaining from jail, overtures to heal a rift in the workers' movement, *Vörös Ujság* pamphlets, and the eventual Communist-Socialist alliance, played a part in this rapid turn of events. However, the Entente played into Kun's hands by issuing an ultimatum to the Károlyi regime on March 19, ordering the Hungarian government to create an eastern demilitarized zone and evacuate all Hungarian troops behind the new demarcation lines. It was believed that, if the demarche was fully implemented, the entire country would be occupied by the Entente, except for a twenty-mile radius around Budapest. Without this ill-timed ultimatum, it is doubtful whether the Hungarian Soviet Republic would have come into being.[15]

The Hungarian Soviet Republic was destined to last only 133 days, but its destabilizing effects lasted a great deal longer. It was based upon the mistaken belief that the transition from capitalism to communism could be accomplished in Hungary within a short time. Encouraged by lack of opposition of former ruling classes to their Communist takeover, Kun and his comrades believed that the bourgeoisie had seen the error of their ways and handed the government over to the proletariat without complaint. The party's economic program was prepared by Jenő Varga, Gyula Hevesi, and József Kelen, on the principle that centralized planning was superior to the anarchy of capitalism. Everything was to be nationalized, and land communally owned. Béla Kun was appointed People's Commissar of Foreign Affairs, a post he was to hold throughout the republic's 133-day existence. Next to hope of Russian military aid, his foreign policy was based on immediate outbreak of world revolution in Central and subsequently Western Europe. Propagandists were dispatched to the successor states of the Habsburg Empire, with the aim of splitting Socialist parties, engineering strikes, and hindering military preparations against Hungary. Kun correctly believed that the only alternative to dictatorship of the proletariat was foreign invasion.[16] The Republic's only embassy—in Vienna—became a hotbed for Communist propaganda. Elek Bolgár and Ernó Bettelheim worked closely with Austrian Communists to achieve their goals.

One week after Kun and their associates created the new republic, Kun's party organ *Népszava* (People's Voice) announced that, in effect, the Hungarian Social Democratic Party had absorbed the Communist Party's secretariat, thus giving up the Communist Party's separate identity. Lenin opposed the idea, and splits in the newly formed party began to form. Led by the extremist Szamuely, doctrinaire Communists objected to this merger, because they had not been consulted. Thus, almost as soon as it was formed, a struggle for power began in the Hungarian Socialist Republic. Kun was forced into a radically revised strategy in order to save the revolution, and improve the situation of a militarily defeated, bankrupt, starving country. Three revolutionary governing council commissions were formed, with a "Hungarian Cheka" led by Otto Kórvin, joined by a private army of the extreme left ("Lenin boys"), who were led by a friend of Szamuely. However, at the end of April the Socialist members of the Revolutionary Governing Council confronted Kun with an ultimatum demanding that he curb these "police" activities. Kun had no option but to return the police to bourgeois detectives. Szamuely, Münnich, Mátyás Rákosi, and many "Lenin boys" were sent to the front to serve as political commissars in the Red Army.[17]

On April 7, 1919, the Budapest Council of Workers' and Soldiers' Deputies met, and elected an executive committee that defeated all Communist proposals. Kun refused the Entente's offer regarding recognition of Armistice demarcation lines that had earlier been agreed to by the Károlyi government. Romania invaded on April 17 and, by the end of April, was at the gates of Budapest. On April 26 Kun offered to resign, and eventually gave in to the workers' committee. An insurgent force was rapidly recruited, which drove the Romanians back and by early June was ready to enter Slovakia. The Communist Party was thus not all-powerful, and it also had to deal with the Socialist faction. It became clear that the Communist drive for control of the united party was doomed from the start. Committed Communists like Rabinovits and József Révai objected strongly to Kun's perceived sellout on behalf of Socialist unity. By the end of May, the situation had become so bad that Kun was ready to settle for maintaining the status quo (no matter how unfavorable), without further loss of Communist strength and prestige. Unlike the Russian Bolsheviks, Hungarian Communists were divided on all manner of critical issues, and unable to speak with one voice and properly control foreign threats.[18]

Results of the first two-and-a-half months of the Soviet Republic made it clear that the only way Kun and his comrades could break through the wall of resistance of other parties, was to prove the Communists' exclusive validity, including in foreign affairs. To this end, Béla Szántó (commander of the Hungarian Red Army, Sixth Division), Mátyás Rákosi, Ferenc Münnich, and Antonin Janousek (head of the Czechoslovak branch of the Hungarian Communist Party) initiated an offensive against the Czech lines defending the Slovakian frontiers. The purpose of this offensive was to reoccupy Eastern Slovakia, and establish a Soviet Republic there. Additionally, Ernő Bettelheim and Ernő Czóbel, aided by local Communists, prepared an armed uprising in

Vienna. Both events were to take place on June 10–15, to coincide with the party congress. However, it was clear that the Socialists were not going to be rushed into indiscriminate acceptance of Communist proposals, as they were before.[19]

The first significant meeting of the "united" party began on June 12, followed by the nine-day meeting of the National Congress of Soviets, which opened on June 16. Despite strenuous arguments by numerous delegates on both sides, no general agreement was reached. It appeared that Kun had incorrectly judged the dynamics of bolshevism in the Hungarian context. Kun recommended Soviet Hungary's compliance with a proposal by Clemenceau, which promised cessation of hostilities by the Entente in exchange for immediate evacuation of Slovakia by the Hungarian Red Army.[20] However, his support of the short-lived Slovak Soviet Republic, and reckless campaign against the church, caused irreversible damage to his regime, demonstrating its lack of public support and superficiality of its control over the proletariat. In response, a Socialist coup was planned for June 24. Although it did not materialize, other uncoordinated groups of plotters launched an armed uprising, which was suppressed within twenty-four hours. The psychological effect of this short-lived uprising, however, showed the government's total lack of public support, and, instead of taking up arms, most members of the Budapest Workers Council—which was then in session—melted away.[21]

This abortive uprising of disillusioned soldiers and workers made a deep impression on members of the government who had become convinced that the revolution was in decline and could not be saved without external military intervention and concomitant terror. Their resignation followed, and a new Revolutionary Governing Council was formed. Measures against Polish Jewish refugees were instituted, with evacuation from the capital of all those not involved with "vital services," universal military conscription, and a Socialist system of wages and incentives. In late March/early April, Szamuely assumed the mantle of leftist opposition, but was outmaneuvered by yet another leftist group.

In the middle of July, the 150-man Federal Central Executive Committee met to review their four months in power. It was apparent that the decision to retreat from Slovakia had been a fatal error, which irreversibly damaged national pride and induced the Czech Army—contrary to the provision of the Clemenceau note—to pursue Hungarian units. The Ukrainian units disobeyed Lenin's orders to establish contact with Hungary, and the Romanian and Polish units sealed off the road to Hungary. Amidst resultant chaos, Kun and several

Communist and Socialist leaders of the failed Republic fled to Austria. The remainder opted to stay in Hungary, awaiting arrest. Szamuely committed suicide at the Hungarian border. The Hungarian Soviet Republic, devised and planned by mostly Jewish Hungarian prisoners of war indoctrinated by Lenin and his Bolsheviks, had lasted exactly 133 days.[22]

Béla Kun was captured and interned in Austria, but released in exchange for Austrian prisoners in Russia in July 1920. He never returned to Hungary. Once in Russia, he rejoined the Communist Party of the Soviet Union. Kun was put in charge of the regional Revolutionary Committee in Crimea, where he and Rosalia Zemlyachka, with Lenin's approval, ordered the execution of about 50,000 prisoners of war who had been captured fighting for the White Army, and anti-Bolshevik civilians. After having been promised amnesty, they had surrendered. Mass arrests and executions occurred while Kun was in control of the Crimea. Between 60,000 and 70,000 inhabitants of the Crimea were executed in the process. Until his execution by Stalin, Kun served in the Communist International.[23]

It is interesting to note that eighteen mostly Jewish leaders of the Hungarian Soviet Republic (including Béla Kun himself) were executed, or died as a result of, the great Stalinist purges of the late 1930s.[24] In the end, their efforts to facilitate the spread of world communism had been destructive and counter-productive.

The results of this ill-fated revolution were catastrophic for Hungary. Apart from ensuing political chaos, Rumania invaded and, at the Treaty of Trianon in 1920, Hungary lost seventy-five percent of its land and thirty percent of its prewar population, mainly to Romania but also to Yugoslavia and Czechoslovakia. Politically, Jews were now front and center in Lenin's Bolshevik, and Hungary's Soviet Revolutions. It became fatally easy to link Jews and Bolsheviks together, facilitating the path toward Hitler's annihilating antisemitism two decades later.

As far as other nationalities were concerned, Czechs, Poles, Southern Slavs, Romanians, and Italians each reacted in their own way, forming Western-style democracies or states led by the military. Leaders such as Tomáš Masaryk, (1850–1937), Nikola Pašić (1845–1926), and Józef Piłsudski (1867–1935) stabilized their respective newly formed countries, after greater or lesser degrees of border unrest (especially in Poland). Between 1918 and 1921, pogroms broke out in Lemberg, Cracow, Pinsk, Vilna, and at least at least 50,000 Jews were murdered in the continuing pogroms in Ukraine.[25]

As was the case with Jews in the German army, defeat led to increased Austrian antisemitism, charges of shirking, war profiteering, and responsibility for the lost war. In 1919 Edmund Daniek published a booklet *Das Judentum im Kriege* (Jewry in the War), in support of Jewish shirking and war profiteering.[26] Although shorter and less detailed than the book published by Alfred Roth/Otto Armin in Germany at the same time, it is filled with the same kind of virulent baseless accusations.[27] Daniek asserted that "the only place free of Jews [*Judenrein*] during the war was the trenches."[28] Jews became members of the Red Cross in order to assure service in the rear and avoid front service, and the vast majority of shirkers were to be found amongst Jews, who used the rabbinate (exempted according to paragraph 31 of the Conscription Law) to dodge military service.[29] He also stated that, by 1916, there had been more than 1,300 attempts to avoid service, using this artifice, in Vienna alone.[30] Galician Jews made widespread use of price gouging, smuggling, and profiteering, especially with sale of food. In addition, they maliciously spread incorrect war rumors, and attempted national recognition of their Jewish "jargon" (Yiddish). Jews were cowardly, unpatriotic, and spread revolutionary propaganda.[31]

Daniek asserted that the great majority of Aryan Ruthenian, Polish, Italian, and Ukrainian refugees were badly accommodated in camps and barracks throughout the country, while Jewish refugees lived in larger cities, making their money from dishonest practices and war profiteering. Jews took over trade in food and other badly needed materials, profiting from price gouging. By autumn 1914, Jewish refugees had stockpiled huge amounts of flour, coffee, sugar, rice, chocolate, cotton, tea, pasta, and many other commodities, withdrawing them from general circulation. The Galician refugees, with their coreligionists still living in the country:

> ... became notorious as the worst kind of war profiteers, who enriched themselves at the cost of a nation in desperate need. They enjoyed regular coffee at their coffee-houses in the Leopoldstadt, and champagne flowed like water night after night, until the early morning hours.[32] The assembly point for all this rejoicing and war profiteering was the Hotel Brauhaus am Semmering, where nightly wassailing at a cost of between 9,000 and 10,000 crowns often occurred. A whole series of Styrian castles was now in the hands of Jewish thieves and war profiteers.[33]

Army contracting was supposedly also controlled by the Jews, who made huge profits from sale of equipment and supplies, with no thought given to quality. There were so many Jews, that one got the impression of visiting a synagogue, not the war ministry.[34] Jews were also active in central war offices, where they flung the door wide open to rich Jewish capitalists, to favor their own industries and products. Daniek found no less than eighty offices controlled by Jews. "The call of the suffering *Volk* becomes ever louder and penetrating: away with the existing system of Jewish centralized economy!"[35]

Jews owned and controlled the banks, profiting hugely thereby. On page 26 Daniek presents a comparison of bank assets between 1913 and 1918. Of course, banks were Jewish-owned, with astronomical profits. Interestingly, Daniek (like Roth-Armin) does not give the sources for his numbers. His pamphlet ends with a ringing justification for antisemitism:

> German Aryans, citizens, merchants, farmers, officials, teachers, and workers who are not social democrats; all who do not want German Austria to fall prey to international Jewry and Social Democratic dictatorship; who are prepared to fight against the delusional idea of socialism; who do not want private property and possessions, obtained by honest labor, to become the objects of Jewish-Socialist pipe-dreams; who are honest, upright members of the German *Volk*: on election day, do not vote for International Jewish socialism![36]

Between 1918 and 1938, some degree of antisemitism (mostly not as extreme as above) was espoused by all Austrian political parties. The long-standing, moderating hand of Emperor Franz Joseph had disappeared. However, in contrast to Germany where the *Reichswehr* was deeply and openly antisemitic and had no postwar Jewish officers, the postwar Austrian army still contained a significant number of Jewish officers, and proved to be quite resistant to antisemitism in its ranks. An elaborate war memorial for fallen Jewish soldiers was erected in the Vienna *Zentralfriedhof* (plate 16) and memorials appeared in synagogues and cemeteries all over the country. Between 1918 and 1938, Jewish political and religious allegiance was solidly in favor of the new Austrian Republic.

In 1932, in the shadow of increasing threats by Nazi storm troopers, and more than a decade after the founding of the *Reichsbund jüdischer Frontsoldaten* in Germany,[37] the *Bund jüdischer Frontsoldaten* (BJF) was formed, as a combined veterans' and Jewish self-help organization. Its founders were Major-General (reserves) Emil Sommer (1869–1947) and First Lieutenant (reserves) Ernst Stiassny. After Adolf Hitler became Chancellor of Germany in 1933, and Austrian Chancellor Engelbert Dolfuss (1892–1934) replaced parliamentary rule with an authoritarian regime, the BJF declared: "It is our duty as front-line soldiers to be prepared at all times, if the government needs militias." After the murder of Dolfuss on July 25, 1934 and his replacement by Kurt von Schuschnigg (1897–1977), leadership of the BJF was taken over by Captain (reserves) Sigmund Edler von Friedmann (1892–1964). During the war, Friedmann had served in Galicia, and then in the heavy artillery section on the Italian Front. Friedmann's goal was to unite disparate left- and right-leaning Jewish organizations in Austria into one organization, excluding all other political considerations. Under his leadership, branches of the BJF were formed all over Austria. By 1938, the BJF had 38,573 members out of an Austrian Jewish population of around 180,000.[38]

The *Anschluss* of March 1938 led to the abrupt and permanent dislocation of Jewish life, and Vienna saw an attack of Jew-baiting such as had not been seen even in any German cities. The BJF was disbanded, and Austria's Jews—veterans and non-veterans alike—had two choices: emigrate, or remain and suffer the consequences which ultimately led, in the majority of cases, to the death camps.

The story of Dr. Bernhard Bardach has been described by Helmut Konrad. Bardach and his wife Olga immigrated to the United States in 1939, to live with their two daughters. Not only, after two decades of loyal military service—including the entire war—did they leave penniless, but his military pension was blocked and cancelled, through the immediate postwar period. The rationale was that "overseas residence nullified pension claims." The fact that remaining in Vienna would have led to imprisonment and the death camps did not seem important, even to postwar Austrian officials. Only after Bardach's death in 1947, did Olga manage to extract a paltry pension from their Vienna bank. As Helmut Konrad puts it, "the bureaucratic shadow of the Holocaust continued to darken Jewish lives long after the end of the war."[39]

As in Germany, many highly decorated Jewish soldiers or Austrian soldiers of high rank were sent to Theresienstadt. There, some of them survived, but the remainder were deported and murdered in Auschwitz.[40]

Let us look at the post-1918 fates of a few of these veterans.

Emil Sommer was born 1869 in Dorna Watra, Bukowina, son of a merchant.[41] After finishing school he performed his one-year volunteer service in the Thirtieth Infantry Regiment in Lemberg. In 1895 he became a professional officer, serving in the infantry. In 1908 he was transferred to the Twentieth Infantry in Vienna, from where he was transferred to the Russian front as captain when the war began. In April 1915, during fighting in the Carpathians, he was taken captive, and spent thirty-three months as a Russian prisoner of war. He was released after the revolution, and served from January 1918 in the infantry on the Italian Front. He was demobilized in 1919, and entered the militia, which was soon absorbed into the *Bundesheer* (postwar Austrian army). During occupation of the Burgenland, he was appointed colonel and commandant of the First Infantry, which was attacked in September 1921 by Hungarian *francs-tireurs*, who killed ten of his men. He retired in 1923 with the rank of colonel, and was named honorary major general by the President of the Republic in 1932 As stated above, he became the first president of the BJF in 1932 but, due to a difference of opinion on the society's role, resigned in 1934. When, after the *Anschluss* in 1938, he was ordered to join a humiliating "cleaning unit," he appeared in full uniform, wearing all his decorations: even the Nazis were humiliated, and sent him home. He was imprisoned several times and finally, in 1942, deported to Theresienstadt with his wife. Both survived. Emil Sommer, as he looked in uniform and subsequently in Theresienstadt, is depicted in plates 17 and 18. He settled in Vienna after the war, but died during a visit to his daughter in the United States in 1947.[42]

Several veterans immigrated to Palestine and helped form the military and political forces of the nascent State of Israel. Sigmund Edler von Friedmann changed his name to Eitan Avisar, became deputy chief of staff of the Haganah, later promoted to *aluf* (major general), and eventually headed the Israeli Defense Force's supreme military court. He died in 1964.[43] Wolfgang von Weisl (1896–1974; see previous chapters), was son of Ernst von Weisl, one of the first Jews to join Herzl's Zionist movement, who transmitted his beliefs to his son. Weisl served as artillery officer during the war. In 1922, after completing his medical studies that had been interrupted by the war, he emigrated to Mandated Palestine and, in 1925, helped found the Israeli Revisionist Party. He was received by Khalif Hussein—then Hedjazi King—Ibn Saud, and Faisal of Iraq, and was the personal physician of King Abdullah I of Transjordan. In 1931 he foretold the rise of Adolf Hitler, and raised money to support the first "illegal" immigrants' ship. He was a military strategist, physician, and medical researcher, and world expert in Islam.[44]

Julius Deutsch (1884–1968) was born in Lackenbach (Austrian Burgenland). His father was a passionate adherent of the Austrian Labor Party, and Julius became acquainted with Victor Adler (1852–1918), founder of the Austrian Social Democratic Party (SDP), at an early age. Julius became a lawyer, working for the SDP in that capacity until the beginning of the war. He was one of the few politicians to come out openly against the war in 1914. However, in early 1915, he joined the Fourth Fortification Artillery Battalion, promoted second lieutenant (reserves) in 1916. His bravery led to him being awarded the Silver Medal for Bravery, the Charles Cross, and the bronze Signum Laudis on the ribbon of the Military Service Cross. He fought on the Italian front; in early 1917 he was transferred to the Romanian and Russian Fronts, and took part in the Battle of Caporetto before being transferred back to Vienna. He ended the war as first lieutenant (reserves).

During the immediate postwar period, Deutsch became undersecretary of the army in the newly established Austrian Republic, and helped establish the new volunteer Austrian Army. He was a committed member of the Social Democratic Workers Party (SDAP), After the war, he served as state secretary for military affairs, and head of the SDP militia, a counterweight to the Christian Socialist militias. After the Christian Socialists won the election in 1934, he was part of the opposition until it was banned in 1934 after murder of Chancellor Dolfuss. From 1936 to 1939 he was a general on the republican side of the Spanish Civil War. He immigrated to Paris in 1939 after the *Anschluss*, where he served as foreign representative of the Austrian Socialists. In 1940 he fled to the United States, where he remained for the rest of the war. After the war, Deutsch was one of the very few Jews who returned to Austria: he died in Vienna.[45]

In the summer of 1921, Avigdor Hameiri left Odessa with a group with a group of writers who, thanks to the lobbying efforts of Bialik, were permitted to leave Russia;[46] later that year he immigrated to Palestine. He spent most of his remaining years in Tel Aviv, where he dedicated himself to literary work, theatrical productions, and a wide variety of journalistic activities. Among other achievements, he established and managed the first Hebrew satirical theater, *Hakumkum* (The Kettle), which from 1927 staged satirical cabarets based on the Central European model. In 1938, Hameiri published a book based upon his 1930 trip to Europe after World War I, during which he saw the grave threat posed by the ascent of Hitler and the Nazis.[47] After the establishment of the State of Israel, Hameiri worked as editor and recorder at the Israeli Knesset. He died in 1970.[48]

As was the case with German Jewish veterans, high war decorations at most delayed inevitable persecution. Siegfried Lateiner (1885–?), a jurist, was awarded the Silver Medal for Bravery First Class; he was promoted to second lieutenant (reserves) in 1916, then to first lieutenant in 1918. Because he was an Austrian citizen, he could still work as a lawyer in Berlin after 1933, at a time when this was forbidden to German Jews. After the *Anschluss*, however, he lost this privilege: He disappeared into *Nacht und Nebel*: the last report in 1940 stated that he had "been deported on an unknown date to an unknown destination." Platoon Leader Gustav Kleinmann, likewise recipient of the Silver Medal for Bravery First Class, was, after the *Anschluss*, deported to Buchenwald, Auschwitz, then further east. His high decoration did not protect him from being deported. He ended the war in Mauthausen, where he was liberated by the Americans. Only twenty-six of the thousands of Jews imprisoned with him (some veterans) survived the war.[49]

Austro-Hungarian chaplains were included in Nazi persecution. After the war, Rabbi Adolf Altmann (chapter 6) returned briefly to his position in Salzburg. In 1920, he was elected *Oberrabbiner* of Trier, one of the oldest Jewish communities in Germany. There, he participated in the great (but tragically short-lived) renaissance in Jewish culture and thought in the Weimar Republic, led by Martin Buber and Franz Rosenzweig. In 1938, Rabbi Altmann, his wife and family immigrated to the Netherlands. In 1943 he and his wife were deported to Westerbork, and then on to Theresienstadt in February 1944. They were deported to Auschwitz, their final destination, in May 1944 where, a few weeks later, Rabbi Altmann died of malnutrition, still staunch in his faith. His wife was gassed shortly thereafter.[50] Rabbi Arnold Frankfurter, chief garrison rabbi of Vienna, was arrested immediately after the *Anschluss* in September 1938 and deported first to Dachau, then to Buchenwald where he was beaten to death on March 10, 1942.[51]

Even when a Jew had been deported to concentration camps or immigrated, the wheels of Nazi bureaucracy ground on remorselessly, extracting everything possible, and then dividing the spoils. Plate 19 lists confiscated rings and jewelry from Rabbi Frankfurter after he had been deported. Rabbi. Samuel Lemberger, most decorated of all Jewish chaplains, emigrated to Mandated Palestine, leaving his property to be auctioned off and divided up by Nazi finance officials. This was the fatherland's thanks for the services rendered (plate 20).[52]

Teofil Reiss (chapters 4 and 5) illustrates vagaries of the fates of these veterans. After the *Anschluss*, Reiss and his wife, together with about 800 other Jews, boarded a train from Vienna, as part of the last illegal transport to Palestine before the war began. However, at the Russian border, Reiss was ordered to get off the train, and shot at with machine guns. Reiss, with twenty other men, fled through the train window, hiding in the nearby swamps. He knew the area well from prior front-line duty, and they managed to get to Lemberg, where he lodged with a local family. There he established himself as a shoemaker, and with his meager proceeds opened a small soup kitchen for refugees. He was joined by Sigi, son of his brother Stefan, and they lived there together for a year. Because Sigi was a Polish Communist, he was one of the first to be arrested by the Russian Army when they marched in to claim their share of occupied Poland. Reiss closed his workshop and labored fruitlessly day and night to find his cousin. They were destined to meet in Fergana four years later.[53]

Russians exiled German-speaking emigrants, including Reiss, to Siberia as "suspects." After two-year captivity, he was allowed to move around freely. A letter from Irkutsk to two of his children who managed to get to Palestine, dated October 26, 1941, states that he was being moved to a warmer climate: After a year of hunger, diseases, cold, and difficult travel conditions, Reiss finally arrived in Tashkent and took up residence in nearby Fergana. At the end of the war, Sigi, who lived in the nearby mountains with a young woman, accidentally met up with Teofil and invited him to stay with them. Teofil went back to the collective farm where he was living, to gather his belongings and wash, but three days of continuous heavy rain made travel through the valley impossible. Teofil contracted typhus, died alone, and was buried in a mass grave.[54]

The *Theresiestadtkonvolut* entry from January 1, 1944 lists fourteen *Prominente*—former citizens of "Greater Germany" (Germany and Austria) and the Czech Protectorate, active in the *jüdische Selbstverwaltung* (Jewish self-government), who served during the World War I.[55] Their fate was the same, irrespective of how bravely they had fought and how many medals they had been awarded. Courage counted for nothing for those who were excluded from the *Volksgemeinschaft*. Even maimed veterans were not spared. Otto Grossman, who had joined in the Austro-Hungarian Army at the age of seventeen, served throughout the war, and was so badly wounded that his one leg had to be amputated, was sent to Theresienstadt in August 1942, where he died two months later at the age of seventy.[56]

The above examples shows the fate of a cross-section of Habsburg Jewish veterans. We must not lose sight of the fact that World War I was the original sin of the twentieth century, and that World War II was merely a continuation of the First, with a twenty-year-long armistice. We are still living with the unresolved problems of World War I. Especially after the war's centennial, we would do well do ponder its causes and effects. This current book attempts to shed light on a group of Jewish veterans, whose fatherland turned on them murderously two decades after the end of the war. Their fate was the same as that of their German compatriots: bravery, loyalty, courage mattered nothing to the annihilating antisemitism of National Socialism. If this book speaks for these long dead and long forgotten soldiers, I am content.

Endnotes

1. B. Bardach, *Carnage and Care on the Eastern Front*, trans. and ed. P. C. Appelbaum (New York and Oxford: Berghahn Books, 2018), 282. Lemberg: Lviv (Ukraine).
2. R. L. Tőkés, *Béla Kun and the Hungarian Soviet Republic. The Origins and Role of the Communist Party of Hungary in the Revolutions of 1918-1919* (New York and Washington: Frederick A. Praeger, published for the Hoover Institute on War, Revolution and Peace, Stanford, CA, 1967).
3. Ibid., 1–23.
4. Ibid., 25–36; T. Szamuely, *A Magyar Kommunisták Pártjának Megalakulása és Harca a Proletárdiktaturáért* (Budapest: Kossuth, 1964), 49–54.
5. Tőkés, *Béla Kun*, 36–47.
6. According to Rauchensteiner (personal communication), this number was between 200,000 and 300,000. No firm statistics are available.
7. Tőkés, *Béla Kun*, 49; G. B. Shumenko (ed.), *Boevoe sodruzhestvo trudyashchikhsya zarubezhnykh stran s narodami Sovetskoi Rossii, 1917-1922* (Moscow: Sovetskaya Rossiya, 1957), 7.
8. It is interesting to note that Kun's parents hired Endre Ady (1877–1919), the greatest Hungarian poet of the twentieth century, to tutor him (Tőkés, *Bela Kun*, 53).
9. B. Khudyakov, foreword to *Uroki proletarskoi revolyutsii v Vengrii* by Béla Kun (Moscow: Gospolitizdat, 1960), 6.
10. Tőkés, *Béla Kun*, 50–62.
11. Ibid., 63–69; Nikolai Ivanovich Bukharin (1888–1938) was a Bolshevik revolutionary, Soviet Union politician, and a prolific author of books on revolutionary theory. He was executed during Stalinist purges.
12. Tőkés, *Béla Kun*, 69–81.
13. Ibid., 82–97.
14. Ibid., 98–122.
15. Ibid., 123–136; M. Práger, T. Hajdu, S. Gábor, G. Milei, and G. Szabö (eds.), *A Magyar Munkásmozgalom Történetének Válogatott Dokumentumai*, vol. 5 (Budapest: Szikra, 1956), 677–679.
16. Tőkés, *Béla Kun*, 137–143; B. Kun, "On the Unity of the Proletariat," *Népszava*, March 30, 1919.
17. Tőkés, *Béla Kun*, 144–160.
18. Ibid., 161–174.
19. J. Weltner, "Party Congress," *Népszava*, June 12, 1919.
20. Georges Clemenceau (1841–1929) was a French politician, physician, and Prime Minister of France during the latter part of World War I.
21. Tőkés, *Béla Kun*, 175–194.
22. Ibid., 194–206.
23. D. Sejdamet, *Krym: Przeszłość, Teraźniejszość i Dążenia Niepodległościowe Tatarów Krymskich* (Warsaw: Nakł. Instytutu Wschodniego, 1930), 128–129; D. Rayfield, *Stalin and His Hangmen: The Tyrant and Those Who Killed for Him*. (New York: Random House, 2004), 83; R. Gellately, *Lenin, Stalin and Hitler: The Age of Social Catastrophe* (New York. Alfred A. Knopf, 2007), 72; Edige Kirimal, "Complete Destruction of National Groups as Groups: The Crimean Turks," *International Committee for Crimea*, accessed March 18, 2021, http://www.iccrimea.org/historical/crimeanturks.html; idem, "Genocide in the USSR: Studies in

Group Destruction," in *Complete Destruction of National Groups as Groups—The Crimean Turk*, ed. N. K. Deker and A. Lebed (Munich: Institute for Studies of the USSR, 1958).
24 Tőkés, *Béla Kun*, 261.
25 P. Kenez, Civil War in South Russia, 1919-1920: The Defeat of the Whites (Berkeley: University of California Press, 1977), 166; F.M. Schuster, *Zwischen allen Fronten. Osteuropäische Juden während des ersten Weltkrieges (1914–1918)* (Cologne, Weimar, and Vienna: Böhlau Verlag, 2004), 419-453. Lviv (Ukraine), Pinsk (Belarus), Vilnius (Lithuania).
26 E. Daniek, *Das Judentum im Kriege* (Vienna: Verlag der deutschnationalen Vereinigung, 1919).
27 O. Armin (pseudonym of A. Roth), *Die Juden im Heere. Eine statistische Untersuchung nach amtlichen Quelle*n (Munich: Deutscher Volks-Verlag, 1919). See P. C. Appelbaum, *Loyal Sons. Jews in the German Army in the Great War* (Portland, OR and London: Vallentine-Mitchell, 2014), 266-270.
28 Daniek, *Das Judentum im Kriege*, 4.
29 Ibid., 4-6.
30 Ibid., 6-8.
31 Ibid., 8-10.
32 Second municipal district of Vienna, heavily populated by Jews before the Holocaust.
33 Daniek, *Das Judentum im Kriege*, 8-17.
34 Ibid., 17-19.
35 Ibid., 20-25.
36 Ibid., 25-32.
37 Appelbaum, *Loyal Sons*, 287.
38 M. Senekowitsch, "Gleichberechtigte in einer großen Armee – zur Geschichte des Bundes jüdischer Frontsoldaten Österreichs 1932-1938," in *Judentum und Militär, 18 Kulturwissenschaftlicher Dialog vom 16. November 2010 veranstaltet vom Institut für Human- und Sozialwissenschaften, Landesverteidigungsakademie Wien* (Vienna: Bundesministerium für Landesverteidigung und Sport, 2012), 55–88; E. Schmidl, *Habsburgs jüdische Soldaten, 1788–1918* (Vienna, Cologne, and Weimar: Böhlau Verlag, 2014), 146-156.
39 Bardach, *Carnage and* Care, 11–14.
40 A. Feuß, *Das Theresienstadt-Konvolut* (Hamburg: Dölling und Galitz Verlag, 2002).
41 Watra Domei (Romania).
42 M. Senekowitsch, unpublished information; Schmidl, *Habsburgs jüdische Soldaten*, 145, 147, 160, 228.
43 Schmidl, *Habsburgs jüdische Soldaten*, 162–167.
44 W. von Weisl, *Die Juden in der Armee Österreich-Ungarns. Illegale Transporte* (Tel Aviv: Olamenu, 1971); Schmidl, *Habsburgs jüdische Soldaten*, 166.
45 "Dr. Julius Deutsch," *Parlament*, accessed April 4, 2021, http://www.parlament.gv.at/WWER/PAD_00208/index.shtml; J. Deutsch, *Putsch oder Revolution? Randbemerkungen über Strategie und Taktik in einem Bürgerkrieg* (Karlsbad: Graphia, 1934), 5–50; idem, *Ein weiter Weg, Lebenserinnerungen* (Zurich, Leipzig, and Vienna: Amalthea-Verlag, 1960), 100–224, 376–412; idem, *Wesen und Wandlung der Diktaturen* (Munich: Humboldt-Verlag, 1963), 74–152; M. Berger, "Fallbeispiel: Dr. Julius Deutsch, vom k.u.k. Frontoffizier zum General der republikanischen Armee," in *Jüdische Soldaten—Jüdischer Widerstand in Deutschland und Frankreich*, ed. M. Berger and G. Römer-Hillebrecht (Munich and Paderborn: Fedinand Schöningh, 2012), 268–272.
46 Chaim Nahman Bialik (1873–1934), Israeli national poet.

47 A. Hameiri, *Masa be'Eropa Haperait* (Tel Aviv: Va'ad Hayovel, 1938). English translation: *Voyage to Savage Europe. A Declining Civilization*, trans. and ed. P.C. Appelbaum (Boston, MA: Academic Studies Press, 2020).
48 A. Holtzman, A., "Hame'iri, Avigdor," *YIVO Encyclopedia*, accessed April 4, 2021, https://yivoencyclopedia.org/article.aspx/Hameiri_Avigdor.
49 Schmidl, *Habsburgs jüdische Soldaten*, 161.
50 M. Altmann, "K.u.k. Feldrabbiner Dr. Adolf Altmann an der Kriegsfront (1915–1918) in Begegnung mit Feldmarschall Conrad von Hötzendorf und anderen Armeekommandanten," special addition, in *Ein Ewiges Dennoch. 12 Jahre Juden in Salzburg*, ed. M. Feingold (Vienna, Cologne, and Weimar: Böhlau Verlag, 1993); G. Steinacher, "Rabbi Adolf Altmann: Salzburg, Meran Trier, Auschwitz," in *Jüdische Lebensgeschichte aus Tirol: vom Mittelalter bis in die Gegenwart*, ed. T. Albrich (Innsbruck and Vienna: Haymon Verlag, 2012), 235–260.
51 Schmidl, *Habsburgs jüdische Soldaten*, 159–196.
52 Österreichisches Staatsarchiv/Archiv der Republik/VA 924, VA 35.248.
53 Uzbekistan.
54 T. Reis, *Tagebuch eines jüdischen Soldaten* (New York: Leo Baeck Institute, DS 135 A93 R45 [1919], 339–368. A Hebrew translation was published in 1995 by Reiss's son and other relatives.
55 Feuß, *Das Theresienstadt-Konvolut*.
56 M. Berger, *Für Kaiser, Reich und Vaterland. Jüdische Soldaten: eine Geschichte vom 19. Jahrhundert bis heute* (Zurich: Orell Füssli Verlag, 2016), 189–191.

Bibliography

Abramson, G. *Hebrew Writing of the First World War.* London and Portland, OR: Vallentine-Mitchell, 2008.

Adjustierungsvorschrift für das k.u.k. Heer, part 7, Normal Verordnungsblatt für das k.u.k. Heer, no. 23. Vienna: Druck der k.k. Hof- und Staatsdruckerei, 1918.

Altmann, A. *A Filial Memoir. Yearbook of the Leo Baeck Institute* 26 (1981).

Altmann, M. "K.u.k. Feldrabbiner Dr. Adolf Altmann an der Kriegsfront (1915–1918)." Part of "Begegnung mit Feldmarschall Conrad von Hötzendorf und anderen Armeekommandanten." Special addition. In *Ein ewiges Dennoch. 12 Jahre Juden in Salzburg,* edited by M. Feingold. Vienna, Cologne, and Weimar: Böhlau Verlag, 1993.

An-sky, S. *The Enemy at his Pleasure. A Journey through the Jewish Pale of Settlement during World War I.* Edited and translated by J. Neugroschel. New York: Metropolitan Books, Henry Holt & Co., 2002.

Appelbaum, P. C. *Loyalty Betrayed. Jewish Chaplains in the German Army during the First World War.* London and Portland, OR: Vallentine-Mitchell, 2014.

———. *Loyal Sons. Jews in the German Army in the Great War.* London and Portland, OR: Vallentine-Mitchell, 2014.

Ardelt, R. G. *Vom Kampf um Bürgerrechte zum "Burgfrieden." Studien zur Geschichte der österreichischen Sozialdemokratie 1888–1914.* Vienna: Verlag für Gesellschaftskritik, 1994.

Armin, O. [A. Roth]. *Die Juden im Heere. Eine statistische Untersuchung nach amtlichen Quellen.* Munich: Deutscher Volks-Verlag, 1919.

Ausubel, N. *Pictorial History of the Jewish People from Bible Times to Our Own Day throughout the World.* New York: Crown Publishers, Inc., 1959.

Baja, B., I. Lukinich, J. Pilch, and L. Zulahy, eds. *Hadifogoly Magyarok Története* [History of Hungarian Prisoners of War]. Budapest: Athanaeum, 1930.

Bardach, B. *Carnage and Care on the Eastern Front. The War Diaries of Bernhard Bardach 1914–1918.* Edited and translated by P. C. Appelbaum. New York and Oxford: Berghahn Books, 2018.

Berger, M. *Eisernes Kreuz, Doppeladler, Davidstern. Juden in deutschen und österreichisch-ungarischen Armeen. Der Militärdienst jüdischer Soldaten durch zwei Jahrhunderte.* Berlin: Trafo Verlag, 2010.

———. "Fallbeispiel: Dr. Julius Deutsch, vom k.u.k. Frontoffizier zum General der republikanischen Armee." In *Jüdische Soldaten—Jüdischer Widerstand in Deutschland und Frankreich,* edited by M. Berger, and G. Römer-Hillebrecht. Munich and Paderborn: Fedinand Schöningh, 2012.

———. *Für Kaiser, Reich und Vaterland. Jüdische Soldaten: eine Geschichte vom 19. Jahrhundert bis Heute*. Zurich: Orell Füssli Verlag, 2015.

Bihari, P. *A Forgotten Home Front: The Middle Class and the "Jewish Question" in Hungary During the First World War*. PhD dissertation, Central European University, 2005.

Bihl, W.-D. "Die Juden." In *Die Habsburgermonarchie 1848–1918*, vol. 3, *Die Völker des Reiches*, edited by A. Wandruszka and P. Urbanitsch. Vienna: Verlag der Österreichischen Akademie der Wissenschaften, 1980.

Biskupski, M. B. B. *Independence Day: Myth, Symbol, and the Creation of Modern Poland*. Oxford: Oxford University Press, 2012.

Blond, K. "Ein unbekannter Krieg. Persönliche Aufzeichnungen als k.u.k. Sanitätsfähnrich in Persien während der Jahre 1915/16." In *Österreichische Militärgeschichte*, vol. 5, *Ein unbekannter Krieg 1914–1916. Das k.u.k. Gesandtschaftsdetachement Teheran von Persien bis nach Wien*. Vienna: Verlagsbuchhandlung Stöhr, 1997.

Bottome, P. *Alfred Adler. A Portrait from Life*. New York: Vanguard, 1957.

Brändström, E. *Unter Kriegsgefangenen in Rußland und Sibirien*. Berlin: Deutsche Verlagsgesellschaft für Politik und Geschichte, 1922.

Breithaupt, G. *Der Kampf ums Dasein. Ein Ausschnitt aus der sibirischen Gefangenschaft*. Berlin: Verlag Carl Curtius, 1919.

Briganti, P. *Il Contributo Militare degli Ebrei Italiani alla Grande Guerra 1915–1918*. Turin: Silvio Zamorani, 2009.

Brodde, G. *Russische Gefangenschaft und die Flucht durch die Bolschewiki*. Siegen: Montanus-Verlag, 1918.

Brusilov, A. A. *A Soldier's Notebook 1914–1918*. Westport, CT: Greenwood Press, 1971.

Budaj, A. *Vallis Judaea—Povijest Požeške židovske Zajednice* [Vallis Judaea. A History of the Požega Jewish Community]. Zagreb: D. Graff, d.o.o., 2007.

Budnitsky, O. *Russian Jews between the Reds and the Whites, 1917–1920*. Translated by T. J. Portice. Philadelphia, PA: University of Pennsylvania Press, 2011.

Bullock, D. *The Czech Legion 1914–20*. Oxford: Osprey Publishers, 2008.

Canaani (Kanani), D. *Le'Nogah 'Ets Rakav* [The Gleam of Decaying Wood]. Merhavia: Sifriyat Po'alim, 1950.

Cartellieri, G. *Hilfplatz D7 vermißt. Erlebnisse eines kriegsgefangenen Arztes*. Karlsbad-Drahowitz and Leipzig: Adam Kraft Verlag, 1936.

Clark, C. *The Sleepwalkers: How Europe Went to War in 1918*. New York: Harper Collins, 2013.

Conrad von Hötzendorf, F. *Private Aufzeichnungen. Erste Veröffentlichungen aus den Papieren des k.u.k. Generalstabs-Chef*. Edited by K. Peball. Vienna and Munich: Amalthea-Verlag, 1977.

Crouthamel, J., M. Geheran, T. Grady, and J. B. Köhne, eds. *Beyond Inclusion and Exclusion. Jewish Experiences of the First World War in Central Europe*. New York and Oxford: Berghahn Books, 2018.

Dainotto, R. M. "The Italian Risorgimento and the Questione Romana." In *The Italian Jewish Experience*, edited by T. P. DiNapoli. New York: Stony Brook University Press, 2000.

Daniek, E. *Das Judentum im Kriege*. Vienna: Verlag der deutschnationalen Vereinigung, 1919.

Davies, N. *God's Playground: A History of Poland*. Revised edition. Oxford: Clarendon Press, 2005.

Davis, G. H. "The Life of Prisoners of War in Russia, 1914–1921." In *Essays on World War I: Origins and Prisoners of War*, edited by S. Williamson and P. Pastor. New York: Brooklyn College Press and Columbia University Press, 1983.

Deák, I. *The Lawful Revolution. Louis Kossuth and the Hungarians, 1848–1849*. New York: Columbia University Press, 1979.

———. *Jewish Soldiers in Austro-Hungarian Society*. Vol. 34 of Leo Baeck Memorial Lectures. New York: Leo Baeck Institute, 1990.

———. *Beyond Nationalism. A Social and Political History of the Habsburg Officers Corps, 1848–1918*. New York and Oxford: Oxford University Press, 1990.

———. *Der k.u.k. Offizier. 1848–1918*. Vienna, Cologne, and Weimar: Böhlau Verlag, 1991.

De Groot, G. J. *The First World War*. Basingstoke, Hampshire: Palgrave Macmillan, 2001.

De Lange, N. R. M. *Atlas of the Jewish World*. New York: Facts on File, 1992.

Deutsch, J. *Putsch oder Revolution? Randbemerkungen über Strategie und Taktik in einem Bürgerkrieg*. Karlsbad: Graphia, 1934.

———. *Ein weiter Weg, Lebenserinnerungen*. Zürich, Leipzig, and Vienna: Amalthea-Verlag, 1960.

———. *Wesen und Wandlung der Diktaturen*. Munich: Humboldt-Verlag, 1963.

De Waal, E. *The Hare with Amber Eyes. A Hidden Inheritance*. New York: Picador, Farrar, Straus & Giroux, 2010.

Dobrovšak, L. "Fragments from the History of the Croatian Jews during the First World War (1914–1918)." *Review of Croatian History* 10, no. 1 (2014).

———. "Fallen Jewish Soldiers during the First World War." In *Jewish Soldiers in the Collective Memory of Central Europe. The Remembrance of World War I from a Jewish Perspective*, edited by G. Lamprecht, E. Leppin-Eppel, and U. Wyrwa. Vienna, Cologne, and Weimar: Böhlau Verlag, 2019.

Dubowski, R. *Seven Years in Russia and Siberia, 1914–1921*. Cheshire, CT: Cherry Hill Books, 1922.

Engle, J. C. "'This Monstrous Front will Devour All of Us.' The Austro-Hungarian Soldier Experience, 1914–15." In *1914. Austro-Hungary. The Origins and the First Year of World War I*, edited by G. Bischof, F. Karlhofer, and S. R. Williamson. New Orleans: New Orleans University Press, 2014.

Epstein, A. *Kriegsgefangenen in Turkestan. Erinnerungen von Georg Popper und Adolf Epstein*. Vienna: Selbstverlag, 1935.

Ernst, P. "Der erste Weltkrieg in deutschsprachig-jüdischer Literatur und Publizistik in Österreich." In *Krieg. Erinnerung. Geschichtswissenschaft*, edited by S. Mattl, G. Botz, S. Karnern, and H. Konrad. Vienna, Cologne, and Weimar: Böhlau Verlag, 2009.

Essèn, R. *Zwischen der Ostsee und dem stillen Ozean. Asiatische Probleme und Erinnerungen.* Frankfurt am Main: Frankfurter Societäts-Drückerei, 1925.

Färber, R. *Unser Kaiser, ein Sendbote Gottes. Predigten zum Allerhöchsten Geburtstage Sr. Maj. des Kaisers Franz Joseph I und aus anderen patriotischen Anlässen.* Mährisch Ostrau: Selbstverlag, 1915.

Feuß, A. *Das Theresienstadt-Konvolut.* Hamburg: Dölling und Galitz Verlag, 2002.

Franzos, K. E. *Moschko von Parma.* Stuttgart and Berlin: G. Cotta'sche Buchhandlung Nachfolger, 1921.

Frojimovics, K., G. Komoróczy, V. Pusztai, A. Strbik, eds. *Jewish Budapest. Monuments, Rites, History.* Budapest: Central European University Press, 1999.

Frühling, M. *Biographisches Handbuch der in der k.u.k. österr.-ungar. Armee und Kriegsmarine aktiv gedienten Offiziere, Ärzte, Truppen, Rechnungs-Führer und sonstige Militärbeamten jüdischen Stammes.* Vienna: Selbstverlag, 1911.

Galantái, J. *Hungary in the First World War.* Budapest: Akadémiai Kiadó, 1989.

Gałęzowski, M. *Na Wzór Berka Joselewícza : Żołnierze i Oficerowie Pochodzenia Żydowskiego w Legionach Polskich.* [In the Footsteps of Berek Joselewicz. Soldiers and Officers of Jewish Origins in the Polish Legions].Warsaw: Instytut Pamięci Narodowej, Komisja Ścigania Zbrodni przeciwko Narodowi Polskiemu, 2010.

Gebetbuch für israelitische Soldaten in Kriege. Vienna: Verlag des israelitischen Kultusgemeinde Wien, 1914.

Gellately, R. *Lenin, Stalin and Hitler: The Age of Social Catastrophe.* New York. Alfred A. Knopf, 2007.

Gitelman, Z. Y. *A Century of Ambivalence. The Jews of Russia and the Soviet Union, 1881 to the Present.* New York: Schocken Publishers, 1988.

Grünwald, M., ed. *Die Feldzüge Napoleons nach Aufzeichnungen jüdischer Teilnehmer und Augenzeugen.* Vienna and Leipzig: Wilhelm Braumuller, 1913.

———. "Rafael König, der erste jüdische Schlosser-Meister Österreichs." In *Die Feldzüge Napoleons nach Aufzeichnungen jüdischer Teilnehmer und Augenzeugen*, edited by M. Grünwald. Vienna and Leipzig: Wilhelm Braumüller, 1913.

———. "Antisemitismus im Deutschen Heer und Judenzählung." *Jüdische Soldaten—Jüdischer Widerstand in Deutschland und Frankreich*, edited by M. Berger and G. Römer-Hillebrecht. Paderborn and Munich: Ferdinand Schöningh, 2012.

Güde, W. "Fallbeispiel: Rabbiner Dr. Alexander Kisch als k.k. Landwehrrabbiner. Zugleich ein kleiner Beitrag über die Anfänge der jüdischen Militärseesorge in Österreich-Ungarn." In *Jüdische Soldaten—Jüdischer Widerstand in Deutschland und Frankreich*, edited by M. Berger and G. Römer-Hillebrecht. Paderborn: Ferdinand Schöningh, 2012.

Gyóni, G. "Just For one Night." In *The Lost Voices of World War I*, edited by T. Cross. Iowa City: University of Iowa Press, 1989.

Hameiri, A. *The Great Madness*, translated from the original Hebrew (*Hashigaon Hagadol*) by Y. Lotan. Haifa: Or Ron Publishing House, 1984.

———. *Hell on Earth*, translated from the original Hebrew (*Bagehinom shel Mata*) by P. C. Appelbaum. Detroit: Wayne State University Pres, 2017.

———. *Of Human Carnage—Odessa 1918-1920*, translated from the original Hebrew (*Bein Shinei Ha'adam*) by P. C. Appelbaum. Middletown, RI: Stone Tower Publishers, and Boston, MA: Black Widow Press, 2020.

———. *Voyage to Savage Europe. A Declining Civilization*, translated from the original Hebrew (*Masa be'Eropa Haperait*) by P. C. Appelbaum. Boston, MA: Academic Studies Press, 2020.

———. *The Great Madness*, revised and edited by P. C. Appelbaum. Middletown, RI: Stone Tower Press, and Boston, MA: Black Widow Press, 2021.

Hank, S., H. Simon, and U. Hank. *Feldrabbiner in den deutschen Streitkräften des ersten Weltkrieges*. Berlin: Hentrich & Hentrich, 2013.

Hecht, D. J. "Feldrabbiner in der k.u.k. Armee während des ersten Weltkrieges"
In *Weltuntergang. Jüdisches Leben und Sterben im ersten Weltkrieg*, edited by M. G Patka Vienna, Graz, and Klagenfurt: Styria Premium, 2014.

———. "Austro-Hungarian Jewish Chaplains between East and West. Rabbi Bernard Dov Hausner (1874–1938) during World War I." In *Jewish Soldiers in the Collective Memory of Central Europe. The Remembrance of World War I from a Jewish Perspective*, edited by G. Lamprecht, E. Lappin-Eppel, and U. Wyrwa. Vienna, Cologne, and Weimar: Böhlau Verlag, 2019.

Herzog, D. *Kriegspredigten*. Frankfurt am Main: Verlag von J. Kauffmann, 1915.

Hoeflich, E. [M. Y. Ben Gavriel], *Tagebücher 1915 bis 1927*. Edited by A. A. Wallas. Vienna, Cologne, and Weimar: Böhlau Verlag, 1999.

Holquist, P. *Making War, Forging Revolution. Russia's Continuum of Crisis, 1914–1921.* Cambridge, MA and London: Harvard University Press, 2002.

Jósza, A. *Háború Hadifogság, Forradalom. Magyar Internacionalista Hadifoglyok az 1917-es Oroszországi Forradalmakban* [War, Military Captivity, Revolution, Hungarian Internationalist Prisoners of War in the Russian Revolutions of 1917]. Budapest: Akádemia Kiadó, 1970.

Jung, P. "Der Militärische Weg Kaspar Blonds bis zu seiner Flucht 1915." In Österreichische Militärgeschichte, vol. 5, *Ein unbekannter Krieg 1914-1916. Das k.u.k. Gesandtschaftsdetachement Teheran von Persien bis nach Wien*.Vienna: Verlagsbuchhandlung Stöhr, 1997.

———. *Der k.u.k. Wüstenkrieg: Österreich-Ungarn im Vorderen Orient 1915–1918*. Graz, Vienna and Cologne: Styrian Verlag, 1992.

Kafka, F. "Eintrag 06.08.1914." In *Tagebücher 1910–1923*, edited by M. Brod. Frankfurt am Main: Fischer Taschenbuch Verlag, 1976.

Kálmán, M. "The Union of Jewish Soldiers under Soviet Rule." In *World War I and the Jews. Conflict and Transformation in Europe, the Midde East, and America*, edited by M. L. Rozenbit and J. Karp. New York and Oxford: Berghahn Books, 2017.

Karniel, J. *Die Toleranzpolitik Kaiser Josephs II*, vol. 9 of Schriftenreihe des Instituts für deutsche Geschichte, Universität Tel Aviv. Gerlingen: Bleicher, 1986.

Karp, J., and M. L. Rozenblit, "Introduction. On the Significance of World War I and the Jews." In *World War I and the Jews. Conflict and Transformation in Europe, the Middle East, and America*, edited by M. L. Rozenblit and J. Karp. New York and Oxford: Berghahn Books, 2017.

Kenez, P. *Civil War in South Russia, 1919–1920: The Defeat of the Whites*. Berkeley: University of California Press, 1977.

Kestenberg-Gladstein, R. *Neuere Geschichte der Juden in den Böhmischen Ländern*, vol. 1, *Das Zeitalter der Aufklärung 1780–1830*. Tübingen: J. C. B. Mohr, Paul Siebeck, 1969.

Khudyakov, B. Foreword to *Uroki Proletarskoi Revolyutsii v Vengrii* [*Lessons of the Proletarian Revolution in Hungary*] by Béla Kun. Moscow: Gospolitizdat, 1960.

Kinsky, N. *Russisches Tagebuch 1916–1918*. Herford: Busse Seewald, 1987

Kirimal, E. "Genocide in the USSR: Studies in Group Destruction." In *Complete Destruction of National Groups as Groups—The Crimean Turk*, edited by N. K. Deker and A. Lebed. Munich: Institute for Studies of the USSR, 1958.

Kisch, E. E. *"Schreib das auf Kisch!" Das Kriegstagebuch von Egon Erwin Kisch*. Berlin: Erich Reiss Verlag, 1930.

Klanska, M. "'Jedes Land hat die Juden, die es verdient.' Karl Emil Franzos und die Juden." In *Karl Emil Franzos: Schrifsteller zwischen den Kulturen*, edited by P. Ernst. Innsbruck, Bozen, and Vienna: Studienverlag, 2007.

Klein-Pejšovšá, R. *Mapping Jewish Loyalties in Interwar Slovakia*. Bloomington, IN: Indiana University Press, 2015.

———. "The Budapest Jewish Community's Galician October." In *World War I and the Jews. Conflict and Transformation in Europe, the Middle East, and America*, edited by M. L. Rozenblit and J. Karp. New York and Oxford: Berghahn Books, 2017.

Kohn, H. *Living in a World Revolution. My Encounters with History*. New York: Pocket Books, 1964.

Kraus, L. *Susreti i Sudbine. Sjećanja iz Jednog Aktivnok Života* [Experiences and Destinies. Memories of an Active Life]. Osijek: Glas Slavonije, 1983.

Lamprecht, G., E. Lappin-Eppel, and U. Wyrwa, eds. *Jewish Soldiers in the Collective Memory of Central Europe. The Remembrance of World War I from a Jewish Perspective*. Vienna, Cologne, and Weimar: Böhlau Verlag, 2019.

Lein, R. *Pflichterfüllung oder Hochverrat? Die tschechischen Soldaten Österreich-Ungarns im ersten Weltkrieg*. Vienna: Lit Verlag, 2011.

Lilien, E. M. *Briefe an seine Frau, 1905–1925*. Edited by O. M. Lilien and E. Strauss. Königstein/Taunus: Jüdischer Verlag Athenäum, 1985.

Lindner, E. *Patriotismus deutscher Juden von der napoleonischen Ära bis zum Kaiserreich*. Frankfurt am Main: Peter Lang, 1997.

Liulevicius, V. G. *War Land on the Eastern Front: Culture, National Identity, and German Occupation in World War I. Studies in the Social and Cultural History of Modern Warfare*. New York: Cambridge University Press, 2005.

Macartney, C. A. *The Habsburg Empire 1790–1918*. New York: Macmillan, 1969.

Mader, H. M. "Judentum und altösterreichische Armee." In *Judentum und Militär. 18 Kulturwissenschaftlicher Dialog vom 16 November 2010*. Vienna: Bundesministerium für Landesverteidigung und Sport, 2012.

Madigan, E., and G. Reuveni, eds. *The Jewish Experience of the First World War*. London: Palgrave Macmillan, 2019.

May, A. J. *The Passing of the Habsburg Monarchy 1914–1918*, vol. 3. Philadelphia, PA: University of Pennsylvania Press, 1966.

McCagg, W. O. Jr. *A History of Habsburg Jews 1670-1918*. Bloomington, IN: Indiana University Press, 1989.

Milei, G., and K. Petrák, eds. *Tanúságtevők Visszaemlékezések Magyarországi Munkásmozgalom Történéből Magyarok a Nagy Oktober Győzelméért 1917–1921* [Witnesses. Recollections of the History of the Hungarian Labor Movement. Hungarians for the Victory of Great October 1917–1921]. Budapest: Kossuth, 1977.

Moll, M. *Die Steiermark im ersten Weltkrieg. Der Kampf des Hinterlandes ums Überleben 1914–1918*. Vienna, Graz, and Klagenfurt: Styria Premium, 2014.

Okey, R. *The Habsburg Monarchy c. 1765–1918. From Enlightenment to Eclipse*. Basingstoke, Hampshire: Palgrave Macmillan, 2001.

Panter, S. *Jüdische Erfahrungen und Loyalitätskonflikte im ersten Weltkrieg*. Göttingen: Vandenhoeck and Ruprecht, 1914.

Pastor, P. *Hungary between Wilson and Lenin: The Hungarian Revolution of 1918–1919 and the Big Three*. Boulder, CO: East European Quarterly, 1976.

———. "Hungarian Prisoners of War in Siberia." In *Essays on World War I*, edited by P. Pastor and G. A. Tunstall. New York: Columbia University Press, 2012.

Patka, M. G., ed. *Weltuntergang. Jüdisches Leben und Sterben im ersten Weltkrieg*. Vienna, Graz, and Klagenfurt: Styria Premium, 2014.

Paul-Schiff, M. "Teilnahme der österreich-ungarischen Juden am Weltkrieg." In *Mitteilungen der Gesellschaft für jüdische Volkskunde*, new series, 3 (1925).

Petrovsky-Shtern, Y. *Jews in the Russian Army, 1827–1917. Drafted into Modernity*. New York: Cambridge University Press, 2014. First published 2009.

Plaschka, R. "Zur Vorgeschichte des Überganges von Einheiten des Infantrieregiments Nr. 28 an der russchischen Front 1915." In *Österreich und Europa: Festschrift für Hugo Hantsch zum 70 Geburtstag*. Graz: Verlag für Geschichte und Politik, 1965.

Práger, M., T. Hajdu, S. Gábor, G. Milei, and G. Szabö, eds. *A Magyar Munkásmozgalom Történetének Válogatott Dokumentumai* [Selected Documents from the History of the Hungarian Workers Movement], vol. 5. Budapest: Szikra, 1956.

Rachamimow, A. *POWs and the Great War. Captivity on the Eastern Front*. Oxford and New York: Berg, 2002.

Rákosi, M. *Visszaemlékezések, 1892–1925* [Memoirs 1892–1925]. Budapest: Napvilá Kiádo, 2002.

Ranglisten des kaiserlichen und königlichen Heeres. Vienna: K.k. Hof- und Staatsdruckerei, 1916.

Rauchensteiner, M. *The First World War and the end of the Habsburg Monarchy, 1914–1918.* Vienna, Cologne, and Weimar: Böhlau Verlag, 2014.

Rayfield, D. *Stalin and His Hangmen: The Tyrant and Those Who Killed for Him.* New York: Random House, 2004.

Rechter, D. *The Jews of Vienna and the First World War.* Oxford and Portland, OR: Littman Library of Jewish Civilization, 2008.

Redlich, J. *Österreichische Regierung und Verwaltung im Weltkriege.* Vienna: Hölder-Pichler-Tempsky AG, 1925.

Reiss, T. T. *In the Line of Fire: A Soldier's Story 1914–1918.* Translated by T. Erez. N.p.: CreateSpace Independent Publishing Platform, 2016.

Roth, C. *The History of the Jews of Italy.* Philadelphia, PA: Jewish Publication Society of America, 1946.

Roth, C., ed. *Encyclopedia Judaica*, vol. 9. Jerusalem: Keter Publishing House, 1971.

Roth, J. *Radetzkymarsch.* Hamburg: Rowohlt, 1987.

Rothenberg, G. E. *The Army of Francis Joseph.* West Lafayette, IN: Purdue University Press, 1976.

———. "The Habsburg Army in the First World War." In *The Habsburg Empire in World War One,* edited by R. A. Kann, B. K. Király, P. S. Fichtner, 74–75. Boulder, CO: East European Quarterly, 1977.

Rozenblit, M. L. *Reconstruction of a National Identity. The Jews of Habsburg Austria during World War I.* Oxford and New York: Oxford University Press, 2001.

———. "Jewish Courtship and Marriage in 1920s Vienna," In *Gender and Jewish History*, edited by M. A. Kaplan and D. D. Moore. Bloomington and Indianapolis: Indiana University Press, 2011.

Rozenblit, M. L., and J. Karp, eds. *World War I and the Jews. Conflict and Transformation in Europe, the Middle East, and America.* New York and Oxford: Berghahn Books, 2017.

Sajó, G., and R.-T. Fischer. "Die jüdischen Soldaten des Kaisers im heiligen Land." In *Weltuntergang. Jüdisches Leben und Sterben im ersten Weltkrieg*, edited by M. G. Patka. Vienna, Graz, and Klagenfurt: Styria Premium, 2014.

Saperstein, M. *Preaching in Times of War 1800–2001.* Oxford and Liverpool: The Littman Library of Jewish Civilization, 2012.

Scheer, T. "Habsburg Jews and the Imperial Army before and during the First World War." In *Beyond Inclusion and Exclusion. Jewish Experiences of the First World War in Central Europe*, edited by J. Crouthamel, M. Geheran, T. Grady, and J. B. Köhne. New York and Oxford: Berghahn Books, 2018.

Schmelzer, A. L. "Die Juden in der Bukowina (1914–1919)." In *Geschichte der Juden in der Bukowina. Ein Sammelwerk*, edited by H. Gold, vol. 1. Tel Aviv: Olamenu, 1958–1962.

Schmidl, E. A. *Juden in der k. (u.) k. Armee 1788–1918. Jews in the Habsburg Armed Forces.* Vol. 11 of Studia Judaica Austriaca. Eisenstadt: Eisenstadt Jewish Museum, 1989.

———. *Habsburgs Jüdische Soldaten 1788–1918*. Vienna, Cologne, and Weimar: Böhlau Verlag, 2014.

———. "Jüdische Soldaten in der k.u.k. Armee." In *Weltuntergang. Jüdisches Leben und Sterben im ersten Weltkrieg*, edited by M. G. Patka. Vienna, Graz, and Klagenfurt: Styria Premium, 2014.

Schoenfeld, J. *Shtetl Memoirs: Jewish Life in Galicia under the Austro-Hungarian Empire and in the Reborn Poland 1898–1939*. Hoboken, NJ: Ktav Publishing House, 1985.

Schuster, F. M. *Zwischen allen Fronten. Osteuropäische Juden während des ersten Weltkrieges (1914–1919)*. Cologne, Weimar, and Vienna: Böhau Verlag, 2004.

Schwake, N. "Nissim Bemoiras." In *Weltuntergang. Jüdisches Leben und Sterben im ersten Weltkrieg*, ed. M. G. Patka. Vienna, Graz, and Klagenfurt: Styria Premium, 2014.

Schweitzer, G. "Hungarian Neolog (Progressive) Rabbis during the Great War (1914–1918)." In *Jewish Soldiers in the Collective Memory of Central Europe. The Remembrance of World War I from a Jewish Perspective*, edited by G. Lamprecht, E. Lappin-Eppel, and U. Wyrwa. Vienna, Cologne, and Weimar: Böhlau Verlag, 2019.

Sejdamet, D. *Krym: Przeszłość, Teraźniejszość i Dążenia Niepodległościowe Tatarów Krymskich* [Crimea: The Past, Present, and Independence Strivings of the Crimean Tatars]. Warsaw: Nakł. Instytutu Wschodniego, 1930.

Senekowitsch, M. "Gleichberechtige in einer großen Armee—zur Geschichte des Bundes jüdischer Frontsoldaten Österreichs 1932–1938." In *Judentum und Militär. 18 Kulturwissenschaftliche Dialog vom 16 November 2010 veranstaltet vom Institut für Human- und Sozialwissenschaften, Landesverteidigungsakademie Wien*. Vienna: Bundesministerium für Landesverteidigung und Sport, 2012.

Shumenko, G. B., ed. *Boevoe Sodruzhestvo Trudyashchikhsya Zarubezhnykh Stran s Narodami Sovetskoi Rossii, 1917–1922* [Military Solidarity of Foreign Workers with the Peoples of Soviet Russia, 1917–1922]. Moscow: Sovetskaya Rossiya, 1957.

Shumsky, D. "On Ethnocentrism and its Limits—Czecho-German Jewry in Fin-de-Siècle Prague and the Origins of Zionist Bi-Nationalism." *Jahrbuch des Simon Dubnow Instituts* 5 (2006): 173–188.

Sondhaus, L. *Franz Conrad von Hötzendorf: Architect of the Apocalypse*. Boston, Leiden, and Cologne: Brill Academic Publishers, 2000.

Späth, B. *Als Kosak und Matrose unter Koltschaks Fahne in Sibirien*. Konstanz am Bodensee: Scheffel Verlag, 1925.

Sperber, M. *God's Water Carriers*. Translated by J. Neogroschel. New York: Holmes and Meier, 1987.

Spomenica Poginulih i Umrlih Srpskih Jevreja u Balkanskom i Svetskom Ratu 1912–1918. [Monument to the Killed and Deceased Serbian Jews in the Balkan and World Wars 1912-1918]. Belgrade: Odbor za podizanje spomenika palim jevrejskim ratnicima, 1927.

Steinacher, G. "Rabbi Adolf Altmann: Salzburg, Meran Trier, Auschwitz." In *Jüdische Lebensgeschichte aus Tirol: vom Mittelalter bis in die Gegenwart*, edited by T. Albrich. Innsbruck and Vienna: Haymon Verlag, 2012.

Steiner, P. "Namensliste der Feldrabbiner in der österreich-ungarischen Armee des ersten Weltrieges." In *Weltuntergang. Jüdisches Leben und Sterben im ersten Weltkrieg*, edited by M. G. Patka. Vienna, Graz, and Klagenfurt: Styria Premium, 2014.

Strachan, H. *The First World War*, vol. 1, *To Arms*. Oxford: Oxford University Press, 2003.

Szabolcsi, L. *Két Emberöltő. Az Egyenlőség Évtizedei* [*Two Generations. The Decades of Egyenlőség*]. Budapest: MTA Judaisztikai Kutatócsoport, 1993.

Szamuely, T. *A Magyar Kommunisták Pártjának Megalakulása és Harca a Proletárdiktaturáért* [The Communist Party of Hungary: Its Formation and Struggle for the Dictatorship of the Proletariat]. Budapest: Kossuth, 1964.

Tőkés, R. L. *Béla Kun and the Hungarian Soviet Republic. The Origins and Role of the Communist Party of Hungary in the Revolutions of 1918–1919*. New York and Washington: Frederick A. Praeger, published for the Hoover Institute on War, Revolution and Peace, Stanford, CA, 1967.

Trebitsch, S. *Chronicle of a Life*. Translated by E. Wilkins and E. Kaiser. London: William Heinemann Ltd., 1953.

Ujvári, P., ed. *Magyar Zsidó Lexikon Kiadása* [*Hungarian Jewish Lexicon*]. Budapest: Pallas-nyomda, 1929.

Verhey, J. *The Spirit of 1914. Militarism, Myth, and Mobilization in Germany*. Cambridge: Cambridge University Press, 2000.

von Weisl, W. *Die Juden in der Armee Österreich-Ungarns. Illegale Transporte*. Tel Aviv: Olamenu, 1971.

Watson, A. *Ring of Steel. Germany and Austria-Hungary in World War I*. New York: Basic Books, 2014.

Winter, J. *Remembering War. The Great War between Memory and History in the Twentieth Century*. New Haven and London: Yale University Press, 2006.

———. *War beyond Words. Languages of Remembrance from the Great War to the Present*. Cambridge and New York: Cambridge University Pres, 2017.

Wolf, G. *Josef Wertheimer. Ein Lebens und Zeitbild. Beitrag zur Geschichte der Juden Österreichs in neuerster Zeit*. Vienna: Herzfeld & Bauer, 1868.

———. *Die Geschichte der Juden in Wien (1156–1876)*. Vienna: Alfred Hölder, 1876.

Wurzer, G. *Die Kriegsgefangenen der Mittelmächte in Russland im ersten Weltkrieg*. Göttingen: V&R Unipress, 2005.

Žáček, W. "Zu den Anfängen der Militärpflichigkeit der Juden in Böhmen im Neunzehten Jahrhundert." *Jahrbuch der Gesellschaft für Geschichte der Juden in der Czechoslovakischen Republik* 7 (1935): 265–303.

Zuckermann, H. *Hugo Zuckermann. Gedichte*. Vienna and Berlin: R. Löwit Verlag, 1919.

Index

A

Adler, Alfred, 10, 113
Adler, Friedrich, 50
Adler, Viktor, 59, 63n10, 64n49
Afghanistan, 272, 275, 277
Albin, Stanislaw, 110
Albrecht, Archduke, Field Marshal, 37
Aleppo, xxvi, 8, 73, 243, 282-83
Alexander, Prince, 144
Alpári, Gyulá, 292
Alsace-Lorraine, 8, 240
Altmann, Adolf, Rabbi, xxxiii, 172, 184, 204-5, 229, 302
Amman, Paul, 5, 150-51, 164
Andarinsk, 257, 263, 265, 267-68
Arbib, Angelo, 148
Armenian genocide, xxvi, 8, 73, 122n28, 171n66, 243, 245, 279, 282-83, 289n141
Arnstein(er), Maximilian, 28
Ashkhabad, 279
Astrakhan, 8, 241
Auschwitz, viii, 229, 249, 299, 302
Austerlitz, Leopold, 37
Austria, passim
Austro-Hungary, passim

B

Bader, Edwin, 15, 151-53, 164
Bader, Lilian, 15, 149, 151, 168
Baeck, Leo, Rabbi, 175, 203
Baghdad, 282
Baikal, Lake, 265, 286n66
Balaban, Majer (Meier) Samuel, 215, 229
Balkans, 6, 73, 127-28, 144, 222
Balnica (Poland), 144
Bardach, Dr, Bernhard, xxiv, xxvii, 2, 5, 9, 11, 14, 62, 68, 103, 113, 164, 174, 234n82, 290, 299
Bark, Piotr, 11
Beer, Peter, 28

Beer Sheba, 166
Belgrade, 37, 73, 88, 128-29, 142-44, 146, 149, 245-46
Berezovka, 256-57, 271, 286n66, 287n76
Bermann (Höllriegel), Richard Arnold, 51, 72-73
Bertisch, Leo, Rabbi, xxvi, 18, 179, 181, 207, 215-18, 221, 229
Bettelheim, Ernő, 294
Bialikamin, 145
Biró, Ákos, 179
Bismarck, Otto von, 30, 32, 128
Blond, Kaspar, xxiv, xxvi, xxxvi, 8, 73, 242-43, 244-45, 278-81, 289n127
Bloch, Abraham, Rabbi, 229
Bloch, Joseph Samuel, 55
Bock, Salomon, xxxii
Bohemia, 3, 16, 25, 27, 30, 32, 39, 49, 115, 175-76, 180, 218, 231n23
Böhm, Vilmos, 7
Bomash, Meer Khaimovich, 11-13
Bores, Albert Izydor, 110
Boroević, Svetosar, Field Marshal, 166
Bosnia-Herzegovina, 3, 128-29, 147
Brändström, Elsa, 239, 271
Breithaupt, Georg, xxiv, 8, 239, 241, 243-44, 257, 271
Brest Litovsk, 70, 123n68, 201, 277, 288n117, 291
Brigido, Graf Joseph von, 25
Brody (Ukraine), x, 10, 13, 49, 104, 189
Brzezany, 84
Buber, Martin, 50, 62n10, 302
Buchenwald, xxxix, 229, 302
Budapest, viii, 2, 15-16, 35, 38, 49-50, 54, 60-61, 67, 72, 81-82, 87, 90-91, 100, 102-3, 111, 165, 176, 178-79, 181, 189, 293-95
Bukhara, 2, 19n3, 241, 287n98
Bukharin, Nikolai, 291, 304n11

Bukowina, viii, xxvi, 6, 8, 16-17, 36, 39, 46n42, 49-52, 57, 60, 67-68, 90, 104-5, 112, 121n17, 123n69, 148, 168, 173, 175, 177, 187, 189, 218, 221, 231n25, 289n124, 299
Bulgaria, 72, 127-28, 145, 283, 285n39
Burg, Meno, xxiv, 29, 70

C

Čačak (Serbia), 88
Carpathians, 10, 77, 84, 103-5, 108, 116, 121n1, 130, 146, 200, 227, 230n7, 239-40, 258, 263, 299
Carpatho-Ruthenia, xxvii, 2, 54, 90
Caspian Sea, 275, 277
Central Asia, xxv, 2, 7, 13, 90, 238, 241-44, 272-73, 275, 287nn98-99, 288n113, 289n123
Cer Mountain, 128-29
Chayes, P.H., xxxiv
Chelyabinsk, 264-65
China, 257, 269, 275, 277, 288n111
Chortkow, 39, 88, 98, 211
Clark, Christopher, 128
Cohen, Hermann, 175
Cohen, Löser, 28
Corfu, 145, 238
Courland (Western Latvia), 9, 71
Cracow, 60, 74, 76, 80-81, 89, 113, 194, 196, 296
Crimea, 296
Crna Bara (Serbia), 140
Croatia, 16, 38, 105, 107, 128, 130, 136
Czechoslovakia, 7, 296
Czernowitz (Černivci), viii, 32, 49, 52, 71, 88-89, 98, 103, 105, 108, 121n17, 278
Czóbel, Ernő, 294

D

Dalmatia, 41, 46n52
Daniek, Edmund, 297-98
Darnitsa, 240, 248, 254
Debreczin, 144
Denmark, xv, 32, 36, 239
Deutsch, A. D., xxxiv
Deutsch, Ernst (Ernő), Rabbi, xxxiii-xxxiv, 180, 205-6, 235n110
Deutsch, Julius, 300-301
Diamant, Béla, xxxiv, 207, 214
Djemal Pasha, 73
Donji Brodac (Bosnia), 134
Dowlatabad, 280

Draginje (Serbia), 142
Drina River, 131, 133, 135-36, 138-39, 239

E

Eastern Luristan, 281-82
Ehrentheil, Adolf, Rabbi, 175
Einhorn, Ignác, Rabbi, 175
Einstein, Albert, 51
Ekaterinburg, 250
England, 44n2, 58
Engle, J. C., 239-40
Enver Pasha, Ismail, 73, 122n28, 166, 171n66
Ephrussi family, 55
Epstein, Adolf, xxiv, 8, 243-44, 273-78
Essén, Rütger, 271
Eugen, Archduke, 144, 204

F

Färber, Reuben, Rabbi, 220-22
Ferda, Rudolf, Rabbi, xxxiii, 180, 229
Fergana, 303
Feuerstein, Avigdor. See Hameiri, Avigdor
Fischer, Eric, 74-75
Fischer, Max Béla, Rabbi, 182
Fleischmann, Karl, 37
Flesch, Philip, 151
Floch, Joseph, 14, 74
France, xiv, xvi, 25, 27, 29, 32, 36, 47n67, 58, 79, 175, 241, 304n20
Frank, J., xxxiv
Frankfurter, Arnold, Rabbi, xxxiii, xxxix, 89, 123n70, 179-81, 229, 302
Frankl, Abraham, Rabbi, 181
Frankl, Franz Bernard, 28
Franz Ferdinand, Archduke, 146
Franz Joseph, Kaiser, vii, xvii, xxiv, 1, 4, 9-10, 14, 30-32, 36-38, 41-42, 49, 51, 55, 58, 85, 108, 114, 144, 154, 157, 181, 184, 196, 213, 231n23, 237n168, 248, 298
Franzos, Karl Emil, 25, 44n8, 176, 231n25
Wilhelm II, 30
Frederick William III, 28, 30
Frederick William IV, 29-30
Freud, Sigmund, 52
Fridman, N. M., 11, 13
Fried, Robert, 112
Friedländer, David, 27
Friedmann, Sigmund Edler von, 299-300
Frühling, Moritz, 36, 39, 42, 56
Funk, Moritz (Ritter von), 40
Funk, Salomon, Rabbi, 179

G

Gałęzowski, Marek, 110
Galicia, viii, xii, xvii, xxvi, 3, 6, 8, 11-12, 16-17, 25, 37, 39, 42, 49-52, 55, 57, 60-61, 67-68, 73, 94, 101, 107-8, 110, 112, 124n108, 148, 153, 168, 173, 177, 184, 186-87, 189, 194, 213, 218, 220-21, 231n25, 234n82, 273, 299
Garibaldi, 147-48
Germany, viii-ix, xv, xx, xxiv 7, 14-15, 17-18, 25, 27, 30, 39, 41-42, 50, 57-59, 61, 70-71, 106, 108, 110, 127, 145, 164, 166, 172, 181, 183, 235nn107-8, 242-43, 265-66, 285n39, 288n110, 288n114, 288n117, 291, 297-99, 302-3
Georg, Prince, 144
Georgi, von, 3
Gersdorff, Werner von, 244, 263-71
Gitelman, Zvi, 50
Goldfand, Samuel, 210
Goldstein, Ignaz, 32-35
Dolfuss, Engelbert, 298-99, 301
Golinski, Ludwig, 193
Goražde, 140
Gorlice, 9-10, 16, 124n94, 189, 233n73, 234n82247
Görz, 37
Greece, 128
Greenberg, Uri Zvi, xxviii, 145-46
Gross, Moses David, Rabbi, 179
Grünfeld, Artur/Arnold, Rabbi, 192-93, 200, 225-26, 229
Grün(hut), Mór, 37
Grünwald, Max, Rabbi, 29
Guastalla, Enrico, 147-48
Gyóni, Géza, 240

H

Habsburg Empire, vii-viii, xxiv, xxvi-xxvii, 27, 67, 72, 109, 120, 172, 290, 293
Hameiri (Feuerstein), Avigdor, xxvii, xxix, xxx, 2, 15, 54, 68, 90-102, 124n102, 146, 243-44, 247-55, 271, 286n63, 301
Harbin, 257
Hausner, Bernard, Rabbi, xxxiv, 211
Hazai, Samu(el), 42
Hecht, Dieter, 211
Herz, Leopold, 42
Herzl, Theodor, 39, 47n67
Hevesi, Gyula, 293
Hindenburg, Paul von, 10
Hindls, Arnold, 52, 243, 255-57

Hirsch, S., xxxiv
Hitler, Adolf, xi, xiii, 245, 296, 298, 300-301
Hödl, Rudolf von, 24
Hoeflich, Eugen, 15, 69
Höllriegel, Arnold, 14, 72-73
Höllriegel, Arnold. *See* Bermann, Richard Arnold
Horowicz, Benjamin Halevi, Rabbi, 179
Hötzendorf, Conrad von, xxv, 3, 204, 233n62
Hungarian Soviet Republic, 7, 242, 290-93, 296
Hungary, passim

I

Italy, ix, xiv-xv, 3-4, 6-7, 15, 29, 31-32, 39, 40, 60, 69, 72, 106, 127, 148-49, 156, 163, 171n60, 172, 174, 178, 184, 226, 231n23, 235n108, 243
Irkutsk, 69, 251, 256, 265, 268, 273, 286n66, 303
Isfahan, 281
Isonzo, xxxiv, 4, 72, 105, 127-28, 148-51, 153-55, 157, 165, 168, 171n60, 174, 184, 206, 211-12, 222, 224
Israel, xxxix, 181, 217-18, 223, 233n70, 236n144, 244, 254-55, 287n98, 300-301
Istanbul, 73
Italiener, Bruno, Rabbi, 174

J

Jancsik, Ferenc, 291
Janja (Bosnia), 133
Janousek, Antonin, 294
Jodłowa (Poland), 187
Josefdorf, 144
Joseph, Archduke, 68
Joseph II, Emperor, viii, xvi, xxiv, 14, 19, 24-25, 56

K

Kafka, Franz, 51, 54, 62n10
Kálmán, Edmund (Ödön), Rabbi, 189-92
Karfunkel, Aron, 177
Karikás, Frigyes, 291
Karl I (Charles I), Emperor, vii, 5, 85
Károlyi, Mihály, Count, 6, 292-94
Kashan, 281
Katowicz, 80
Kazakhstan, 8, 288n111
Kazan, 250
Kazimierza Wielka (Poland), 196
Kefalov, K. D., 13

Kelémen, Adolf, Rabbi, xxvii, xxxiv, 17, 227-29
Kelen, József, 293
Kerensky, Alexander, 108, 125n129253, 286n59
Kermanshah, 282
Khabarovsk, 272
Kiev, 7, 11, 70, 240, 248, 253-54, 273
Kinsky, Nora, Countess, 239
Kisch, Alexander, Rabbi, 175-77
Kisch, Bruno, 177
Kisch, Egon, xxxi, 2, 53, 120, 128-45, 168
Kishinev, xxvii, 51, 58
Klaber, Isidor, 146, 149
Klapka, György, General, 175
Kleinmann, Gustav, 302
Kohn, Hans, xxiv, xxix, 8, 54, 242, 272-73
Kohn, Isidor/Israel, 226
Kokand, 8, 241, 244, 275, 277, 288n113
Konrad, Helmut, 299
Kórvin, Otto, 294
Kossuth, Ludwig, 31, 45n30, 230n17
Koszyce (Poland), 196
Kovno, 11-12, 234n82
Kozhukhovo, 240
Krak, Ensign, 100
Krasne (Poland), 81
Kraśnik (Poland), 79, 194, 196
Krasnoyarsk, 256, 265, 273, 291
Kraus, Lavoslav, xxiv, 2, 6-7, 72, 107-9
Kriegler, Alfred, 245
Kun, Béla, 6-7, 72, 242, 291, 293, 296
Kunfi, Zsigmond, 7
Kunszentmárton (Hungary), 189
Kurdistan, 281-82
Kurrein, Viktor, Rabbi, 212-13
Kyrgyzstan, 8, 288n99, 288n113

L

Landler, Jenő, 7, 292
Landau, Ezekiel (Yechezkel), Rabbi, 25, 177
Lateiner, Siegfried, 301
Latzi the Gypsy, 251
Lazarevac, 142
Lebovics, Hirsch, Rabbi, 183
Lemberg (L'viv), viii, xxvii, 7, 11, 29, 49, 60, 71-72, 75, 80, 88, 101, 105-6, 111-13, 118, 146, 149, 157, 161, 184, 188-89, 211-13, 234nn82-83, 241, 263, 273, 289n120, 290, 296, 299, 302
Lemberger, Samu(el), Rabbi, xxxix, 213-14
Lena River, 256
Lenin, 109, 286n63, 288n117, 291, 293-96

Leopold II, 27
Lešnica (Serbia), 131, 133
Levi, Leopold Rosenak Sali, 203
Levi, Rodolfo, Rabbi, 178
Levy, Arthur, Rabbi, 183, 185-86, 203
Lieben, Fritz, 52, 74, 155
Lilien, Ephraim, 53
Link, Samuel, Rabbi, 207-10
Lipica Dolna (Ukraine), 85-87
Lipolist, 141
Liulevicius, Vejas Gabriel, 9
Łódź, 11, 185
Löw Leopold, Rabbi, 175
Löwenstein, Jack, 115
Löwi, Richard, 200
Lublin (Poland), 79, 110, 194
Lueger, Karl, 9
Lukács, György, 7

M

Macedonia, 128
Maendel, Maximilian, 37
Magyar, Ludwig, 165
Manchuria, 257, 273
Mändel (Mändl), Fritz, 3
Maniów (Poland), 145
Mahidascht, 282
Mährisch-Ostrau, 80, 220
Mannheimer, Noah, 31
Margel, M., xxxiv
Margolis, 94-98, 100-102, 248-49, 251-53
Maria Theresia, 30
Masaryk, Tomáš, 5, 7, 85, 123n56, 296
Masurian Lakes, 9, 71
Mauthausen, 302
Mechner, Adolf, 10, 103-5, 155, 164
Mehmet V, Sultan, 73
Meier-Graefe, Julius, 254
Mengele, Josef, 250
Mesopotamia, xxvi, 2, 8, 242, 279, 281-82
Mladenowac, 246
Mongolia, 266, 268-69, 286n66
Moravia, 3, 16, 32, 39, 49, 57, 180, 218
Moscow, xxvii, 8, 240-41, 248, 255, 263, 265-67, 291-92
Münnich, Ferenc, 291, 294

N

Nagelberg, S., xxxiv
Nagy, Imre, 241
Nahavand, 282
Napoleon, xxiv, 27, 147

Natt, Hugo, 9-10, 42
Neipperg, Erwin, Graf, 42
Netherlands, 302
Neumann, David, 15, 68
Nisch, 245-47, 285n36
Nizhneudinsk, 251, 254
Nizhny Novgorod, 249
Novibazar, 245, 247, 285n35
Novosibirsk, 243, 255-56, 273

O
Ob, 255-56
Ochser, Schulim, Rabbi, 223-24
Odessa, 11, 247, 254, 265, 286n63, 301
Oesterreicher, Tobias, 37
Ofutak, 144
Omsk, 251, 265, 271, 291-92
Oppenheimer, Heinrich, 31
Orenburg, 252, 278
Osh, 8, 244, 272, 275-76
Ostjuden, xxvi-xxvii, 1, 6, 8, 10-11, 60-61, 67-68, 71, 78, 90, 117, 127, 262, 271
Oświęcim (Poland), 220
Ottolenghi, Giuseppe, 148
Ottoman Turkey, 8

P
Padua, 147
Palestine, xxvii, 127, 166-67, 179, 247, 279, 300-303
Pály, 93, 95-99, 102, 248, 251, 254
Pamir Mountains, 8, 272
Pašić, Nikola, 296
Perm, 250
Persia, xxvi, xxxvi, 2, 8, 242, 277, 279-82
Peter, King, 144
Petrograd, 291
Petrov Grob, 143
Piave, 10, 74, 109, 149-56, 160-64, 166, 170n47, 225, 238
Pick, Alois, 42
Piedmont, 147
Pilsen (Czech Republic), 208
Piłsudski, József, Marshal, 7, 17, 108-110, 125n133, 296
Pinsk, 7, 296
Pitreich, Heinrich von, War Minister, 175
Pius VII, Pope, 147
Plaschkes, Siegfried, 42
Pogány, József, 7, 292

Poland, viii-ix, 6-7, 16, 22n51, 25, 55, 108, 110, 122n33, 124n94, 125n133, 187, 196, 215, 234n82, 255, 278, 296, 303
Pollak, Josef, 27
Pomerania, 17
Popper, Lipót, 31,
Popper, Georg, xxxv, 244, 273-76
Pór, Ernő, 291
Potiorek, Field Marshal, 140-41
Prague, 3-4, 25-26, 28, 37, 44n2, 49-50, 53-54, 60, 67, 72, 79-80, 106, 129-30, 140, 145, 157, 159, 168, 176-77, 179, 193, 211, 215, 224, 261, 272-73
Prussia, viii, xiii-xiv, xxiv, 1, 28, 32, 36, 42, 175
Przemyśl, xxv, xxxv, 7-8, 13, 42, 88, 111, 215, 234n82, 239-41, 256, 258, 262, 273
Pugliese, Emanuele, 148

Q
Qum, 280-81

R
Rabinovits, József, 291
Radetzky, Field Marshal, 29
Rákosi, Mátyás, 240, 294
Rawitz, Adolf (Dolu), xxvii, xxxi, 14, 149, 157-64
Reed, John, xxvii, 10
Reiner, Max, 105-6
Reiss, Teofil, xxiv, xxvii, xxx, 11, 15, 68, 75-90, 110, 155-57, 302-3
Rome, 147-48, 178
Rosenduft, Samuel, 258-60, 265-66, 281
Rosenfeld (Rozsay), József, 31
Rosenthal, Friedrich, 111
Rosenzweig, Arthur, Rabbi, 224-25
Rosenzweig, Franz, 302
Roth, Joseph, x-xiii, xix, 43
Rovighi, Cesare, 147-48
Rozenblit, Marsha, xix, 3, 90
Rubens, Julius, 244, 257-71
Rudnyánszky, Endre, 291
Russia, passim
Rzeszów, 72, 79, 187

S
Šabac (Serbia), 144
Sacerdoti, Angelo, 178
Salar River, 273
Samara, 242-43, 265, 272, 278, 287n89
Samarkand, 272-73
Sandomierz (Poland), 198

Sarajevo, 73, 146-47
Sava River, 135-37, 143, 145-46, 239
Sayansk, 252
Sazonov, Sergei Dmitrievich, 11
Schapira, Aron, 73
Scheer, Tamara, 9, 40, 43
Schlesinger, Sámuel, Rabbi, 183
Schmelzer, Arieh Leon, 52
Schnitzler, Arthur, 9, 43, 53, 63n26
Schoenfeld, Joachim, 153-54
Schünemann, Max Otto, 281, 289n135
Schuschnigg, Kurt von, 299
Schwarz, Carl, 37
Schwarz, Gabriel, Rabbi, 181-82
Schwarz, M., xxxiv
Schwarcz, Moritz, 245-47
Schweiger, Albert, Rabbi, xxxiv, 200-201, 229
Schweiger, Yizhak, Rabbi, 200
Schweitzer, Eduard, 36
Segall, Isidore, Dr., 10, 42, 113
Segre, Roberto, 148
Semipalatinsk, 252
Serbia, ix, 2-3, 49, 58, 87-88, 111, 122n27, 123n63, 127-31, 134, 137-38, 140-42, 144-45, 147, 149, 168, 169n29, 174, 181, 183, 238-39, 243, 245, 247, 285nn38-39
Shatsk, 249, 253, 286n47
Sieniawa (Poland), 5, 189
Siberia, xxvii, 2, 8, 105, 239-242, 251, 254, 264, 266, 271-73, 275, 286n66, 288n104, 291, 303
Silesia, 17, 39, 49, 177
Singer, Heinrich, 29
Sicher, Gustav, Rabbi, 193-99
Slavonia (Eastern Croatia), 16, 28, 130, 136
Slovakia, 72, 106, 233n80, 294-95
Slovenia, 6, 166, 171n60
Sniatyn, 153
Sommer, Emil, xii-xii, xix, xxxviii, 298-300
Sonderling, Jakob, 203
Spain, 63n33, 239
Sperber, Manès, 51
Spitzer, Siegfried, 2, 106
Stanislau, 88, 215
Stanisławów, 184
Staszów (Poland), 197-98
Steiner, Peter, 179
Stepojevac, 143
Stiassny, Ernst, 298
Straucher, Benno, 175
Struga, 245-46, 285n36
Stürgkh, Karl von, 51, 58, 64n47

Sweden, 239
Szánto, Béla, 294
Szántó, Jozef, Rabbi, 175
Szamuely, Tibor, 7, 291
Szilágyi, Imre, 291

T

Talaat, Pasha, 73
Tannenberg, 9, 60, 71
Tänzer, Aron, Rabbi, 174, 201, 203
Tarnogród (Poland), 78, 188-89
Tarnów, 11, 22n55, 74, 78, 89
Tashkent, 8, 241, 244, 273-78, 303
Tauber, Meir, Rabbi, xxxiv, 179, 184-89, 205-7, 214, 219, 229
Tehran, 279-81
Teplitz, 224
Teplitz-Schönau, 213
Theresienstadt, xxxviii, 299-300, 302-3
Tisza, Count, 59, 64n51, 135, 169n14
Tito, Josip Broz, 7
Tomsk, 251, 291
Transbaikalia, 2, 8, 243, 256-57
Transylvania, 7, 213
Trieste, xxxiv, 25, 72, 162, 165, 214-15
Tuchów (Poland), 13
Turkestan, xxvi-xxvii, 1-2, 8, 239-42, 272-282, 288n111, 289n123, 291
Tuscany, 147
Tyrol, 3, 6, 16, 31, 89, 127, 128, 138, 152, 168, 208, 218

U

Ub, 142
Ugreshskaya, 240
Ukraine, viii, xxvii, 7, 22n5189, 100, 106, 110, 121n1, 122n34, 123n68, 153, 166, 174, 222, 230n7, 230n12, 231n25, 233n80, 286n63, 296
United States, xii, xiv, 38239, 244, 287n98, 299-301
Urals, 6, 250, 255, 265, 278
Uralsk, 252
Üsküb, 245
Ussuriysk, 257
Uzbekistan, 8, 19n3, 283n98, 288n111, 288n113

V

Vántus, Károly, 291
Varga, Jenő, 7, 292-93
Velino Selo (Bosnia), 135-36

Venice, 147, 168, 227
Verkhoyansk, 251
Verona, 147, 178
Vienna, passim
Vilna, 7, 11, 16, 204, 296
Višegrad, 140
Vitebsk, 11
Vladimir-Volynsky, 72, 74, 117, 220-21
Vladivostok, 242, 257, 273
Volhynia, 10, 74, 110, 122n34
Vyatka, 250

W
Waldstein, Michael, 42
Weisl, Wolfgang von, xix, 52, 300
Wiener, Karl, 28
Wilkomir, 12
Windischgraz (Slovenj Gradec), 60
Winter, Alexander, Rabbi, 173
Wola Michowa (Poland), 145
Wolf, Gershon, 25, 38
Wolf, Nathan, 9-10, 42

X

Y
Yakutsk, 251

Z
Żabno (Poland), 195
Zagreb, 181
Zagros Mountains, 281
Zaklików (Poland), 196
Zakrzów, 78
Zamość (Poland), 74, 80
Zemlyachka, Rosalia, 296
Zminjak, 141
Zweig, Stefan, 50, 53, 62n5
Zuckermann, Hugo, 115-16

Praise

"Peter Appelbaum's impressive research contributes to a profound understanding of not only the Austro-Hungarian military as an institution, but also of the social history and Jewish emancipation and identity in the Habsburg empire from the late 18th century. For the first time, a number of important sources, especially on Austrian military Rabbis and the fate of Jewish POWs during and after World War I, are made accessible to the English-speaking reader. Appelbaum's comprehensive approach makes *Habsburg Sons* as relevant for the expert as it is fascinating for the interested reader."
— *Michael Haider, Director, Austrian Cultural Forum New York*

"Jewish soldiers fought in all European armies during the First World War. We are in Peter Appelbaum's debt for telling the story of Jews in the Austro-Hungarian army, and for bringing out their dignity and their pride in being both Jewish and Austrian. This is a part of Austrian history the Nazis could never erase."
— *Jay Winter, Charles J. Stille Professor of History Emeritus, Yale University*

"*Habsburg Sons* brings to light a wealth of sources documenting the experience of World War I for Jewish soldiers, prisoners of war, and military chaplains across a vast empire that was home to one of the world's largest Jewish communities. A meticulously researched and deeply moving book."
— *Derek Penslar, author of Jews and the Military: A History*

"This book fills a painful gap in research. The leading specialist on the subject writes in his typical style with a mixture of profound scientific analysis and vivid rendering of the central sources."
— *Dr. Georg Wurzer, author of*
The Prisoners from the Central Powers in Russia During WWI

"'We had such a beautiful Army, it was the most beautiful Army in the world. And what did they do with the Army? They sent them to war!' This quip, which could easily have represented Jewish humor, is well known in Austria today. Although a joke, it reveals that even a hundred years ago, war was considered a legitimate means in the pursuit of securing political interest. Following the explosion of ethnic nationalism in the whole of Europe and the catastrophe of the Second World War, this multi-ethnic approach of the Habsburg Monarchy became questionable, if not dubious. Appelbaum's latest work on diversity, presented here, deploys the example of Jewish soldiers and their devoted loyalty to illustrate how a multi-ethnic and religiously grounded State, can be viable—despite its subsequent political destruction. The confirmation of this principle of inclusion and diversity is presently observed in the existence of the European Union."

— *Ministerialrat Magister rer.soc.oec. Martin Senekowitsch, Oberst der Reserve*